With Scarcely a Ripple
Anglo-Canadian Migration into the United States and
Western Canada, 1880-1920

Much of the development of regions and communities on both sides of the United States–Canada border resulted from migration. *With Scarcely a Ripple*, the first study to link persistence, immigration, internal migration, and return migration, looks beyond the narrowly defined geographical and temporal boundaries of the aggregate census to clarify the social, economic, and demographic adjustments made at the turn of the century by both transient and persistent Anglo-Canadian migrants.

Using a prosopographical approach that combines descriptive exposition, quantitative tabulation, and structural analysis, Randy Widdis determines the geographical and social origins of migrants, the distance and direction of migration corridors, and geographical destinations in both the United States and Canada. The study provides a new view of the invisible Anglo-Canadian, one of the largest and least understood immigrant groups in the United States. Widdis's results show that there were many differences between Anglo-Canadians, and that their experience in the United States was much more complex than is usually assumed.

With Scarcely a Ripple not only contributes to our understanding of the dynamics of intra-regional, inter-regional, and return Anglo-Canadian migration but also interprets this movement in terms of the paradox of an emerging Canadian identity and a developing integration with the United States. It offers a historical geographical perspective on a subject that, in this era of free trade and globalization, is more relevant than ever.

RANDY WILLIAM WIDDIS is associate professor of geography, University of Regina.

McGill-Queen's Studies in Ethnic History
Donald Harman Akenson, Editor

McGill-Queen's Studies in Ethnic History
Series Two: John Zucchi, Editor

Picnic, Walsh County Old Settler's Association, 1910
(State Historical Society, North Dakota Heritage Center/E731)

With Scarcely a Ripple

Anglo-Canadian Migration into the United States and Western Canada, 1880–1920

RANDY WILLIAM WIDDIS

McGill-Queen's University Press
Montreal & Kingston · London · Ithaca

© McGill-Queen's University Press 1998
ISBN 0-7735-1733-2

Legal deposit fourth quarter 1998
Bibliothèque nationale du Québec

Printed in Canada on acid-free paper

This book has been published with the help of a grant from
the Humanities and Social Sciences Federation of Canada,
using funds provided by the Social Sciences and Humanities
Research Council of Canada.

McGill-Queen's University Press acknowledges the
financial support of the Government of Canada through
the Book Publishing Industry Development Program for its
activities. We also acknowledge the support of the Canada
Council for the Arts for our publishing program.

Canadian Cataloguing in Publication Data

Widdis, Randy William, 1953–
    With scarcely a ripple : Anglo-Canadian migration into the
United States and Western Canada, 1880–1920

(McGill-Queen's studies in ethnic history)
Includes bibliographical references and index.
ISBN 0-7735-1733-2

    1. Canadians, English-speaking–United States–History.
2. Canadians, English-speaking–Canada, Western–History.
3. United States–Emigration and Immigration–History.
4. Canada–Emigration and immigration–History.
5. Migration, Internal–Canada–History. I. Title. II. Series.

JV7225.W53 1998   304.8'73071'089112   C98-900675-1

Typeset in 10/12 Baskerville by True to Type

For old presbyopic goalies with bad knees

Immigration to Western Canada: All Are Welcome
(Saskatchewan Archives/R-A12402)

3rd Street, Grand Forks, 1882
(State Historical Society, North Dakota Heritage Center/A4043)

Contents

Tables

Maps and Figures

Acknowledgments

Over the past two decades I have received considerable financial support, encouragement, and constructive criticism from individuals and agencies in both Canada and the United States. Space limitations and a poor memory prohibit me from thanking all those who helped to make this book a reality. I apologize to anyone I neglect to mention in these acknowledgments.

I am grateful to the Social Sciences and Humanities Research Council of Canada, the Fulbright Program, the Association for Canadian Studies, Queen's University, and the University of Regina for the awards which supported me during the research and writing of this study. This book has been published with the help of a grant from the Humanities and Social Sciences Federation of Canada, using funds provided by the Social Sciences and Humanities Research Council of Canada.

My voyage would never have been possible without the guidance provided by those academics who influenced me so much during my undergraduate and graduate careers. Among this group I must note John Warkentin, J. David Wood, Conrad Heidenreich, Skip Ray, Louis Gentilcore, Andy Burghardt, Darrell Norris, Victor Konrad, David Gagan, Peter Goheen, Eric Moore, George Lovell, Allan Fell, Donald Swainson, Marvin McInnis, and especially Brian Osborne, my supervisor at Queen's University, who has continued to support me in his capacity as mentor and friend over the years. For favours both great and small I also wish to thank Phil and Cheryl Hoffman, Jay Nuttal, Richard Harris, David Howes, John Campling, Jeannette Rice, John Belec, Sam and Marie Arsenault, Judy Wiesenger, Evelyn Peters, Dianne Brydon, Gord Taylor, Pam Navickas, John Adams, Alice Kulikoff, Don and Jo Ann Parkerson, the late Peter Knights,

David Davenport, Bruce Elliott, Walter Nugent, John Clarke, Alan Brunger, Wayne Moodie, Allan Catchpole, Bob McCalla, Hugh and Lynne Millward, Ken Aitken, and David Smith. I am particularly grateful for the friendship and encouragement so generously provided by Gerard Bouchard. I would also like to thank the anonymous reviewers operating on behalf of the Social Sciences Federation for their comments and encouragement.

The staff of the relevant libraries, court houses, and archives, too numerous to mention, contributed enormously to the completion of this project. Special thanks are due to George Hepner, Harvey Miller, and the rest of the staff and students in the Department of Geography at the University of Utah where I spent six months engaged in research and teaching. All of them went out of their way to make me feel at home during my time in Salt Lake City. I also want to express my gratitude to the staff at McGill-Queen's University Press for their assistance and patience. I am especially indebted to Donald Akenson for his sage council, encouragement, and friendship over the years.

Several students, secretaries, and technicians at Queen's and Regina provided assistance in producing maps and figures: Mark Publicover, Ross Hough, George Innes, Margaret Somerville, Donna Glass, Shelly Shannon, David and Merle Ackerman, Mark Cote, Frank Abramovic, Hugh Nelson and, especially, Lorena Patino. I also have to thank David Hampsten for allowing me to use his 1901 map of Grand Forks, North Dakota.

For all her support through the years and particularly for the summer of 1985, I thank Helen Roberts. As always, I acknowledge the love and support of my mother, father, and brothers. Finally, I wish to thank my wife Julee and my step-children Jennee and B.J. for making my life so much more than an academic journey. When Julee and Jennee chose to leave their home in Utah and follow me north "across the line," my personal voyage acquired new meaning. Together, we continue to explore and respect both our similarities and differences. I can only hope that others on this continent do the same.

The Voyage

It's not what you see, it's what you find.

– Anonymous

The context in which this book takes place represents more than just an academic interest in a subject that has too long been ignored; it reflects the incredible changes that have occurred in our world during the past few years. As centralized states topple across Europe and nations join together in economic trade blocs, monolithic national identities are vanishing and the meanings of borders are changing. The rhetoric of the day, regional conflicts notwithstanding, would have us believe that ahead lies a new world order, a new internationalism, with its chief allure a dynamic, integrated global economy that knows no boundaries. The dismantling of the Iron Curtain, the transformation of western Europe and North America into economic suprastates, the intensification of a world economy, and the internationalization of popular culture have prompted some to believe that boundaries of all types – geopolitical, economic, cultural – are no longer relevant or desirable.

Yet borders are important for states that will continue to occupy peripheral positions because such boundaries symbolize theoretical sovereignty in a world increasingly dominated by economic superpowers and giant transnational corporations based in North America, Europe, and Asia. As Canada faces a host of challenges posed by this new world order and begins a fresh chapter in its relationship with the United States, the meanings assigned to the border it shares with its southern neighbour have particular relevance for many Canadians regardless of political and economic philosophy.

One might question what this new world order has to do with this study of Anglo-Canadian intracontinental migration at the turn of the twentieth century. At the start of my dissertation twenty-one years ago I embarked on a exploratory voyage in a largely unfamiliar sea. Relatively few Americans have contemplated their relationship with Canada and even fewer American historians have examined the Canadian immigrant experience, despite the fact that Canadians in 1900 represented the third-largest ethnic group in the United States after the Irish and the Germans. And although the relationship with the United States serves as a barometer by which Canadians measure their evolving identity and is a major, if not the dominant, focal point for a plethora of historical, literal, symbolic, and psychological interpretations of Canadian identity – or at least an Anglo-Canadian identity – few Canadians have considered the importance of migration in linking people and communities on both sides of the border and the role of mobility in shaping the development of both Canadian and American regions. The actual or perceived rapidity with which Anglo-Canadians assimilated and the significant difficulty in examining this group given the absence of passenger lists and the imprecision of U.S. census data are the reasons most often given for the neglect demonstrated of this topic. I was cautioned, and rightly so, that I might drown in a research ocean with few landmarks to offer guidance along the way.

Yet despite these well-intentioned warnings, I decided to set sail into this aqua incognita. Every grail requires a journey. My only reference point, besides a strong feeling that this story is not as straightforward and unremarkable as commonly believed, was my lifelong fascination with Canadian-American relations. In order to proceed, I needed to discover sources and devise strategies that would allow me to follow Anglo-Canadians through both time and space in order to develop a better understanding of the demographic, social, and economic adjustments made by those who moved on and those who stayed behind. Tracing migrants, however, is difficult, as researchers are restricted by their inability to operate behind the narrowly defined geographic and temporal boundaries present in the census. Tracing individuals across large areas of North America is particularly difficult because censuses were not designed for either cross-jurisdictional or cross-temporal linkage.

The breakthrough occurred when I discovered a little used record, the U.S. Petitions for Naturalization, a source which goes beyond the census because it contains information on origin and destination points, birthplace, family composition, mode of travel, date of emigration, residence in America, and occupation. My dissertation investigated Canadians emigrating to urban centres in northern New York State. Subsequent research has focused on long-distance, primarily rural-rural migration to the Red River valley of North Dakota and both the return migration of Canadians from the United States and the internal migration of Canadians, primarily from Ontario and Manitoba, to Saskatchewan. In this work, I have devised a number of tracing strategies, using a variety of sources in addition to the Petitions for Naturalization, to follow individuals and families: manuscript censuses, directories, local histories, border crossing records, tax records, homestead records, family histories, genealogies, and oral histories.

The approach taken in this project can be described as prosopographical, a fusion of fact and theory, of the qualitative and quantitative, of structure and agency, and of broad survey and biography. No one strategy or method, I decided, was appropriate to present this story. Descriptive exposition, quantitative tabulation, and structural examination were modes of analysis deemed appropriate to organize the information. The qualitative dimensions of this migration both in Canada and the United States were explored by examining Canadian and American newspapers, journals, and literature in order to discern attitudes held by the native population towards foreigners, to monitor any expressions of Canadian consciousness which surfaced during this period, and to identify any possible vehicles for this developing consciousness. The use of genealogies allowed me to move beyond these more traditional modes and develop a life-history approach which gets us closer to the individuals involved. Five well-documented genealogies of Bay of Quinte families introduced different family groups who served as *dramatis personae* of the monograph. These genealogies provided an opportunity to study the mobility and persistence experiences of pioneer eastern Ontario families and their descendants (over nine hundred descendant families) throughout the course of the nineteenth century and, when linked with other records, allowed me to trace land ownership and occupation over time. By this device, the study was able to personalize, characterize, compare, and contrast the experiences of Anglo-Canadian persisters and movers.

When I began this voyage, I felt alone; I no longer do. A growing interest in Canadian studies in the United States reflects a different attitude on the part of some Americans towards their relationship with Canada, an attitude shaped and directed by the economic, cultural, and political forces associated with the changes that I mentioned previously. The reality of a North American free trade bloc has prompted Americans to reconsider their relationships with Canada and Mexico. At the same time, Canadians have intensified their compulsive fascination with the United States. In light of this increased interest, the scope of this research extended beyond my initial curiosity about the Anglo-Canadian migrant experience and led me to consider broader questions about assimilation and identity.

The present context prompted me to consider the variable Anglo-Canadian immigrant experience in terms of the forces that served to integrate this group into the larger American community and the forces that ensured their continuing ties with family, friends, and a Canadian identity. The concepts by which I framed this discussion of Anglo-Canadian migration – regional separation, cultural diversity, Canadian-American relations – constituted the framework in which to examine this larger question of identity. The unavoidable question to emerge from this study, one that I was unable to answer satisfactorily, is: did the migrants have any Anglo-Canadian identity to retain or give up when they moved to the United States? Unfortunately, the data, tracing strategies, and modes of analysis did not allow me to fully appreciate the interior experiences of individual migrants. I faced the dilemma that all other researchers of historical migrations confront, the paucity of data and the necessity of inferring a great deal from a limited set of sources. And I would argue that this predicament is made even more difficult by the "invisible" nature of this particular immigrant group.

Nevertheless, the project has revealed much about a movement for which more than broad impressions have yet to be given. Canadians and Americans need to know more about this phenomenon, as it played a major role in shaping the development of families, communities, and regions on both sides of the border. Our understanding of the dynamics and consequences of Canadian intracontinental migration, not only in terms of its effects on the individuals involved, but on the communities of origin and destination as well, have been improved. And I would like to believe that this story will provide Canadians with a better understanding of themselves and their relationship with the United States. For ultimately, this is a voyage that I believe we all must take.

PART ONE
Contexts

Bath Town Hall
(Public Archives Canada/Pa-87853)

Introduction

Je ne demande pas ou menent les routes; c'est pour la trajet que
je pars.

                      – Anne Hébert
           "L'Ange de Dominique," *Le Torrent*

In an interview conducted in his later years, James Pappa of Watertown,
New York, observed: "I was ambitious and anxious to overcome my many
deficiencies, hence I worked long hours and hard, making the most of my
evenings by studying, thus endeavouring to compete with those my own
age." Recalling his early years in Watertown, he added: "If I were to place
on paper the record of the first few years of my experience in this city in
my effort to make good, it would take much valuable space."[1] James Pappa
did make good. This Canadian immigrant from Newburgh, Ontario, established himself in the community and eventually became mayor of Watertown, one of New York's fastest growing urban centres at the end of the
nineteenth century. He is also distinctive because, unlike so many of the
almost two and a half million Canadians settling in the United States
between 1860 and 1900,[2] he left a record of his early migration experience.

James Pappa was born in Newburgh on 24 July 1852, the son of a Canadian-born merchant tailor and an English-born mother. He was the
youngest of four children, all maintained in "comfortable circumstances."
Following in the footsteps of his older brother, a typesetter in the office of
the Kingston, Ontario, *British Whig*, he became a printer. His first job was
with the Newburgh *Beaver*, a four-page weekly. James left the paper after
seven months, disillusioned that he never received a cent of the $1.50
weekly wage promised to him. Apparently Pappa was not attracted by any
of the few remaining opportunities available in Newburgh, including
clerking in a store, driving a stagecoach, or working in a foundry or carriage plant. Like many others, he decided to move on to greener pastures
south of the border. His father was involved in a vessel business with

James's uncle in Oswego and often spoke of the many opportunities in the United States. In September of 1871 the nineteen-year-old James left for Oswego. His route took him through Watertown where he stayed at the Globe Hotel. Exploring the town, James happened to pass by the Watertown *Daily Times* and he decided to make an application for work. At that point, Pappa's good luck was about to begin:

S.M. Washburn, the foreman, was the first and only person I ever asked for a job. Fortunately, as I learned later, Foreman Washburn was a former Canadian printer of Belleville, Ontario. This fact was doubtless in my favour and I was told I might report for work at 1 in the afternoon. I was there on time. This was my first introduction to the good people of Watertown and 12 years later I made it my permanent home and became an American citizen by naturalization.[3]

After his experience at the Newburgh *Beaver*, the salary he first received, $1 per day, must have seemed like a fortune to the young man. He was soon promoted to foreman in the book department of the job printing plant. A short time later, the *Daily Times* sold the building and the job plant to the Hungerford Printing Company, and Pappa was promoted to the business office. He subsequently became a member of the editorial staff where he reported on the city markets and compiled the "Looking Backward" column.

As James became established in his career, his involvement in the city increased. A member of the Odd Fellows fraternity for over twenty years, he was also involved in municipal politics. In 1901 he ran, successfully, as the Republican candidate for mayor, and after serving his two-year term, was elected supervisor of the second ward on two different occasions. Pappa's life in Watertown was a satisfying one. His voyage was smooth and short.

In many ways, James Pappa's story is representative of Canadian emigration to the United States. Many left home because of unfavourable circumstances and moved to American cities and rural communities because of better prospects and the presence of friends and relatives. And it is also likely that their fellow expatriates hired many Canadians like James. His story supports the commonly held assumption that anglophone Canadians adapted easily to American society and as such disappeared into the mainstream of American life with scarcely so much as a ripple. Yet little can be said about the typical Canadian immigrant experience. No immigrant has received less attention in the historical literature than the "invisible" Canadian.[4]

There has been little detailed examination of migration between Canada and the United States even though history attests to the intermingling of the Canadian and American peoples during periods of both peace and conflict. A possible reason for this neglect is the historical assumption of an American "unit of expansion." The great emphasis placed upon the role of the frontier in shaping the settlement of the North American continent has blinded many to the myriad of influences outside the frontier process that affected development – urbanization and industrialization, and the cultural transfer of ideas and values. Both the Canadian and American experiences are lumped together in this model and differences between the two countries and within each individual nation are hidden in this view of settlement as a wave of western expansion.[5]

This significant flow of people out of Canada directly affected the social and economic lives of both those who participated in the movement and those who did not. Varying in intensity, time, and space, it was nonetheless an omnipresent phenomenon for much of the nineteenth century. As such, it has engendered considerable scrutiny; and yet the historical literature has tended to stress the general rather than the particular. Macro-scale research has centred on the dimensions and causes of the migration, ignoring the consequences of the movement for the individuals involved.[6] Micro-scale studies that have concentrated on the consequences of migration have focused almost exclusively on the experiences of French Canadians, whose presence in America has facilitated such detailed analysis.[7]

The focus in migration research has long been on the transatlantic migration of Europeans to the new world, a phenomenon replete with romantic associations of national development. Canadians, both French- and English-speaking, but particularly the latter, were not believed to have experienced the social dislocation which European groups encountered upon migration. As a group, there was no overwhelming desire to flee; Canadians were not subject to the same levels of discrimination, political prejudice, or overwhelming poverty as were Jews and Irish. They did not have to face a long and arduous sea voyage, the rotten food and sickening conditions of steerage. Once they arrived in the United States, they did not encounter the crowded and confused circumstances that greeted European immigrants at such reception points as Ellis Island. The distances travelled were often so short that the prospect of permanent separation from family and friends was practically non-existent for most Canadians.

Because they shared the same language and many of the same cultural, historical, and economic conditions with the Americans, it is assumed that anglophone Canadians found it easier to adjust to American society than other immigrant groups. They were not bound by the same religious ties, a distinctive culture, or a shared sense of destiny as were the French Canadians in New England. Because these Canadians were of the same stock as many Americans and held similar beliefs and values, their presence as a distinct ethnic group was rarely noticed. Anglo-Canadian social institutions were rare as cultural fragmentation and dispersed employment reinforced a traditional lack of unity which characterized most Canadian ethnic groups at home and abroad.

Yet this flow of people invites examination for several reasons. The very nature of the movement suggests that it may have played a major role in the development of particular communities on both sides of the border. The areas from which migrants came tended to be older and well-settled, although there were exceptions, predominantly rural enclaves, experiencing economic stagnation or decline. Often these regions lost population to nearby American urban centres. For many of these American communities, Anglo-Canadians constituted one of the largest sources of labour for their expanding industry. The districts which experienced this drain probably suffered greatly because of this loss, although this out-migration may have served as a safety-valve, relieving pressure due to unfavourable human-land ratios.

The migration was for many, particularly the young, a movement off the farm or from the small town into larger industrial cities, a process which must have presented many problems and challenges to the individual. It seems facile, moreover, to view anglophone Canadians as a homogeneous group; they came from different regions, classes, religions, and occupations. And they had experienced different conceptions of government, social welfare, ethnic heritage, and economic organization than had their neighbouring Americans. The presence or absence of such differences shapes this exploration of migration experiences and constitutes a major area of inquiry among those interested in the discovery and elaboration of the Canadian identity.

Attachment to local identity plays a significant role in the migration experience. For many Canadians, the family and its kinship network may have proven to be more important than any loyalty to occupation or ethnic group. Investigation may reveal that the pattern of localized ties, so important in Canada, was repeated in America. Regional cross-border linkages may have also played a role in creating a variable migration experience.

Geographical origin is not enough to define the Anglo-Canadian experience; an effort has to be made to understand the "Canadianness" of the migrant population. In this context, several difficult questions emerge. How did Canadians view Americans and Americans view Canadians and what role did these viewpoints play in the adaptation process? Did conditions, institutions, and events encountered at home and in their new locations serve to reinforce a feeling of non-Americanism, which may have been equated with a sense of being Canadian? These experiences have to be structured within these questions of identity. The monitoring of the Canadian consciousness during this turn-of-the-century period is framed by the usual barometers by which we assess our identity (or lack of identity): regional separation, cultural diversity, and our relationship with the

United States, particularly in the context of immediate cross-border interactions. Post-migration experiences of Anglo-Canadians are examined in terms of individual responses, group cohesion, and societal interaction as conceptualized in terms of the family, community, and the "ethclass," that is, the social class segment within an ethnic group to which people relate.[8] Because of the fact that so many Canadians returned from the United States to Canada, albeit to a different part of the country from which they originated, this story is rounded out with an analysis of returning Canadians to Saskatchewan as well as an investigation of internal migration to this same province.

Our voyage begins in Canada by examining the political-economic and socio-cultural contexts of this migration, searching the historic-geographical and psychological characteristics of Canadian identity during the nineteenth century; examining the dimensions and regional variations of emigration to the United States; reviewing the theories and conceptual debates underlying the study of mobility and rural transformation; and centring on the context of emigration from a regional perspective, focusing in particular on the Bay of Quinte region of Ontario and the experiences of the genealogical families chosen for study. The attention then shifts to three major destinations chosen by Anglo-Canadian migrants, primarily from Ontario, where the experiences of this group are compared and contrasted with others in the specific contexts of those particular locations.

1 Where is Here? The Problem of Identity

> If the national mental illness of the United States is megalomania,
> that of Canada is paranoid schizophrenia.
> – Margaret Atwood, *Journals of Susanna Moodie*

It is fashionable in socio-psychological history to look back and discover or invent identifications and attachments to place. Individuals and groups conceptualize their identity within the context of place – the household, the community, the region, the nation. Conceiving a feeling of "who-ness" in terms of a sense of "where-ness" is a voyage of discovery everyone takes. In this passage, the voyager searches for frames of reference which facilitate the development of attachments to place and, in doing so, creates structural and psychological boundaries. These boundaries, in turn, serve to delineate territories which are deemed necessary to both physical and psychic survival. And survival is dependent on the strength or vulnerability of the borders that separate the individual or group ("us") from others ("them").[1]

Borders – socio-economic, geopolitical and psychological – have always played a role in the development of an Anglo-Canadian identity. These boundaries represent structural centripetal and centrifugal forces that both unify the country and pull it in different directions. Such contradictory energies have created a country that is in itself a paradox. And trying to make sense of this paradox is in many ways a schizophrenic task. Yet try we must, for not to do so would leave out an important part of our story, the role of identity in the migration experience.

ISLANDS IN A SEA: REGIONAL SEPARATION AND CULTURAL DIVERSITY

To most Canadians, the search for identity is made difficult by the fact that the country has been divided by what Hugh MacLennan has called the "two solitudes." Through much of Quebec's history, language, faith, and the family have acted as the triad of French-Canadian culture and have served to protect both the interests and the identity of this group.[2] Yet while French Canada can identify with its distinctive religion, art, literature, and other indigenous cultural traits, there is no comparable monolithic "English" Canada. Profound cultural and regional differences separate this large but amorphous group, differences based on ethnicity, class, religion, and history. The fact of being "non-French" and the perception of being "non-American" have been the principal characteristics identifying anglophone Canadians.

The panoply of attachments existing in this country has always countered a pan-Canadian identity: allegiances to region, to ethnic group, to religion, to outside interests. While not a collection of warring tribes, Canadians have always erected boundaries that have shaped the contours of the Canadian identity. What effects these borders have had is the subject of much debate and confusion.

Regional Borders   Regionalism is a narrow prism through which to view a political landscape but history teaches us that regional differences in this country are the consequence of distinct historical development and geographical distance. The regional dimension of Canadian life has been and continues to be a major factor in the development of the Canadian identity, a fact eloquently expressed by the giant of Canadian literary criticism, Northrop Frye.

Through a lifetime of study, Northrop Frye unconsciously adopted a historical geographical approach to the study of Canadian identity. He views the elusive question of identity as nothing more than an expression of culture, including the human imagination. Since the imagination – that is, the ideas by which we live – is so shaped by personal experience and perception, in a country as large and diverse as Canada, identity is not a Canadian but a regional question. The tension between national unity and regional identity, Frye believes, means that the important existential question perplexing Canadians is not "Who am I?" but rather "Where is here?"[3] He emphasizes the fact, later elaborated upon by R.C. Harris, that there was no temporally and spatially continuous settlement experience as in the United States. Small communities and regions, geographically isolated from one another, ensured a development of what Frye calls a "garrison mentality" and Harris terms an "island archipelago."[4]

Both Harris and Frye express their views of the historical geographical essence of Canada in the form of metaphors, the former seeing Canada as a collection of islands in a stormy sea called Confederation and the latter comprehending the country in the form of a cartographical metaphor – that is, using the legend and conventions of a map.[5] To Frye, each voyager (Canadian) in search of the national image (Here) is involved in a journey that has no arrival; the map is not yet complete. The individual identifies and interprets ideas, events, and experiences largely within a geographic frame, which enables him to orient himself in time and space. Individuals interpret who they are by defining from where they speak. Self-identity can only be discovered in the context of community yet is not ontologically prior to community. Individual values are both enabled and constrained through those of the community, however defined. Yet it is this ambiguous process of definition or placement that creates an ontological crisis for the individual.

He asks himself "Where is here?" but this leads him still into uncharted territory. In this quest the voyager must recognize that there is a body of cultural assumptions, framed by regional/local consciousness, involved in the appreciation of the nature of Canada which acts as a filter through which the imagery passes. Frye reasons that an individual's "Here" is neither static nor complete but continually evolves as new ideas, events, and experiences permeate one's consciousness.

To Frye, every part of Canada is a separation, segregated from every other along several grounds.[6] Complicating matters for the individual is a pluralistic ethos which admits the possibility of a multiplicity of communities. Canada as a "community of communities," a society where differences do not have to be adversarial, where unity in diversity is seen to be the essence of a collective identity, poses conceptual challenges to its members who more readily and easily align themselves with the immediate – the group, the locality, the region. Separation doesn't have to imply segregation, but exclusion and/or inclusion is often what results.[7]

What effect the physical environment has had on both unifying and dividing the country has also been a subject of considerable discussion, much of it centring on the theme of environmentalism. A tradition of cultural environmentalism evident in Canadian literature attributes both national and regional character to the shaping forces of terrain and climate. It is the reality of Canada's geography, many argue, that has nurtured strong regional identities which act as barriers against national unity. Those communities on the periphery are still marginalized and isolated from the mainstream.

Canada's earliest European agriculturalists were limited to patches of suitable farmland, fishermen were huddled in protective coves, and lumbermen were scattered in isolated camps. This discontinuous settlement experience, which produced isolated communities and retarded a common identity, created a different frontier experience in Canada than in the United States, one in which "European social formations were bent ... by non-European space."[8]

Cultural Borders   Regional separation within Canada, however, is not just related to geographical isolation; cultural plurality based on language, religion, and ethnicity also serve as centrifugal forces. Culture is shared and transmitted between generations through the medium of language. The English-French duality is a basic reality of Canadian existence but even among Canadians who share the same language, English, religious and ethnic differences, often exacerbated by geographical isolation, have created boundaries both between and within regions.

The whole question of ethnicity and ethnic identification is extremely problematical. Akenson suggests that anglophile Canadian is perhaps a more suitable designation than Anglo-Canadian because included in this group is a multiplicity of ethnic and religious subgroups: English, Scottish, Welsh, Irish Protestant, Irish Catholic. It is essential, in his opinion, to know ethnic origin as well as place of birth because "ethnicity is a perduring cultural characteristic" which has influence over the generations.[9] This is no doubt true but it is impossible to discern, for example, the degrees of Irishness and Canadianness in the second and third generation Irish-Canadian. It is fashionable to dwell on the limitations to Canadian identity (association with British traditions, the dominance of American culture), but to ignore the shaping forces of time and place on the individual psyche is to neglect at least half of the story.

However, developing theories of relationship between individual behaviour and ethnic background is difficult. Ethnicity is an abstract, heuristic device that is used to create boundaries of inclusiveness and exclusiveness. Yet it is important to separate ethnic identity (who am I?) from the traits associated with ethnicity (what am I?). Most researchers focus simply on the ethnic – those aspects of culture (speech, dress, custom) that people recognize as setting a group apart from the rest. The subjects of this study were for the most part second- or third-generation Canadian. Yet at the same time, one could say that they were also third- or fourth-generation Irish or English or Scottish. Whether Anglo-Canadians at the turn of the twentieth century looked upon themselves as resolutely Canadian or predominantly British is difficult to discern, although impressions may be garnered from a reading of papers, letters, and editorials relating to various issues such as, for example, the Boer War.

Only a small number of Europeans settled in the less friendly environment of Canada during the initial peopling phase of North America. They were a composite of ethnic and religious groups, all carrying their own cultural baggage. During the sixteenth and seventeenth centuries the North American colonies were just another destination available to mobile Europeans responding to political and religious fragmentation, enclosure and the commercialization of agriculture, population pressures, and the lure of cheap and available land overseas. Bailyn describes this movement as "a spillover – an outgrowth, an extension – of ... established patterns of mobility."[10] Most of those who came to Canada during the French regime were unemployed men, soldiers, girls from poorhouses, and criminals. After the conquest, the more ambitious settlers from Britain usually chose the United States, while the Maritimes and Ontario attracted the poor who came to Canada because of cheap passage in the hold of a timber ship. And many of this group within a very short time made their way to the United States.

The deep division between anglophones and francophones continued in the post-Confederation period. The two solitudes produced religious confrontation between Protestants and Catholics and a low degree of intermarriage. "The French Canadians, who supplied a good deal of the labour force and a little of the agricultural produce of the St. Lawrence trading system, had a different attachment to place, different views of the relationship of an individual to society, and different conceptions of government and of themselves in the world than had the English-speaking businessmen in Montreal and the English-speaking farmers of Ontario."[11] Events such as the hanging of Louis Riel and the removal of the French language from the legislatures of both Manitoba and the North-West Territories and the elimination of French in the public schools in the 1890s did nothing to bridge the cultural division. Class differences so evident in Quebec between the anglophone merchants of Montreal and Quebec City and the poorer, predominantly rural French-Canadian habitants also served to magnify the two solitudes.

Outside Quebec, the majority of the population at the turn-of-the-century period was of Anglo-Celtic ethnicity (60.6 percent in 1871, 58.8 percent in 1881, 57 percent in 1901, 55.5 percent in 1911). In 1871, the Irish comprised the majority of persons of British Isles origin in Canada (40.1 percent), followed by the English and Welsh (33.5 percent) and the Scots (26.1 percent). Thirty years later, the English and Welsh were the largest group (41.2 percent), followed by the Irish (32.3 percent) and the Scots (26.1 percent).[12] While the population was predominantly British in origin, religion served to create divisions. The obvious differences that split Canada led some to believe that the idea of Canada was an absurdity. Goldwin Smith argued that loyalty to the group superseded any fealty to "English" Canada:

When Canadian nationalists say that patriotism is a good thing, they are told to keep their wisdom for the copy-books; and the rebuke would be just if those who administer it would recognize the equally obvious truth that there can be no patriotism without nationality. In a dependency there is no love of the country; no pride in the country ... In a dependency every bond is stronger than that of country, every interest prevails over that of the country. The province, the sect, Orangeism, Fenianism, Freemasonry, Odd Fellowship, are more to the ordinary Canadian than Canada."[13]

In rebuttal, nationalists contended that national sentiment was starting to unfold "like a flower ... Its vegetation has, indeed, been slow. Individual nationalities have mitigated against it. Local jealousies and heartburnings here, and mediaeval politics there, have trammelled its growth and screened it from the light. But its power and cohesiveness are being felt at last, and already it is binding the scattered communities of British America together in the bonds of a common cause, a common language, and a common destiny."[14] However, the common destiny would have to rest upon more than metaphorical arguments; economic, political, and cultural foundations were needed to counteract deep regional and cultural divisions.

Economic Borders   Well into the nineteenth century, "pre-industrial methods of production and distribution still fostered a strong localism in British North American life."[15] Differences in settlement policy, resource base, social organization, and level of urbanization and industrialization contributed greatly to local and regional variations in economic development. The link between economic development and the formation of identity at the national, regional, and local scales has most often been understood from the functional approach, which adheres to the metropolitan-hinterland interpretation of staples theory. In this approach, "Canada is organized into a series of regions that link together strong metropolitan centres of capital and hinterlands of staple exploitation."[16] The fact that investment from foreign and domestic metropolises was never effectively coordinated under a national policy of economic development only served to exacerbate regional differences associated with history and geography.[17]

European powers saw profit in the new world in the exploitation of staple resources, native wealth and labour, and a barter trade, and exploration was aimed at this end. In the Maritimes, staple resources such as fish, timber, and furs were exploited for European markets. Access to Europe, the West Indies, and America counteracted to a significant extent a limited hinterland and small local markets. Settlements were developed as small colonial links in a metropolitan chain with no one centre asserting its dominance within the region. Small urban centres with limited regional hinterlands were more closely linked with outside metropolises than with each other.

This external focus reinforced the meagre development of the region's inhospitable interior, so that the majority of the population did not experience significant gains in their standard of living. There was no canal age in the Maritimes as in the Canadas, further retarding the improvement of communications with the region's hinterland. Samuel Cunard's decision to move his steam packet service from Halifax to Boston because of the latter's superior connections to the interior of the continent did much to retard the development of a dominant metropolis within the region.

The major lure for Maritime provinces to enter Confederation was the promise of a railway connecting the region with the interior. Eventually the Intercolonial Railway was built but it never achieved the volume of traffic anticipated. To the chagrin of Maritimers, it soon became obvious that central Canadian financial interests were both unable and unwilling to provide the capital needed to fund development of the region. By the end of the first decade of the twentieth century, the region was well on its way to "deindustrialization in the name of economic efficiency."[18]

The National Policy of the Conservative government has been interpreted as an economic instrument used by metropolitan interests based in central Canada to develop the West as colony of central Canada.[19] During the economic troubles of the 1880s, western farmers sold grain on an unprotected world market but were forced to buy expensive goods produced in central Canada. This cost-price squeeze, the monopoly power of the Canadian Pacific Railway, and federal control of prairie crown lands all fostered anger and a sense of regional alienation in the West.

A growing disillusionment prompted threats of secession from a number of hinterland newspapers. In 1885 the Manitoba *Free Press* reacted in the following manner to the suggestion that Newfoundland was considering joining Confederation: "If the people of Newfoundland know when they are well off, they will give the Dominion a wide berth. There are few provinces, if any, in it today that would not rejoice to be out of it, and that would not forever stay out if they were." In a similar vein, the Halifax *Morning Chronicle* in May of 1886 welcomed the first secessionist campaign in Nova Scotia with the following words: "We thrived before we endured the exactions of the Canucks, we shall thrive when we are once again free from their exactions."[20]

With the improvement of the economy in the 1890s, regional tensions declined and more confidence was expressed in the view that Canada was economically strong enough to survive. The Maritimes, however, did not share in the general prosperity and a legacy of regional antipathy towards central Canada was firmly established.

J.M.S. Careless views the development of the Canadian frontier as an expression of metropolitan interests searching for staples. During the colonial period, Canadian centres such as Quebec City, Montreal, and Halifax served as entrepôts but eventually developed their own regional hinterlands. In the nineteenth century, Toronto and other centres would come to acquire their own hinterlands. At the same time, American metropolises such as Boston, New York, Chicago, St Paul, and San Francisco created their own links with Canadian regional hinterlands, although London remained the dominant external metropolis for much of the period.

Because the drive for Confederation was urban-directed, Careless maintains that metropolitanism promoted an emerging national identity and helped shape regional sentiments. "Because regional centres became branch locations of national businesses and industries, most located in central Canada," he reasons, "they shared in national attitudes and identity."[21] Yet while metropolitan interests were expanding, a poorly developed native culture, at least in Anglo-Canada, and political differences were working against the development of a national identity.

Attempts to Create Cultural Bridges   While Confederation brought the colonies together in a political alliance, it could not unite them spiritually. That could only take place over the course of time with the development of economic linkages and the evolution of an indigenous culture shared by the inhabitants of all regions. The major problem with Confederation, according to Frye, was its impoverished cultural basis. Instead of relying on a native cultural base, Canada "was thought of, however unconsciously, as a British colony and a Tory counterpart of the United States, with French and indigenous groups forming picturesque variations in the background."[22] At Confederation, Canada outside Quebec did not really have a culture either in the sense of a shared heritage of historical memories and customs or in terms of artistic creation through literature, music, architecture, scholarship, and the applied arts.

Anglo-Canadians could only draw upon a meagre reservoir of symbols and myths for guidance. Symbols help us interpret who or what we are and what we can be and myths are particularly important because they transform secular history into sacred legends. Anglophone Canada by the turn of the twentieth century had relatively few myths around which emotions, beliefs, memories, and nostalgia had been ritualized, the exceptions being the trek of the Loyalists northward and the idea of Canadians standing up to the Yankees during the War of 1812. But even the myth of the Canadian David standing up against the American Goliath gives way to the reality of Canada being defended largely by British troops and Indian loyalists and the irony that trade between regions on both sides of the border continued largely unabated even as armies crossed that same line.

Culture needs roots from which to grow. At Confederation, these roots were confined largely to regions and locales. Through a combination of exogenous metropolitan influences and indigenous social processes, regional cultures had developed over time. People were moulded by both what they left behind and what they experienced in the new world. Many view this process as a "simplification" of Europe overseas. While Hartz argues that the mechanism of simplification was the emigration of fragments of the larger European society – fragments whose backgrounds facilitated their adjustment to their new environments – Harris and Meinig believe that the simplification of Europe overseas had to do more with the nature of the environments immigrants encountered rather than their own backgrounds. Regional cultures were not simple transplants but developed over a considerable period through processes of adaptation to the local environment, cultural selection, and interactions with people of other races and ethnic groups.[23]

No strong national culture existed which would provide citizens of the new country with a common frame of reference. For Anglo-Canadians, heritage was primarily of British rather than native origin, a point often noted in the literary journals of the period. In 1875 Jehu Mathews declared: "It has been almost always remarked by travelers in our own country that the national spirit was very strongly developed in Canada – that is to say the spirit of the glorious British nationality." That same year, William Norris remarked: "While over eight tenths of the population of Canada are native-born, the number of native Canadians, or men imbued with Canadian sentiments, in power, are very few."[24]

A poor development of social communication among the regions contributed largely to this lack of clarity in Canada's self-conception. Symbols lie at the core of culture but they first have to be created and then communicated to others. Before the development of moving pictures, radio, and television, literature and art served as the most important mediums of communication in society, transforming the material of culture into a mythology with which people could identify as their own.

While some Canadian-born authors wrote of Canada as a nation as early as the 1830s, Marchak argues that most Anglo-Canadian literature prior to 1930 was written by British visitors and Scottish Presbyterian ministers, both groups expounding the values of the imperial empire while not reflecting on the different cultural roots and values of a diverse indigenous population. "The resulting fictional portrait of Canadian development," she insists, "is a highly selective and predictably inaccurate portrait."[25] Pre-Confederation literature, published in journals such as *The Maple Leaf or Canadian Annual* (1847–9) and the *Anglo-American Magazine* (1852–5) romanticized the past, particularly as it related to British conquest and development of empire. The superiority of British institutions and the magnificence of the Canadian landscape were common themes appearing in the poems, short stories, articles, and novels of the period. To a large extent such literature was directed towards the prospective immigrant and thus served as a tool of propaganda for the state. The inferiority of American society always accompanied such discussions. Yet it was during this time that the maple leaf, the beaver, snow, and other elements of the Canadian environment were developed as national symbols.

Post-Confederation literature, according to Marchak, ignored non-British groups, racism, and poverty and presented romantic and unrealistic portraits of the immigrant experience. Why this was the case was due to "the fact that Canada remained a colony long after [its] 'declaration of independence'."[26] Colonial symbols continued to dominate despite increased efforts among Canadian writers to develop indigenous symbols, myths, and themes in novels and journals such as the *New Dominion Monthly*

(1867–9), the *Canadian Monthly and National Review* (1872–82) and *This Week: A Canadian Journal of Politics, Society and Literature* (1883–96). The literature appearing in these journals was more aggressively nationalistic, focusing on romanticized images associated with the Loyalists, Queenston Heights, the Battle of Lundy's Lane, the repulse of the Fenians, and other historical episodes of Canadian settlement.[27] Poetry and short stories portrayed ordinary Canadians – farmers, fishermen, lumbermen – as heroic characters. Figures who perhaps were more deserving of the label heroic – Isaac Brock, Maisonneuve, Laura Secord, D'Arcy McGee – attained some degree of mythical status in the literature.

Certain nationalists asserted that a national vision was starting to develop in the minds of the country's citizens. The small Anglo-Canadian Canada First movement of the late 1860s and early 1870s, developed by William Foster, a political writer for the Toronto *Telegram*, R.G. Haliburton, and others, believed that Canada as a nation would in time take precedence over sectional and regional interests. The group published their views in political articles, fiction, and poetry. Deterministic and anti-American in tone, they emphasized the country's northern climate and geography and focused on selective and simplistic symbols. The image of "the true north strong and free" rested on the argument that the northern environment would produce a hearty race of people with characteristics that would lead them to assume an important role not only within the empire but in the global theatre as well.

Anglo-Canadian writers operated within two literary frames of reference: the British and the American. By mid-century, influenced by their distinct environment and by their close proximity to the United States, Canadian writers had become committed to revitalizing British civilization within a new world setting. The passion for all things British diminished over time, although many were not ready to break all links with the old world. Those who supported imperial federation were convinced that Canada would renew an imperialism that would in turn protect Canadian independence in North America.

This argument was perhaps most effectively made in Sara Jeanette Duncan's 1904 novel, *The Imperialist*. The significance of this novel, according to Allan Smith, lay in the "manner in which it explored the tension which arose from Canada's situation as a community of the New World with strong and vital links to a community of the Old."[28] From this position, Duncan and others maintained, Canada was well suited to avoid the excesses of both British and American societies.

Nationalists such as Charles Mair believed that within a short period of time, a sense of nationality had managed to take root: "It [Canada] has traditions and a history of which it may be proud; but it has a history to make, a national sentiment to embody, and a national identity to carry out. There was a time when there was no fixed principle or national feeling in

Canada; when men were Englishmen, Scotchmen, Irishmen, or Frenchmen, and when to be a Canadian was almost to hang your head. But that time has passed away."[29]

Yet powerful obstacles existed which retarded the development of myths, symbols, and ideals which would articulate a national experience. Most fundamental was the element of time. Canada was only thirty-three years old in 1900 and not all provinces at that time had joined Confederation. Not enough time had passed for the country to develop a strong sense of history and a set of traditions which reflected a national rather than a colonial experience. While the population growth of French Canadians was due more to natural increase than immigration, a significant proportion of anglophone Canadians at the turn of the century were immigrants. And even though the overwhelming percentage of Anglo-Canadians were native-born, many came into the world as British citizens – that is, they were born before 1867. Further, many of this group were only one or two generations removed from their immigrant ancestors. A few of the Fathers of Confederation, particularly Macdonald and to a lesser extent Cartier and Brown, would eventually acquire the legendary status ensured by the passage of history, but the fact that Canada was born out of compromise rather than revolution dulled the process of myth-making.

The Canadian West never gripped the imagination of Canadians as the American West had captivated the minds of Americans. The ingredients of an Anglo-Canadian national identity were based primarily on a British cultural tradition. Yet imperialist sentiment and British tradition were not enough to counteract strong regional sentiments and increasing American penetration. As a result, Anglo-Canadians struggled to find their own vision of human order. This conflict is evident in the literature that evolved over time.

Much of the literature was regional as opposed to national in character, a quality Cappon argues to be "an extension of the economic and social reality of Canada's situation as 'hinterland' to first the British and then the American 'metropolis'."[30] Many of the Canadian-born writers of the period were attached geographically and emotionally to their region which, for most of this group, had been a colony during their formative years. In 1875 Roswell Fisher noted that "the feeling of Canadianism is not yet sufficiently strong enough to override all conflicting local feelings and interests."[31] Any ideas that were developed about a national identity were shaped by the writer's regional context.

Most importantly, Canadian literature had little influence on the public because most during this period had little time for reading and reflection. Unfavourable copyright laws, a small readership, cheaper and more readily available American and British literature, and a high illiteracy rate resulted in hardships for Canadian writers and a restricted capability for developing and communicating native ideas, interpretations, and symbols.[32]

I believe that the border has become a symbol for this country. We are, as Russell Brown states, a country "encoded by borders."[33] While identity is moulded to a significant extent by a regional consciousness shaped by cultural plurality and geographical isolation, the frame used by the voyager to orient himself in territory is bounded east and west by the rest of Canada and north and south by his transborder relationship with the United States.

BORDERS AND METAPHORS: CANADIAN-AMERICAN RELATIONS

It is evident upon examination of metaphors used to describe the border that different meanings have been offered regarding Canadian-American relations. Canadians, particularly anglophone Canadians, have tended to view the border as a dividing line or shield, protecting a fledgling culture from a dominating presence. The metaphor of the *border as shield* symbolizes that, for Canadians, our relationship with the United States has played a major role in developing what symbols we do have. This is an important consideration given the reality of living in an environment dominated by American symbols, icons, and myths.

Quebec exists largely as a nation because of its unique culture, reinforced by language, and its association with a distinctive historical geography, but anglophone Canada has always struggled to find its niche within the continent. For this group, the Canadian-American border takes on an even greater meaning. It is understood as an interpreted emotional experience, a symbolic marker defining a Canadian community.

The most striking aspect of the border as shield metaphor is its oppositional character. As Anthony Cohen wisely states, "boundaries are relational rather than absolute; that is, they mark the community in relation to other communities."[34] The border serves as the basic reference point for historical, literal, symbolic, and psychological interpretations of an Anglo-Canadian identity. Yet identity is a problematical concept; it is heavily contextual, difficult to measure, and changes over time and according to milieu. What is constant in the Canadian experience is that all groups in different regions and at different times have interpreted their identity vis-à-vis their relationship with the United States. And in this context, the border is the emotional and ideological focal point for the never-ending debate over the nature of these relationships.

This is the basic premise of Patrick McGreevy's examination of the contrasting meanings assigned to the Niagara border region by citizens from both countries. McGreevy metaphorically describes the border as a "wall of mirrors, reflecting back different meanings to Canadians and Americans, meanings that in turn reflect different ideologies of nationalism." Canadians take much better care of their side of this border region in comparison to Americans because Niagara symbolizes the "front entrance to the house," the place where Anglo-Canadian nationalism begins; whereas for Americans, this place represents "the back alley where the trash is kept," the place where America's manifest destiny ended with the War of 1812.[35] Yet as McGreevy readily admits, the meanings assigned to the border by citizens living on both sides are not so clearly distinguishable at other places because of different experiences. There was no similar militaristic conflict along the St Croix River (despite the antics of the drunken Fenians in 1866) or the 49th parallel. The strong commercial links between the Maritimes and New England and the east-west flow of trade and migration into the West paralleling the transcontinental railway resulted in a different transborder experience for these Canadian regions and generated different interpretations of the significance of the border.

Political forces of integration and separation have had a significant impact on Canadian-American relations. Discussion often centres on what can be termed the genesis thesis: the United States was a product of revolution, created by rebels who wanted to limit the role of government and for whom the only inalienable entitlement was "life, liberty and the pursuit of happiness," whereas Canada was created by a process of evolution, its constitution emphasizing "peace, order and good government."[36] This different political culture is viewed not simply as something inherited from Britain but rather as something organic, evolving from the Tory-Whig debate and the act of revolution itself in the American colonies. Lipset maintains that both Canada and the United States were created by revolution, with America inheriting Whig ideas and ideals and Canadians inheriting Tory ones.[37] Likewise, Frye views Canada "as a country that grew out of Tory opposition to the Whig victory in the American Revolution, thus forming in a sense, something complementary to the United States itself."[38]

Loyalism is seen by many as the dominating ideology of nineteenth-century Anglo-Canada; in fact, considerable discussion of Canadian political culture is centred around its role. How one interprets loyalism plays a major role in subsequent interpretation of the developing political culture of Canada. The literature on the role of loyalism is divided roughly into two camps: those who view the Loyalist tradition as embracing both conservatism and an intense anti-Americanism and those who argue that Loyalists were really liberal Americans with a "Tory touch." The former position, stemming from Louis Hartz's "fragment theory" and associated most clearly with the views of S.F. Wise, contends that what made Canada, at least anglophone Canada, unique from the United States, was its Tory character.[39] To Wise, loyalism suggested more than just loyalty to the British monarchy; it "meant as well adherence to those beliefs and institutions the conservative considered essential in the presentation of a form of life different from, and superior to, the manners, politics and social arrangements of the United States."[40] Drache suggests that the country was settled by those who were either exiled or fleeing revolution and it was this counter-revolutionary legacy "which fundamentally altered not only the liberal democratic character and institutions but class relations as well."[41]

As an ideology, loyalism measured its values of social order and respect for authority against the American example. According to Cheal, while "Americans were regarded as an unstable people, erratic and unpredictable, and consequently careless of law and order ... the Loyalists stood for the recognition of law rather than rebellion, for the unity of Empire rather than a separate existence for colonies, for the British constitution rather than republicanism and for a hierarchical society in which the classes possessed, and recognized, different rights and privileges."[42] Government intervention supported by Tory collectivist traditions was to be the hallmark of this new society. Horowitz suggests that both socialism and toryism, from which the former was derived, share two features in common: the rejection of liberal notions of a society devoted to individualism and equality of opportunity, and a sense of community superseding individual desires.[43]

Environmentalists believe it was the underlying force of the frontier that ultimately strengthened the liberal principles of freedom and individuality even in a society where much faith was placed on traditional conservative values. Clark believes that urban dwellers were more attached to conservative British values than the more numerous and politically apathetic countryside residents. In response, Wise argues that eventually the Tory convictions developed by the elite were accepted by the inarticulate majority.[44] But studies by Errington and others show that while the Tory elite were most vociferous in criticism of all things American and praise of all things British, many of this same group, particularly those involved in business, expressed admiration for American economic achievements and continued to foster connections with their southern neighbours.[45] This "Federalist-Loyalist alliance" argument suggests that even though Loyalists were loyal to Britain, most were shaped by the more liberal environment into which they were born and raised, although one might argue that the thousands of blacks, Indians, and Germans who composed a significant percentage of this migration were not raised in such a milieu. And once in the Canadas and the Maritimes, Loyalists continued to be affected by cross-border flows of peoples, goods, and ideas. Proximity, relative ease of communication, trade, kith and kin connections, and some basic liberal beliefs combined with conservative ideals to provide a basis for this alliance.[46]

While the War of 1812 left a residue of anti-Americanism in Upper Canada, it had little effect in the Maritimes, where mutually beneficial ties with New England continued largely unabated. But over time, even in

Upper Canada the rate of development in the United States won grudging respect, especially among those who sought reform. Much of William Lyon Mackenzie's social ideal was Jeffersonian in origin. Both sides in the 1837 rebellion looked south for vindication of their actions; for reformers, "the United States illustrated the advantages of democratic reform [while] conservatives ... pointed to American social and political disorder, to the lack of talent the electoral system provided for government, and to diminishing religious sentiment in society."47 Yet as the two sides squabbled over issues, they were laying the foundation for an emerging colonial ideology, an amalgam of British and American ideas and ideals that would produce an Upper Canadian political culture.

Confederation, to a large extent, resulted from the dynamics of the political culture of Ontario, shaped significantly by the patriotism deriving from loyalism.48 In fact, only Ontario supported Confederation. Quebec entered the union reluctantly. In the Maritimes, Joseph Howe and other anti-Confederates saw Confederation as a menace, threatening the economic and political integrity of the smaller provinces.

Nationalists in the post-Confederation era constantly worried about the threat of American annexation. Jehu Mathews believed that because Canada could never defend itself against the United States if the latter chose to invade, it was therefore necessary to maintain loyalty to a supportive Britain: "Hence the stubborn fact that the Canadian nationality would be dependent for its existence on the forbearance of the United States remains unshaken and indisputable. Such a species of 'Independence' is no desideration for any nation; and people who admit that Canada would occupy such a position should not seek either directly or indirectly to make Canadians covet it."49

From Manitoba, Charles Mair expressed worry over the possibility of American expansion into the Canadian West as American wheat lands were becoming exhausted:

It is not surprising that Americans should advocate annexation. Bad as their system of government is, they love their country, and by every means in their power encourage the growth of a national sentiment which, not withstanding its glaring faults, is an honour to the Yankee. But it is surprising that there should be even a few Canadians in Canada – for Canadians, of whom there are thousands in the U.S. are almost to a man opposed to it there – who with the repulsive characteristics of American political and social life constantly before them, advocate the incorporation of the young and vigorous Dominion with the moribund and unhealthy fabric of the huge Republic.50

Throughout the entire nineteenth century, discussion of political annexation was greatest during times of economic downturn. It was during these periods that some people favoured economic reasoning over social and political arguments. Strong economic links connected adjacent Canadian and American border regions and it was these bonds that continentalists referred to in making their case for either commercial or political union.

Over time 1841 proved to be a landmark year for Canadian-American economic relationships even though it signalled an immediate change in the relationship between Britain and her Canadian colonies. For some period, Britain had found protected trade with Canada to be increasingly expensive to maintain. In 1841 Sir Robert Peel was elected prime minister and over the next few years his government brought in legislation to dismantle protection. The repeal of the Corn Laws in 1846 combined with higher tariffs imposed by the United States produced considerable agitation, especially in Montreal, where in 1849 many of the city's anglophone merchants signed an Annexation Manifesto and riots resulted in the burning of the Parliament Buildings.

The end of British protection forced the Canadian elite to implement responsible government and consider the possibility of a confederation. It also signalled the beginning of the great Canadian debate over free trade, a polemic taking place not only in the political corridors of colonial capitals but in the local taverns, clubs, and newspapers as well. Pro-annexation arguments appeared in the newspapers, such as that made in an 24 October 1849 edition of the Prescott *Telegraph*: "The causes of the present state of feelings are clear enough. The first and chief of them is the complete annihilation of every tie of interest between us and the people of England. We are foreigners to them, they are foreigners to us ... On the other hand, as we recede from all social alliance or commercial intercourse with England, we rapidly advance in forming and cementing those connexions with the United States." Similar statements were made from time to time during the period but they were overshadowed by arguments made against annexation.

With the movement towards reciprocity, the annexation debate disappeared for a time only to reappear later in the century. The 1854–66 Reciprocity Treaty, a limited nineteenth-century free trade agreement in natural resources and some agricultural products, was popular in Canada as it coincided with an upturn in the Canadian economy. Yet prior to the signing of the agreement, many distrusted the motives of the Americans, including the editorialist of the 10 May 1848 edition of the *Constitutional* and Bathurst, Johnstown, and Dalhousie Districts' *General Advertiser*: "Should the United States ever consent to trade with us upon reciprocal grounds, we should view it with distrust and alarm, for we may then be assured that she is activated by one motive only, viz; that she perceives us falling from Great Britain and therefore – being hostile to that country and anxious for self-aggrandizement – she opens her arms to receive us."

Yet for many, reciprocity was seen as giving British North America the best of both worlds – access to American markets and political independence. Communities along the New York side of the St Lawrence were also in favour of reciprocity during the mid-century period, anticipating expanded trade and free navigation of the river. Centres such as Ogdensburg and Massena, important transfer points for Canadian goods entering the United States, stood to gain from an increase in cross-border traffic.

Protectionist sentiments in Congress and anger towards Great Britain's support of the South during the Civil War led to the abrogation of the Reciprocity Treaty in 1866. After its cancellation, Canadians were faced with some difficult choices. Having earlier lost their favoured trading status with Britain, Canadian colonies now worried about lack of access to the American market, one much larger than their domestic markets. This proved to be a major impetus to Confederation the following year. Yet interest in reciprocity continued for another forty four years, with both Conservative and Liberal governments being unsuccessful in their dealings with the Americans. Americans, for their part, realized shortly after Confederation that the political meaning Canadians assigned to the border meant that any economic relationship between the two countries would have to reconcile with this reality. This certainly was the message in the 1871 report on Canadian-American relations produced by Senator J.N. Larned, who stated: "The circumstances which make the common boundary of the two countries an actual barrier instead of an imaginary line are under their control, not ours. It is for them to determine which affects them most importantly, their political association with Great Britain or their commercial and industrial association in interest with the United States."[51]

The National Policy was not the Conservatives' first choice of economic policy. They wanted reciprocity with the United States but only on terms perceived as favourable to Canada. Macdonald was never able to achieve such terms so in order to stimulate a domestic market he instituted a policy of protective tariffs. Support for the National Policy was not only encouraged by the desire to create a domestic manufacturing sector and to protect Canada against the economic power of America, "it was also motivated by a wish to imitate the United States: if this is a contradiction, it is a very Canadian one."[52]

Economic uncertainty characterized the 1873–96 period and calls for one form of annexation or another re-emerged. Poorly developed transportation linkages among Canadian regions promoted the feeling among certain Canadians that north-south economic connections were more natural and desirable. Nobody championed the call for economic union more than Goldwin Smith who, along with Erastus Wiman, a wealthy Canadian-born businessman living in New York City, headed the Commercial Union movement. In a number of articles and his book *Canada and the Canadian*

Question, Smith argued that Canada could only become a great manufacturing country if it gained free access to the American market.[53] This, he maintained, would result from a union with the United States:

Canadian nationality being a lost cause, the ultimate union of Canada with the United States appears now to be morally certain; so that nothing is left for Canadian patriotism but to provide that it shall be a union indeed, and not an annexation; an equal and honourable alliance like that of Scotland and England, not a submission of the weaker to the stronger; and at the same time that the political change shall involve no change of any other kind in the relations of Canada with the mother country.[54]

In presenting his case, Smith cited a number of factors he believed were leading to a stronger relationship between Canada and the United States: the extension of American-owned railways into Canada, the emergence of New York City as the pleasure and business capital of Canada, American ownership of Canadian vacation property, the increasing circulation of American periodicals in Canada, and the increasing number of cross-border family linkages resulting from extensive Canadian migration to the United States. Smith also listed factors he considered as weakening the relationship between Canada and Great Britain: distance, divergence of economic interest, divergence of political character, and the powerful attractive force of the nearby United States. Wiman worked on the American side to spark interest in the possibility of a commercial union that he described in the following manner:

If the barbed wire fence, which, in the shape of a customs line, now runs athwart the continent, could be lifted, made of uniform height, and stretched around the continent, commercial union would be achieved. The height of this line, in other words, the tariff, would have to be regulated in Washington. Of course, the Canadians object to this, and say that it is taxation without representation ... There are, however, not a few who feel that the elimination of the tariff entirely from the politics of Canada would not be an unmixed evil, and it would be worth the attempt to see whether or not the enormous gains which Canada would make under commercial union would not be more than compensation for the loss of the privilege of tariff-making. It is claimed that whatever would be good for Massachussetts in the shape of taxation on imports, would certainly be advantageous to the Maritime Provinces. Whatever would suit New York and Ohio in the shape of tariff would certainly suit Ontario and Quebec; while, if Minnesota and Montana prospered, Manitoba and the Northwest would enjoy equal advantages, and that which precisely fitted the Pacific slope would suit British Columbia. It may be difficult to achieve, but, if commercial union stands or falls upon the right of the American people to regulate the tariff of the whole continent, my own impression is that, with time and patience and liberty on the part of the United States, the Canadian people would accept such a tariff as would benefit the United States, because it could not fail to benefit them also.[55]

Smith's opinions and the brash way in which he presented them did not endear himself to Canadians. While many desired some form of reciprocity, they equated commercial union with absorption into the United States. Nevertheless, economic uncertainty in the immediate post-Confederation era, particularly in the Maritimes, promoted new calls for annexation but, more significantly, a renewed desire for reciprocity with the United States. While both Conservatives and Liberals supported it, even after the National Policy was enacted, there was considerable disagreement as to what form it should take. Macdonald favoured reciprocal trade covering natural products only, while the Liberals in the late 1880s came to support the idea of an unrestricted reciprocity, a concept pushed by their spokesman, Sir Richard Cartwright. They believed that economic prosperity resulting from free trade would strengthen Canada as a country and lessen the threat of annexation. The Conservatives argued that unrestricted reciprocity was really a version of Goldwin Smith's commercial union and that would lead to annexation. Such a possibility struck fear into the hearts of Canadians and the Liberals were defeated in the election of 1891.

It was not only the phobia about annexation that accounted for the Conservative victory. The passing of the McKinley tariff in 1891, closing much of the American market to Canadian interests, combined with American reluctance to enter into free trade negotiations seriously, further hindered the reciprocity movement in Canada. The economic prosperity of the late 1890s and early 1900s also served to bolster confidence in the National Policy.

Admiration for and emulation of American economic success enabled American capital to circumvent the tariff by establishing branch plants in Canada. Ironically, American interest in Canada increased after protective tariffs were established. American capital could more effectively tap the Canadian hinterland with branches and takeovers. In 1897, 25 percent of American foreign investment was in Canada and by 1913 there were 450 American branch plants in the country.[56]

This increasing investment was one of the reasons that prompted Sara Jeanette Duncan to write *The Imperialist*. In this classic portrait of turn-of-the-century Canada, Duncan, through the words of the young Lorne Murchison, an idealist running for political office on the grounds of a rejuvenated British Empire, warns of a "new" threat of invasion:

We often say that we fear no invasion from the south, but the armies of the south have already crossed the border. American enterprise, American capital, is taking rapid possession of our mines and our water-power, our oil areas and our timber limits ... The trades unions of the two countries are already international. American settlers are pouring into the wheat-belt of the Northwest, and when the Dominion of Canada has paid the hundred million dollars she has just voted for a railway to open up the great lone northern lands between Quebec and the Pacific, it will be the American farmer and the American capitalist who will reap the benefit. They approach us today with all the arts of peace, commercial missionaries, but the day may come when they will menace our coasts to protect their markets unless by firm resolve and whole-hearted action now, we keep our opportunities for our own people.[57]

The book's message – that Canadians should be wary of pursuing commercial union with the United States at the expense of forsaking historical and spiritual ties with Britain – underscores the position that Anglo-Canadians found themselves in during the Victorian period. Imperialist arguments did not appeal to pragmatic people and lost their impact in light of Britain acting to sever its colonial ties with Canada. Canadians, at the turn of the century, had to define a new relationship with the United States, an association defined not only economically and politically, but spiritually as well.

CANADIAN-AMERICAN RELATIONS: A BORDERLANDS INTERPRETATION

The nature of these linkages is the focus of the Borderlands Project, an interdisciplinary research and compiling effort whose directors, despite claims to ideological neutrality, take the ideological position that "North America runs more naturally north and south than east and west."[58] The borderlands concept, developed years ago in other settings but only adopted recently by scholars interested in Canadian-American relations, serves as a worthwhile albeit polemic framework in which to view the complexity of the Canadian-American relationship.

An important symbol of this country, as I have argued, is the border. Yet in this context we can distinguish between borders as lines symbolizing differentiation and as places or zones of mediation. It is the latter view in which the concept of borderland is included. While borders separate, borderlands are regions of interaction where functional relationships are established which are acceptable for intercourse. Various economic, social, and family networks that serve to integrate communities on both sides of the boundary create borderlands. The idea of borderlands takes on a decidedly geographical flavour, seeing its primary features as "revealed in the dialectic between boundary as a political demarcation, and region as a geographic entity."[59]

Members of the Borderlands School typically depict the two constituent spatial units of these regions as peripheral within the context of their respective nations and therefore particularly subject to foreign influences emanating from the adjacent country. The border itself is seen as a determining force in the sense that all who live along such a geopolitical boundary share a common experience resulting from geographical propinquity and functional interdependence. It is this transnational interaction that sets borderlands apart from interior zones. While borderlands proponents concentrate on similarities occurring within the transborder region, others focus on expressions of difference. Borderlands are regions of both similarity and difference, a duality of dualisms; what is emphasized often reflects underlying ideology.

I believe the most important contribution of the borderlands concept to an understanding of the historical geography of Canadian-American relations is that *it returns the symbol of border to the fact of place*. Our propensity in this country to discern the border as a shield should not blind us to the powerful and sometimes overwhelming forces which serve as a bridge between us and the United States. Yet at the same time, the Canadian-American border/borderland is a complex line/place. Borderland communities certainly are "spatially proximate" as Victor Konrad, a major proponent of the borderlands thesis states, but the degree of economic and social integration varies both spatially and temporally.[60] Borderlands are organic; they evolve over time to become different kinds of places. Examination of historical interactions within and interpretations of Canadian-American borderland regions reveals such differences. The configuration of borderland regions can only be fully comprehended with reference to particular historical and geographical contexts.

Greater New England   Graeme Wynn has provided the most detailed historical geography of what is in many ways the most pronounced borderland region. He describes pre-Revolutionary Nova Scotia as part of a wider economic and cultural unit whose constituent parts were linked by ties of trade and kinship.[61] Although these connections weakened somewhat during the nineteenth century, the Maritime colonies continued to trade timber and fish products with the "Boston" states in what he chooses to call "Greater New England." Wynn adopts the core-periphery model developed by Meinig and divides the region into a core (Massachusetts), a domain (southern Nova Scotia and New Brunswick, Maine, and Connecticut), and a distant sphere (Prince Edward Island, Cape Breton, and northern New Brunswick and Nova Scotia). Boston served as the metropolis of this transborder region.

Using this framework, Wynn identifies several "Greater New Englands." The first he designates a greater New England of experience produced by seasonal and permanent movement of people from both sides back and forth across the border carrying goods and ideas which served to integrate the region and produce a common outlook. Over time, this movement became increasingly one-way but managed to maintain its directional focus in spite of the western fever gripping North America. Despite the embargo imposed during the War of 1812, trade persisted and continued to expand until Confederation, stimulated greatly during reciprocity and the American Civil War. Even with the end of reciprocity and the introduction of National Policy tariffs, trade continued, particularly in fish, which was allowed duty-free into the American market between 1873 and 1885. American capital flowed north into the Maritimes as Americans purchased land and invested in lumbering, sawmill and coal industries and in power companies and street railways.[62]

Wynn also identifies a greater New England of the primitive and romantic. The image of the Maritimes as a pristine wilderness attracted New Englanders, creating a vacation hinterland for the more urban and densely populated New England core. Borrowing from the frontierists, Wynn argues that a ready availability of land, isolation, and pioneer conditions combined with proximity to the United States to create a greater New England of attitudes and artefacts which resulted in a relative decrease of British manners and customs.[63] Wynn does recognize that, over time, the Maritimes did develop regional, national, and even imperial sentiments which found expression in the region's culture. Towards the end of the nineteenth century the British connection strengthened, but Wynn doesn't say much about central Canada replacing New England as the Maritimes' core and what influence that had on the shaping of this borderland region.

The St Lawrence Borderland Region   The Borderlands Project has identified a St Lawrence borderland region based on interactions between the St Lawrence valley of southern Quebec and New England. Much of the research emphasizes the out-migration of French Canadians facing unfavourable conditions at home and focuses on themes such as the role of the family in adaptation and assimilation. Earlier migrants settled as farmers in northern Vermont or worked in the lumber camps of Maine, but increasingly they migrated in greater numbers and worked in mill towns such as Manchester, New Hampshire, and Lynn, Massachusetts. Just as the Maritimes, Quebec served as a hinterland of reserve labour for New England but its relationship with its neighbouring American region differed in some significant ways. While Maritimers and New Englanders were united by language and common ethnic stock, Quebeckers were distinct and as such were viewed differently by their hosts. This cultural divide meant that New England capital and ideas would have much less impact in Quebec than they did in Atlantic Canada.

The Great Lakes Borderland Region   In his 1813 gazetteer, Michael Smith estimated that 80 percent of the 136,000 white settlers in Upper Canada came from the United States, with only 25 percent having been born or descended from Loyalists.[64] This flow was soon reversed as Upper Canadians, particularly from southwestern Ontario, began to flood into Michigan during the 1830s and into other Great Lakes states shortly thereafter.[65] While many of these original migrants were intent on farming, those who followed were inclined to settle in the rapidly expanding cities of the region. This migration often occurred in stages, followed definite streams, and was directed to a great extent by the presence of family and friends.

The natural water route connecting Ontario with New York and the Midwest facilitated this movement of people – a corridor later extended and reinforced with the development of a railway network that crossed the border at several points. The construction of the Erie Canal, completed in 1825, was partly a reaction to complaints made by those Americans forced to pay shipping duties at British-controlled Great Lakes and St Lawrence ports. The canal served to integrate the interior with the Atlantic trade of the eastern seaboard. In response, the British built the Welland and Rideau canals, not only as preventative measures against the threat of American invasion but as a means to secure Canadian transportation routes to and between the Great Lakes. Competition in this borderland region for the Great Lakes hinterland spurred the development of extensive canal systems on both sides of the border, which in turn stimulated the cross-border flow of entrepreneurs and investment. Both American and Canadian vessels and cargoes passed through lake and river ports such as Port Colborne, Oswego, and Cornwall.[66]

The railways first augmented and then replaced the canal system and served to strengthen intra- and international links. The same serve-and-volley pattern of response to transportation expansion continued. After the Americans built the Erie Railroad in the early 1850s, the British constructed the Grand Trunk Railway. The Grand Trunk used a different gauge track to the American lines but as the flow of goods crossing the border increased, the company changed its track to match the American lines in order to expedite this movement. The Grand Trunk was a direct channel into America's most expansive market at the end of the nineteenth century and served to further link Ontario with its neighbours.

Unlike the Maritimes, which never developed a regional metropolis to counteract the pull of Boston and the increasing control of Montreal, Ontario would generate a more mature urban system centring more over time on Toronto. The growth of Toronto, Hamilton, and other cities nullified to some degree the pull of nearby American metropolises even during the long period of recession in the latter part of the century. Macdonald's National Policy of protective tariffs stimulated industrial development in these centres and in southern Quebec as well. Yet ironically it was these same tariffs that would increase the flow of American capital into Ontario in the form of branch plant investment. As time passed, Ontario would increasingly become an extension of the American midwestern manufacturing belt.

The Great Plains–Prairie Borderland Region   The Great Plains–Prairie borderland region, extending roughly from a line paralleling the 98th meridian in the east to the Rocky Mountains in the west and from the Kansas-Nebraska border in the south to the parkland belt of the prairie provinces in the north, differs markedly from other borderland regions. From a geographical perspective, this appears to be the most homogeneous of all the transborder regions. Physical uniformity is ensured by a grassland ecosystem and an extreme continental temperate climate, although there are widely divergent soil types, vegetation, and surface features on the local scale. The borderland economy is predominantly rural and agrarian and is dominated by grain production. The region is also characterized by low population density and geographical isolation from markets. Unlike some other transborder regions, there is little continuous settlement along the boundary in this region.

The kinds of interactions taking place over time as well as similar geographical conditions have resulted in a considerable degree of borderland convergence. North-south intermingling occurred well before European settlement as the American and Canadian fur-trading systems converged along the upper Missouri River at the villages of the Mandan and Hidatsu Indians in what is now west-central North Dakota.[67] In the early 1800s the Hudson's Bay Company began purchasing oxen in the St Paul market to pull carts loaded with provisions purchased in the United States. The Red River colony established by Lord Selkirk in 1820 was supplied with livestock from south of the border until 1833. After that date, the colonists in turn supplied livestock to farms and urban centres in Minnesota.[68] Western Canada, or Rupert's Land as it was then known, was further integrated into a north-south economy when steamboats first descended the Red River to Fort Garry in 1859 and the railroad reached St Paul soon after. The Hudson's Bay Company began to import its goods by way of the United States, resulting in the decline of York Factory on Hudson Bay as a principal port of entry into Rupert's Land.[69]

The Red River–St Paul oxcart trade grew considerably by the 1840s and expanded to include the carrying of mails. A more reliable courier service was organized in 1853 and two years later a monthly service was established between Red River and Pembina right across the border. Attempts to develop a Canadian route through northern Ontario proved unsuccessful and so the colony depended entirely upon the US post office at Pembina. Outgoing mail had to be paid in US stamps sold in Fort Garry. In 1870 an agreement was signed with the US post office for transmission of closed mails between Winnipeg and Windsor by way of Pembina, St Paul, and Chicago.[70]

Settlement in western Canada was discouraged in part by the reports of various surveys which described the prairies in unfavourable terms. In particular, the report of the John Palliser expedition (1857–60) did much to bring about an interaction of British and American ideas about the plains. British explorers who were part of this expedition were influenced greatly by the American perception of the region as a desert.[71] Eventually perceptions would change and the region would be described in a more favourable light, but settlement continued to be almost non-existent because of the lack of a railway connection and the magnetic attraction of the American West.

Before the building of the Canadian Pacific Railway (CPR), St Paul served as the gateway to the northwest. So it was only logical that Minnesota capitalists wanted to extend their empires into Canada with the development of railway networks and settlement schemes. St Paul and Chicago competed for control of the northern plains and many politicians and businessmen in these centres saw the Hudson's Bay Company monopoly as a barrier to realizing their dreams.

Railroads beyond Chicago began bridging the Mississippi River in the 1850s and served to direct rather than follow settlement. Canadians moving west to Manitoba and the North-West Territories had to pass through American territory before the building of the CPR. Most travelled via the Grand Trunk Railway which was extended from Sarnia to Chicago in the 1860s. There they transferred on to trains travelling to St Paul, at which point they boarded stagecoaches that carried them to Red River settlements. Settlers then travelled by land or steamboat to Fort Garry. This movement was greatly expedited when railroads were extended from St Paul to the Dakotas.

I.G. Baker and Company of Benton, Montana, located at the head of navigation on the Missouri River and functioning as the gateway to the Whoop-Up Trail reaching Fort Macleod and Calgary, dominated the commerce of the Canadian plains for almost twenty years. Canadians complained about the monopoly of the company, believing that much of their money was financing the building of Benton. The monopoly of Benton and the grand schemes of the St Paul capitalists were ended with the building of the CPR. Control of the region passed into Canadian hands and Winnipeg came to replace Benton, Chicago, and St Paul as the key metropolis of the Canadian west.[72]

As was the case in the Great Lakes region, transportation played a key role in development of both east-west intra-national and north-south international linkages. American penetration into the grasslands region by navigable waterways and then by railroad combined with occasional utterances of Manifest Destiny, provoked Canadians to create the province of Manitoba in 1870 and complete the CPR in 1886. A transplanted Canadian, James J. Hill, built the first railway infiltrating the Canadian prairies, the St Paul, Minnesota and Manitoba. The CPR itself was modelled upon earlier American examples of government-subsidized, land-grant railways. In 1876 the Northern Pacific Railroad reached Winnipeg. In order to prevent local traffic from being drawn off to the United States, the CPR diverted its originally planned route through the parkland belt southwards. A branch of Hill's Great Northern Railroad reached Portage la Prairie in 1888. In response, the CPR built the Soo Line connecting its main line near Moose Jaw with St Paul and Duluth. The irony of these developments, as McIlwraith notes, is that "the Canadian Pacific, supposed to be the staunch axis of nation building, was displaying its true continental business stripes."[73] The importance of railways in directing settlement is illustrated in the linearity of the settlement pattern both east-west and north-south, further reflecting uniformity within this borderlands region.

Before the Canadian West experienced its settlement boom in the late 1890s, population movement within the borderland region was predominantly north-south as expensive goods produced in central Canada, depressed wheat prices, excessive transport and credit costs, and high mortgages drove Manitobans out of the province. Yet the majority of Canadians settling in the Dakotas, western Minnesota, and Montana came from eastern Canada, particularly Ontario, and not from Manitoba or the North-West Territories. Elsewhere, most Canadian emigrants originated within their respective borderland regions. Also significant is the fact that unlike other transborder regions, movement was predominantly south to north, reflecting the closing of the Great Plains frontier and the opening of the western Canadian frontier. This reverse migration took place after 1896 and was the direct result of Canadian economic expansion and American land hunger.[74] Department of Immigration propaganda made use of American mythology such as the agrarian ideal and the Horatio Alger stereotype in their attempt to lure American farmers. Yet at the same time, they focused on those differences between the two societies that were deemed to be most attractive, contrasting in particular the law and order image of Canada with the wild and lawless reputation of the American West.[75]

Indeed, strong forces linked people living on both sides of the international boundary within this borderland region. Many prairie communities are named after both famous and ordinary Americans. Similar problems such as land use in an area of recurring drought, similar farmers' organizations, persistent agrarian radicalism, relations with eastern centres, transportation, investment in a frontier environment, and even a plains culture, gave unity to this part of North America.[76] Americans brought with them experience and capital needed to develop western Canada. Among Harvey's list of American-born founders of enterprises among Canada's business elite, fourteen established their companies on the prairies between 1850 and 1920.[77] Of this number, twelve were based in Winnipeg, one in Calgary, and one in Cardston, Alberta, indicating that Americans with large amounts of capital were attracted to the largest city in the region where they could invest in land and construction. Yet although this group generally had more capital than European immigrants, Hansen and Brebner argue that American homesteaders were those unable to purchase property at home and thus were poorer than their fellow countrymen who chose not to move.[78] But in a land where capital was in short supply, the relative wealth of Americans compared to other immigrants was immediately noted.

American capital, technology, and settlers made significant contributions to the development of the Canadian West although there is considerable debate as to the nature and degree of their impact. Bruce Shepard has shown that American technology, including the steel plough, barbed wire, and the self-binding reaper, along with dryland farming techniques, facilitated the move into drier regions and the development of the wheat monoculture. American farm implement companies such as International Harvester would eventually follow American settlers into western Canada.[79]

Much debate centres on the impact of American influences on the development of the ranching industry in southwestern Saskatchewan and southern Alberta. Revisionists challenge the traditional assumption that the Canadian ranching industry was primarily a product of American capital and technology and argue that government support, British capital, and the presence of the Northwest Mounted Police created a conservative community devoted to Victorian ideals and produced an environment much different than the American-style frontier. This position in turn has been challenged by those who, while not denying eastern Canadian and British institutions and values, maintain that in order to cope with a challenging environment ranchers found it necessary to adopt American practices and employ American labour. While acknowledging that both the Canadian and American cattle industries owed a debt to British capital, the 1891 and 1901 censuses reveal that one out of every five cattlemen working on the Alberta range were Americans and experienced American foremen were essential to the Canadian industry in terms of their abilities in handling workers and monitoring markets and prices.[80]

While integration within this region has occurred because of a common hinterland syndrome, migration, and capitalist forces, it is also a region where, in Frances Kaye's words, "contrasts are most precise simply because the two cultures, the two nations, meet face to face on a territory differentiated only by that political abstraction, the border."[81] The contrasts that do exist can be attributed to different settlement histories, different political systems, different urban systems, and different core-periphery relations.

While Lipset in his original version of *Agrarian Socialism* attributes the success of the Co-operative Commonwealth Federation in Saskatchewan to the isolation produced by the organization of the province into rural and urban municipalities, he later places more emphasis on the impact of political structures, in particular arguing that the Canadian federal system and the parliamentary form of government provided the opportunity for the emergence of third parties in Canada in ways that were not possible in the United States. In response, Schwartz argues that farmers' movements were just as significant in the United States as in Canada and points to the fact that third parties in Canada have only had success at the regional level. This is certainly true but the fact remains that this particular third party was successful on a large enough scale to capture power in the province of Saskatchewan. Lipset also stresses the differential impact of a revolutionary versus counter-revolutionary tradition at the national scale. Schwartz concedes the value of this thesis, arguing that "when there were borrowed elements, these were transformed in directions affected by both national and local conditions." This points to the importance of considering the effects of culture in interpretation of this particular borderland region.[82]

In this context, attention must be placed on Canadian policies which fostered a degree of ethnic cohesiveness in the face of Anglo-conformity. European immigrants and eastern Canadian migrants, particularly from urban-industrial working-class backgrounds, carried values and ideas that would prove to be supportive of socialist movements on the prairies. Social and ecological conditions may also have bolstered agrarian movements. The isolation produced by government support of ethnic bloc settlement, combined with low population densities and a dispersed settlement pattern, may have played some role in the evolution of rural class consciousness.

Historical and geographical factors have hindered urban development on both sides of the border but not to the same extent. While the image of the desert was eventually abandoned in favour of a more acceptable view of a farming frontier, the northern plains was never regarded as the promised land. That was the symbol attached to California and the Pacific Northwest or, in the case of Mormons, Utah. But for many Europeans and North Americans, the Canadian prairies held the promise of a "new Eden" and "the Last Best West." The east-west flow of trade and migration into the West which paralleled the transcontinental railway was viewed by Canadians as an important, if not the key, ingredient in the development of the nation.

Urban development reached a greater level of intensity on the Canadian side of the 49th parallel. Winnipeg emerged as the regional metropolis with the rest of Manitoba and the North-West Territories as its hinterland. Parallel urban development in Alberta was ensured somewhat by the great distance separating this part of the prairies from Winnipeg, but the latter would continue to have considerable hold over Saskatchewan well after the province was established in 1905. Geographically, Winnipeg was ideally situated to assume the role as the gateway city for the Canadian West. Indeed, natives of that city viewed the prairies as their hinterland just as central Canadians did.[83]

Accessibility also favoured links between border communities on the American side and Winnipeg. Even though a dependency relationship developed between the prairies and central Canada, whereby prairie centres relied to a significant degree on the fortunes of eastern metropolises to which they were subordinate, a regional urban system based on the railway evolved, yet no comparable system would develop on the American side. There, urban centres functioned primarily as commercial outposts for Minneapolis–St Paul and other large cities encircling the region. Manitoba, Saskatchewan, and Alberta were more subordinate to the metropolitan cores of eastern Canada than any adjacent American region, even though they were integrated into the Canadian and world economies to a significant part through the efforts of American entrepreneurs and as a result of diffusion of innovations from south of the border.

While Bruce Shepard quite rightly scolds "nationalist" historians who criticize the over-emphasis on similarities and the disregard of differences, he downplays the significant distinctions between the Canadian and American plains as noted by Paul Sharp, the very person he is defending. In his balanced article entitled "The Northern Great Plains: A Study in Canadian-American Regionalism," Sharp argues that "similarity does not imply identity" and notes the following differences which distinguished the two societies within this trans-border region:

Many extraregional relationships and many heritages from older societies were far too powerful to be affected by environment. Nationalism, the most pervasive influence in modern society, was unaffected by its movement into a plains environment and created Canadian plainsmen to the north and American plainsmen to the south. Each possessed loyalties outside the region that prevented a complete identification of common problems ... The rush of settlement into the Canadian West never outran organized government as it so frequently did in the American West ... Constitutional difference places far greater powers in the hands of the central government under the Canadian confederation than in the American system. Litigation over water rights in the semiarid West was avoided in Canada by the denial of riparian rights, the rejection of the doctrine of appropriation, and the acceptance of the legal principle that water was the property of the Crown. Stronger ties with Europe through the Imperial relationship and a continuing inmigration from the mother country provided a further source of difference. A conscious emphasis upon English culture reflected the recency of the transition and the immaturity of Canadian culture. On top of this, the frontier experience was too brief to have more than an ephemeral influence, and civilization in western Canada sprang up nearly full grown, possessing a twentieth century sophistication. Yet it was true that society on the northern plains, Canadian and American, was the heir of many cultures, the copy of none.[84]

So while Sharp emphasizes the strong connections between the West and both the rest of Canada and Britain, Shepard offers a somewhat immoderate conclusion that "ultimately ... the Canadian Plains did not become part of the United States, despite the tremendous American influence upon the region's evolution, because the settlers who moved north did not demand it."[85]

The Pacific Borderlands Region   As in other borderland regions, actions perceived as aggressive resulted in defensive responses. Competition over the fur staple created an environment where almost any movement was viewed as a threat. Thomas Jefferson suspected that the British wanted to colonize the Columbia River basin and in response sent Lewis and Clark to discover and map the most direct and practical water route across the continent. The Hudson's Bay Company and its rival, the North West Company, many of whose employees were from Montreal, were first into the region and on that basis regarded this part of the continent as one to whose trade they were entitled. The Americans, on the other hand, considered the Oregon Territory as their own on the basis of the terms of the Louisiana Purchase of 1803 and by virtue of the discovery of the mouth of the Columbia River by Captain Gray. The North West Company dominated the land-based fur trade in the region by virtue of David Thompson's 1811 discovery of the Athabaska Pass through which he made his way to the Pacific Ocean. They merged with the Hudson's Bay Company in 1821 and held undisputed control of the trade until the American Fur Company of St Louis moved into the region in the 1820s. American settlers intent on farming began to flood into the region in the late 1830s. In 1841 the British reluctantly ceded the territory south of the Columbia River to the United States but then attempted to secure their position by sponsoring colonization of the territory north of the Columbia with migrants from Red River. This scheme failed and Americans continued to pour into the region. Yet even while the British were attempting to dissuade Americans from settling north of the Columbia, they were supplying colonists in the Puget Sound area.[86]
    While both the British and the Americans first entered the region in order to exploit the fur staple, the latter were more committed to agricultural settlement and would soon begin to dominate in population and power. A Canadian northwoods fur-trade culture developed in the east. Composed of an amalgam of English capital, Scottish leadership, and French-Canadian–Indian labour, it was unsuited to conditions in this region. George Simpson, the governor of the Vancouver Island colony, adopted some features of the more mobile and ruthless American fur-trade

culture and initiated a series of reforms which, Meinig argues, produced a variant of the Canadian culture, which he calls a Pacific subculture.[87]

In 1843 the Americans formed a provisional government in the Willamette Valley which claimed on paper a territory that extended from California, then a Mexican possession, to Alaska, which was under Russian control. Yet in practical terms, this government only managed that territory west of the Cascades and south of the Columbia River. Eventually, in-migration and natural increase extended the American presence north of the Columbia where they increasingly complained about the monopoly of the Hudson's Bay Company. Finally, in 1848 the international border was extended along the 49th parallel from the Rockies, with the British losing control of their hold on the Puget Sound region. In order to consolidate their position north of the 49th, the Hudson's Bay Company founded a colony on Vancouver Island with Victoria as its capital.[88]

The discovery of gold along the Fraser by 1858 had attracted thousands of Americans, particularly from California. In response, the British sent the Royal Engineers regiment to the region where they established the mainland colony of British Columbia. The British requirement that all miners, regardless of origin, purchase a licence at Victoria angered the Americans, even though California had earlier passed a law requiring non-Americans intending to mine to purchase more expensive licences than native-born. With the end of the gold rush, immigration ending, construction ceasing, and real estate prices falling, Victoria experienced a depression. The pressure to join the United States was great even after Vancouver Island and the mainland merged in 1866.

The arguments for annexation were many and powerful. Britain had virtually washed its hands of these distant colonies and Canada was far away beyond a formidable mountain barrier. The United States' presence was, on the other hand, felt both geographically and economically. Sandwiched between Alaska to the north, purchased by the United States in 1867, and Washington Territory to the south, British Columbia realized that it soon had to reach a decision about its political future. The economy was in transition as lumber and coal were replacing gold and furs as the major staples. In many ways, British Columbia was part of a greater Pacific Northwest, a region with San Francisco as its chief metropolis and Victoria as a northern outpost serving the hinterland. The coastal trade between San Francisco and Victoria began in 1854 with the former providing the latter with many of its required goods. Until it joined with the mainland in 1866, Victoria was a free port and American goods paid no duty there, unlike on the mainland. It served as an entrepôt for Vancouver Island, the mainland, and to some extent the neighbouring states and Alaska. Letters from British Columbia were prepaid with full American postage and then sent to San Francisco where they were treated as American mail. Telegraphic communication between British Columbia and the rest of the world was for a period of time carried over American lines.[89]

In addition to these strong north-south connections, pro-annexationists contrasted the presence of a strong, growing, and proximate American market with a hypothetical Canadian market thousands of miles to the east. They pointed out that, with annexation, access to an already existing transcontinental railway would be confirmed, free trade would be guaranteed, the colony's debt would be assumed by the federal government, and its inhabitants would be assured a representative and responsible government. In response, the pro-confederationists argued that Canada also promised to assume the colony's debt, provide representative and responsible government, and negotiate reciprocity with the United States. Canada also vowed to build a transcontinental railway linking British Columbia with eastern markets if the colony agreed to join Confederation. At least on paper, the pro-annexation arguments appeared much stronger than those favouring Confederation and yet British Columbians chose to join Canada.

This decision was certainly an act of faith, but it would be too simple to dismiss it as an act of blind faith. While both the Victoria and the mainland colonies were tied to San Francisco and the states within its hinterland, it is facile to view the colonies as completely dependent commercial appendages. British capital and markets had more influence than is commonly believed. Commercial interests feared that local trade protected by tariffs would be hurt by American competition. More importantly, settlement of the colonies by Britons and eastern Canadians ensured that the British connection would remain strong. Many of those Americans present during the gold rush returned home after it ended. Canada was favoured over the United States because it promised to preserve a political system and laws which the colonists respected.[90]

Yet even after British Columbia chose to join with Canada, new economic links continued to enforce the north-south connection. American capital and mining technology was initially prominent in the Kootenays after gold was discovered there in the early 1890s. American branch lines penetrated as far as one hundred miles north of the border by 1910, serving Canadian mines at Trail, Crowsnest, and Cranbrook. Yet eventually American capital was replaced by British and eastern Canadian funding. The east-west linkage was further strengthened as British Columbia became the major supplier of lumber for the expanding market of the prairies. The penetration of American capital did not pick up again until after the end of the Second World War.[91]

ANGLO-CANADIANS IN NORTH AMERICA IN
THE LATE NINETEENTH CENTURY

If economic concerns were the only basis for political decisions, then it is very likely that Confederation would not have taken place and that the economic forces joining adjacent American and Canadian regions would have inevitably led to annexation. Yet while Canada hoped to duplicate the historical experience of the United States in economic terms, it did not choose to mirror the social development of its southern neighbour. For much of the century, Britain served as the chosen social model. Yet the milieu in which Canadians found themselves guaranteed that they would never be "British" North Americans; a very different environment and direct relationships with the geographically proximate United States ensured this. A different historical experience, one shaped to a considerable extent by the European connection, and an environment less amenable to a contiguous settlement process, meant that Canadians were not simply "British" (or "French") Americans.

The evolution of Canadian society during the nineteenth century can be viewed in organic terms; that is, the succession of presents during this period are weighed against the past and the future. The past was linked to the British Tory traditions of collectivism and authority while the future was represented by the new world environment of liberalism, individualism, and opportunity, a milieu most often but perhaps incorrectly associated with the American frontier. Anglo-Canadian society evolved as an amalgam of British and American societies. Over time, Canadians were increasingly occupied with the material affairs and the mobility opportunities of their new world and yet in the hearts of many ran the undercurrent of respect for and allegiance to Britain. What many wanted was a society with values somewhere between unthinking conformity and the absolute pursuit of self-interest, a society neither completely British nor completely American, but somewhere in between and combining the best of both.

Prior to Confederation, authority, sentiment, and mercantilism bound Canadians to Britain; yet over time, kinship ties, economic links, and joint social affairs brought Americans and Canadians closer together. However, Canadians and Americans remained divided over certain economic, political, and social issues at the national level. Newspapers reveal evidence of a Canadian inferiority complex, reflecting not only perceived status vis-à-vis the United States but chagrin over the indifference of Britain. The 11 July 1849 edition of the Prescott *Telegraph*, commenting on the Fourth of July celebrations in nearby Ogdensburg, asked:

Why is it that of all days in the year, the 4th of July calls out the largest of our town and country population for recreation and pleasure, we do not understand: yet such is the fact. We, poor Canadians, have no great event to commemorate – we have no national birthday, no fact or deed over which the hearts of the people can hold jubilee, and bear in fresh and grateful remembrance. Ah no! We are not a nation; only a small bunch, of no importance to the parent trunk. Neglected, almost discarded, by the mother, estranged from each other by internal dimensions, and positively despised by the outer world – yet mighty in our own contracted imaginations.

Yet while Canadians suffered from an inferiority complex, they also chafed at what they took to be an American superiority complex. One can only imagine how citizens of Prescott reacted upon reading the 7 July 1848 editorial of the Ogdensburg *Daily Sentinel*: "What should it [Canadians celebrating the Fourth of July in Ogdensburg] mean but that the people of Canada, sick of the eternal twaddle about the 'divine right of kings' and becoming 'inoculated with the infection of liberty', are determined to follow our republican example. Old England will need more soldiers than she has in Canada now, to repress the spirit of Reform that pervades the Canadian colonies. They will have Independence, and after independence, look out for Annexation."

By Confederation, Canadians had developed strong ideas about American society, and while they admired much about the Republic, particularly its economic accomplishments, there was still much that they disdained. Journalists and writers such as John Dafoe, John Willison, and John Hopkins believed it was "Britishness" that distinguished Canada from the United States and provided a better political and social philosophy.[92] Yet they also recognized that the North American environment played a major role in the development of Canadian social values. In this context, Canadians were influenced by American ideas on equality and were more egalitarian in their views on social status than were the British. American models and ideas also had profound effects on religion and education in Canada. Over time the Canadian school system mirrored the American system in its movement away from classical liberal arts to training children in skills.

With time, there appeared a greater number of calls for developing a society that would be distinguished by Canadian values. In 1872 Thomas White stated: "We must cultivate a spirit of self-confidence and self-reliance. The course of Canada has been the tone of depreciation in which its own sons have been apt to speak of it. If we would have a nation worthy of its name, we want a national spirit where with to build it up. Let us have faith: faith in the country itself, faith in its resources; faith in our power to develop them; faith in the institutions we possess; and faith in the destiny before us." Three years later, Roswell Fisher made a passionate plea for Canadians to take responsibility for their own future: "Further, individually and nationally, we must so shape our growth and course, keeping what is best, throwing off what is worst, in the qualities of the different people from which we sprung, to form in the future a nation, at once united and strongly marked, which shall not be British, nor American, but something different, something better than either – in a word, Canadian."[93]

A basic reality of the period, however, was a massive outflow of people southwards, a fact that was very much in the minds of politicians and citizens. Economic pragmatism triumphed over sentiment. The country was going through some economic turmoil during the period and the opportunities south of the border were well known. It has been estimated that American industrial wage levels were 60 percent higher than those in Canada during the turn-of-the-century period.[94] Such movement only served to fuse more closely together peoples living in borderland regions. Yet many still adhered to the belief that Canada was still a morally superior society. Granatstein and Hillmer talk about a popular novel of the period which "told the tale of a young man who sought the larger horizons of the United States; finding fame and fortune there, he returned home to retrieve his Canadian sweetheart. This was the quintessential Canadian parable. Opportunities for success and a better way of life to the south, there could be no doubt. But goodness, still, resided in Canada."[95]

Nonetheless, while many Canadians associated moral and political superiority with Canada and Britain, the truth is that the country became increasingly Americanized over time. By the 1880s most of the reading material circulating in Anglo-Canada was American authored, a fact that disturbed a number of Canadians, including James Douglas Jr: "As purveyors of news, the American newspapers altogether outstrip the English ... but in pandering to the low tastes of the multitudes for horrors ... as a rule, English newspapers discuss the topics of the day more fully and calmly than do the American ... It is to be regretted that our own papers have imitated the American rather than the English type." As early as 1873, J.W. Langley, writing in the *Maritime Monthly*, recognized that American literature, characterized by a lack of social distinctions and a greater freedom from political and social institutions than European literature, had a greater influence on Canadian literature than did that of Europe.[96]

The cheapness of American publications and the operation of postal, customs, and copyright regulations facilitated American dominance and retarded the development of Canadian publishing. Smith, in fact, argues that American culture constituted the principal element in the central (Ontario and Anglo-Quebec) Anglo-Canadian cultural milieu while the Maritimes enjoyed a cultural and intellectual life superior to that of central Anglo-Canada. He even goes so far to say that many Canadians could only visualize their country in terms borrowed from the United States. American newspapers, journals, and novels, he argues, "brought Canadians into close contact with the life of the Republic and so at once enlarged the frame of reference within which they felt themselves to be operating and heightened their consciousness of themselves as inhabitants of the North American continent."[97]

Smith makes some cogent points but perhaps he overstates his case. While influenced greatly by American goods, technologies, myths, and ideas, Canadians did not see their place in North America in exactly the same way that Americans did. Canadians from different regions and groups formed variable ideas about society and their relationship with the United States. Many continued to hold dear certain of the social and political principles inherited from Britain but realized that a strong Canada was necessary to ensure the continuance of those same ideals. But their view of Canada continued to be framed by island perspectives. The islands in the late nineteenth century were shrouded in the fog of ignorance and the few bridges that had been constructed were in danger of collapsing from too little structural support. Yet this archipelago of solitudes, created within an institutional framework which in many ways furthered division, slowly developed associations that transcended differences and strengthened ties even in the face of developing north-south integration. That this was a struggle there is no doubt; yet it was in this effort that Canadians discovered what they shared in common and constructed bridges.

2 Charting the Voyage: National and Regional Perspectives of Migration

"The meat of the buffalo tastes the same on both sides of the border."
– Sitting Bull,
quoted in *Between Friends*, NFB documentary

MIGRATION AND THE GREAT TRANSFORMATION: PHILOSOPHIES, THEORIES, AND CONCEPTUAL DEBATES[1]

Migration originates in transformations of social and economic structures in both the sending and receiving societies, but it is perpetuated and shaped by social networks and individual or familial decisions. Thus the critical theoretical problem for the researcher is "to determine not only how individual actions combine to produce ... social consequences ... but also how individuals' values and orientations are historically and culturally produced by the manifold structural relations in which they are embedded."[2] Critical to theorizing about human activity is an understanding of the interrelationships between social structures and the mechanisms by which these structures are translated into action while at the same time recognizing the autonomy humans have from structural forces. And however universal structures and processes may be, outcomes vary widely according to local circumstances and historical context.[3]

Historical-structural analyses treat migration as a locally specific outcome in which larger political-economic forces and ideology play a major role. This is certainly evident in theories of Canadian emigration to the United States during the latter half of the nineteenth century. In Canada, the debate over causes and impacts has raged between two groups, one influenced by neo-classical economics and the other by the neo-Marxian perspective. This has resulted in different interpretations, from the push-pull explanation that sees migration in terms of costs and benefits, to the core-periphery paradigm that views migration as part of the development of capitalism.[4]

The core-periphery explanation describes the development of metro-politan and hinterland relationships between regions and across national boundaries and outlines the history of how the United States came to replace Britain as the economic core for the Canadian periphery. From such a perspective, Montgomery claims that it was the influx of immigrants into the labour force rather than technological development that account-ed for higher levels of wealth produced at the turn of the twentieth century in North America.[5] He views the entire northeastern region of the continent from New York and Boston to Montreal and Toronto to Chicago and St Louis as an international core area into which flowed a massive number of people from peripheral regions of Europe and North America. The hinterland included the Atlantic provinces, rural Quebec and, to some extent, eastern Ontario. Montgomery sees this migration as an interregional process, international in scope and resulting from the development of the factory stage in industrial capitalism.

The debate rests upon two dialectically opposed visions of this para-digm: the neo-classical perspective which views core-periphery exchanges as mutually beneficial because of the trickle-down mechanisms of the mar-ketplace; and the neo-Marxian view which sees core-periphery relations as unequal and exploitative because of the unequal exchange mechanisms inherent in capitalist markets. Those who favour the former view suggest that this emigration, resulting from a depressed Canadian economy and an expanding American industrial economy, served to link Canadian peripheral origins with American metropolitan destinations and join both regions in a reciprocally favourable relationship. Those who adhere to the latter perspective insist the Canadian capitalist class was dominated by a commercial bourgeoisie which favoured short-term investment in the sale of staple goods over long-term investment in manufacturing. This resulted in industrial underdevelopment and retarded the goal of the National Pol-icy to develop a domestic manufacturing sector, doing little to arrest the flow of persons attracted to the higher wages paid in American industries.[6]

Although these perspectives differ, both view this migration in terms of the transformation of social and economic structures taking place in Cana-da and the United States and downplay how human agency shapes and alters this movement. The role of migrant social networks in shaping and channelling this particular migration is an example of how internal human agency serving as an important contingent cause. Transcontinental chain migrations of kin and friends, generated by individuals responding to changes occurring in society, altered the very societies whose structures shaped these decisions. This reinforces Pedroza-Bailey's assertion that "the theoretical and empirical challenge now facing migration is to cap-ture individuals as agents and social structure as both delimiting and enabling."[7]

Theories of this migration, regardless of ideological underpinnings, are related to the transformation of rural society with the growth of industrial capitalism. Perhaps the major theme of study for nineteenth-century North America is the absorption of semi-autarchic economies and local cultures into increasingly broader regional, national, and international contexts. In their attempts to examine this process known interchangeably as "urbanization," "modernization," or "The Great Transformation," scholars have been concerned primarily with mobility, family structure, and class relationships, particularly in the larger cities. While some studies have shed light on the relationship between demographic, economic, and social structures of rural populations and the institutional environment in which these populations evolved, much research into Canada's rural past continues to be dominated by perspectives which disregard the ways in which different levels of community responded and adjusted to change.

No one interpretation adequately explains the changing relationships between town and country during the nineteenth century. In the United States the debate has focused on the nature of the transition to capitalism in rural America. Kulikoff suggests that there are two sides in the discussion, one influenced by neo-classical economics and the other by British social history.[8] The former group, whom Kulikoff calls the "market historians," stress the impact of market forces on human behaviour and explain the spread of market processes through rural society.[9] The latter group, labelled "social historians," seek "to uncover patterns of economic and social behaviour and to relate their behaviour to the social relations of production and to social and political consciousness."[10] The market historians view early American farmers as pre-nascent capitalists while the social historians argue that "most exchange was for the immediate use of the farm household or its neighbours." Yet, as Kulikoff rightly notes, the two sides are not that different; the controversy really boils down to "the degree of local self-sufficiency and the extent of market exchange rather than the fact of exchange."[11]

Growing crops for changing markets certainly signalled changes in farm production but it does not necessarily indicate fundamental changes in the nature of rural society. Farmers in North America experienced early capitalist development and participated in commodity markets almost from the beginning of settlement but even though they sold their surpluses to regional and foreign markets, most output was for family or local consumption. Yet from the outset the desire for land and the pursuit of economic opportunity were present in most regions of North America. And with striking rapidity the market became a driving force, an agent of change penetrating all levels of society.

In Canada, historical debate has focused on the relative merits of the staples thesis and metropolitan theories of development. Modernization theory has been the central organizing frame for this discussion. The centre and margin dichotomy of Innis, the exploitation and dependency of

Lower, the entrepreneurship of Creighton, and the metropolitanism of Careless all picture the countryside as a passive entity, shaped by urban centres at different levels of the hierarchy. This process of increasing domination is most clearly articulated in the metropolitanism theory of Careless.[12] The metropolitanism theory views both smaller centres and their hinterlands as peripheral. In this dependency relationship, the hinterland serves as a pool of labour, where raw materials and capital are exploited and controlled by the metropolitan core. Also implicit in this relationship is the assumption that the penetration of urban and market values and institutions combines with new inventions and means of communication (postal service, telegraph, telephone, automobile) to erode the local institutions and values of rural communities.

Both Careless and his followers[13] base much of their interpretations of metropolitanism on the four stage model of urban development created by the economist, N.S.B. Gras. Gras's stages include the creation of a marketing system for a city's territory with an establishment of warehouses, wholesaling and exchange facilities; a period of manufacturing growth either in the city or the hinterland but directed by the former; the improvement of the transport system to gain urban centres better access to their hinterlands and other urban places; and the development of financial institutions to service both hinterland trade and the external world.[14]

Geographers have also examined the process of modernization, the most notable interpretation being the central place theory developed by Christaller,[15] which ranks communities according to their abilities to support certain market threshold levels. Vance has criticized central place theory for its emphasis on internal forces and retail gravitation.[16] His mercantile model suggests an exogenic system, whereby cities grow in relation to their long-distance ties as well as their particular linkages with surrounding hinterlands.

In summary, researchers studying changes taking place during the period of the "Great Transformation" have for the most part adopted one of a number of different explanations of the modernization perspective. As in the interpretation of emigration to the United States, ideology plays a major role in how scholars view this process. Those who see modernization in a favourable light view it as a progressive process whereby traditional rural communities give way to a new urban-industrial society. Those who adopt the Marxist perspective, on the other hand, portray modernization as a process whereby people come to exist for production rather than creating a society where production exists for people. Rural areas are seen to have become increasingly dependent on the metropolis, from which economic, political, and socio-cultural decisions effectively subjugate the countryside.

Both the Marxist and neo-classical modernization interpretations of the transformation of rural society share a similar feature. Both views assume that social change in rural areas paralleled urban and industrial trends. But can we presume that characteristics of urban society, traits primarily associated with large cities, provide satisfactory models for understanding both rural life and change in rural society? American rural historians are now seeking to unravel the complex transformations of rural society free of a controlling metropolitan bias. They have questioned the organizational principles of metropolitan dominance and central place theory subsumed within the modernization perspective.[17] How well do they explain the changing relationships taking place in rural society during the nineteenth century? While the economic, political, and social context provided by the development of capitalism is the framework for the study of both rural and urban society, the precise ways in which these forces affected individuals or local social groups depend on a number of local features. We need to focus on the processes of human interaction between town and country and the experiences of people in both settings.

While it is true that rural communities and small towns were integrated right from the beginning into larger regional, national, and international systems of production, in their own right, they played an essential role in satisfying the need for community.[18] Residents of small communities needed the cooperation and business of the surrounding farm population in order to survive. A smaller population pool ensured more ties of friendship and kinship and encouraged a sense of community and, perhaps in some cases, a regional identity. Indigenous capital development, not originating from the larger metropolis, also played a role in changing relationships between different groups in the countryside.[19]

Just as modernization and metropolitanism have been spatially over-generalized in the examination of transformation, so have been Marxist and neo-classical perspectives in terms of analysing migration. A region's development milieu often affects various components of the migration process. Market conditions, for instance, vary from place to place, reflecting economic growth and decline at national, regional, and local levels. Migration is one of the many processes of economic and social differentiation which accompany societal transformation, although it certainly played a major role in the development of communities on both sides of the border. How we view this transformation is particularly important in examining the context for migration, a movement of people resulting in large part from economic, social, political, and geographical forces interacting with local conditions. How, then, are we to interpret mobility in our attempt to understand the context for migration?

Mobility is to be recognized not only as a *dependent* variable, reflective of social change, but also as an *independent* variable, functioning as an agent of change. Those who accept the latter view see geographical mobility as the spatial expression of the presence or absence of opportunities for social mobility. In nineteenth-century North America, "geographical mobility was assumed to be synonymous with social mobility, and both appeared to be natural by-products of the breakdown of local barriers to industrial improvement under the impact of North America's characteristic, unlimited space, especially socio-economic space."[20] Those who accept the former view argue that mobility may be seen as being determined by the structure of society as well as the individual characteristics of the movers. In the countryside, the changing market and land pressures played a major role in prompting movement; in the city, the industrialization process exerted greater control on the individual, creating new opportunities for those who could adapt and placing severe restrictions on those who could not.

Mobility was part of and reaction to the passage of western societies from the pre-industrial or proto-industrial stage to the industrial age. Because mobility and changes in the dominant modes of production are mutually interactive and vary according to the phases in which local, regional, and even national economies find themselves, "there is little that can be said on theoretical or a priori grounds."[21] The attempt to construct theories of migration dates back to E.G. Ravenstein, the first scholar to search for regularities in the movement of human populations.[22] But Ravenstein never assigned the status of scientific laws to his hypotheses. His statements are generalizations derived from examination of the 1871 and 1881 censuses for Britain and, to a lesser extent, western Europe and North America. Because his principles are empirical regularities and not laws, his inductive approach lacks theoretical grounding.[23] Yet it is on the basis of his empirical regularities that subsequent scholars have attempted to construct deductive theories of migration.[24]

Ravenstein was an observer of late nineteenth-century Victorian society, and his generalizations reflect that time. Migration is a contextual process, and any effort to construct a theory of migration has to understand the social context within which individuals form images of their world and make decisions whether to migrate. Those who have adopted Ravenstein's principles in their attempts to build migration theory are misguided because any such theory will fail to provide critical insights into the causes and effects of mobility in particular circumstances. Nevertheless, it is useful to establish generalizations in the context of theories of social change and explore migration as one of a myriad of processes of social and economic differentiation which accompany societal transformations.[25] This necessitates empirical research to reveal the different courses of mobility in particular times and places.

Yet while mobility may be regarded as a product of major processes operating upon and within nineteenth-century society as well as being itself an important dimension of this society, its role has been over-emphasized. People possessed a strong sense of localism centred on family and an extended network of family and friends. Strategies were devised not only to assist family members choosing to emigrate but also to ensure that others would remain. The continuous presence of family members during this period of tremendous change "also may have played an important role in the historical experience of communities where there were high levels of transiency."[26]

LAND, ECONOMY, AND SOCIAL CHANGE IN NINETEENTH-CENTURY ONTARIO: THE CONTEXT OF EMIGRATION

Ontario on the eve of Confederation was a predominantly rural society and was described by many of its observers in largely idyllic terms. This idea of peace and tranquillity served to reinforce an image of conservatism, stability, and attachment to place. Certainly the loyalist legacy was part and parcel of this conservative ideal, an image which remained strong in the face of a developing sense of reform and liberalism in the province. Although the desire for independence was shared by many and attachment to the old country weakened over time, there remained a fierce and loyal pride in the British Empire. Indeed, Ontarians viewed their own role in imperialistic terms; they were to be the locus of power in the new empire known as the Dominion of Canada.

Conservatism and loyalism were compatible with the idea of a pastoral society composed of sturdy yeomen farmers surrounded by comfortable houses and a real sense of community. Despite the development of commerce and the gradual growth of industrial centres, Ontario was a rural society in the nineteenth century and rural was synonymous with all the characteristics associated with conservatism. It was a "place to stand" as well as a "place to grow."

Even in the face of events that brought about significant alterations in people's lives and how they saw themselves in the changing society, this model of Ontario continued to dominate. Warkentin designates the 1880s, a time which witnessed dramatic changes associated with modernization and the greatest outflow of people at any time in its history, as the climax in the development of the conservative, complacent Ontario. "It was," he describes, "a pleasant, open society, in which the individual had considerable freedom within the social mores of the time; if things got too dull for one's taste or if one felt constricted by the customs, one could always leave, as many did."[27]

This image of a contented society, reinforced by the loyalist tradition and a conservative ideal, masks the truth somewhat. In reality, Ontario in the late nineteenth century was anything but a one-dimensional society. People did not move just because of boredom. Perhaps Warkentin and others have overestimated the openness of Ontario society.[28] Certainly people had the freedom to move geographically but the lack of freedom, whether it be in the ability to acquire land or in obtaining a decent paying factory job, may more appropriately account for decisions to move.[29]

Land Policy   By 1855 almost one million people either owned or occupied land considered suitable for agriculture in Ontario. In less than fifty years the agricultural frontier had ceased to exist, and settlement and development had taken place in spite of unenlightened land policies and significant emigration. At the beginning of settlement a wide distribution of accessible property enabled farm households to control most aspects of production. Farm households were largely self-sufficient during the pioneer period, although most began producing for local markets almost immediately. The local exchange of goods and services dominated, although Upper Canada's colonial status ensured significant long-distance exchange with Great Britain. Families supplied many of their own needs by consuming their own products and entering into networks of exchange with neighbours.

Two major developments influenced Ontario agriculture during the early part of the century: the increasing unavailability of land, and exploitation of the wheat staple. The ubiquity of land speculation within Upper Canada has been well noted in historical literature. Gates, for example, suggests that in 1825 about 62 percent, or five million of the eight million acres granted to that date in the province, were in the hands of speculators.[30] Land policy lay at the root of this situation. In 1791 Upper Canada was virtually a colony without people, industry, or institutions (of European origin). Population was the first prerequisite for development but this presumed some kind of mechanism – a land policy – for assembling people. The government therefore sought to establish a system whereby settlement could proceed effectively. Each township was divided into 200-acre lots, with two in every seven lots being reserved for the crown and clergy respectively. The remaining crown land was to be given as "free" grants of 200 acres, though settlers were required to pay small survey and registration fees.

From the outset, however, certain groups of Loyalists were entitled to more land; military men, depending on rank, could accumulate up to 1,000 acres.[31] The government was also responsive to bloc settlements sponsored by companies and individuals who would assist groups of settlers in return for land.[32] The purpose of the system was to get as many families on the land as quickly as possible, and its beauty, to its creators, lay in its simplicity and cheapness.

The free-grant policy was designed to prevent middlemen and speculators from trafficking in land but, in reality, speculation was encouraged. From the beginning the government used land in lieu of cash to reward many people for many different things. For example, after 1818 surveyors were reimbursed for their duties with a percentage of the land surveyed.[33]

As Johnson has shown, many who received land in this way viewed it not as the means to an agricultural life but as capital "to be accumulated and spent as needed."[34] Settlement duties were not enforced with any rigour until 1820. As a result, thousands of acres were never developed for settlement and those intending to farm found it increasingly difficult to acquire land. This was not a serious problem when land was readily available, but as population pressure increased, the existence of large unsettled tracts of land came to be seen as retarding the settlement of the colony. The proportion reserved for the crown and the clergy alone was approximately 28 percent of the total land area of the southern Ontario. The action of private land speculators thus exacerbated the problem of institutional speculation that already existed.

The impact of such activity was recognized very early in the settlement process, as revealed in Gourlay's comments on speculation as a barrier to successful settlement:

In Canada large proportions of land are set aside for the future purposes of government; large proportions are set aside for the maintenance of a dominant church, which has not even a chance of being established; and large proportions are given away and in favour for fees of office to individuals who never think of cultivating but who depend on sales at a remote period of time while actual settlers are, in consequence, removed so far apart, that it is impossible for them to cultivate with economy and profit.[35]

Gourlay's opinion was not shared by everyone. D'Arcy Boulton, a large landholder and speculator himself, praised the speculative practices of land entrepreneurs as a spur to the development of the agricultural economy: "It [speculative activity] is the best method to improve capital and allows the settler, after establishing his own personal farm, to acquire other land, improve it, and sell it and make a profit."[36]

Agriculture   While emigration increased as it became more difficult for people to obtain land, the sheer numbers entering the province and high rates of natural increase moved settlement along at a pace which more than offset the numbers leaving. But agriculture was undergoing a fundamental structural change during this period as mixed farming was replacing wheat cultivation. The importance of wheat cultivation in Ontario has been the subject of much discussion. Innis argues that wheat cultivation led to the development of railways which in turn stimulated an increase in settlement. McCalla and George assert that this interpretation oversimplifies our understanding of agricultural development in Ontario and neglects certain important factors, including the expansion of wheat before the completion of the canals and railways, the important role played by rivers and roads in moving staples, and the appearance of railways when wheat production and immigration were actually declining. Many other commodities were produced and marketed, winter wheat was not widely grown, and only on larger farms was a marketable surplus of wheat produced. Forest products actually outranked wheat and flour in Upper Canada's export economy.[37]

Ontario was well on its way to establishing a mixed farm economy by the 1840s, with wheat playing a central but not exclusive role. Commercial agriculture developed with the transition to production for the growing domestic market. While earlier in the century farmers were not completely dependent on the market but rather took advantage of market opportunities as they arose, by mid-century they often had to borrow money to shift to production for the growing urban market. This created new problems of having to pay for credit, land, labour, and machinery. By the early 1840s land in Upper Canada sold for £3 to £5 an acre and the cost of clearing, building, and stocking a farm added considerably to the total. In addition, mortgages at 12 to 15 percent were expensive and difficult to acquire. Increases in improved land and real estate values, as well as the development of dairy and fruit production, were signs of increasing commercialization.

Rural industrialization outstripped urban industrialization in many parts of the province at mid-century. Farmers still laboured on their own property but those with larger operations increasingly integrated wage labour into their business.[38] In Gagan's opinion, the socio-economic transition which accompanied commercialization and the shift to a mixed farm economy was shaped by a series of forces during the 1860s: decreasing production values, market dislocation, blight, overpopulation in some areas, and land shortages. These forces combined to drive the least adaptable farmers to emigrate, to propel farm labourers and surplus towards the city, and to motivate marginal farmers to seek wage-paying jobs in both town and country. "This shakeup," Gagan states, "which favoured well-established farmers who would underwrite the transition to the new regime of capital intensive, mechanized mixed farming to service a domestic market ... also marginalized smallholders and tenant farmers who became the motive power behind the diffusion of industrialization throughout the towns and villages of Ontario after 1870."[39] Yet the opportunity to acquire land still existed in the province during the 1860s, at least in certain parts such as central Ontario.

Canada's Reciprocity Treaty of 1854 with the United States accelerated the shift from wheat to mixed farming and dairy production. The transition was further induced by problems of wheat midge experienced by Ontario farmers during the 1850s. The mixed agricultural economy received a boost with the American Civil War as the North required Ontario wool, cheese, beef, and mutton to clothe and feed the troops. A tax placed on whiskey increased beer consumption in the northern states during this same period and stimulated barley production in nearby Ontario.[40] By the mid-1880s barley had replaced wheat as the major cash crop in the province, but the substitution of corn for barley in beer-making in the United States and the growing competition of barley production in Iowa and Wisconsin reduced Ontario's American barley market and the passing of the McKinley tariff in 1891 effectively closed the door on this same market.[41]

Land soon became more expensive and difficult to acquire. Despite this, relatively few chose to rent property. In 1871 only 15.3 percent of all Ontario farms were tenant-operated, the majority in the older settled areas around the lakes near the larger cities. Tenants were generally young immigrants operating smaller farms and producing lower yields.[42] Renting was not seen as a viable option and so many moved elsewhere in the province, particularly Bruce and Grey counties, where newly opened land was selling cheaply, or they left for the United States. Those who persisted were often forced to borrow money or to mortgage land, crops, or livestock in order to make the shift to commercial mixed farming.[43] Mortgages were increasingly negotiated with merchants, bankers, and lawyers while previously they had been arranged with neighbours and family.

Industrialization   Pre-industrial rural manufacturing took place primarily in small cottage manufactories where artisans practised specialized skills. Sawmills and grist-mills dominated the rural landscape, and tanneries, carding mills, breweries, metal foundries, and other small enterprises supplied local markets with consumer goods. Over time, rural households increasingly purchased manufactured goods produced in the larger centres. Eventually, small-scale rural manufacturing, supported by families and the local exchange of goods and services, became less important as demands for larger-scale manufacturing necessitated great amounts of capital and larger numbers of wage labour.

Yet industrialization in Ontario proceeded at a relatively slow pace, particularly when compared to that of the United States. The primary sector (food, construction, unfinished producers), although declining in importance, remained dominant throughout the latter half of the nineteenth century and the tertiary sector developed at a much greater rate than the secondary sector (consumer and finished producer goods).[44] Industrialization did not expand significantly until the increase of American investment early in the twentieth century.

Different interpretations of Ontario's industrial development are offered in the historical literature. Naylor believes that the political and economic elite invested their money in the traditional exploitation of staples and commercial markets, thus leaving few funds for industrial capital formation and retarding the development of industrialization. Drummond views Ontario's industrial revolution quite differently, arguing that industrial development increased significantly after 1871 and that the transformation of Ontario to an urban-industrial society was virtually complete by 1914. Although local industries had emerged before the tariff, industrialization, in his opinion, really took off after the implementation of the National Policy.[45]

Whatever interpretation one accepts, the fact remains that industry in Ontario was experiencing a fundamental transition from the primary processing of staples to the increasing production of consumer and producer goods. By 1891, under the protection of the tariff the province began to specialize in producer goods such as agricultural machinery and increased the number and variety of consumer products offered to its expanding population. Although the period 1873–93 is generally viewed as one of economic uncertainty, there were some years of relative growth, notably at the end of the 1870s and the beginning of the 1880s. In fact, there are some tangible signs of growth in the province during the period: wages rose by 68 percent between 1880 and 1900 and public deposits in Canadian banks jumped from $41 million in 1881 to $50 million in 1891.[46]

But the degree of development differed not only between the various regions of Canada but within Ontario as well. Industrial growth was greater in the area surrounding the head of Lake Ontario, with extensions into the Grand Valley and Middlesex County. By 1891 a manufacturing belt had formed including York, Wentworth, Waterloo, Brant, and Middlesex counties, taking advantage of agglomeration economies and the multiplier effect.[47] Those communities less favoured in terms of location and economies of scale did not share in growth; indeed, many experienced stagnation and decline. Smaller lake ports suffered greatly after the McKinley tariff reduced the grain export trade.

Despite increases in wages, there is evidence to suggest that this did not translate into significant improvements in living standards for Ontario workers: "In 1855 the Ontario Bureau of Statistics estimated that the average mechanic with a family of 4½ would spend annually $216 for food, $90 on fuel, $72 on rent, and $86 for clothing. The total of $464 left him with a mere $30 spending money." The majority of workers were non-unionized and the labour unions that did organize during the period were too weak to enforce better wages and working conditions.[48] Ontarians were well aware of the substantially higher wages paid in nearby American cities, a fact that no doubt entered into the decision-making of those choosing to emigrate. And even though the larger centres benefited from the tariff that gave rise to the expansion of manufacturing, the supply of labour exceeded the demand, a reality of life at this time which served to push people out of the province.

Urbanization Industrialization spurred urban growth in Ontario, yet urban centres originally developed as places supplying goods and services for an agricultural population. Before Confederation, urbanization tended to be extensive rather than intensive. A string of small port towns existed with no one centre dominating. London was the only town of significant size before 1850 not along the St Lawrence or the lakes. By 1842, Toronto had emerged as the largest settlement (14,000), followed by Kingston (6,000), Hamilton (3,000), and London (2,000).[49]

Urban development was dictated by geography, particularly transportation. Towns functioned as collection centres for the staples of the surrounding hinterland and as distribution centres for imported goods. Early in the century, location by water, whether it be the St Lawrence or Lakes Ontario and Erie, was the prerequisite for growth. The construction of a canal system, followed by railways at mid-century, marked a new stage of urban development. The railways in particular spurred the growth of inland towns as distribution and market centres. Those communities bypassed by the railways stagnated and declined.

Urbanization became more intensive during the second half of the century with improved transportation, increasing immigration, the end of the agricultural frontier, and the development of industry. Various towns in eastern Ontario such as Kingston, Gananoque, and Brockville had long before established their presence as market centres. But the advantages of early settlement were undermined by the disadvantages of geography. These communities were faced with a hinterland of limited agricultural potential, ephemeral resources, and transitory settlement and thus were unable to keep up with the growth occurring in urban centres elsewhere.[50] Ports close to Toronto such as Cobourg, Port Hope, Port Credit, Whitby, and Oakville lost almost all their export trade to the larger centre.

Population concentrated in the larger cities where opportunities were perceived to be greater. Toronto, in particular, benefited from its site and situation: it was centrally located, it had a good agricultural hinterland, it offered a larger array of services than other places because of its role as capital, and it had an excellent harbour.[51] By the middle of the 1850s the city had become the focus of railway development in the province, connected by the Grand Trunk to Montreal, the Great Western with New York through Hamilton and Buffalo, and the Northern with the trade of the upper lakes. The central location of Hamilton and its superior harbour ensured that city's growth, particularly after the development of the iron and steel industry at the end of the nineteenth century.[52]

Land Ownership   The transformation taking place in Ontario society during the nineteenth century also involved fundamental changes in social structures and social integration. However, one element of Ontario society, the value placed on ownership of land, remained constant throughout most of the century and was regarded as a basis for assessing social status and social integration. Property, land for agricultural purposes, was seen as the key to independence, upward mobility, and family security for much of the period. How much land an individual held was a barometer of how successful his efforts at ensuring independence for his family had been. Land was a symbol of security; it meant many things to different people but it was seen by all as the means to a better life. Indeed, property ownership has been regarded by some as a common denominator in Ontario society.[53]

Yet in reality, a functional approach to property was adopted by many. Settlers were frequently advised that once their property was improved to the point of production, they should consider selling their holdings in part or in whole and invest capital in more land or in mortgages. Accumulation of capital through the sale of land allowed one to expand farming operations, move on to what was perceived to be a better environment, or even to abandon agriculture in favour of urban life. To many, land was a commercial commodity and farmers, as well as merchants and speculators, participated in what Johnson calls "the Upper Canadian national game."[54] Such an attitude contributed significantly to the environment of mobility that characterized not only Ontario but all of North American society.

Yet land ownership and accumulation also encouraged persistence for many. For some there was little room for attachment to land in such a dynamic society, while for others ownership was associated with independence, egalitarianism, and stability. In early Ontario land was one resource that was ample and could be exploited by a population poor in capital and skills but rich in the ability to work. What emerges from various pioneer reminiscences and travel accounts is that the most important goal of the pioneer was independence from other people and institutions.[55]

An Open Society?   Right from the beginning of settlement, John Graves Simcoe, the first lieutenant-governor of the colony, wanted to create a society which would be a loyal remnant of the empire. The key to fulfilling this objective was the attraction of well-to-do individuals who would accept the responsibility for establishing settlements in return for large grants of land. Although the plan failed, the precedent for a landed hierarchy was established.

Upper Canadian society was stratified on the basis of amount of land owned, occupation, education, and wealth. The practice of awarding large grants of land to privileged individuals ensured that certain families and their descendants would occupy the top layer of society. The so-called Family Compact, a name used by people of that period and scholars today to refer to a province-wide social and political aristocracy that was linked through marriage and business, together with local elites, held considerable power in the colony. Yet opportunities for upward movement existed, primarily through the acquisition of land and the development of business.

The degree of openness in Upper Canadian society has been subject to much debate. Rural areas were more fluid as acquisition of land allowed individuals and their families the means to improve their standard of living and status. The gulf between small and large landholders was bridged to some extent by a middle class composed of artisans and proprietors. Urban communities were more strictly defined with a more rigid social structure composed of a commercial elite, a small emerging middle class, and a large proletariat.

The importance of the agricultural frontier in the social formation of pioneer Ontario is difficult to ascertain. Even though Upper Canada was a colony and therefore controlled to a significant extent by Britain, it also offered economic opportunity to anyone investing labour and capital in developing the local economy. The state co-opted the efforts of a conservative oligarchy supported by extensive grants of land by inviting them into the administration of political, social, and economic control. Yet the ease of acquiring property, at least during the initial settlement phase, was the key to mobility. Advancement on an individual basis was possible but less accepted were challenges to authority.[56]

However, access to cheap, available land became more difficult after the first generation of settlement resulting in a more structured rural sector. A poorly supported and unsuccessful attempt at rebellion in 1837–8 is testimony to a growing sense of frustration shared among Upper Canadians over land policies, speculation, and the oligarchic nature of government. Ontarians of this period were increasingly influenced by new world ideas of individual freedom, many coming from the neighbouring republic. Liberal ideas and the geographical reality of the frontier ensured a looser social context. And yet at the same time, the liberalism of Ontario was much different than that existing in the United States. Ontarians, for the most part, remained strongly attached to the empire and accepted a larger and more paternalistic role for government. The failure of the rebellion to garner popular support is evidence of these feelings.

Government land grants and settlement policies in Upper Canada produced social inequality by creating a class of landless wage labourers who provided a cheap and available industrial workforce. This growing proletariat was supplemented by the large inflow of Irish emigrants fleeing the potato famine during the 1840s. Yet despite the development of a landless proletariat in both urban and rural communities during the mid-century period, there is little evidence of the formation of working-class consciousness in the province until after Confederation, when branches of groups such as the Knights of Labor, the Patrons of Industry, and the Grangers started appearing in Ontario centres.

Responses to Industrial Capitalism   Ontario farmers at mid-century were becoming more aware of the increasing control that the interests of capital had over their lives. They, along with the skilled labourers and factory hands working in the towns and villages, began to question the guiding hands of commercial capitalists. Both the Dominion Grange of the Patrons of Husbandry and the Grand Association of the Patrons of Industry were outgrowths of American movements, the former entering Ontario in 1874 and the latter coming into the province from Michigan in 1889. These organizations attempted to organize farmers into co-operative ventures designed to protect their rights to a just return for their labour and to reduce the influence of urban capitalists. Through co-operation, it was hoped that farmers could have more control over prices paid for their products and costs of the goods they purchased. Both groups feared the social costs of industrialization and adhered closely to the agrarian myth of the primacy of farming in society.

The Patrons declared their political intentions from the beginning and in 1894 actually managed to have seventeen members elected to the Ontario legislature. The Grange, on the other hand, was not a political organization even though it was concerned with political questions. In the first issue of their journal *The Granger* in 1875, the directors of the movement lamented the inequality in political power existing in the country: "The truth is, the legislation of the country is shaped and controlled by less than 1/10 of the population. It is made in the interest of capital, instead of the interest of the people. And this is the reason there is so much suffering among the industrial classes today." Both organizations were sympathetic to the needs of the urban proletariat and in the 1890s attempted to create an alliance with urban labour groups which would bring about a new brand of politics concerned with questions of social justice.[58] Yet they were never able to capture control of the Ontario market or gain much support among the population.

As the factory system expanded after mid-century, conflict between labour and capital escalated in the province, as evidenced in the increasing number of strikes in the 1870s and 1880s. While international unions first appeared in Canada in the 1850s, it was the arrival of the American-based Knights of Labor in 1881, a labour organization that was simultaneously a trade union, political reform body, and fraternal lodge, that signalled the rise of a new labour movement. The Knights attracted close to two-thirds of Ontario's labour force and in response the government enacted some conciliatory factory and workmen's legislation. Eventually, the Knights were defeated as employers retaliated with harassment of workers, but they paved the way for the future development of a powerful Canadian labour movement.[59]

The Search for Consensus: Church and School   The debate between church and state and the final victory of volunteerism represented important events in Upper Canada. The debate involved the search for a consensus regarding the role that institutions should play in people's lives. The population of the colony was divided among religious as well as national backgrounds. The Protestant tradition promoted privatism, and a streak of fundamentalism placed a premium on egalitarianism in spiritual matters. Many immigrants who had previous unfavourable experiences with state and church controls on their lives treated the intrusion of the state into matters of individual religious freedom with hostility.

Simcoe's model of Upper Canadian society called for an alliance between church and state in which the former would indoctrinate people with conservative ideals that the latter would put into practice. But the majority of immigrants during this period were not Anglicans but Lutherans, Baptists, Quakers, and Methodists who opposed any church-state alliance. For much of the first half of the nineteenth century, Roman Catholic and Protestant dissenters, divided by factionalism and along ethnic lines, united in their attempt to deny Anglican claims to function as the official church of the colony. Bishop Strachan's effort to assert the control of the Anglican church was assisted by the government, who decreed that only the Church of England had the right to use their share of the clergy reserves to support the church and clergy. But Egerton Ryerson, the leader of the Methodists, and others made the relationship between church and state a political issue.

Following the introduction of responsible government, church and state were largely separated. Governor General Sydenham, by the 1841 Act of Union, decided all churches should share the clergy reserves. In 1854 the clergy reserves were abolished, the money and interest being invested in the Municipality Funds of Canada West and Canada East. While tension continued over government support of Roman Catholic schools, religious strain gradually eased towards the end of the century.

The search for consensus not only characterized religion but education as well. Debate arose over who should be responsible for education and what philosophy the system was to be based upon. Simcoe wanted to provide a grammar school and university for sons of the political and religious elite and set aside half a million acres for the support of education. During the pioneer period only the affluent could afford to send their children to the small number of private schools established in the province or to private teachers or have them taught at home.[60] Yet over time, a rudimentary system was slowly put in place. The 1807 District Grammar School Act provided for the establishment of one grammar school in each of Upper Canada's administrative districts, but they proved to be too inaccessible in terms of distance and costs of room and board for the average family. Communities who paid teachers built a scattered network of schools. But attendance was poor as children were regarded as a valuable source of agricultural labour during the pre-industrial period.

Reformers and Tories argued over the philosophy of schooling, with the former wanting non-sectarian education and the latter favouring an Anglican-dominated system. With the Union of the Canadas in 1841, a Common Schools Act was passed which called for a liberal general education system. This centralized education and stimulated a common curriculum. The 1841 act envisaged separate schools but as part of a common school system. By 1853 separate schools were guaranteed a distinct existence from the public school system but given no financial aid other than tax support. Ten years later an act was passed that increased public funds for separate schools. In 1870 the Compulsory School Act was passed providing compulsory education for children aged seven to fourteen. By the end of the century, basically all the pieces of the public school system had been put in place.

Population Trends and Demographic Responses   While experiencing an economic and social transformation, Ontario was also affected by profound changes in the composition, distribution, and dimensions of population. Population is both an independent and a dependent factor, modified and transformed by social and economic systems. Increases or decreases of population relative to resources influence age at marriage, fertility, and systems of land inheritance. Family and kinship are affected by changes in the economy, class relations, production methods, ideology, religion, and political governance; yet these components are in turn altered by modifications in family composition or behaviour.[61] In pre-industrial agrarian society, age at marriage and fertility were influenced by factors such as inheritance systems and class relations of land-ownership which governed the availability of land. The intricacies of these relationships are difficult to establish and yet are fundamental to understanding the transformation taking place in Ontario society during the nineteenth century.

Four waves of immigration populated Ontario during the first half of nineteenth century: first the Loyalists (*c.* 1780–93), then the Americans (*c.* 1790–1812), followed by migrants from the British Isles (*c.* 1816–35), and finally the Europeans, primarily from Ireland, who emigrated to Canada in the aftermath of the potato famine (*c.* 1847–55). Somewhere between five thousand and eight thousand Loyalists, many American-born and coming from the frontier areas of nearby American colonies, particularly New York, and two to three thousand Amerindians settled in what was to become Upper Canada. Lands were made available to the white settlers in newly surveyed townships along the St Lawrence River, eastern Lake Ontario, and the Niagara River, while the Six Nations Indians were offered land along the Grand River.[62]

Loyalists in Upper Canada were soon followed by other American immigrants, the late Loyalists, a restless group of land-seekers attracted by cheap crown land. By 1812, 80 percent of the almost one hundred thousand people in Upper Canada were of American origin, and at least three quarters of this group were neither Loyalists nor their descendants.[63] After the War of 1812 the government, in an environment of growing attachment to the crown and distrust of the United States, passed legislation making it difficult for Americans to purchase crown land, effectively reducing, although not completely ending, the in-migration of this group.

Following the Napoleonic Wars in Europe a massive wave of immigrants came to North America, a considerable number finding their way to Ontario. The rise of industrialization, the modernization of agriculture, and the enclosure movement created a mobile population in Britain and in the face of periodic depressions and population pressure, the government strongly supported out-migration as a means of alleviating social problems.[64] Upper Canada was the primary destination for those immigrants coming to Canada, although many of this number, taking advantage of cheaper passage rates to Canada, soon afterwards crossed the border into the United States. From 1815 to 1865 well over a million of British emigrants entered British North America and in the years between 1825 and 1842, the population of Upper Canada tripled to 450,000. The majority of the Britons settling the colony during this period hailed from the northern and western peripheries (Ireland, Scotland, northern England) of the British Isles. By 1842 the Irish were the largest ethnic group in Canada, with native-born and first-generation comprising over 25 percent of the population.[65]

Following the disastrous potato famine, an estimated 729,868 Irish came to North America during the period 1846–9, almost 30 percent arriving in Canada. As Akenson shows, the majority of this group coming to British North America were not the "polluted" lumpenproletariat of Irish society but were relatively well-off tenant farmers from the north-central part of the country decimated by the potato failure.[66] Protestants, carrying with them skills associated with farming as well as with craft production, settled primarily in the countryside of Ontario. Irish Catholics, fewer in number and predominantly of peasant origin, took up subsistence farming, with more over time employed in the labour markets associated with the building of canals and railways as well as urban construction. Later, Canada drew heavily upon the industry-related backgrounds of immigrants of English and Scottish origins.[67] During the first half of the nineteenth century Ontario experienced considerable population growth as a result of high fertility as well as immigration, expanding from 158,000 in 1825 to 952,000 in 1851.[68] At mid-century Ontario had one of the highest birth rates in the world, although there was significant regional variation. Fertility rates were lower in the older settled areas along the St Lawrence and the Niagara peninsula and higher in the more recently settled interior.[69] Children were regarded as an economic asset to the pre-industrial farm. It has been estimated that during the pioneer period it would take one hard-working immigrant labouring by himself over thirty years to create a fifty-acre farm, so obviously children were regarded as a valuable source of labour.[70] During this period, the efforts of the male off-spring were usually rewarded with either inheritance of the family farm or gifts of land nearby.

Early marriages and large families placed considerable pressure on household heads to acquire property for children. As land became more scarce and expensive, parents found it more difficult to provide for their children. Each child deserved a reward for his or her contribution to the household, but it became increasingly obvious that most families could no longer dispense equal shares. Excessive subdivision of holdings created farms that were not viable, especially as farm sizes increased in response to commercialization.

A number of strategies were adopted by families to deal with increasingly unfavourable population/land ratios. Those who could afford it purchased nearby land for their children. This alternative became less viable as land increased in price. Inheritance practices were modified to ensure the continuance of the family farm and the care of parents. Under this system, the family farm was transferred to a single heir who then became responsible for fulfilling the parents' responsibility to the rest of the children. This heir, who was often but not always the youngest son or the last one to marry, was left with the burden of providing dowries for his sisters, dispensing cash shares to his brothers, and, in the event of the death of his father, supplying his widowed mother with an annual income. In order to fulfil these responsibilities, heirs sometimes sold some of the land and divided the money amongst their siblings; others sold all of the land, distributed the capital to family members, and moved away. Some went into mortgage debt and others avoided their responsibility by simply giving the land to another sibling or someone else.[71]

Demographic responses included fertility reduction and marriage at a later age. Fertility declined earlier in Ontario than in Quebec, first in urban centres and shortly thereafter in rural areas.[72] Family formation was also related to the changing nature of the economy. As the goal of obtaining a farm could only be achieved after a period of wage labour or out-migration, this led increasingly to marriage postponement and declining fertility.[73] As society urbanized, such trends continued.

These strategies were designed to secure the cohesiveness of the family unit; such a goal was obtainable, either through persistence or mobility. Land was the key to security; if it was readily available, persistence was largely ensured; if not, then mobility became more likely. As land became less available and agriculture experienced a fundamental transformation, mobility became an important part of a strategy not only to secure the cohesiveness of the family but in some cases to ensure the maintenance of community as well.

As suitable agricultural land in Ontario was taken up, young people increasingly moved to urban centres to find employment in the expanding industrial and tertiary sectors. Those wishing to continue farming moved farther north where land was still available at a reasonable price. Yet by the 1880s frontier-ward intra-provincial migration had virtually ceased and urban-industrial growth could not keep pace with an increasing population. It has been estimated that at least 180,000 people in the 1880s, 200,000 in the 1890s, and 205,000 in the 1900–10 decade, many of them young women, left Ontario's countryside. Ontario had the highest rate of population increase of all the provinces during the second half of the nineteenth century; its population grew by 122 percent between 1851 and 1891.[74] Yet a series of economic slumps was almost immediately followed by surges in emigration by an extremely mobile population. In the last forty years of the century more people were leaving the province than arriving. Yet for all those who left, many more stayed.

DIMENSIONS AND REGIONAL VARIATIONS OF MIGRATION

A Macroscopic View: The Published Censuses

A certain amount of emigration had always taken place during the nineteenth century, starting with disenchanted Loyalists returning to their former homes. But by the 1850s economic change, high rates of natural increase, and progressively unfavourable population/land ratios conspired to increase the flow out of the country. A movement that started out as a steady trickle had turned into a raging flood during the last four decades of the century, with the greatest loss occurring in the 1880s (Table 1). It has been estimated that over the period 1861–1931 the net migration of Canadian-born to the United States totalled 2,080,000. By 1900, nearly 788,000 Anglo-Canadians comprised 8 percent of America's foreign-born.[75]

The period 1873–96 was characterized by a succession of economic slumps, varying in intensity and by region, and corresponding increases in emigration to the United States. The tariff, which had been designed to achieve a domestic market for Canadian manufactures, was struggling to achieve its purpose in the face of uncertain global markets. According to Easterbrook and Aitken, the National Policy only achieved success "when the best lands in the United States had been alienated, her agricultural surplus reduced by her growing domestic market, and her forest resources nearly exhausted."[76] A recovery in the world economy by 1896 resulted in an increase in the selling price of exports, a decrease in the cost of transporting prairie wheat, a greater demand in industrial Europe for foodstuffs, and an increase in immigration to Canada.

The published Canadian censuses, available from 1851 onwards, and

Table 1   Two Different Estimates of Canadian Emigration during the Nineteenth Century

Example 1: Maximum and Minimum Estimates (in thousands) of Immigration, Emigration, and Net Migration for Canada, 1851–1911

Decade	Immigration	Emigration	Net migration
1851–61	209–486	86–332	+(123–180)
1861–71	187–266	370–436	–(150–191)
1871–81	253–353	293–440	–(40–85)
1881–91	448–903	602–1110	–(150–205)
1891–1901	249–326	364–510	–(115–181)
1901–11	1,111–1,782	317–1,067	+(715–810)

Source: W.E. Kalbach and W.W. McVey, *The Demographic Bases of Canadian Society* (Toronto: McGraw-Hill Co. of Canada, 1971), 41.

Example 2: Migration of Canadians to the United States

Year	Canadian-born living in the US	As a % of the US population	As a % of the US foreign-born population	As a % of the Canadian population
1850	147,711	0.6	6.6	6.2
1860	249,970	0.8	6.0	7.9
1870	493,464	1.3	8.9	13.9
1880	717,157	1.4	10.7	16.6
1890	980,938	1.6	10.6	20.3
1900	1,179,922	1.6	11.4	22.0

Source: Ralph E. Vedder and Lawrence E. Galloway, "Settlement Patterns of Canadian Emigrants in the United States," *Canadian Journal of Economics* 3 (1970), 478.

the published American censuses, available from 1790 onwards, contain only the crudest types of aggregate information. The birthplaces of individuals are listed but only by country, province, or state of birth. From such data the researcher can only establish gross patterns of migration, but this information is useful nonetheless.

The published census has been used by economists and economic historians in their assessment of the displacement and demand-side theses of Canadian emigration. One disciple of the displacement thesis, Paul Coats, bases his support of this hypothesis on the location patterns of Canadian-born migrants living in the United States in 1920.[77] Canadian migrants did not go to those parts of America which were expanding most rapidly, as they would have done if demand forces were the determining factor. Instead they went to areas of previous emigration, many locating near the border, awaiting an opportunity to return home.

Vedder and Galloway support the demand-side argument based on their examination of the American decennial censuses for the period 1850 to 1960.[78] The empirical results of testing their gravity model reveal that both

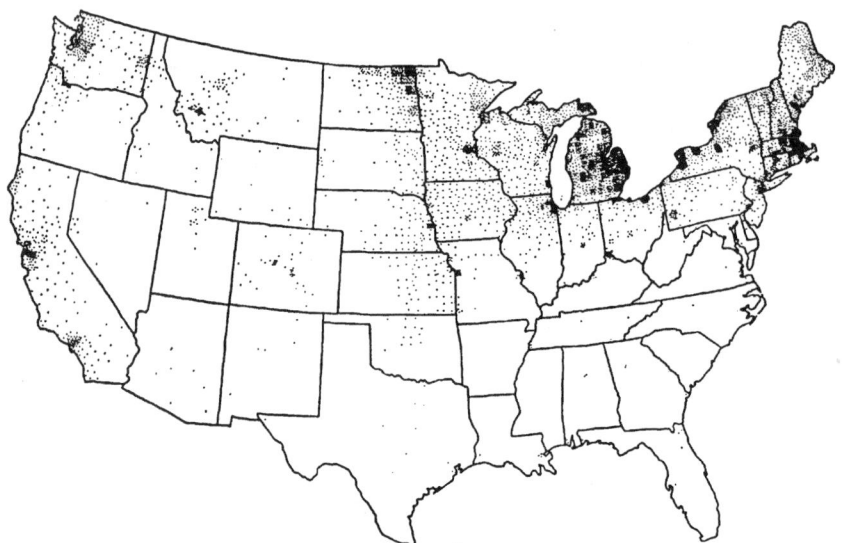

Map 1: English-Canadian Settlement in the United States, 1900

Source: Rowland Berthoff, *British Immigrants in Industrial America* (Cambridge, Mass.: Harvard Univesity Press, 1953).

French- and English-speaking Canadians have been quite responsive to income differences in the demand for labour. They conclude that Canadian emigrant labour mobility patterns have conformed to the demand theory, which posits that resource allocation is improved by resources moving towards those sectors of the international economy where the returns to such resources are highest.

The published American census also illustrates the short-distance nature of Canadian migration to the United States during the latter half of the century. Using the published census as a source of evidence, Berthoff was able to construct a map of English (-speaking) Canadian settlement for the year 1900 which clearly reveals that migration among this group was generally short-distance in nature (Map 1).[79] The tendency for Canadians to locate in adjacent border regions is evident not merely at the national scale but at the state scale as well, as illustrated in Map 2, which shows Canadian settlement in New York State in 1880.

Migration fields earlier in the century were more widespread as Canadians responded to the availability of agricultural land in a number of locations. By 1880, however, the agricultural frontier of America had retreated west into Kansas, Nebraska, and Texas, territories not readily accessible to young Canadians. Yet improvements in transportation reduced the importance of distance as a factor in migration decisions as nearby American

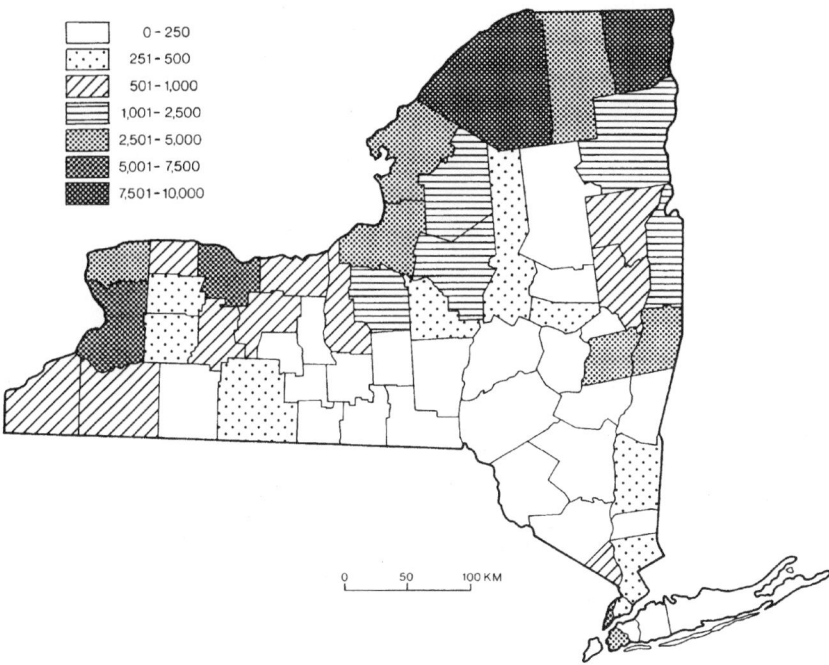

Map 2: Number of Canadian-Born by Counties, New York State, 1880

regions were made even more accessible after the middle of the nine-teenth century by regular railway and steamer service. The increasing concentration of Canadians in border states is attributed in part to the job opportunities, levels of per capita income, and population densities of these areas. Anglo-Canadians were also drawn to nearby American regions by expectation of employment in a familiar occupation. Some 49 percent of the Canadian workforce in the United States in 1880 were engaged in manufacturing, mechanical, or mining industries, 26 percent were in the professional and personal sector, 21 percent were employed in agriculture, and 9 percent were engaged in trade and transportation. Over fifteen thousand carpenters and twenty-two thousand domestics comprised more than 4 percent and 6 percent respectively of Canadians employed in the United States. Young single women employed as domestics tended to move to the nearest American cities. In fact, there were more women than men among Canadian immigrants at the turn of the century in cities such as Boston, Detroit, and Chicago. Young single males were more likely to move greater distances to lumbering and mining frontiers of the midwest, western interior, and far West.[80]

Although the distribution patterns revealed in these maps emphasize the effect of distance upon migration, the attraction of large centres is also noticeable. Much of the short-distance nature of Canadian migration during this period can be explained by the fact that the majority of Canadians lived relatively close to the major industrial centres of the American northeast and midwest. In 1880 Canadians, primarily from Ontario, comprised 23 percent of the foreign-born population in Detroit, 14 percent in Rochester, 12 percent in Buffalo, 12 percent in Syracuse, and 6 percent in Chicago.[81] Although they generally moved short distances to New York State, Michigan, Illinois, and other midwest states, Ontarians were the Canadians most likely to travel farther afield. Maritimers, the majority moving to the New England states, alone constituted 22 percent of the foreign-born population of Boston in 1900.[82] In 1880 one-third of New Brunswickers in the United States lived in Maine, many employed as lumbermen, with smaller proportions joining fellow Maritimers, Ontarians, and Québecois in the lumber camps of northern Michigan, Wisconsin and Minnesota. By the 1880s Nova Scotians alone comprised 12 percent of the population of Gloucester, Massachusetts, and made up an even greater percentage of that community's fishing fleet.[83] A small percentage, however, pursued agricultural opportunities in the upper midwest and Great Plains. The majority of French Canadians migrated to New England where many worked as labourers in the mills of cities such as Lynn, Lowell, and Manchester. Yet despite the predominance of short-distance migration, considerable numbers of Anglo- and French-Canadians gravitated towards such distant centres as Kansas City, Los Angeles, and San Francisco.

A Macroscopic View: Canadian Border Entries to the United States

The Index to Canadian Border Entries to the United States, described in Appendix 1, sheds more light on Canadian emigration to the United States than the published censuses. From this source, two random samples, each including one thousand individual cases, were generated, the first examining the migration patterns and characteristics of Anglo- and French-Canadian-born and those from other countries emigrating to the United States from Canada between 1895 and 1924, the second focusing specifically on the characteristics and movement patterns of Anglo-Canadians over the age of 15 moving to the United States during that same period. The data derived from these two samples are summarized here. Besides examining attributes of the migrants themselves, I was able to explore the regional dimension of this particular flow. Yet because the index is arranged alphabetically and not geographically, it is difficult to trace in detail the experiences of migrants from specific Canadian origins to particular American destinations. In addition, the majority of records refer to Canadians emigrating after 1910, thus missing the period of greatest Canadian out-migration to the United States.

Random Sample of Migrants Born in Canada and Elsewhere.   Almost half the random sample were born in Canada, the majority coming from Ontario and Quebec, with approximately 10 percent arriving from the Maritime provinces and only a handful hailing from western Canada. Other important countries of origin included England, Russia, Italy, Scotland, the United States, Sweden and Norway. Yet while only 44.9 percent of the sample were born in Canada, 58.4 percent were Canadian citizens, indicating that 25 percent of those born outside the country had acquired Canadian citizenship before moving to the United States. Roughly two-thirds of the Canadian-born were Anglo-Canadians. Of those born outside Canada, those from the United States were by far most likely to acquire Canadian citizenship. Other birth groups distinguished by significant citizenship rates were the Romanians, English, Armenians, Scots, and Irish.

A significant proportion of these migrants had previously lived in the United States.[84] This group included those who first came to the United States and then moved to Canada and those who emigrated to Canada, moved to the United States, and then returned to Canada for either a considerable period of time or just to collect their family and possessions and return to the United States. For many, the movement captured in the border entries represented scouting expeditions in which they would test the waters, so to speak, and if they found them favourable then the decision was made to leave their homeland.

Almost 86 percent of those born in the United States moved from Canada as Canadian citizens. Some migrants, those born in China, Australia, and Ireland in particular, passed through both the United States and Canada en route to another destination. In the case of the Chinese, several moved from Vancouver to board ships in Seattle and San Francisco bound for destinations such as Cuba. A few Italians previously living in Canada travelled to New York where they embarked on ships returning to Italy.

As expected, males dominated this particular migration. Females were relatively numerous in the Canadian-born flow, reflecting the fact that this migration for many was short-distance in nature and did not result in permanent separation from family and friends. In fact, many Canadian-born females were moving to join husbands or family members who had previously emigrated to the United States. Eleven of this group were nurses moving to occupy positions in hospitals in cities such as New York and Chicago. Just over half of all migrants were married and yet many of these same individuals travelled alone either, in the case of men, to settle in some community before sending for their family, or, in the case of women, coming to join their husbands. The majority of single women travelling alone came to the United States to take up positions as domestics, labourers, and nurses. Many of this group were pushed from farms by physically-demanding labour and lured to Canadian and American cities where they anticipated an expanded social life and a greater degree of financial independence. Children accompanied many of the married women travelling without their husbands.

For the time period chosen, the majority of migrants entered the United States between 1910 and 1919 – although proportionately equal numbers arrived in the 1920–4 interval. Not all these migrants from Canada were granted entry. Surprisingly, Canadians had a higher rate of rejection than migrants born in northern Europe, although they lagged behind those born in countries such as China, Hungary, Turkey, India, Persia, and Italy. The majority of debarred Canadians declared very small amounts of money on their manifests, a fact that no doubt resulted in their being denied entry. Among this group, those listed as French Canadians were slightly more likely to be turned back than those designated as Anglo-Canadians.

Kin and kith connections influenced the location decisions of all nativity groups. Fifty-four percent of the migrants were joining relatives and almost 19 percent were joining friends. When queried about the location of their closest relative or friend, 42.2 percent listed the same place within North America in which they last lived, 28.9 percent answered the same country outside North America in which they lived, 9.4 percent responded the same province or state but not the same community in which they previously lived, 5.4 percent replied another province or state than the one in which they lived, and 0.6 percent listed some other country than the one from which they came. Almost 14 percent did not fit into any of these categories.

Perhaps the most striking difference among nativity groups moving from Canada to the United States was their occupational profile. Among the thirteen nativity groups numbering over ten persons, the Finns were most heavily concentrated in the unskilled labour category, followed by the Italians, Austrians, Norwegians, Swedes, Belgians, Russians, Irish, Chinese, Canadians, Scots, English, and Americans. The group showing the highest percentage of semi-skilled workers was the Norwegians, followed by the Swedes, Austrians, English, Canadians, Scots, Americans, Irish, and Russians. Among skilled workers, the Scots ranked first, followed by the Belgians, Russians, English, Americans, Irish, Canadians, Swedes, Italians, and Austrians. Among the six nativity groups with over ten individuals represented in the clerical category, the Irish ranked first, followed by the Scots, English, Canadians, Americans, and Russians. Among these groups represented in the business category, the Chinese ranked well above the rest, followed by the Belgians, Scots, English, Canadians, and Italians. In the professional category, the Irish once again ranked first, followed by the Americans, Chinese, English, Canadians, Scots, and Russians. In the farmer group, the Americans ranked well above the rest, followed by Belgians, Norwegians, Swedes, Canadians, Austrians, Russians, and English. Finally, in the wife category, which may be viewed as synonymous with housewife, the Russians ranked first, followed by the English, Americans, Canadians, Irish, Scots, Belgians, Norwegians, Swedes, and Italians.

Canadian-born more closely approximated patterns exhibited by British- and American-born migrants, but unlike these groups, they did not deviate greatly from the average, neither ranking very high nor very low. They were most under-represented in the business and unskilled categories and most over-represented in the clerical and farmer classifications. French Canadians were more concentrated in the blue-collar categories and less represented in the farmer, clerical, and professional sectors than Anglo-Canadians.

While the small sample size may be questioned in terms of its representativeness, it does add to our understanding of transatlantic migration by presenting evidence regarding the intermediary migration of Europeans sojourning in Canada before moving to the United States. As mentioned, Canadian emigration to the United States reached its apogee during the 1880s, a decade of economic stagnation and decline. Those arriving in Canada from the United States and Europe were also sensitive to these conditions and moved on to greener pastures south of the border. While less than 50 percent who arrived in Ontario during 1879 passed through the province to other parts of North America, transients far outnumbered persisters for the next eleven years. Over time, the numbers arriving from Europe via Halifax and the St Lawrence River decreased while the proportions passing through Ontario, primarily by train, increased. Reports submitted by the commissioner of the Department of Immigration to the lieutenant-governor of Ontario attributed the increase in the number of immigrants moving on to the United States to the revival of trade and manufactures in the United States during the early years of the decade and a great demand in the neighbouring republic for domestics in the large cities and farm labourers in the midwest and Great Plains states. Improving conditions in the province towards the middle of the decade slowed the turnover rate, but a reduction of wheat prices and the more general use of machinery resulted in a decrease in wages of labourers. Towards the end of the decade an increase in railway fares between New York and Chicago resulted in larger numbers of immigrants passing through Canadian ports and over Canadian railways to the western states.[85]

Yet while many of the sample migrants during the 1895–1924 period only passed through Canada, others took up residence in the country and a significant number of this group acquired citizenship before moving south. And some lived in both countries before making the move recorded in these records. Thus to picture Canada simply as a temporary step in a larger-stage migration process is perhaps misleading, at least to some degree. Canada did serve as a sieve through which immigrants passed on to the United States, but this passage was not as direct or swift as many believe.

Random Sample of Anglo-Canadian Migrants   Just as in the previous sample, most Anglo-Canadian-born migrants were young males who carried relatively small amounts of money, applied for entry after 1909, and intended to join family or friends. The total proportion of males engaged in blue-collar occupations was also similar to the prior sample, although relatively fewer were classified as unskilled labourers and many more were designated semi-skilled. Higher wage positions in the United States were particularly attractive for Canadian blue-collar workers.[86] Almost 40 percent of females were classified as housewives. Among those women working outside the home, the greatest numbers were employed in the unskilled category, almost half of these working as domestics and servants. There were several instances where women working in these positions indicated in their manifests that they were joining employers in cities such as New York and Detroit.

Not surprisingly, the unskilled were more likely to hold less money than other occupational groups while those who comprised the "other" category (speculators, gentlemen, retired people) and farmers were more likely to hold greater sums of money. Somewhat surprising are the small amounts of money carried by those classified as professionals and businessmen. Again, many belonging to these categories may have chosen not to carry all of their money with them or it may be that other factors such as stage in life cycle may explain their apparent lack of capital. For example, some of those classified as professionals, doctors for instance, had just graduated from medical school and were travelling to the United States to take up their first position.

Over 80 percent of those who applied for entry intended to live permanently in the United States. Again as in the previous sample, a significant number of Anglo-Canadians previously resided in the United States (35.1 percent). While the majority of this group spent less than two years in the United States, almost 15 percent had previously lived in that country for more than ten years. As was the case for the previous sample, kin and kith connections played an important role in this migration. When asked what parties they were joining, almost 52 percent declared relatives, 15.5 percent stated friends, and 5.6 percent identified their employers.

In order to explore the regional dynamics of this particular migration, analysis now focuses upon provincial or origin and state or destination characteristics. The vast majority of migrants in the sample came from Ontario. The United States also drew a considerable number of Anglo-Canadian migrants from the Maritimes, especially during the 1920–4 period when rural decline combined with industrial collapse to accelerate the out-migration of young people. Quebec was relatively less important as a source region as the majority of migrants from this province were francophones. Manitoba was the major source of emigrants from western Canada.

Sources of out-migration that had emerged in the late nineteenth century continued to be important for the first two decades of the twentieth century although more migrants came from places more distant from the border, a reflection of Canada's development of its interior. In addition, more Anglo-Canadians were born in urban centres than before, reflecting the increasing pace of urbanization in the country. This was especially true for those migrants born in southern Ontario, the major source region for emigration. Toronto, Hamilton, London, Brantford, St Catharines, and Kingston were just some of the cities from which migrants originated. Yet most migrants to the United States came from rural communities. A proportionately high out-migration from Bruce and Grey counties and the Ottawa-Huron tract continued into the twentieth century. Migration for many was a step-wise process involving a number of moves on both sides of the border.

Last places of residence before movement to America suggests that there were internal rural-to-urban movements within and between Canadian regions and a chain process of departure. In the Canadian west, farmers' sons, many who had been working for other farmers or living at home, were leaving in greater numbers for centres such as Winnipeg, Regina, Saskatoon, Calgary, and Edmonton. The spread of settlement farther west reflects increasing migration of families from eastern Canada and Manitoba. On the west coast, Vancouver grew in population partly in response to this internal migration. Movement from fishing villages and small agricultural centres into growing centres such as Halifax, St John, and Sydney is also evident, although many Maritime migrants continued to live in their birthplaces until their migration to the United States.

Movement from small towns and farms into cities was most pronounced in southern Ontario. Significant movement took place from interior rural townships and small communities in eastern, central, and southwestern Ontario into the cities. Next to Saskatchewan, where three out of four migrants last resided in a community different from that in which they were born, Ontarians were most likely (59.7 percent) to move from their birthplace to some other location in Canada before emigrating to the United States. Anglo-Canadian Quebeckers ranked next in terms of mobility (53.8 percent), followed by migrants from Alberta (50.0 percent), Manitoba (45.2 percent), New Brunswick (44.7 percent), Nova Scotia (37.0 percent), Prince Edward Island (31.2 percent), and British Columbia (25.0 percent).

A significant percentage of Ontario, Quebec, and Manitoba migrants who remained in their birthplace until their move to the United States resided in the largest cities of their respective provinces. For example, while Toronto was the last destination for many Ontarians from elsewhere in the province, 84 percent of those migrants born in this city remained there until their move to the United States. Relatively high persistence rates within the Maritimes may be explained in part by the stagnating economy in the region and the lack of urban-related opportunities. For many, urban migration meant movement across regional borders to cities in central Canada or New England. The high persistence rate within British Columbia is explained in part by the fact that most migrants were born in Vancouver and Victoria and therefore did not participate in the urbanward stage migration common in other parts of Canada and by the fact that most of them left Canada at a very young age. For most British Columbians in the sample, emigration to the United States represented the first stage in their migration histories.

As stated, Anglo-Canadian migrants were relatively young. Migrants from New Brunswick tended to be older than other provinces while those from the west tended to be younger. Many young men from the prairies seeking the bright lights of the city chose to move to American destinations such as Chicago and Minneapolis. It is likely that some of this group were directly descended from American immigrants coming to Canada at the turn of the century.

Single migrants were in the majority for all provincial groups, dominating particularly in Saskatchewan, Alberta, and British Columbia. Marital status correlates with age for these provinces just as it does for New Brunswick which, besides having the oldest migrants, also had the greatest percentage of widowed migrants. Migrants from Ontario followed most closely the average occupational profile for the sample in total. The sample migrants displayed an adaptation to more urban forms of employment than the generation preceding them. Prince Edward Island and Manitoba were the only two provinces with farmers comprising more than 10 percent of the occupations. Migrants were predominantly blue-collar, although those provinces with the largest cities, Ontario and Quebec, were over-represented among the clerical occupations, reflecting the fact that many of the migrants from central Canada came from cities such as Montreal, Toronto, and Hamilton where such employment was more prevalent. While migrants from Nova Scotia, New Brunswick and Quebec, were over-represented among the unskilled category, those from Ontario were under-represented and showed greater representation among semi-skilled and skilled occupations, reflective perhaps of the more advanced industrial development of this province. The numbers from Saskatchewan and Alberta are so small that any comment is hardly worth making, but the fact that none of the six migrants from these agricultural provinces listed their occupations as farmers is interesting. Two were farm labourers and the other four pursued other urban-related occupations.

Few migrants carried much money with them; this was particularly the case for the young men from Saskatchewan, Alberta, and British Columbia. Yet the differences among the provinces were not significant. While over 80 percent of the migrants intended to live permanently in the

United States, notable percentages from the Maritimes and Manitoba declared that their stay in the United States would only be temporary. Although the motives of these individuals are unknown, it is likely that some were just visiting friends or relatives while others were just testing the waters of opportunity south of the border before deciding to cut their ties with their homes.

Maritimers were most likely to have previously lived in the United States, migration across the border being seen as a temporary but regular occurrence. Indeed, a number of Maritimers spent time in the United States working in lumber camps, factories, and fishing ports, presumably to make money to send home. Migrants from western Canada were less likely to have previously lived in the United States, a reflection of the young age and stage of life cycle of those from British Columbia and Saskatchewan and, perhaps, the commitment of a significant percentage of Manitobans to farming, an occupation which may not have permitted them to search for opportunities elsewhere. The familiarity with opportunities available in nearby American cities combined with the presence of kith and kin in these same communities and the close proximity to people at home explains in part the large numbers of Ontarians and Quebeckers previously living in the United States. The fact that most of these same migrants declared their moves to be permanent suggests that previous trips south were meant to establish grounds for their subsequent permanent migration.

Individual motivations remain hidden and so any interpretation is purely speculative. It may be that for many the border was largely irrelevant in social terms. Family and friends in the United States and a relatively easy entry into America may have encouraged such a pattern. On the other hand, the fact that many had lived previously in the United States for considerable periods and yet chose to retain their Canadian citizenship and return to Canada may be seen as evidence of an attachment to their homes and a reluctance to relinquish their Canadian connections.

Most Anglo-Canadians travelled alone; this was particularly the case for the young single men from British Columbia, Saskatchewan, and Alberta. Those not travelling alone usually were accompanied by one other person, in most cases a spouse. Older migrants from Ontario, New Brunswick, and Quebec were more likely to have their children with them. Most Anglo-Canadians were granted entry, with Manitobans, Quebeckers, and British Columbians having the highest rates of rejection. Most of those denied entry either had little or no money in their possession or did not indicate that they were joining anyone at their destination.

Most migrants filled out their manifests upon crossing the border, although a number chose to do so at American consulates or upon leaving port in Canadian cities. A few did not complete this task until they reached destinations south of the border, perhaps at points where they disembarked from trains (for example, Albany or Minneapolis). Places of manifest served as portals into America as migrants primarily from adjacent Canadian regions passed through these openings on their way to neighbouring American destinations.

Detroit was by far the most important entrance to America, not only for migrants from southwestern Ontario but for those from other parts of Canada. It also served as a portal for migrants journeying to Michigan destinations, the most significant being Detroit itself, as well as locations elsewhere in the midwest and farther west. Port Huron served much the same function as its larger neighbour to the south. Migrants from northern Ontario and Manitoba entered at Sault Ste Marie, Michigan, and International Falls, Duluth, and Rainier, Minnesota. Most Manitobans signed their manifests in Winnipeg, although five did so at Pembina, North Dakota, and another two at Neche, North Dakota. Anglo-Canadians from Saskatchewan and western Manitoba entered the United States via the Soo Line at Portal, North Dakota. Migrants from Alberta, other prairie provinces, and elsewhere in Canada crossed at Sweetgrass and Gateway, Montana, as well as at Eastport, Idaho, Marcus, and Northport, Washington State. Like their Manitoban counterparts, most British Columbians signed their manifests at home but some did so upon their crossing at Sumas and Blaine, Washington.

For the most part, Canadians planned to settle in American cities in adjacent states although some were attracted to more distant localities, particularly in California. Anglo-Canadian migration in the early years of the twentieth century took on a configuration exhibiting four principal regional components: one linking the Maritime provinces and, to a lesser extent, Quebec, to New England; the second connecting Ontario and, to a lesser extent, Quebec, to midwestern states and New York State; the third linking the eastern prairies to the midwest and the Great Plains states; and the last connecting the western prairies and British Columbia to the Pacific states, particularly Washington and California. While much of this movement in the 1880s and 1890s was rural-urban in direction as well as in job orientation, considerable numbers continued to farm in the United States. Yet for the sample period most migrants held occupations not related to farming. As well, many more came from larger urban centres, although a significant percentage were born and last lived in small towns and continued to practise skills and occupations learned in such settings, such as carpentering, blacksmithing, and so on. Of those states that were the destination of ten or more Anglo-Canadians, Montana, Minnesota, Washington, North Dakota, Wisconsin, and California were most attractive to migrants involved in farming, reflecting the importance of agriculture and perhaps the greater availability and affordability of land in those areas.

Many of those classified as professionals, including a relatively significant percentage of women working as nurses, located in cities such as New

York City, Boston, and Detroit. Although attracting fewer businessmen than a handful of other states, almost 37 percent of Canadians belonging to this category settled in Michigan, most taking up residence in Detroit, Port Huron, and other urban centres. Washington, Ohio, California, and New York were other states both absolutely and relatively important as destinations for businessmen. Among the most important destination states, Michigan, California, and New York attracted the greatest absolute and relative percentages of clerical workers, most locating in the larger urban centres. Relatively large proportions of unskilled and semi-skilled workers locating in more rural states such as Montana, Maine, Minnesota, Wisconsin, and North Dakota were engaged in rural-based occupations such as fishing, lumbering, carpentering, and blacksmithing. Both rural- and urban-related occupations were practised by Canadians settling in Michigan, New York, Illinois, and Massachusetts. Those working in skilled trades such as machinists and iron workers, primarily from Ontario, Quebec, and the Maritimes, settled in Michigan and New York State.

Thirty-eight cities attracted 62 percent of the sample migrants and among this number, over 76 percent settled in just ten cities, demonstrating the magnetic attraction of America's largest centres. Detroit itself drew over one-third of the total sample from all over Canada, although the majority were born in southwestern and south-central Ontario. With the spread of railways throughout the western United States after the middle of the nineteenth century, Detroit became the key entry point into the American west. Rural-urban stage migration within Canada and the fact that a significant percentage of migrants were born in cities such as Toronto, Hamilton, and London meant that many of those who would eventually arrive in the Michigan metropolis were already familiar with urban life and would bring with them a mix of skills they had learned or refined in Canadian centres. The typical migrant was young (almost 82 percent were less than 36 years of age) and carried little money (almost 80 percent carried less than $100), although 14 percent were wives who for the most part either travelled with their husbands who held the family's money or were planning to join their husbands and so did not carry the full extent of the family's capital. Many Canadians coming to Detroit were blue-collar and clerical workers, either single or recently married with young families, and thus had not yet been able to accumulate much in terms of possessions and capital. The opportunities presented in a rapidly expanding city such as Detroit, where the automobile industry was just beginning to assert its dominance, combined with the relatively low cost associated with such a short-distance migration and the close proximity to family and friends both in this city and back in Canada made this destination a particularly attractive location.

The allure of the near and the familiar remained strong for the majority of young men and women leaving Canada. While far-off destinations such as Los Angeles, Seattle, San Francisco, Spokane, and San Diego attracted people from all over Canada, most continued on well-worn paths to nearby American destinations. Boston, Cambridge, Portland, Brookline, Worcester, and Dorchester continued to pull in Maritimers, reinforcing a long tradition of population movement across the line into New England. Indeed, it has been estimated that the exodus of people from this part of Canada, most of them young, totalled somewhere between 75,000 and 122,000 a decade between 1880 and 1930.[87] Massachusetts and Maine absorbed the bulk of the migrants. Like the Ontarians who located in Detroit, Maritimers carried their occupations with them to New England centres. Women worked as domestics, fishermen carried on their way of life in New England fleets, lumbermen continued to labour in the Maine woods, and carpenters worked in both house and boat construction. And as the rest of their Canadian counterparts, Maritimers generally did not carry much capital with them to the United States.

Anglo-Quebeckers were more widespread in their location decisions, moving to New England mill towns such as Worcester, nearby metropolises such as New York and Boston, midwestern cities including Chicago and Detroit, traditional regions for Quebec migration such as the upper peninsula of Michigan, and rapidly expanding western cities such as Seattle and Los Angeles. Ontarians also dispersed throughout the United States although, as was the case for Detroit, the more important destinations drew migrants from specific parts of the province. Buffalo attracted Ontarians from the adjacent Niagara region and nearby southwestern and south-central Ontario while New York City's migration field was more far-reaching, befitting a city of its size and drawing power. Niagara Falls drew all of its migrants from Ontario, the majority from the adjacent Niagara region and nearby south-central and southwestern Ontario. Rochester attracted Ontarians primarily, many travelling across the lake from south-central and eastern Ontario. The migration field of Chicago was similarly broad, luring Canadians from Ontario and Quebec as well as a notable percentage from Manitoba. While Los Angeles drew people from all over Canada, although most notably Ontarians, Seattle, at least in this sample, was even more broad in its spatial coverage, attracting considerable percentages from British Columbia, Quebec, and New Brunswick.

CONCLUSIONS

Whereas census-based research shows that the predominance of short-distance migration and the gravitation of long-distance migrants towards centres of industry and commerce generally apply at the aggregate level, other aspects of migration behaviour are more difficult to ascertain at this scale of analysis. Investigation of the Index to Canadian Border Entries gives us greater insight into this movement. These records reveal that many moved in stages on the Canadian side before crossing the border. This movement can also be seen as a typical example of chain migration based upon kinship, as the majority of migrants stated their intention to locate in communities in which relatives or friends were living. Anglo-Canadians were shown to share many of the characteristics of European-born immigrants, particularly those coming from Britain, Ireland, and other northern European countries.

This emigration can be viewed as evidence of capitalist economic relations changing rural life and as part of the larger process of internationalization of labour markets. The index reveals that while Canada served as an intermediary stage in a larger transatlantic migration from Europe to the United States, it represented for many Europeans more than just a brief sojourn. A significant number acquired Canadian citizenship before moving on to the United States, indicating that many had spent a considerable time in Canada and had developed some attachment to the country. The records also reveal that both European- and Canadian-born migrants, particularly the latter, were able to scout American opportunities before making a firm commitment to move. Many of those declaring their intention to reside permanently in the United States had lived there previously. Indeed, it is likely that many of those migrants who stated their crossing to be temporary were involved in this process of exploration.

The evidence also suggests that for many Canadians, both anglophone and francophone, migration to the United States was not permanent, despite what they claimed when signing their manifests. There were clear patterns of seasonal migration between Canadian regions and neighbouring states, particularly for Maritimers and less so for Ontarians and Quebeckers working in the lumber camps of Maine and the upper midwest and the fishing villages of New England. While many of these temporary migrants did settle permanently in the United States, others came home again, although not always to the communities in which they were born. Also significant is the specific nature of migration streams whereby communities on the Canadian side were directly attached via a process of chain migration to communities across the line. Most did not venture far beyond the border and, when possible, they went back, either to visit or to live.

The broad contours of our voyage have been established. I will now focus on a small region to see how individuals and families reacted and responded to the transformation occurring in society. By doing so, I hope to capture not only the outward patterns of their mobility but also to gain insight into their interpretation of the changes affecting their lives.

PART TWO
Movers and Persisters

Front Street, Belleville, c. 1900
(Public Archives Canada/C7117)

Introduction

The boundary line between Canada and the United States is a
typically human creation; it is physically invisible, geographically
illogical, militarily indefensible, and emotionally inescapable.
                                 – Hugh Keenleyside, *Canada and the United States*

In section one, national and regional contexts of migration and the
conditions and circumstances influencing Canadian identity during the
nineteenth century were reviewed. This section attempts to evaluate the
importance of context in shaping transitions occurring in the Bay of Quinte
region. The area is observed as it transformed from a frontier to a settled
rural place and attempted to adapt to the forces of modernization. Particular focus is placed on how individuals and families confronted, adapted,
and shaped that change. As well, this analysis recognizes that continuity
also characterized responses to internal and external developments.

Chapter three investigates the changing relationships between Belleville, the largest urban centre, and its immediate hinterland. Belleville
developed as a rural service centre functioning as a central place that
processed and traded products from its local hinterland and distributed
incoming finished products to the same hinterland. It continued to serve
primarily as a distribution centre throughout the century despite its
increasing size, a greater diversity of functions, and its efforts to attract
industrial development. Eventually the city was left behind by others in the
drive to industrialize. The story of Belleville is unique and yet the experience of this urban centre is representative of many other Canadian towns
undergoing stagnation and decline in the late nineteenth century.

While the Quinte region constitutes the specific locational context for
considering the interrelated themes of mobility and rural transformation,
the investigation of migration and persistence experiences of four generations of Quinte families in chapter four allows us a clearer insight into how
Anglo-Canadians adapted to change. Genealogies constitute the starting
point for this strategy and thus deserve some critical comment here.[1]

Of all our records, census manuscripts are used most often to interpret the changes taking place in Ontario during the nineteenth century.[2] While this source remains the backbone of historical demography in Anglo-Canada, there are intrinsic deficiencies and chronological limitations which restrict its use. The censuses vary greatly in terms of information as the criteria for data collection varied over time. For example, the 1851 and 1861 censuses do not include information on tenure. Detailed information on agricultural production is not available after 1871. There are no specific fertility or nuptiality data beyond born and married in the census year so scholars resort to identifying vital rates through examination of age and determining fertility by calculating child-woman ratios.[3] Census-based synoptic studies of Ontario are only possible for the second half of the nineteenth century. While they focus on distributions of population at a single point in time, record linkage of censuses capture to some extent change over time. But such an approach is limited, given the decennial collection of the material and the highly mobile nature of the population.

For the pre-census period, generally felt to be the frontier era in Ontario, demographic analysis is even more difficult. During its pioneer period, Ontario was on the fringe of the British Empire and relatively little organized data collection took place. Recourse, therefore, is made to a scattered collection of other sources, including parish registers, assessment rolls, property deeds, directories, and local histories. Yet it is rare to find comprehensive collections of data describing the initial demographics of communities in Ontario.[4]

The problems associated with the limited set of sources available make it difficult to examine the dimensions of social change in rural nineteenth-century Ontario and to respond to Bouchard's request for "a double reform of demographic history."[5] In order to develop a longitudinal perspective and to integrate historical demography with the social history of Ontario's rural population, it will be necessary to discover sources which move beyond the confines of the census-based cross-sectional approach.

The life-history approach has become the accepted strategy among a small group of scholars devoted to migration analysis at the micro-level. This research is reflective of the shift from cross-sectional and one-community–oriented studies to what Hagerstrand in geography and Hareven in history term "life-course" analysis.[6] In this approach, changes in the life-course are in part the result of changed needs for real and human capital in the economy. Mobility is seen as a response to changing opportunities, and these changes are mediated by the family and its cycle of procreation, marriage, and mortality. Thus, a major focus of life-course migration analysis is on the significance of landholding, marriage, and inheritance structures in generating selectivity amongst both migrants and persisters. The approach emphasizes individual experiences in context and shows how the lives of individual Canadians, just like the country itself, are in a constant state of becoming, embedded in familial, institutional, and cultural contexts that mould individuals and in turn are shaped by people.

In the study of the interplay between individuals and the family, and families and society, concern is with life-course transactions, how the individual passes through different family settings and different family roles. The genealogical-based approach is essential to this endeavour as it is one of the best ways to relate individuals to their families and socio-economic and physical environments. Well-documented genealogies enable us to study the mobility experiences of pioneer families and their descendants and, when linked with other records, also allow us to trace land ownership, occupation, and other economic and demographic indicators.

Bruce Elliott's study of Irish migration to Canada is the major Canadian example of large-scale life-course analysis using a genealogical method.[7] Elliott concentrates on a well-defined group who shared a common origin and left good records of themselves, making it possible to locate, identify, and trace their experiences. The success of his venture strengthens the cause of the genealogical approach to the study of migration, but sceptics might wonder as to the utility of this strategy for examining the mobility experiences of less well-defined native-born groups moving internally within North America. Residential persistence among immigrant groups often depended on the processes of chain and cluster migration that had been capable of transplanting culturally homogeneous and often kinship-related populations to North America in the first place. Such transplanted communities were often reinforced by a strong institutional focus and settlement among their own kind. Availability of land was a major factor in ensuring residential and, to a certain degree, cultural stability.

On the other hand, frontiers that changed quickly with the rapid settlement of land discouraged community formation and persistence among immigrants. Native-born North Americans were similarly affected, but were less likely to be influenced in their location decisions by any sense of maintaining transplanted communities. Subsequent generations of immigrants who did not share the emigration experience and were affected more directly by the assimilative forces present in their new homes were more likely to be less attached to their communities of origin. Yet the maintenance of kinship and other ties based on business, religion, or other factors may have played an important role in the mobility decisions of this group.

Genealogies specify the particulars of lives over time and space within the context of kinship and with their longitudinal focus transcend the limits of the cross-sectional census-based approach. In this way, the genealogical approach moves beyond the life-cycle model and its residential information allows one to investigate lifelong geographical mobility and note the importance of kin in migration. Equally important is the genealogical investigation of persistence and the development of community as researchers increasingly realize that despite the tremendous mobility that characterized nineteenth-century North America, many individuals remained in place and played a key role in the development of community, particularly in the rural context.

Yet while completed genealogies can provide the kind of data that migration, community, and transformation studies require, they can be criticized on several grounds as to their representativeness. By and large, genealogies are secondary compilations based on primary sources and many of the earlier genealogies are highly unreliable, reflecting the poor state of record collection techniques that existed in the past. The majority of published genealogies are often testimonies to social status and, in a minority of cases, religious or racial purity. Recent genealogies are more reliable and detailed in nature as researchers take advantage of more sophisticated compilations of records and expand their pedigree charts to include full-scale biographies.

While legitimate concerns can be raised regarding the representativeness of published genealogies, they should not detract in any way from the value of the genealogical method to historical research. Upon examination of thirty different genealogies, both published and unpublished, I selected the five which were most thorough in terms of geographical and biographical information and which satisfied the various criteria of representativeness. At the initial point of settlement of the Bay of Quinte region during the 1780s and 1790s, a hierarchy of landowners was established among the predominantly Loyalist population. While field officers received 1,000 acres, privates were entitled to 100 acres only, which later increased to 200 acres. Non-Loyalists were also granted 200 acres, although settlers were required to pay survey and settlement fees. The five families chosen belong to these landholding groups. Their members are relatively independent and fairly representative of that society at the beginning of settlement. One progenitor was an ensign who was granted 850 acres; two were privates who received 100 acres; the fourth was a sergeant who never received a grant in the Quinte area; and the last died in a Loyalist refugee camp in Quebec before obtaining his grant.

Unfortunately, none of these genealogies are complete. Missing and in some cases false genealogical information, combined with the loss and destruction of personal sources (for example, assessment rolls, property records) in both Canada and the United States impeded the tracing procedure, hindering in particular the attempt to compare and contrast the economic status of persisters and movers. Significant gaps in information still exist but the results demonstrate the potential of the genealogical-based linkage approach for mobility research.[8] While the selected case histories do not allow me to draw broad conclusions about societal processes, they nonetheless are illuminating and reveal much about the circumstances and consequences of migration, persistence, and community development.

3 Continuity and Change in the Quinte Region

This is border country.

– Margaret Atwood, *Surfacing*

Regional separation within Canada and different transborder experiences between these regions and their American neighbours have combined to produce a diverse migration story. Generalizations can be made about the condition of Canadian society as a whole but to achieve a deeper understanding about societal transformation and mobility, it is necessary to explore the structure and dynamics of society within the specific historical context of the region. The Bay of Quinte region in east-central Ontario (Map 3), the home of the five genealogical groups acting as dramatis personae of this monograph, serves as the case study for exploring these themes.[1]

THE PIONEER PERIOD, 1784–1840

The Bay of Quinte region was among the first to be settled in Ontario by the United Empire Loyalists and their families, who established an agrarian-based society along the bay and the St Lawrence River. The region is part of the St Lawrence Lowlands and is underlain by sedimentary rocks. The soil is glacial till of various kinds with an abundance of lime. The topography varies from relatively flat to moderately rolling with some low-lying, poorly drained areas and sandy sections, particularly in Prince Edward County. A generally favourable climate moderated by the lake now supports tree fruits and canning crops on light-textured soils. Forage crop and mixed-crop production, beef production, and dairying are carried out on intermediate and heavy-textured soils. Generally, the region is distinguished by intermediate-textured soils, some with serious drainage problems and some susceptible to significant erosion. Yet there are sections of

Map 3: Bay of Quinte Region

excellent first- and second-class land in Prince Edward County and Sidney and Thurlow townships. Sandy areas along the lake in Prince Edward are only marginal for farming, while there are some sections throughout the region which are totally unsuited to agriculture because of poor drainage. To the north in the Laurentian Shield, the quality of land and the suitability of climate diminish rapidly.[2]

After the initial settlement of Adolphustown in 1784, a frontier elite developed quickly throughout the area and succeeded in establishing social control. It was a landed, military-based group supported by extensive grants of land awarded to them as Loyalists and soldiers.[3] From this base, certain members extended their operations into mercantile activity and staple exploitation. Government grants also resulted in rapid settlement. In Hastings County, much of the land in the first six concessions of Thurlow Township was taken up by 1800. Thurlow received its first settlers in 1789 when some fifty people crossed over from Prince Edward County to settle, most in the neighbourhood of Foxboro.[4] The more attractive lands in Sidney were also being occupied, although the steep hills in the rear of the township deterred settlement and made access to the front difficult. Tyendinaga was still controlled by the Mohawk Indians and remained so until 1819 when the first four concessions were surrendered to the government. The remaining portion of the township was sold by the government on behalf of the Mohawks in 1840.[5]

By 1790 the days of scarcity were over for Quinte farmers. The Midland District was producing more wheat than it consumed and surplus was sold at the Kingston market. In fact, farmers of Sidney and Thurlow by 1793 had enough pork to spare to furnish the military garrison at Kingston with a surplus of 480 barrels.[6] Although a ready market existed at Kingston, Quinte farmers were hampered by the lack of roads; produce was transported by bateaux to Kingston but westerly winds slowed the trip back home.

Improving transportation would prove to be the key to development of the Quinte region. By 1800 Dundas Street had been opened from York (Toronto) to the Bay of Quinte but this road crossed the isthmus to Prince Edward and the bay by ferry to Adolphustown, so that inhabitants of Sidney and Thurlow were left to provide roads for themselves. The Danforth Road, opened by statute labour between Kingston and York by the end of the first decade of the nineteenth century, connected both these townships with the colony's two largest markets, but this was a dirt road that was largely impassable for long periods of the year. As a consequence, Hastings County farmers did not have ready access to markets for their produce. In fact, pioneers had to travel to Napanee in order to have their grain milled, a distance of some thirty miles from the mouth of the Moira River, the location of what was to become the site of Hasting's primary settlement, Belleville.[7]

While pioneers in Sidney and Thurlow had limited accessibility to market, they were not entirely dependent on markets for disposal of produce. Farms still produced most of what was required in terms of food, clothing, tools, harnesses, and furniture. Yet conditions were ripe for the development of mercantile activity to serve the growing population, augmented by the so-called Late Loyalists, who were attracted by the 200-acre grants awarded by Simcoe in his 1792 proclamation, and the influx of British immigrants after the War of 1812. The Loyalists, Late Loyalists, and British migrants that settled the region had experienced early capitalist development in their former homes. In America, Loyalists and Late Loyalists had for the most part been petty producers who grew much of their own food but also participated in local and regional commercial markets. A commercial inclination existed among the pioneer population in the Quinte region which was to be exploited by those who took advantage of large landholdings and speculative practices to develop a regional market and create new centres of commerce.

Three such individuals were Captain John Walden Meyers and James and Simon McNabb, the most important players in the early development of Belleville. The first settler of what was to become the city of Belleville was Asa Wallbridge, who built a log cabin on the banks of the Moira in the early 1780s. But the first business at this site was the log trading post established by Captain George Singleton, a Loyalist from Fredericksburg Township.[8] In 1789 Singleton sold his land to John Taylor who the following year sold part of his parcel to Captain John Walden Meyers, a Loyalist from Albany, New York. With his son, Meyers erected a dam on the river and built Thurlow's first industries, a lumber and grist mill, providing Hasting's farmers with an alternative to the long trip to Napanee or Kingston. Meyers expanded his trade business and began to export flour, grain, lumber, potash, and other items to Kingston and Montreal in bateaux and Durham boats. He also built a distillery and erected an inn and a small settlement, known interchangeably as Thurlow village and Meyer's Creek, began to grow.

In 1800 the McNabb brothers moved from York to Thurlow and soon established links with such leading Kingston merchants as Richard Cartwright and Donald McDonnell. In 1802 James and Simon constructed a dam near Meyer's mills and in 1804 built their own saw and grist mill and a cloth factory. The brothers shipped flour, potash, and other Hastings produce to their Kingston partners who forwarded these items overseas to Britain. With such assistance, they were soon involved in a fierce competition with Captain Meyers. In 1811 James dissolved his partnership with Simon and devoted his efforts to politics. In 1816 he organized a petition to make Thurlow village a town site. Later that year the settlement was surveyed by Samuel Wilmot and was renamed Belleville after Mrs Anna Bella Gore, wife of Lieutenant-Governor Francis Gore.[9]

Belleville became the major market for Thurlow, Sidney, and Prince Edward County farmers, the latter crossing the bay by ferry. Early merchants such as Captain Meyers and William Bell made great profits because they controlled the movement and pricing of provisions and the export of agricultural produce. They bought grain from Hastings farmers, milled it into flour, and then sold it at a high profit to the military at Kingston. By 1812 two grist mills had been built above Belleville on the Moira, Reed's at Corbyville and Canniff's at Cannifton.[10] While these villages could provide some of the services and markets which hitherto had been located at Kingston and then Belleville, they were never able to compete with the lakeshore communities. Because of its central position on the Bay of Quinte and its situation at the mouth of the Moira River, Belleville was ensured of a growing primacy in the region. The key to growth was the development of a transportation system that would link Belleville and its surrounding hinterland with regional, national, and international markets.

The entire Quinte region was at a disadvantage during the pioneer period as travellers and merchants preferred to sail directly from York to Kingston, bypassing the bay and avoiding the slow and often difficult passage via the Dundas and Danforth roads. However, a significant event in the history of Belleville and the Quinte region took place in 1818 when the steamer *Queen Charlotte* sailed from Kingston up the Bay of Quinte and down the St Lawrence as far as Prescott. Within five years, five steamships sailed the bay and gradually the Durham boat and the bateaux disappeared. The coming of the steamships increased the importance of Belleville as a port and market town and made it easier to export the produce of its hinterland. By 1830 William Weller's stagecoaches from York were connecting with Bay of Quinte steamers at Carrying Place and this became the common way of travelling in summer. But while transportation links gradually improved, it was only with the arrival of the Grand Trunk Railway in the 1850s that Belleville citizens felt their community could break out of its perceived position as a backwater settlement.

After the War of 1812 the pace of British immigration to Upper Canada increased and a considerable number of the immigrants found their way to the Quinte region. One hundred and fifty-four landowners held land in Thurlow Township in 1820, the average holding being 256.4 acres.[11] The 1818 response to Robert Gourlay's questionnaire identified a lack of a yeoman population and insufficient money invested in agriculture as the major factors retarding development.[12] Land was the major source of capital in money-scarce Upper Canada and farmers often borrowed to finance their farm's expansion, their major source at this time being the local store. Yet even as late as 1839, not one store existed in Thurlow Township outside of Belleville.[13] According to William Hutton, an Irish-born farmer settling in Sidney Township in 1834, farmers could not always get cash for their produce in Belleville. In a letter written to his brother-in-law and dated 25 June 1834, Hutton complained: "You are occasionally obliged to take groceries or other goods out of the store, if you require them, and credit the merchant until the article is forwarded."[14]

By the 1840s, Belleville had become a booming lumber centre and it was the development of this staple, rather than wheat, that would play the most important role in the future prosperity of the community. Lumbering actually began as early as 1804 in Thurlow. It was especially attractive to farmers wishing to supplement their income in the winter months. But there was little effort to develop the industry beyond the local level as markets were distant and transportation was difficult. The Napoleonic Wars and the War of 1812, however, created a demand for Canadian timber for shipbuilding. In the early 1820s timber on public land was legally opened for anyone who paid a fixed scale of fees. The new system spurred the lumber industry, providing full-time employment for lumbermen and part-time employment for farmers. By 1839 there were eight sawmills in Thurlow as opposed to only four grist mills.[15]

Wheat certainly played a major role in the development of the local economy, although Quinte farmers never specialized in wheat to the point where they excluded other crops. William Hutton speaks enthusiastically about the regional market: "The market of Belleville (which town contains about 1,000 inhabitants) is a good one; prices of grain being rather better, and that of other things nearly the same as Toronto. Besides having a home [Quinte] consumption of beef and mutton, and butter and milk, we have Kingston market within reach, where there are 4,800 inhabitants, and a good meat market."[16]

Belleville grew steadily, if not spectacularly, during the 1830s and 1840s, reaching a population of 1,926 by 1844. The population would more than double by 1850, reflecting the impetus given the community by an expanding lumber industry and the imminent arrival of the Grand Trunk Railway. It was these two developments that allowed Belleville to extend its hinterland and solidify its role as the major urban centre along the bay.

BELLEVILLE AT MID-CENTURY, 1840–1880

That noted observer of Upper Canadian society, Susanna Moodie, was generally impressed with the Quinte region at mid-century although she felt that the area suffered from its geographical isolation:

By a simple inspection of the map of Upper Canada, it will be seen, that as the Bay of Quinte was out of the general route of steamers, and too near the lower end of the lake navigation, it did not suit the views of the parties most interested to direct emigration to its shores. Thus the beautiful Bay of Quinte, with the most fertile land on its shores, and scenery which exceeds in variety and picturesque beauty that of any part of Upper Canada, Hamilton and Niagara alone excepted, has been passed for years for situations much less desirable or attractive to European settlers."[17]

The lack of accessibility was deemed by many observers to be the major hindrance to development of the region and so Quinteans placed considerable importance on the building of the Grand Trunk Railway in opening markets for the region and furthering development of the hinterland. The immediate townships surrounding Belleville were largely dependent on agriculture while forest exploitation was dominant in the rear townships of Hastings and Lennox and Addington. Belleville was well situated to be the major port for the export of these products and thus experienced significant growth during the mid-century period (Table 2).

Wheat production suffered when wheat midge struck the region in 1849 but by this time farmers were already diversifying. The Bay of Quinte area had emerged as a leading cheese producer by 1850, partly on account of the failure of the wheat crop but also because of the migration of Americans from nearby upstate New York who were familiar with the process of cheese-making. However, it was not until 1866 that the first cheese factory in the Belleville district was built in Sidney. It was organized along the lines

Table 2 Changing Populations in the Bay of Quinte Region, 1824–1901*

Canadian divisions and subdivisions	Population in									Change over periods (%)							
	1824	1830	1839	1851	1861	1871	1881	1891	1901	1824–1830	1830–1839	1839–1851	1851–1861	1861–1871	1871–1881	1881–1891	1891–1901
LENNOX AND ADDINGTON																	
ADDINGTON	7,202	8,104	9,341	14,353	16,120	16,396	16,314	14,900	13,421	12.5	15.3	53.7	12.3	1.7	-0.5	-8.7	-9.9
Adolphustown	610	659	671	718	801	756	737	720	544	8.0	1.6	7.0	11.6	-5.6	-2.5	-2.3	-24.4
Amherst island	253	391	804	1,287	1,270	1,189	1,089	938	821	54.5	105.6	60.1	-1.3	-6.4	-8.4	-13.9	-12.5
Ernestown[a]	3,063	3,370	3,445	5,111	5,450	4,233	3,961	3,597	3,317	10.0	2.2	48.4	6.6	-22.3	-6.5	-9.2	-7.8
Fredericksburg, N	2,434	2,408	2,585	3,166	3,376	1,722	1,720	1,659	1,523	-1.1	7.4	22.5	6.6	-4.6[b]	-0.1	-3.5	-8
Fredericksburg, S	–	–	–	–	–	1,497	1,340	1,125	1,103	–	–	–	–	–	-10.5	-16.0	-2
Richmond[c]	842	1,276	1,836	4,071	3,450	3,341	3,241	2,888	2,563	51.5	43.9	121.7	-15.3	-0.6	-5.5	10.6	-11.6
Napanee	–	–	–	–	1,773	2,967	3,680	3,433	3,143	–	–	–	–	67.3	24.0	-6.7	-8.4
Bath	–	–	–	–	–	601	546	530	407	–	–	–	–	–	-9.2	-2.9	-23.2
PRINCE EDWARD	8,132	9,794	14,018	18,887	20,869	20,366	21,044	18,889	17,864	20.4	43.1	34.7	10.5	-2.4	3.3	-10.2	-5.4
Ameliasburg	1,380	1,642	2,342	3,286	3,487	3,304	3,451	3,079	2,585	17.0	42.6	40.3	6.1	-5.2	4.4	-10.8	-16.0
Athol[d]	–	–	–	1,621	1,823	1,740	1,573	1,204	1,187	–	–	–	12.5	-4.6	-9.6	-18.4	-7.6
Hallowell	2,637	3,182	3,545	3,203	3,629	3,554	3,704	3,380	2,924	20.7	11.4	-9.6	13.3	-2.1	4.2	-8.7	-13.5
Hillier[e]	976	1,450	2,120	2,963	3,153	2,224	2,192	1,890	1,647	46.6	46.2	39.8	6.4	-29.5	-1.4	-13.8	-12.9
Marysburg, N	1,343	1,468	2,396	3,512	3,852	1,794	1,700	1,430	1,213	9.3	63.2	46.6	9.7	2.1[f]	5.5	-15.9	-15.2
Marysburg, S	–	–	–	–	–	2,140	2,205	1,643	1,342	–	–	–	–	–	3.1	-25.5	-18.3
Sophiasburg	1,796	2,052	2,604	2,734	2,857	2,702	2,646	2,341	2,095	14.3	26.9	5.0	4.5	-5.4	-2.1	-11.5	-10.5
Picton	–	–	1,011	1,569	2,067	2,361	2,975	3,237	2,698	–	–	55.2	31.7	14.2	26.0	10.5	12.5
Bloomfield	–	–	–	–	–	–	–	–	521	–	–	–	–	–	–	–	–
Wellington	–	–	–	–	–	517	598	555	652	–	–	–	–	–	15.7	-7.2	16.6

Table 2 (continued)

Canadian divisions and subdivisions	Population in									Change over periods (%)							
	1824	1830	1839	1851	1861	1871	1881	1891	1901	1824–1830	1830–1839	1839–1851	1851–1861	1861–1871	1871–1881	1881–1891	1891–1901
HASTINGS	3,844	4,962	8,925	19,812	25,433	27,124	30,154	32,254	30,252	29.0	79.9	122.0	28.4	6.6	11.2	7.0	-6.2
Sidney	1,730	2,145	3,192	4,574	5,082	5,264	4,842	4,685	4,430	24.0	46.8	43.3	11.1	3.6	-8.0	-3.2	-5.3
Thurlow	1,762	2,444	3,746	4,469	4,864	5,186	4,922	4,817	4,210	38.7	53.3	19.3	8.8	6.6	-5.1	-2.1	-12.6
Tyendinaga[g]	,352	,373	1,987	6,200	7,812	7,573	7,832	5,135	4,743	6.0	432.7	212.0	26.0	3.1	3.4	-34.4	-7.6
Belleville	–	–	–	4,569	6,277	7,305	9,516	9,916	9,117	–	–	–	37.4	16.4	30.3	4.2	-8.1
Deseronto	–	–	–	–	–	–	–	3,338	3,527	–	–	–	–	–	–	–	5.7
Trenton[h]	–	–	–	–	1,398	1,1796	3,042	4,363	4,217	–	–	–	–	28.5	69.4	43.4	-3.3
REGION	19,178	22,860	32,234	53,052	62,492	63,886	67,512	66,043	61,537	19.2	41.2	64.3	17.7	2.3	5.7	-2.2	-6.8

Sources: Upper Canada House of Assembly, *Journal*, 4th Session, 9th Parliament, 1828. Appendix. Population of Midland District, 1824; Upper Canada House of Assembly, *Journal*, 1st Session, 11th Parliament, 1831. Appendix. Population Returns for Midland District, 1830; Upper Canada House of Assembly, *Journal*, 5th Session, 13th Parliament, 1839. Appendix, vol. 1, pt. 1. Population Returns for Midland District, 1839; *Census of Canada, 1851*, vol. 1, Table 1, 4–25; *Census of Canada, 1861*, vol. 1. Table 2. 58–71; *Census of Canada. 1931*, vol. II. Table 12. 61–77.

* Changing census boundaries account for some of the notable population changes. (a) Bath was included as part of Ernestown until 1871. (b) This population change figure includes both North and South Fredericksburg in 1871. (c) Napanee was part of Richmond until 1861. (d) Athol was part of Hallowell until 1840. (e) Wellington was part of Hillier until 1871. (f) The population change figure includes both North and South Marysburg in 1871. (g) Deseronto was part of Tyendinaga until 1891.
(h) Before it was incorporated in 1852, most of Trenton lay in Murray Township, Northumberland County.

of the so-called American system whereby a number of farmers united in a syndicate, chose a board of directors, and appointed one of their members to act as a manager, who in turn provided a building and equipment and hired a cheese-maker in return for a commission, usually two cents a pound, on all the cheese produced. The rest of the proceeds were then divided among the patrons in proportion to their supply of milk.[18] Thus, indigenous capital development, largely in response to a growing urban market but developing from within the region, resulted in the creation of a viable rural industry in the region.

Rye production was also important in the region at mid-century. About 85 percent of the rye grown in the province in 1850 was produced in the region, chiefly because of a large distillery in nearby Kingston. Dairying on a commercial basis did not develop in the province until after mid-century but Quinte emerged as one of the leading dairy areas. The tax placed on whiskey in the United States, which had the effect of increasing beer consumption in the northern states during the Civil War years, result-ed in barley becoming one of Ontario's principal exports. By the mid-1880s barley had replaced wheat as the major cash crop in Ontario, although this overthrow of "King Wheat" had taken place much earlier in the Quinte region. Much of the region's barley was shipped across the lake to Oswego and then sent to large American breweries. Hastings and Prince Edward became well known for the quality of their barley.

Yet it was the forest industry that proved to be more valuable to the region in terms of export value. In 1851 almost 15 million feet of sawed lumber was exported from Belleville and Trent Port (Trenton) to the American market, bringing in over $290,000 and providing employment for hundreds. The lumber industry stimulated development not only in Belleville but also in other towns throughout the region, such as Trenton and Deseronto. By 1856 there were almost sixty water mills on the Moira River, about thirty-five being sawmills, and many other mills on the Salmon and Trent.[19] Steam mills gradually replaced water mills, making it impos-sible for some industries to locate away from the principal waterways.

In 1846 Belleville had four flour mills, four grist mills, one iron foundry, two carding and cloth-dressing mills and three tanneries. Fourteen years later Belleville's industries included three agricultural implements facto-ries, two axe and edge tool factories, two distilleries, seven carriage-makers, four flour mills, five iron founders, five lumber companies, and three sawmills. The two largest employers were Flint and Yeoman's, and Bogart's, both lumber companies. The former employed ninety men and operated between ninety and one hundred saws, capable of manufactur-ing 75,000 to 100,000 feet of lumber every day, while the latter firm employed over fifty men.[20]

Belleville was not alone in its dependence on the lumber industry. Lum-ber companies and sawmills were the dominant employers in most com-

Table 3   Exports from Belleville to the United States during Year ending 20
September 1872

Product	Amount	Value($)
Lumber	59,169,527 ft.	538,380.05
Lathes	9,858,300 pieces	10,837.20
Pickets	224,565 pieces	1,210.22
Heading	1,215,900 pieces	2,354.75
Staves	1,284,800 pieces	4,321.80
Railroad Ties	111,894 pieces	22,378.80
Shingle Bolts	3,082 cords	11,508.25
Posts	1,433 cords	2,996.00
Square Timber	11,730 ft.	1,173.10
Floats	18,912 ft.	1,323.91
TOTAL ALL LUMBER PRODUCTS		596,484.08
Horses	48	6,156.00
Cattle	78	1,423.16
Sheep	4,325	10,865.27
Barley	234,342 bus	224,547.12
Rye	29,262 bus	20,801.15
Peas	26,184 bus	18,219.41
Buckwheat	875 bus	667.19
Eggs	2,184 doz	270.94
Skins	8,949	6,735.62
Scrap Iron	339,000 lbs.	4,935.00
Household Effects		13,355.50
Miscellaneous		2,393.85
TOTAL		908,009.40

Source: Report from the American Consul in Belleville Regarding Exports from Belleville
to the United States. Belleville *Intelligencer*, Friday, October 11, 1872, p. 4.

munities, large and small, throughout the region. Almost 66 percent of
the total value of exports shipped from Belleville to the United States during the year ending September 20, 1872 were lumber products (Table 3).

While Belleville had the largest sawmills west of Ottawa in the 1860s and
was full of optimism for the future, it relied on an industry that was soon
to decrease greatly in importance. The preferred stands of pine and oak
were overcut and companies had to proceed farther north. It became
increasingly clear to Belleville residents that in order for the town to tap
the major resource of its hinterland and to increase its importance as a
central place in the Toronto-Montreal corridor, railways would have to be
built. The Grand Trunk linked Belleville and the Quinte region with major
cities east and west and provided employment for many of its citizens, but
it was felt that the key to the city's future was the building of a line to the
north that would not only tap the products of the forest but develop the
iron ore mines at Marmora and provide Belleville with a direct connection

to the Canadian west. One of the earliest smelters in Upper Canada was opened at Marmora in 1821 but it was small in scale and hampered by poor transportation connections. The distance from the ore deposits in Madoc and Marmora was only thirty-four miles but it took a wagon carrying ore twenty-four hours to make the trip from Marmora to Belleville in 1850. The same trip by train would only take four hours and the cost would be reduced from 9p per ton mile to a fraction more than 1p per ton mile.[21]

The Grand Junction Railway (GJR), incorporated by the Grand Trunk Railway in 1852, was to be built as a loop line from Belleville via Peterborough to Toronto. It was hoped that the line would haul lumber, carry western grain, and help develop minerals in northern Hastings, in that way ensuring terminal status and growth for Belleville. Belleville was envisioned as the Lake Ontario outlet for the Hudson River–Erie Canal system and with railway development it looked to become the major import-export node in the system as it extended farther into the continent and the Canadian hinterland. But the Grand Trunk faced severe financial difficulties during the decade, and in 1870 the charter was surrendered to a group of businessmen, including Billa Flint, D.D. Bogart, and Henry Corby. These three individuals, all involved in the processing of the region's staples, the first two producing lumber products and the latter distilling whiskey and milling flour, believed that a line to the interior was vital to the growth of the town. Flint expressed his hopes in a letter written to the editor of the Belleville *Intelligencer* dated 3 May 1872: "If 3 ½ feet gauge is going to bring to Toronto $500,000 of lumber and produce for shipment in one year [via the Toronto and Nipissing Railway], what will a 4 foot 8 ½ inch or 5 foot 6 inch gauge do for Belleville, the best shipping point for lumber and produce along the whole line of Lake Ontario?"

Flint and his colleagues were obviously worried about the future of their town despite two decades of growth and prosperity. An examination of Belleville's relative industrial standing for 1870, afforded by the industrial manuscript census data collected by Bloomfield et al.,[22] reveals that these men had good reason to fret. Table 4 shows that Belleville was not undergoing the same degree of industrial expansion that other centres of comparable and smaller size were experiencing. The largest employers in 1870 were the H.B. Rathbun saw and flour mill, Flint and Yeoman's steam sawmill, and G. and J. Brown's iron foundry, employing ninety, forty-five, and forty-five respectively.[23] Not one of these industries ranked in the top fifty-two firms in terms of numbers employed, although Flint and Yeoman's did rank fortieth in amount of water and steam power used.[24]

In 1850 manufacturing accounted for 18 percent of the total Gross National Product of Canada but over 50 percent of this consisted of the products of saw and grist mills. While the percentage of the total GNP accounted for by manufacturing was not that different in 1870, saw and

Table 4   1879 Industrial Rankings for Belleville

Criteria	Belleville Data	Ranking	Ontario Average
1) Industrial Employees as a Percentage of Total Population	12.51%	61	13.91%
2) Capital per Establishment	$2803.63	49	$3333.94
3) Average Wage per Employee	$ 233.86	83	$ 271.51
4) Average Value of Product per Establishment	$7945.74	57	$10685.09
5) Wages as a Percentage of Total Production	26.37	27	19.89
6) Average Number of Employees per Establishment	8.96	23	7.83

Source: Elizabeth Broomfield et al., *Industry in Ontario Urban Centres* (Department of Geography, University of Guelph, 1986), 51–5.

grist mill products were down to about one-third of the total while larger-scale iron and steel plants and textile industries were more in evidence.[25] The directors of the proposed Grand Junction Railway were convinced that rail lines to the interior were the only means by which the city could industrialize and reduce its dependence on processing of timber and agricultural products. But not all felt the same way, as evidenced in an unsigned letter written to the editor of the *Intelligencer* and dated 22 November 1872 which accused the directors of building the feeder line to fulfil their desire of ruining this town. Opposition was further strengthened upon the completion of the 1875 investigation of the town's financial affairs in response to the shortage in the treasury discovered under the tenure of Robert Perry Davy as treasurer. The investigation made public that the three largest financial investments were the Belleville and North Hastings Railway, another scheme proposed by the directors of the Grand Junction; the $100,000 bonus given to the Grand Junction Railway, with payment due in 1890; and $50,000 awarded to the Grand Trunk Railway for construction of workshops, half delivered and the other half due upon completion.[26]

Despite the controversy, the Grand Junction line connecting Belleville and Peterborough was finished in 1879, and the following year the Belleville and North Hastings Railway was completed connecting Madoc Junction near Stirling to Madoc and Eldorado.[27] The Belleville *Intelligencer* editorial of 20 January 1880, commenting on the completion of the GJR to Omemee and the connection of Belleville to the Midland Railway, enthusiastically claimed that this enterprise "would open the shortest route between Belleville and all points east, and the northwest, and thereby prove of great advantage not only to the locality but to the largest part of the province." The same editorial also called for the swift completion of the North Hastings line, finished later that year, as it would help increase the development of the Marmora iron mines and extend the hinterland of Belleville's merchants:

As every ton of iron ore shipped hence will benefit the city, as every man employed in the mines and on the railways will to some extent increase the trade of our merchants, it is clearly to the interest of the ratepayers that the line [Belleville and North Hastings] should be extended. Further it will open up to unrestricted trade with the city a fine agricultural region in the northern townships, the inhabitants of which now have to find a market elsewhere.

So the citizens of Belleville pinned their hopes on the railways which were to open up the city's hinterland to industry and trade and secure the city's vital position in the grain route from Georgian Bay to the Atlantic. But even while the hopes of some remained high, others were becoming more frustrated by the lack of development. Billa Flint, who had long been involved in the lumber business with his partner Horace Yeomans, realized that if the city was to prosper in the face of a declining lumbering industry and a world recession, it would have to use the resources of its immediate hinterland and the accessibility to these resources afforded by the newly constructed railway lines to attract new types of heavy industry. In a letter to the *Intelligencer* dated 6 February 1880, Flint argues for the building of a smelting works:

I reference more to the necessity of having a Smelting Works established in Belleville ... I trust that the citizens of Belleville will not let the present favourable opportunity slip by, and, Rip Van Winkle like, go to sleep for another 20 years, until they may wake up to find that the opportunity has passed by, and nothing is left but Rip's lean half-starven dog to remind them of their loss ... I am sure that Mr. Kent [the potential developer of the iron and glass works] would prefer Belleville if he gets the encouragement he ought to have, and now while the whole is within our grasp. I do hope and trust that he will not allow Kingston, Port Hope, Toronto or any other place to take the lead and thereby deprive us of what I believe is a rare chance to not only obtain smelting and glass works, but also rolling mills, steel works and the manufacture of heavy and shelf hardware, and by such means soon double the population of our city, and also to keep in the country a vast amount of money which has now to go yearly to support manufactories in England and the United States.

Six months later, the editorial of June 28 commented on the "sad" history of Belleville's efforts to attract a smelting works. A few years before, the city awarded a bonus of $75,000 to a Mr Pardee of Hazelton, Pennsylvania, to erect a smelting works in Belleville, but depression in the iron trade caused the failure of the project. Despite the pleas of Flint and the

Intelligencer for support of the smelting works, their efforts came to nothing. The editorial scolded the citizens for their lack of enterprise:

There is no other place in Ontario so favourably situated as is Belleville with regard to the iron smelting business. Connected by railway with the finest iron mines on the continent; with limestone located within the city; having water communication with all ports on both sides of the lakes; there is no condition wanting to the manufacture of iron ore on the cheapest possible terms. But unfortunately the spirit of enterprise seems lacking in our midst, and we fear that the golden opportunity will be allowed to pass, namely that of making our city the site of the first iron smelting furnace in Ontario. Nature has given every possible advantage to our city and if Toronto or any other place be allowed to take the lead in the matter, it is the fault of our own people.

Immediately a committee was set up to figure out ways to attract industrial development. At its first meeting, several members voiced their opinion that both high taxes and a decrease in property values were due to a lack of industrial enterprises and the dollars they would deliver to the coffers of the community. The committee was particularly interested in attracting an iron and smelting works which would take advantage of the ore deposits of north Hastings and the new railway connection to these deposits. Some favoured the city taking stock and issuing debentures for a municipally-owned iron company. Thomas Wills argued that the key to industrialization was to ensure water power from the Moira and questioned whether Belleville could maintain competition against England in terms of iron production. T.C. Wallbridge, barrister and sawmill owner, agreed with Wills and was of the opinion that a smelting works would not last six months because it could not compete with Scottish manufactures of iron.[28]

Nothing came of this committee and shortly after, the paper delivered one final editorial on iron smelting: "Strangers look on at amazement at the spectacle of the rich iron ores of North Hastings leaving our doors on the way to the United States, where heavy duties are paid on them, where they are manufactured, and whence they return in large part to Canada, either as pig iron, hardware, or in some other form. Thus our neighbours receive all the benefits which ought to flow to Belleville, were the ores reduced here. Surely there is a lack of enterprise here."[29]

DECLINE AND ADJUSTMENT, 1880–1900

Belleville was never to realize the hopes and dreams held by many of its citizens. The town developed as a distribution centre handling staples and continued to function in that capacity. Great hope was placed on the processing of the iron ore deposits of north Hastings, but it was not to be.

Table 5   Population and Industrial Growth of Belleville, 1851–1901

| | | Industrial Statistics | | | |
Year	Population	No. of Establishments	Employees	Value of articles produced ($)	% Increase in value of articles produced
1851	4,569	–	–	–	–
1860	6,277	–	–	–	–
1870	7,305	102	914	810,465	–
1880	9,516	132	964	1,091,208	34.6
1890	9,916	197	1,095	1,214,095	11.3
1901[1]	9,117	24	543	558,950	–

Sources:
Population Statistics
1851 Canada. Board of Registration and Statics, *Census of the Canadas*, 1851–2, I, 48.
1860 Canada. Board of Registration and Statics, *Census of the Canadas*, 1860–61, I, 58.
1870 Canada. Department of Agriculture, *Census of Canada*, 1870–71, I, 21.
1880 Canada. Department of Agriculture, *Census of Canada*, 1880–81, I, 67.
1890 Canada. Department of Agriculture, *Census of Canada*, 1890–91, I, 48.
1890 Canada. Census and Statistics Office, *4th Census of Canada*, 1901, I, 22.

Industrial Statistics
1870 Elizabeth Bloomfield et al., *Industry in Ontario Urban Centres: Accessing the Manuscript; Census.*
    Research Report No. 1, Department of Geography, University of Guelph.
1870 Canada, Department of Agriculture, *Census of Canada*, 1870–71, III, 290–445.
1890–1901 Canada. Census and Statistics Office, *4th Census of Canada*, 1901, III, 327.
[1]1901 census only includes information for establishments employing 5 or more persons.

The world depression was experienced locally and money was scarce for investment. Both population growth and industrial growth slowed considerably during the 1880s and the situation worsened during the next decade (Table 5). An examination of the pecuniary strength and credit ratings of Belleville businesses for the years 1864, 1871, and 1891 shows that while the number of businesses grew in proportion to the population, the percentage of firms with pecuniary strength of less than $2,000 and with low credit ratings increased also (Table 6).

The lumber trade declined as the timber stands became depleted. The high costs of transportation, the inefficiency of production, and overwhelming competition and lower prices in the market caused all efforts to establish an iron industry either at Belleville or nearer the mines at Marmora to fail.[30] After 1880 flour milling and the farm produce export trade declined. Barley had replaced wheat as Ontario's major cash crop and the accessibility of the Quinte region to the Erie Canal–Hudson River route and its superior barley crop gave the area an advantage. But the substitution of corn for barley in beer-making and the growing competition of barley production in Iowa and Wisconsin hurt Quinte farmers and in 1891 the McKinley tariff effectively shut the door on the American market.[31]

Table 6 Pecuniary Strength and Credit Ratings of Belleville Businesses, 1864, 1871, 1891

Pecuniary strength	1864 no. of businesses	1864 % of businesses	Pecuniary strength	1871 no. of businesses	1871 % of businesses	Pecuniary strength	1891 no. of businesses	1891 % of businesses
less than $2,000	73	51.4	less than $2,000	124	55.4	not known	28	8.0
$2,000–5,000	28	19.7	$2,000–5,000	53	23.7	less than $500	131	37.5
$5,000–10,000	17	12.0	$5,000–10,000	20	8.9	$500–1,000	27	7.7
$10,000–25,000	14	9.9	$10,000–25,000	17	7.6	$1,000–2,000	42	12.0
$25,000–50,000	9	6.3	$25,000–50,000	6	2.7	Total $2,000	200	57.2
more than $50,000	1	0.7	more than $50,000	4	18	$2,000–5,000	48	13.8
	142	100		224	100	$5,000–10,000	35	10.0
						$10,000–20,000	21	6.0
						$20,000–40,000	10	2.8
						$40,000–75,000	5	1.4
						more than $75,000	2	0.6
							349	100

Credit rating	1864 no. of businesses	1864 % of businesses	Credit rating	1871 no. of businesses	1871 % of businesses	Credit rating	1891 no. of businesses	1891 % of businesses
unlimited	0	0	unlimited	0	0	high	0	0
high	8	5.6	high	4	1.8	good	5	1.4
good	50	35.2	good	70	31.3	fair	19	5.5
fair	50	35.2	fair	80	35.7	limited	211	60.5
difficult to rate	34	23.9	difficult to rate	70	31.3	difficult to rate	114	32.7

Source: Public Archives of Ontario, Dun and Bradstreet Reference Books, 1864–1978.

An examination of the newspaper for the year 1891 reveals quite a change in attitude towards what avenues of opportunity the town should exploit. A letter from the chairman of the Industrial Committee, dated 10 February 1891, reveals how earlier grand plans for large iron-smelting works had been replaced by a strategy favouring small-scale processing of agricultural products. The letter recommended that tax exemptions for ten years and free sites be granted to persons operating a canning factory manufacturing at least 100,000 cans yearly. While town leaders earlier lamented the fact that Hastings was losing money in sending iron ore to the United States, they were now upset with the hold of the Picton fruit-processing plants over Hastings: "Is all Hastings fruit to be sent over the bridge to Picton? Let us make our market here and not there."

Shortly after, a group of individuals emerged to take advantage of the offer made by the Belleville Industrial Committee. Ironically, it was not Belleville or Hastings residents who stepped forward but three citizens of Picton who proposed to establish a canning factory in Belleville with a year-ly capacity of 500,000 cans and paying out annually in wages at least $7,500.[32] They planned to employ for the first five months of the year at least twenty-five boys and fifty to seventy-five women and proposed to invest at least $7,000 in starting and equipping a factory. They were even willing to become citizens of Belleville and to show their sincerity gave the city a first registered lien on a mortgage for $3,500. Billa Flint must have thought it typical that once again Belleville failed to attract capitalist devel-opment from within its own community.

The Quinte area was developing a regional specialization in food pro-cessing at the very same time that other parts of the province, particularly the area surrounding Toronto and the Grand Valley region, were attract-ing heavy industry. The litany of industries for the city of Belleville in 1900 – six agricultural implements factories, one brewery, two butter and cheese makers, three cheese exporters, one distillery, three flour and grist mills, two marble works, one woollen mill, one canning factory, one paper man-ufacturer, one rolling mill – attest to the city's continuing reliance on pro-cessing rural products.[33]

Yet Belleville was not alone in its continuing reliance on staple extrac-tion and export. Gilmour shows that, even by 1891, Ontario was still an economy dominated by staples with a stagnant secondary sector squeezed between a falling primary sector and an increasing tertiary sector. But there did exist within the province a notable variation in the relative importance of secondary manufacturing to local economies. Gilmour's analysis reveals that a greater percentage of the labour force in the Quinte region was employed in the primary sector than in the province as a whole.[34] Table 7 illustrates that the percentage of those employed in indus-try in the region actually decreased during the 1851–81 period.

The evidence demonstrates the increasing peripherality of the Quinte

Table 7   Changing Employment Rates by Sector: prince Edward, Hastings, and Lennox
and Addington Counties, 1851–81

Census division and occupation sector	1851 No	1851 %	1861 No	1861 %	1871 No	1871 %	1881 No	1881 %
PRINCE EDWARD								
labour	1,813	36.6	1,198	27.0	794	14.2	862	13.0
rural (including)								
farmer	1,800	36.3	1,916	43.2	3,018	54.9	3,894	58.6
farmers (only)	1,800	36.3	1,903	42.9	3,018	54.9	2,988	44.9
industry	583	11.8	457	10.3	353	6.3	505	7.6
retail	340	6.9	446	10.1	664	11.9	501	7.5
construction	297	6.0	245	5.5	323	5.8	323	4.9
commerce	47	1.0	44	1.0	141	2.5	213	3.2
communication & transportation	53	1.1	109	2.5	207	3.7	271	4.1
government	27	0.5	15	0.3	29	0.5	45	0.7
finance	0	0.0	7	0.2	14	0.3	34	0.5
TOTALS	4,960	100	4,437	100	5,603	100	6,648	100
HASTINGS								
labour	2,321	30.6	2,393	23.2	1,756	12.6	2,636	15.0
rural (including)								
farmer	2,978	39.3	4,795	46.6	7,816	56.1	9,281	53.5
farmers (only)	2,898	38.2	4,098	40.1	7,619	54.7	7,122	40.6
industry	743	9.8	812	7.9	902	6.5	1,505	8.6
retail	762	10.1	1,144	11.1	1,674	12.0	1,846	10.5
construction	562	7.4	717	7.0	754	5.4	973	5.6
commerce	122	1.6	77	0.8	496	3.6	598	3.4
communication & transportation	74	1.0	191	1.9	387	2.8	572	3.3
government	20	0.3	74	0.7	68	0.5	141	0.8
finance	1	0.01	26	0.3	81	0.6	70	0.4
Totals	7,683	100	10,229	100	13,934	100	17,722	100
LENNOX & ADDINGTON								
labour	1,775	35.4	2,463	33.8	1,307	12.8	1,423	11.0
rural (including)								
farmer	1,768	35.2	2,972	40.8	6,369	62.5	8,301	64.2
farmers (only)	1,731	34.5	2,829	38.8	6,254	61.4	6,271	48.5
industry	465	9.3	527	7.2	528	5.2	1,037	8
retail	461	9.2	617	8.5	1,008	9.9	1,000	7.7
construction	280	5.6	359	4.9	453	4.4	524	4.1
commerce	182	3.6	60	0.8	237	2.3	281	2.2
communication & transportation	50	1.0	261	3.6	229	2.2	253	2.0
government	35	0.7	17	0.2	30	0.3	69	0.5
finance	1	0.02	8	0.1	29	0.3	46	0.4
TOTALS	5,018	100	7,284	100	10,190	100	12,924	100

Sources: *Census of Canada*; James Gilmour, *Spatial Evolution of Manufacturing, Southern Ontario, 1851–1891* (Toronto: University of Toronto Press, 1972).

region vis-à-vis the urban-centred regions of Toronto, Hamilton, and London. Belleville was distant enough from Toronto to offer some competition to metropolitan interests and ensure that it would not become merely an economic satellite. The process of integration into the larger Toronto-based economic and social region was not as overwhelming for Belleville as it was for those communities situated to the west. Although the effects of metropolitanism were experienced, local institutions and values were not replaced entirely by "those generated and appropriate to the dominant metropolitan centre."[35]

TOWN AND COUNTRY RELATIONS:
BELLEVILLE AND THURLOW

This discussion of continuity and change in the Quinte region concludes with a brief examination of the relationship that existed between Belleville and the surrounding township of Thurlow during the latter part of the nineteenth century. Two questions will be addressed briefly: What type of people did the declining town of Belleville attract from the surrounding countryside? and how did Belleville and the rural township of Thurlow differ in terms of family structure at the end of the century?

By 1871 Thurlow Township reached a population peak of 5,264. Over 81 percent of the farmers owned their land; a growing local market was centred in Belleville, the demand for the area's cheese was increasing, and farmers found a ready market for their barley across the lake in Oswego. The industrial profile of the township (Table 8) shows that there existed a diversity of small-scale rural industries, the most important enterprises in terms of value of production being Henry Corby's grist mill ($37,500) and distillery ($20,000), William Lingham's grist mill ($39,654), and James Canniff's flour and grist mill ($32,000). Not only could Thurlow farmers bring their wheat to one of the six flour and grist mills in the township, they could also choose to patronize one of three such establishments in Belleville. Low-order goods and services were available in Cannifton, Foxboro, and several other small villages throughout the township, with banks and higher-order services present in nearby Belleville.

Yet Thurlow was to feel the effects of many of the same developments which signalled the change in fortune for Belleville. The township was hurt by the decline of the lumber and flour trade in the 1870s. Most of the sawmills and grist mills closed during the decade. The cessation of the American barley market combined with soil depletion and a world-wide recession to further the decline of the local economy. Although tenancy increased minimally between 1870 and 1890, larger numbers of land occupiers and a greater proportion of smaller holdings may be interpreted as signs of an increasingly unfavourable human/land ratio (Table 9).

Another obvious indication of declining fortune was the loss of popula-

Table 8   Industrial Profile, Belleville and Thurlow, 1871

| | Thurlow (pop – 5,264) | | | Belleville (pop – 7,305) | | |
| | Firms | | No. of | Value of | Firms | | No. of | Value of |
Industrial establishments	no.	%	employees	production($)	no.	%	employees	production($)
Flour & grist mill	6	12.8	18	163,396	3	2.9	7	51,000
Paper mill	1	2.1	10	4,500	0	0	0	0
Saw mill	3	6.4	64	50,000	3	2.9	158	101,000
Brick manufacturer	1	2.1	45	13,000	0	0	0	0
Stave factory	1	2.1	3	1,500	0	0	0	0
Blacksmith shsp/forge	9	19.1	15	5,950	5	4.9	22	17,650
Lime kiln	2	4.3	9	7,625	1	1.0	5	1,350
Tannery	4	8.5	13	18,225	0	0	0	0
Weaver	4	8.5	13	18,225	0	0	0	0
Boot & shoe shop/ maker	5	10.6	5	2,510	9	8.8	55	21,800
Cheese company	1	2.1	4	14,885	0	0	0	0
Carriage & waggon maker	4	8.5	30	14,300	6	5.9	48	29,850
Distillery	1	2.1	6	20,000	0	0	0	0
Cabinet shop	1	2.1	1	430	3	2.9	23	36,600
Millinery/ dressmaking shop	1	2.1	2	350	7	6.9	33	10,000
Hand loom operator	3	6.4	4	1,100	0	0	0	0
Gas company	0	0	0	0	1	1.1	4	7,700
Potash manufacturer	0	0	0	0	2	2.0	21	25,500
Plaster business	0	0	0	0	1	1.0	4	4,500
Carpenter/joiner	0	0	0	0	5	4.9	15	26,350
Cloth dyeing	0	0	0	0	1	1.0	1	1,500
Brewery	0	0	0	0	2	2.0	7	9,000
Woollen manufacturer	0	0	0	0	1	1.0	5	1,500
Bakery & confectioner	0	0	0	0	4	3.9	44	46,400
Soda factory	0	0	0	0	2	2.0	3	4,500
Sewing machine maker	0	0	0	0	1	1.0	16	9,000
Stone ware	0	0	0	0	1	1.0	7	16,000
Sash, door & blind factory	0	0	0	0	5	4.9	31	28,300
Axe factory	0	0	0	0	1	1.0	25	26,000
Marble dealer	0	0	0	0	2	2.0	6	6,500
Cigar maker	0	0	0	0	1	1.0	6	2,000
Foundry & machine shop	0	0	0	0	4	3.0	108	100,000

Source: Canada, Department of Agriculture, *Census of Canada, 1870–71*: III, 290–445.

tion experienced by Thurlow. The population of the township decreased
5.1 percent in the 1870s, 2.1 percent in the 1880s, and 12.6 percent during the 1890s. A final signal of economic decline, or at least stagnation, is
afforded through an examination of the probate records available in the

Table 9   Changing Holding Sizes and Tenure Profile, Thurlow Township, 1851–91

a) Changing Holding Sizes

					Number of Occupiers of				
Years	*less than 10 acres*	*%*	*11–50 acres*	*%*	*51–99 acres*	*%*	*100–199 acres*	*%*	*more than 200 acres* *%*
1851	107	(21.7)	60	(12.2)	197	(40.0)	133	(122.9)	16	(3.2)
1871	95	(16.2)	115	(19.6)	235	(40.1)	123	(21.0)	18	(3.1)
1891	247	(33.8)	102	(14.0)	209	(28.6)	139	(19.0)	33	(4.5)

% change			
Holding Size	*1851–71*	*1871–91*	*1851–91*
less than 10 acres	–5.5	17.6	12.1
11–50 acres	7.4	–5.6	1.8
51–99 acres	0.1	–11.5	–11.4
100–199 acres	1.9	–2.0	–3.9
more than 200 acres	0.1	1.4	1.3

b) Changing Tenure Profile

Year	*Total occupiers[1]*		*Owners*		*Tenants*	
1851	493	(100)	–		–	
1871	586	(100)	477	(81.4)	103	(17.6)
1891	730	(100)	584	(80.0)	145	(19.9)

% change			
Tenure	*1851–71*	*1871–91*	*1851–91*
Total occupiers	–	–	–
Owners	–	–1.4	–
Tenants	–	2.3	–

Sources: Census of Canada, 1850–51, vol. II, table VI, 20–1; 1870–71, vol. III, table XXI, 38–9; 1890–91, vol. II, table XVI, 276–7.

[1] includes employees as well

Archives of Ontario (Table 10). While many people did not register a will, the probate records on file are revealing. They indicate, at least for value of personal estate and effects, a gradual decline in the proportion of estates valued at greater than $1,000. However, too much should not be made of these signs of decline. Analysis of the genealogical families in the next chapter reveals that many Quinte residents made adjustments for changing conditions and continued to persist in the area.

Table 10   Value of Personal Estate and Effects from Thurlow Township Probate Files, 1859–1900

Value of Personal Estate and Effects	1859–69		1870–79		1880–89		1890–1900	
	no.	%	no.	%	no.	%	no.	%
unknown or none	1	3.6	2	4.0	0	0	3	3.4
$1–250	1	3.6	3	6.0	6	12.2	17	19.5
$251–500	11	39.3	13	26.0	11	22.4	21	24.1
$501–750	0	0	8	16.0	7	14.3	14	16.1
$751–1000	3	10.7	3	9.0	10	20.4	4	4.6
$1001–1500	3	10.7	13	26.0	4	8.2	12	13.8
$1501–2000	3	10.7	2	4.0	2	4.1	5	5.7
$2001–5000	5	17.9	2	4.0	7	14.3	6	6.9
more than $5000	1	3.6	4	8.0	2	4.1	5	5.7
Totals	28	100	50	100	49	100	87	100
Average (known)	$1,487.48		$2,188.65		$1,436.01		$1,733.79	
Standard Deviation	1,643.98		4,246.50		2,271.47		4,183.66	
Coefficient of Variation	110.52		194.02		158.18		241.30	

Value of Real Estate from Thurlow Township Probate Files, 1890–1900[1]

Value of Real Estate	Number	%
None	24	27.6
$1–500	4	4.6
$501–1,000	6	6.9
$1,001–2,000	18	20.7
$2,001–3,500	16	18.4
$3,501–5,000	9	10.3
$5,001–10,000	9	10.3
more than $10,000	1	1.1
Total	87	100
Average (known)	$3,059.40	
Standard Deviation	2,268.2	
Coefficients of Variation	74.14	

Source: PAO List of Probate Files, Surrogate Court Wills, Thurlow, 1859–1900.

[1] real estate values were, for the most part, not indicated until the 1890 decade.

Table 11 shows the distribution of all males in Thurlow for the year 1881 and in Belleville for the year 1891 by occupational classification and lists the ten most frequent occupations in both communities for those particular years. The data indicate that Thurlow was very definitely a rural society, with farming being by far the most popular occupation. Belleville had a

Table 11a   Distribution of Males by Occupational Classification, Thurlow (1881) and
Belleville (1891)[1]

Occupational category	Thurlow (1881) no.	%	Belleville (1891) no.	%
1. rural operator	857	58.7	72	2.7
2. manufacturer	12	0.8	37	1.4
3. professional	41	2.8	164	6.0
4. merchant/business	26	1.8	355	13.1
5. semi-skilled and skilled	262	17.9	1,032	38.0
6. clerical	30	2.1	436	16.1
7. unskilled	225	15.4	599	22.1
8. private	9	0.5	20	0.7
Total 1–8	1,461	100.0	2,715	100.0
9. unknown/not apply/retired	1,014	41.0	1,785	39.7
Total	1,461	59.0	2,715	60.3
	2,475	100.0	4,500	100.0

[1] Not including retired, unknown and not apply categories (N = 1014)

Table 11b   Ten Most Frequest Occupations, Thurlow (1881) and Belleville (1891)

Thurlow	no.	%	Belleville	no.	%
farmer	750	51.3	labourer	385	14.2
labourer	166	11.4	clerk	177	6.5
farm labour	85	5.8	carpenter	127	4.7
carpenter	49	3.4	carter/teamster	96	3.5
blacksmith	41	2.8	blacksmith	66	2.4
gardener	27	1.8	railroad engineer	60	2.2
brickmaker	21	1.4	salesperson	54	2.0
college student	21	1.4	agent	50	1.8
servant	19	1.3	lawyer/attorney	46	1.7
carter/teamster	13	0.9	grocer	45	1.7
	1,192	81.6		1,106	40.7
Total all occupations	1,461	100.0	Total all occupations	2,715	100.0

Source: Canada, Thurlow Township Manuscript Censuses, 1881, 1891; Belleville Manuscript Censuses, 1881, 1891.

more diverse occupational profile, with a significant percentage of males employed in tertiary positions. Yet labourer was the largest single occupation. The Grand Trunk was one of the city's largest employers and hired many unskilled people to work in repair crews. The prevalence of carpenters and blacksmiths is interesting only in that most farm boys learned to use a saw and to shoe a horse and thus were prepared to take up these jobs upon movement to the city.

Data were collected for every male resident of Thurlow in 1881 (N=2,475) and every male resident of Belleville in 1891 (N=4,500) and

Table 12   Thurlow Male Residents (1881) in Belleville (1891)

Characteristics	1881	1891
1. Age groups		
0–4	10.9	0
5–9	25.7	0
10–14	13.9	10.9
15–19	9.9	25.7
20–24	15.8	13.9
25–29	5.0	9.9
30–34	2.0	15.8
35–39	5.9	5.0
40–44	3.0	2.0
45–49	2.0	5.9
50–54	1.0	3.0
55–59	1.0	2.0
60–64	3.0	1.0
65–69	1.0	1.0
70–74	0	3.0
75–79	0	1.0
80–84	0	0
85+	0	0
2. Position within household		
head	22.6	30.7
eldest son	20.4	22.8
middle son(s)	21.5	12.9
youngest son	20.4	11.9
only son	10.8	5.9
relatives	2.2	7.9
not related	1.1	5.0
domestic servant	0	1.0
sibling of single head	1.1	2.0
3. Occupational category		
rural operator	16.8	5.0
manufacturer	0	1.0
professional	2.0	3.0
merchant/business	0	3.0
semi-skilled and skilled	15.8	42.6
clerical	4.0	9.9
unskilled	3.0	13.9
private	4.0	5.9
not apply	50.5	15.8
unknown/no occupation	4.0	0
4. Most numerous occupation		
1881 N = 50		
farmer	26 (N=13)	
carpenter	8 (N=5)	
blacksmith	6 (N=3)	
butcher	4 (N=2)	
1891 N = 85		
labourer		9.4 (N=8)

Table 12 (continued)

Characteristics	1881	1891
no occupation		5.9 (N=5)
teamster/carter		4.7 (N=4)
clerk		4.7 (N=4)
blacksmith		3.6 (N=3)
carpenter		2.4 (N=2)

Source: See Table 11.

those who made the move from Thurlow to Belleville during this period were traced on the basis of name, date of birth, birthplace, and religion (Table 12). Only 105 or 4.2 percent of the 1881 Thurlow male residents were living in Belleville in 1891. This short-distance migration was composed primarily of young couples and their children. Over 26 percent of those who held an occupation in Thurlow were farmers. In addition, a number of carpenters and blacksmiths made the move.

Most of the Thurlow residents lived in nuclear family units in Belleville although a few did reside with relatives or boarded. The majority found work in a semi-skilled or skilled position although a considerable proportion were employed as labourers and carters. The information is sketchy but does suggest that Belleville in 1891 only attracted people from nearby Thurlow with poor economic resources and little in the way of skills and capital. Clearly, they could not provide the investment dollars so desperately called for by the city's elite. While certain Thurlow citizens earlier in the century had contributed greatly to the community in terms of investment and energy – individuals such as Henry Corby Jr (distiller and mill owner), J.J. Flint (police magistrate, barrister, and mayor), Roswell Leavens (magistrate and merchant), Alexander Sills (businessman), and Ashael Vermilyea (boot and shoe merchant and city councillor) – fewer were attracted to a city which was clearly stagnating.[36]

The nuclear family was the normal form for both 1881 Thurlow and 1891 Belleville, although a greater percentage of Belleville households than expected were composed of extended families, a form associated with rural societies (Table 13). The close proximity of Thurlow and Belleville perhaps explains this characteristic. Newly arrived migrants from Thurlow may have lived with relatives for a time before establishing their own households. The stem family was more common in Thurlow but the percentage of this type of household is relatively insignificant. A considerable number of males boarded in both communities, the majority being young and single.

Table 14a presents comparative age-specific marital fertility rates for women of Thurlow in 1881 and their counterparts in Belleville in 1891.

Table 13   Household Types to which Males Belong, Thurlow (1881) and Belleville (1891)

	Thurlow		Belleville	
Household type	no.	%	no.	%
nuclear	2,037	82.3	3,636	80.8
extended	148	6.03	350	7.8
stem[1]	57	2.3	36	0.8
stem/extended[2]	12	0.5	10	0.2
solitaire[3]	29	1.2	33	0.7
no family[4]	61	2.5	83	1.8
board[5]	131	5.3	352	7.8

Source: See Table 11.
[1] Married son(s) and his/their family(ies) living with parents
[2] Married son and his family living with parents and other relatives
[3] Widowed, single
[4] No nuclear family, but co-resident with siblings or relatives
[5] Not related to head

Belleville women between the ages of 35 and 39 in 1891 displayed a greater fertility rate than Thurlow women of the same age cohort ten years earlier. More revealing is Table 14b which shows that the proportion of Thurlow women under the age of 25 who had conceived two or more children was only slightly higher than the proportion of Belleville women who had borne more than one child before their 25th year. Belleville women under the age of 25 were, however, far more likely to have no children than their Thurlow counterparts. Whether this is due to later age at marriage can only be determined by further census analysis. What is most striking about the behaviour of women between the ages of 25 and 29 is that the percentages of Belleville and Thurlow women in this age category who had two or more children were almost identical, even though the former were still more likely to have no children than the latter.

CONCLUSION

Belleville did not develop as a classic colonial entrepôt like Kingston or Toronto. It was not planned in advance of general settlement nor was it developed for strategic purposes. Like many other Canadian communities, it developed as a collection centre for the staples of the surrounding hinterland and as a distribution centre for imported goods. Right from the beginning of settlement, Belleville acted as regional branch of European and then Montreal and Toronto sources of credit, supply, and transportation. Yet residents of this community and its hinterland lived and interacted with buyers and sellers in their specific region.

Table 14   Comparative Demographics, Thurlow and Belleville, 1881 and 1891

a) Number of Children not yet 10 Years per 1,000 Married Women
by Age Cohort, Thurlow (1881) and Belleville (1891)

	15–19	20–24	25–29	30–34	35–39	40–44
Thurlow 1881	0	1,170	1,825	2,142	1,756	1,479
Belleville 1891	667	1,000	1,809	1,930	1,784	1,229
Rural - Urban Difference*	–	14.5	0.9	9.9	–1.6	16.9

*% by which urban fertility ratio is lower than rural ratio.

b) Distribution of Rural and Urban Wives Aged 15–29 by Number of Children
1881, 1891 (percentages)

	Thurlow (1881)	Belleville (1891)
Cohort age 15–24		
no children	33.0	42.5
1 child	32.0	27.4
2 or more	34.0	30.1
Cohort age 25–29		
no children	10.9	17.2
1 child	30.7	23.4
2 or more	58.4	59.3

Source: David Gagan, Hopeful Travellers: Families, Land and Social Change in Mid-Victorian Peel County, Canada West (Toronto: University of Toronto Press, 1981), 131, 133; also see Table 11.

The community grew as a commercial market town dependent on the expansion of its import-export role and the development of its inter-regional trade. The former function tied the fortune of Belleville with that of its hinterland and for much of the century the town prospered under this relationship. The processing and exporting of lumber, wheat, and other agricultural produce and, to a lesser extent, minerals, linked Belleville with the surrounding region. But the community was never really able to develop an interregional trade of manufactured goods. With changing world markets and a declining resource base, Belleville desperately attempted to break out of its staple dependency and industrialize. The city pinned its hopes on the promise of the rails but that potential was never fully realized. Its geographic isolation, always a problem, a limited agricultural hinterland, a lack of investment capital, and commercial rivalry of other centres combined with changing markets to seal Belleville's fate as a declining second order centre.

The fortunes of Belleville and its hinterland were directly intertwined. While both were directly and indirectly influenced by outside metropolitan forces, they were inextricably connected in the import-export, staple-producing relationship. The city never received a significant influx of capital from elsewhere but continued to develop on the basis of local firms tapping the hinterland. When the fortunes of Belleville changed, rural communities in the region suffered even more as less local money was available for expansion. Local elites were unable to attract outside investment and because most of them were involved so directly with the declining import-export function, they did not have the capital to develop growth industries. While domestic industries did develop in Ontario during the nineteenth century and were not entirely derivative from staples production, the export of such staples, in Marjorie Cohen's words, "are not to be undervalued for their role in the development of the Ontario economy and to the development and ultimate decline of smaller urban centres in particular."[37]

What is most interesting, at least in the context of this book, is to consider how rural Quinte residents dealt with the declining fortune of their major market centre. It is easy to assume that because the fortunes of both hinterland and urban centre were so closely connected, the rural sector would invariably feel the effects of change even more than the town. But many chose to remain at home despite the fact that Belleville and other smaller centres offered much less than Toronto, Hamilton, New York, Buffalo, Syracuse, Chicago, or even other rural frontiers in the way of opportunities. Farmers in the region adjusted to changing markets and developed their dairying, cheese-making and fruit-growing interests. And towns such as Belleville offered incentives for cheese-making and fruit-processing factories to locate in their midst.

This reinforces the point that modernization should be viewed as a contextual process. Smaller urban centres experiencing stagnation or decline at the end of the nineteenth century were not all incipient metropolises. Some of these centres might have opened their arms to rural interests and rural types of production. Upon deeper inspection, we might find in some of these places a blending of new urban traits and traditional rural values. The important message is that we need to free ourselves from the pervasive influence of an aspatial, large-scale perspective of modernization and realize that local conditions modified modernization forces.

While a widespread exodus from Quinte and the rest of rural Ontario did take place during the latter part of the nineteenth century, many persisted in place because of extensive economic and social ties to family and the community. Even though attention is focused on the experiences of those who left, an integral part of my story is the experiences of those who stayed behind. The genealogical study of the five Quinte families explores persistence as well as geographical mobility among these groups through the context of change and continuity occurring in the Quinte region during the nineteenth century.

4 Change and Continuity among Four Generations of Quinte Families: A Genealogical Window

Joy stifles all sound except
The noise of our new wilderness
We take the first steps
Of our refuge.
– Francis Itani, *Rentee Bay: Poems from the Bay of Quinte*

As all good novelists know, the best way to dramatize large issues is to bring them down to a human scale. The same is true of historical research. This chapter views the impacts of social and economic change in a rural environment through the experiences of those who responded to this transformation. In meeting this goal, the geographical focus moves beyond the Bay of Quinte region of Ontario to include those places to which members of three successive generations of the selected families chose to locate. The investigation functions as a window through which we can attain an impression of the intracontinental migration associated with the opening of a succession of frontiers and the transformation of society. At the same time, the analysis also presents a detailed study of a place and its persistent population over time, allowing us to compare and contrast the experiences of both persisters and movers.

INITIAL LOYALIST SENTIMENT OF THE QUINTE REGION

We begin our story with an account of the Loyalist migrations to the Bay of Quinte region. Although the broad parameters of settlement were presented in the last chapter, it is important to establish the context of colonization, as initial circumstances proved to be influential in determining subsequent patterns of mobility.

Our tale commences with the dawn of political independence for the American colonies. During the years of the American Revolution (1776–83) and its aftermath, citizens who were loyal to the crown were driven from their homes. At the end of the war, Loyalist troops and refugees travelled from every part of the American colonies to destinations on both sides of the Atlantic. The majority, however, moved north into what remained of Britain's American empire, travelling by ship, wagon, and foot to Nova Scotia, Quebec, and the new colonies of New Brunswick and Upper Canada. Most decided to re-establish themselves in areas already settled, but a sizable number chose to move to the recently surveyed townships along the St Lawrence and Niagara rivers and the Bay of Quinte.

The first European to see this part of Ontario was Samuel de Champlain who spent the winter of 1615–16 along its sheltered coastline recovering from wounds inflicted at the hands of the Iroquois.[1] The French, however, never made any significant effort to settle outside Quebec and so the land surrounding the bay remained in the hands of the Mississauga Indians until they agreed to surrender this territory to Britain prior to the coming of the Loyalists. There were several waves of Loyalist migrations to Canada during the course of the Revolutionary War, but the greatest came at the end of the hostilities. In 1783 thousands left New York for Nova Scotia, the Bahamas, and Lower Canada (Quebec). While Loyalists wintered at various Quebec encampments and rendez-voused at the north end of Lake Champlain, Sackett's Harbor, Oswego, and Niagara, surveys were carried out in what was to become Ernestown, Fredericksburg, and Adolphustown townships.[2] The three townships of what was shortly to become Prince Edward County – Sophiasburg, Ameliasburg, and Marysburg – were surveyed in 1785, while Sidney and Thurlow townships across the bay in the future Hastings County were surveyed in 1787 (Map 4).[3]

While Nova Scotia received the more wealthy and educated Loyalists from New York City, Boston, and other seaboard cities and towns, 80 percent of Loyalists settling in that part of Quebec which subsequently became Upper Canada were frontier farmers from the Hudson and Mohawk river valleys. This group included American-born, Palatines from the German states, Huguenots from France, Quakers from England, and Catholics and Protestants from England, Ireland, and Scotland. Over 50 percent of eastern Ontario Loyalists were of Scottish background. Another group of Loyalists settling in the Bay of Quinte region were Six Nations Iroquois under the leadership of Joseph Brant who came to Canada in 1793–4 after losing their lands to the New York Land Company. Land purchased by the government from the Mississaugas was conveyed to the Iroquois and named after Brant's Indian name – Tyendinaga.[4]

The Loyalists tended to be recent immigrants to the United States and thus more inclined to retain their European-based culture and traditions and less likely to be Americanized. In addition, the ethnic and cultural background of these recent immigrants isolated them to some extent from the mainstream of colonial society, a fact, Potter-MacKinnon reasons, "that helps to explain why they remained loyal and why a patriarchal family structure was more likely to persist."[5]

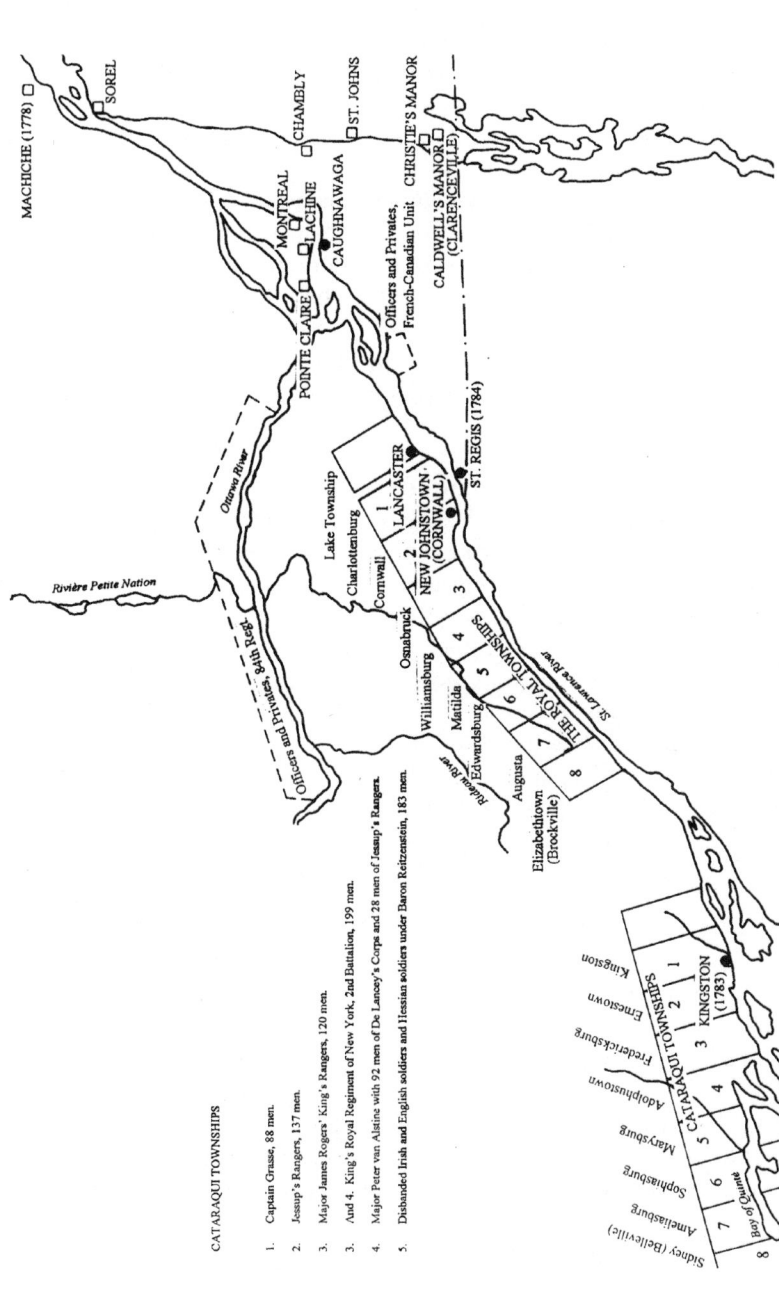

Map 4: Original Loyalist Settlements in Eastern Ontario

SOURCE: Compiled largely from figures in the Haldimand Papers, PAO MS 622

A volume entitled *Pioneer Life on the Bay of Quinte* published in 1904 provides some insight into the origins and circumstances of migrants settling this region of Ontario. Although this source has many limitations, it gives us some idea about origin, distance, and direction of migration, occupation, and persistence characteristics of pioneer settlers.[6] Of the 177 original settlers listed in this book, 108 were American natives and the remainder were European-born. All the American-born arrived prior to 1820 while 46 percent of the European-born came after this date. Over 90 percent of the European migrants were born in Britain, but the Quinte region was not necessarily their first destination. Many who settled before 1800 were Loyalists, thus signifying that they had settled for some time in the American colonies.

Of the American-born settlers, it is possible to locate 65 percent by county or city of origin. The majority (81 percent) came from New York State, particularly Dutchess County (Table 15). Many of the latter were members of Major van Alstine's regiment during the Revolutionary War who later settled in Adolphustown Township. The family articles reveal that their migration to Upper Canada was often no more than one or two generations removed from their European-born ancestors.

Nearly all the Loyalists who migrated to the Quinte area did so directly, although there is evidence that some took up residence in the Maritimes or Quebec before moving to Upper Canada. Of the ninety-three family case studies in which underlying motives for each individual's decision to move are available, fifty-two were forced to flee because they were Loyalists, eleven migrated as children of Loyalists, and seventeen followed family members to Canada. More generally, from the information presented in the case studies, it is possible to identify three types of motives which underlie the movement of people to the Quinte region: military (expulsion of the Loyalists); administrative (for example, in response to the free land policy in Upper Canada); and personal (for example, following a brother).

The Oswego route was adopted by most of the families emigrating to the Bay of Quinte region, many of them choosing to come across the ice by sleigh in winter. The greatest number of migrants who arrived before 1820 settled in Adolphustown and Ernestown townships in Lennox and Addington County; in Sophiasburg, Hallowell, and what would become Hillier townships in Prince Edward County; and in Sidney Township in Hastings County. Since most of the Quinte migrants were Loyalists, the majority in the sample moved directly on to their land grants. Quite a few of the Loyalists were commissioned officers during the war and thus were entitled to extensive grants. At the other end, some non-Loyalists came to the area with very little and were forced to work as farm labourers for years before acquiring property.

Not surprisingly, farming was the most common category among the

Table 15   American Source Areas for Quinte Settlers, 1780–1820

Birthplace	1780–89	1790–99	1800–09	1810–19	Totals
NEW YORK					
Albany	1	–	1	–	2
Orange County	–	1	–	–	1
Dutchess County	9	10	9	2	30
New York City	1	2	1	–	4
Haverstraw	1	2	–	–	3
Long island	–	2	2	2	6
Herkimer County	–	–	–	2	2
Westchester County	2	–	–	1	3
Jefferson County	–	–	–	1	1
Madison County	1	–	–	–	1
Catskill Mountains	–	–	1	–	1
Celina	–	–	1	–	1
Saratoga	–	–	1	1	2
Yonkers	–	1	–	–	1
Other	7	3	–	–	10
NEW JERSEY					
Sussex County	1	–	–	–	1
Lambertville	–	–	1	–	1
Piscataqua	1	–	–	–	1
Other	1	1	2	1	5
RHODE ISLAND	1	1	–	–	2
VERMONT					
Manchester	–	–	1	–	1
Arlington	–	1	–	–	1
Other	2	1	–	2	5
MASSACHUSETTS					
Pembroke	1	–	–	–	1
Boston	–	2	–	–	2
CONNECTICUT					
Stamwich	–	–	1	–	1
Storrington	–	–	–	2	2
Other	–	–	2	–	2
MARYLAND					
Baltimore	–	–	1	–	1
PENNSYLVANIA	–	1	–	–	1
MAINE	–	1	–	1	2
Totals	29	29	24	15	97

Source: *Pioneer Life on The Bay of Quinte* (Toronto: Rolph and Clark Ltd., 1904).

Quinte pioneers both before and after the move. The fact that 43 percent were involved in farming before the move and 73 percent afterwards reflects an obvious adjustment to conditions on a new frontier, devoid of urban centres that could provide opportunities for skilled trades. The migrants came from areas where the demand for urban-based services was already well established, so many of them were involved in occupations other than farming before they moved.

The Loyalists in the *Pioneer Life on the Bay of Quinte* volume were a small fraction of the thousands who first settled the region in the fall of 1783 and the spring and summer of 1784. The Cataraqui or Quinte townships were populated largely by those Loyalists who had fought in the Northern or Canadian Division under the command of Sir Guy Carleton and General Haldimand. The main units of this division operating out of Montreal were Sir John Johnson's Royal Yorkers, John Butler's Rangers, Major Edward Jessup's Loyal Rangers, and a small unit of the King's Rangers commanded by Major James Rogers. Kingston Township was settled by the band of Loyalists under the command of Captain Michael Grass, while Ernestown was allotted to the remainder of Jessup's Rangers, who for the most part settled further east along the St Lawrence in Edwardsburg, Augusta, and Elizabethtown townships.[7] Two hundred and four people settled in Ernestown. Fredericksburg, the third township, was settled by Major Rogers and 259 of his followers while the fourth township, Adolphustown, was the destination for 258 men, women, children, and servants under the command of Major Peter van Alstine.[8] Amherst Island, situated at the estuary of the Bay of Quinte and called Isle de Tant by the French, was first claimed by the Mohawk Indians accompanying Sir John Johnson. They soon after leased their rights to the island to Colonel Crawford, who in turn transferred his right to his superior, Sir John.[9]

In Prince Edward County almost all of Marysburg Township was settled by Captain Archibald McDonnell and his party of 153 men, twenty-nine women, sixty-nine children, and two servants in the fall of 1784. They were accompanied by twenty-nine Hessian soldiers and their families constituting seven women, nine children, and three servants.[10] Most of this party were classified as military claimants rather than Loyalists, meaning they received a reward for service rather than collecting compensation for ceded property in the United States.[11] Many of the discharged German soldiers returned home or settled elsewhere, while others, upon learning that the title deed to their free land would only be transferred to them upon paying a sum of £5, also left. Sophiasburg was settled by Loyalists from Adolphustown and Fredericksburg accompanying Peter van Alstine and Late Loyalists who arrived in 1796 after van Alstine was granted 500 acres along Lake of the Mountain. Ameliasburg was not assigned to any specific Loyalist unit and was settled in various parts by a few who bought land from the Mississaugas. Likewise, Sidney, Thurlow, and Richmond townships were not assigned to any Loyalist unit and were settled largely by the sons and daughters from the Loyalists of older townships along the bay and from elsewhere who had drawn land there, and Late Loyalists.[12]

While waiting for the drawing of lands, the Loyalists lived in military tents. Once the lots were selected, settlers were given a location ticket called script which included both the name of the recipients and the number of their lot. At this point, Loyalists and their families attempted to locate their property, a difficult task given that surveyor markers were the only directing signs available.[13] The government provided rations until 1786 while the settlers cleared land and planted their crops. Mutual assistance was necessary for survival during the first few years in the wilderness, especially during the 1788–9 season when wheat rust and drought brought on what has been called the "Hungry Year." Nevertheless, the settlers managed to survive this crisis and set about constructing an agricultural society out of the forest. It was a society that was both tolerant and structured, "with clear social distinctions, an authoritarian political system, and conservative values."[14]

Yet the Quinte frontier was a transient environment. Only twenty-five of the forty-eight households established in Adolphustown Township by 1784 were present a decade later. The generous allotments apportioned to military claimants, Loyalists and their families, and the bonds of kinship and marriage were concomitants of persistence, a finding for Adolphustown supported by the fact that 63.7 percent of the original settlers designated in the Quinte volume, who were for the most part Loyalists, persisted in place (Table 16). Sixty-four people in the region held more than 350 acres in 1799, with certain Loyalists and military officials controlling well over 1,000 acres. Included among this latter group were Richard Cartwright, Peter van Alstine, the Reverend James Stuart, Joseph Forsyth, Archibald McDonnell, Dr James Latham, Christopher Robinson, William Atkinson, J. Reilly Smith, R. Porter, Joseph Bunbury, and Richard Pilkington who owned 5,691 acres, 5,615 acres, 2,978 acres, 2,400 acres, 2,276 acres, 2,000 acres, 1,800 acres, 1,250 acres, 1,200 acres, 1,200 acres, 1,200 acres, and 1,177 acres respectively in Prince Edward County; Fraser Vandebogaart, A. McGuin, and William Coffin who owned 2,000 acres, 1,400 acres, and 1,200 acres respectively in Hastings County; and William Crawford who held 1,460 acres in Lennox and Addington.[15]

Yet, as revealed in Table 17, the average holding size in the region during the initial settlement period was considerably less than 1,000 acres; the smallest parcels were in Adolphustown, Ameliasburg, and Fredericksburg. It is likely that the surplus of males in Adolphustown during the initial period of settlement as noted by Norris was typical of this frontier region as a whole. Norris's interpretation of Adolphustown's population dynamics – "large farm households augmented by unmarried male immigrants, family completion occurring about two decades after marriage among pre-

Table 16   Persistence Characteristics of Original Settlers, 1780–1820

Township where migrants first settled	Persisters	Those who moved			Totals
		Once	Twice	Three or more times	
PRINCE EDWARD COUNTY					
Ameliasburgh	4	2	–	–	6
Athol	5	1	–	–	6
Hallowell	16	3	1	–	20
Hillier	9	2	–	–	11
Marysburgh	4	1	1	1	7
Sophiasburgh	19	3	–	–	22
Big Island	1	1	–	–	2
LENNOX & ADDINGTON COUNTY					
Adolphustown	15	16	2	–	33
Amherst Island	–	–	1	–	1
Ernestown	4	3	–	–	7
North Fredericksburgh	1	–	–	–	1
South Fredericksburgh	–	2	1	–	3
FRONTENAC COUNTY					
Kingston	1	–	–	–	1
HASTINGS COUNTY					
Sidney	15	1	–	–	16
Thurlow	1	1	–	–	1
Hungerford	1	–	–	–	1
NORTHUMBERLAND COUNTY					
Brighton	1	–	–	–	1
Cramahe	–	1	–	–	1
Haldimand	1	–	–	–	1
Murray	1	–	–	–	1
URBAN CENTRES					
Kingston	1	8	2	1	12
Belleville	–	1	–	–	1
Bath	1	–	–	–	1
Totals	100 (63.7%)	47 (29.9%)	8 (5.1%)	2 (1.2%)	157

Source: See Table 15.

1794 settlers, and a subsequently stable and aging population" – was also representative of the entire region. These conditions reflected increasingly limited opportunities to establish new farms and resulted in the greater out-migration of young adults.[16]

Having set the scene, attention is now focused on Martin Denyes, Joseph Morden, Alexander Laughlin, William Hudgins, and William Ruttan and

Table 17 Changing Holding Sizes in the Quinte Region, 1800 and 1820

				No. of landowners owning (acres)						
Township	Total acres owned[1]	No. of landowners	Average holding (in acres)	less than 100	100– 199	200– 399	400– 499	500– 749	750– 999	more than 1000
1800										
Sidney	32,325	132	244.9	1	28	76	18	7	1	1
Thurlow	32,450	132	245.8	0	12	98	16	3	2	1
Ernestown	37,350	180	207.5	4	97	58	9	8	4	0
Fredricksburgh	38,819	303	128.1	0	260	40	3	3	1	0
Adolphustown	9,773	78	125.3	10	57	10	0	1	0	0
Richmond	21,550	93	231.3	0	16	34	10	2	0	1
Marysburg (1790)	37,400	239	156.5	19	145	56	10	7	0	2
Sophiasburg (1790)	28,200	146	193.2	24	45	59	10	8	0	0
Ameliasburg (1790)	6,950	56	124.1	18	25	13	0	0	0	0
1820										
Sidney	38,286	164	233.5	1	20	22	10	3	4	2
Thurlow	39,486	154	256.4	2	21	104	13	10	1	3
Ernestown	71,482	228	313.5	24	91	80	13	7	7	6
Fredricksburg	44,037	246	177.6	14	133	80	10	5	1	2
Adolphustown	11,664	59	190.9	3	28	20	5	2	0	0
Richmond	26,022	98	265.5	2	14	66	9	3	1	3
Marysburg	39,129	184	212.6	26	88	56	3	2	4	5
Sophiasburg	33,681	135	249.5	10	29	76	10	6	1	3
Ameliasburg	63,421	185	342.8	13	47	90	9	8	4	14
Hallowell	51,140	145	352.7	11	30	65	16	7	6	10

Sources: Rosa Eaton, "The Early History of Prince Edward County" (MA thesis, Queen's University, 1934), 17–28; PAO, RG A-IV, vol. II Schedules Midland District 1800, and Schedules under Assessment Act 1820.

[1] Not including reserves, glebes and empty lots.

three generations of their descendants. We can observe how these family groups reacted to changes occurring in the region, emphasizing in particular their strategies of geographical and social mobility and inter-generational property transfer (Table 18).[17]

THE DENYES FAMILY

The Loyalist settlement along the Bay of Quinte in the summer of 1784 was conducted as a military campaign. The objective was to get people on the land as quickly and efficiently as possible and it was felt that the senior officers would serve as effective administrators until such time as civil authority could be established. Sir John Johnson's second battalion of the Royal Regiment of New York and Major James Rogers's King's Rangers, both incomplete units, were allocated Township Number 3, later renamed Fredericksburg. Martin Denyes, a private in the King's Rangers, was among those assigned lots in the township.[18] He was a descendant of a Dutch family who had emigrated to America at an early date, probably about 1610, where the family took possession of land along the Hudson River just south of Albany. At the beginning of the Revolutionary War the 26-year-old Martin joined the Loyalist forces and fought in many skirmishes. After the disbanding of the Rangers in 1784, Martin, his new wife Ruth, and his step-daughter Sara settled on lot 19 in the third concession of Fredericksburg. The regulations of 1784 entitled Denyes to 100 acres and it was on this property that Martin and Ruth raised three boys and two girls. The pioneer died in 1809 at the age of 59.

All three sons of Martin Denyes settled close to each other in Thurlow Township, breaking off ties with their father's homestead in Fredericksburg Township. Martin had left his oldest son John 50 acres of the homestead in Fredericksburg with his choice as to whether to farm the front or the rear. The other 50 acres he left to his youngest boy Jacob. He also instructed John to pay the middle son, Peter, $50 when he came of age. As Martin had died comparatively young, John bore heavy responsibilities for the care of his brothers and sisters as well as his mother. This obligation and the financial burden it entailed, combined with rapid settlement and subsequent increasing land prices in Fredericksburg, may have prevented John from expanding his farming operations and ultimately prompted him to dispose of his property. He moved to Ernestown Township where he purchased the northern three-quarters of lot 7 in the fifth concession, consisting of 150 acres, from Jonathan Jackson for £80. In 1828 John sold 125 acres of this property to Seth Irish for an undetermined figure and in 1833 he sold the remainder of his property, along with some free grant land in Alwick Township, Northumberland County, and used the funds to purchase lot 10 in the seventh concession of Thurlow from George Fraser for $200.

Table 18 Number of Descendants by Generation: Quinte Families

Generations	DENYES				MORDEN				LAUGHLIN				HUDGINS				RUTTAN			
	Males		Females		Males		Females		Males		Females		Males		Females		Males		Females	
	No.	%	No.	%	No.	%	No.	%	No.	%	No.	%	No.	%	No.	%	No.	%	No.	%
1st	3	75.0	1	25.0	4	100	0	0	3	60.0	2	40.0	10	90.9	1	9.1	7	87.5	1	12.5
2nd	17	41.5	24	58.5	20	69.0	9	31.0	18	50.0	18	50.0	29	50.0	28	49.1	30	55.6	24	44.4
3rd	70	47.3	78	52.7	79	50.0	79	50.0	94	49.0	98	51.0	74	44.0	94	56.0	81	52.6	73	47.4
Total	90	46.6	103	53.4	103	53.9	88	46.1	115	49.4	118	50.6	113	47.9	123	52.1	118	54.6	98	45.4

Sources:

1. Drury Denyes, *The Denyes Family, 1750–1982* (Bloomfield, Ontario, 1982).

2. Unpublished Morden family genealogy (Lennox and Addington Historical Society Museum, Napanee, Ontario); unpublished Morden Family genealogy compiled by Marjorie Van Damme.

3. Unpublished Laughlin family genealogy compiled in 1955 by M.F. and E.R. Laughlin (Lennox and Addington Historical Society Museum, Napanee, Ontario).

4. Charles L. Proctor, *200 Years of Hudgins, 1776–1976* (Picton: Picton Gazette Co. Ltd., 1976) and the Burleigh Collection, series II, Families, box 7 housed in the Queen's University Archives.

5. *Pioneer Life on the Bay of Quinte* (Toronto: Rolph and Clarke, 1904) (reprinted in Canadian Series, No. 20, Belleville: Mika Silk Screening Ltd., 1972); unpublished Ruttan family genealogy compiled by H. Stevenson (Lennox and Addington Historical Society Museum, Napanee, Ontario); the McIlreath Papers housed in the Kingston Public Library; a letter dated August 8, 1988 sent to the author by Mrs Mary Pazuick of Trail, BC.

At some undetermined time after the War of 1812 Peter, who had not been awarded any land in his father's will, moved to Thurlow Township. His name does not appear in the property records until 1835, which suggests that he either rented land to farm or worked as a labourer, more probably the latter. In 1835 Peter used money saved from farm labour to buy lot 13 in the ninth concession from the Canada Company. Thirty years later, Peter bought lot 18 in the ninth concession and in 1870 moved to Sidney Township after selling the farm to his son Albert.

In 1826 Jacob followed his brother John to Thurlow and, using the £150 made on the sale of his Fredericksburg property to Stephen Warner, purchased the northeast quarter of lot 7 in the eighth concession from Phoebe Benninger for an undisclosed amount of money. Anna, the boys' sister, and Sara, their half-sister, were bequeathed half their mother's wearing apparel each and Anna was willed one cow, four sheep, one cherry table, one red chest, one little wheel, one feather bed, two pillows, one sheet, one bed quilt, one blanket, and one calf. Anna married Jacob Young of Fredericksburg and they had no children. No record exists of Sara.

THE MORDEN FAMILY

Joseph Morden was born in England about 1740 and came to America as an early age.[19] One of the genealogical sources mentions a claim that his father was George Morden, who came to America around 1743, settling forty miles above Philadelphia. Another version states that his father was James M. Morden, a Yorkshireman, who also settled outside Philadelphia. Both James and George Morden purchased land in Bucks County, Pennsylvania, in the 1750s. James made a will in 1758 naming his sons as George and James. Whether the relationship was that of father and son, or of two brothers settling near one another, is unknown. *Pioneer Life on the Bay of Quinte* lists James as the father of Joseph but the available evidence points to George as the more probable ancestor.

Joseph Morden married Laurania Howell in the early 1760s. She lived in Walpack, New Jersey, just across the Delaware River from Mount Bethel, Bucks County. It is believed that Joseph moved to the Mohawk River valley in 1768 with his wife and two boys. In New York he rented land from Samuel Holland in the New Philadelphia Bush near Johnstown. He managed to clear 70 acres during the seven years that he held this property. During this time, Joseph and Laurania had two more boys and two girls.

The American Revolution would bring an end to Joseph's plans. Johnstown, which was founded by Sir William Johnson, who died in 1774, was recognized as a Tory stronghold. When the alarm was raised in 1776 that a patriot force under Colonel Dayton was on its way to seize Sir John Johnson, William's son, Joseph Morden, was among those who rallied around Sir John, enlisting in the Royal Yorkers and marching to Montreal to join the Canadian Division. Only the men joined this trek, leaving behind the women and children to care for the farms as best they could. Laurania unquestionably relied on her two oldest sons, James and Richard, age 14 and 12, to help her in this task. Before long their farm was confiscated by the rebels and Laurania and the children made their way to New York City, at that time still in Tory hands.

Joseph, meanwhile, formally re-enlisted in the first battalion of the King's Royal Regiment of New York on 19 June 1776 along with his brother Daniel. Both undoubtedly were distraught with the news of the execution of their brother Ralph, hanged in Pennsylvania for assisting a friend escape to the British. Another brother, Moses, served as a non-commissioned officer in the New Jersey Volunteers. Both Joseph and Daniel saw action in a number of skirmishes but it was smallpox that claimed Joseph's life at the Montreal encampment of the Royal Regiment on 24 November 1777. Laurania later married Matthew Forrest, who was also a member of the King's Royal Regiment, and at the end of the hostilities she, her new husband, and six children made their way to Prince Edward County. The four sons of Joseph settled in Sophiasburgh and Ameliasburgh townships. Joseph Jr and his wife Margaret Huffman had no children and disappeared from the records after selling the land the former received as a son of a Loyalist.

THE LAUGHLIN FAMILY

Alexander Laughlin, the son of a weaver, was born in 1756 in Stirlingshire, Scotland.[20] In 1774 the 18-year-old Alexander emigrated to America. He landed at New York City, travelled up the Hudson River to Albany, and finally settled in Ballstown, Saratoga County. Like many of his neighbours, Laughlin remained loyal to the crown and in 1777 went to Albany and enlisted with the Royal Americans, later renamed the Loyal Rangers. The Rangers were under the direction of Major Edward Jessup, who held over 100,000 acres in upstate New York.[21] Shortly after enlisting, Alexander was captured by the rebels and was held prisoner for over two years. He was released in late 1780 but found it impossible to rejoin the British. So he returned home and on 24 December 1782 married a woman named Mary (last name unknown). In 1788 Alexander and his family crossed on the ice from Cape Vincent to Kingston and then made their way to Ernestown where others of Jessup's corps had settled. There he settled on his 100-acre Loyalist grant (the west half of lot 18, concession 2). In 1806 Laughlin purchased lot 28, concession 3 in Ernestown from a Mrs Elizabeth O'Neil and lived there until his death in 1822. He and Mary had seven children, two of whom died in infancy.

John, Alexander's oldest son, was born on 16 September 1783 in Albany County, New York, and in 1788 accompanied his parents, his brother

James, and his sister Mary to Ernestown Township. Upon purchase of lot 28 of the third concession in 1806, Alexander gave to John the pioneer homestead (west half lot 17, the second concession of Ernestown). Prior to that date, John had married Elizabeth Stover. He sold the property to Harriet Booth on 24 October 1836 and at some later date moved to Sheffield Township in Lennox and Addington County. The records show that he received lot 1, concession 2 (200 acres) from the crown on 25 June 1849.

James, the second son, was born in May of 1786 in New York State. He accompanied his parents when they moved to concession 3 of Ernestown and continued to live at home even after marrying Elizabeth Davy in February of 1810. On 29 September 1818, Alexander gave James lot 28, where he remained for the rest of his life. Elizabeth died in 1824 and James married her sister Mary. James's sister Mary was born in New York State shortly before the family left for Canada. She married John Lake of Ernestown, the son of a Loyalist, and they relocated to Loughboro Township in Frontenac County. Under an order-in-council dated 27 February 1818, Mary was granted 200 acres as a daughter of a Loyalist. The location of the land allotted to her was lot 28, concession 8, Collingwood Township, Simcoe County. Yet she and her husband sold the property they received as their Loyalist legacy and remained on the farm in the vicinity of Battersea for the rest of their lives.

Mary's younger sister, Hannah, was born on 19 November 1790 in Ernestown. In 1807 she married Martin Stover Jr, the son of a Loyalist, and they lived in Ernestown. Martin served as a private in the Addington Militia during the War of 1812 and was killed in action in 1814. After his death, their children became military pensioners and Hannah became the guardian. She then married Benjamin Boyce, a farmer living in Fredericksburg, on 13 October 1814.

Alexander's youngest child, Jacob, also served in the War of 1812, participating in the skirmishes at Fort Niagara and Lundy's Lane. At the time of his discharge in March 1815, his residence was given as Camden East. On 28 May 1816 Jacob married Ruth Johnson and their residence is listed as Ernestown. Under an order-in-council dated 8 March 1820, Jacob, listed as living in Camden Township in Lennox and Addington County, was allotted 200 acres as a son of a Loyalist. His assigned land was lot 20, concession 13, Dover Township, Midland District. Jacob continued to live in the neighbourhood of Yarker where he worked as a labourer. Of note is the fact that he and his children became known as McLaughlins.

THE HUDGINS FAMILY

According to the Kingston, Virginia, Parish Register, William Hudgins was born on Gwyn's Island in Gloucester and Mathews Counties, Virginia, in

1758.[22] His family farm was situated on Chesapeake Bay. William was appointed sergeant in Colonel Saunders's Troop of Light Dragoons. His brother John was a member of the same troops but died in action. In 1781 William was captured by the rebels and confined as a prisoner of war in Philadelphia for more than two years. In 1783 a prisoner exchange freed William and he removed to New Brunswick where he was granted 200 acres on the east side of the St John River in York County, Southampton. There he married a woman named Rachel (last name unknown). Together they raised eleven children. On 10 April 1799 William paid his neighbour Anthony Manuel £15 for lot 40 (200 acres). Ten years later William and his wife sold lots 39 and 40 to Stephen Peabody for £125 and migrated to Upper Canada.

They first lived at Coles Point in Adolphustown Township. William joined the local militia at the outbreak of the War of 1812 and for his service received the right to considerable land. Yet according to Proctor's genealogy, Hudgins was unable to profit from this as the records of his military service were destroyed when York was burned by the Americans in 1813. In 1814 William and his family moved to South Marysburg. He and his descendants filed several petitions for land grants in Upper Canada but they were unsuccessful, possibly because William had been bestowed and sold his New Brunswick grant. A petition dated 20 July 1818 for lot 8 in concession 2 of Fredericksburgh was refused on the grounds that a petitioner had to be a resident of Upper Canada prior to 1798 in order to be granted land as a Loyalist. Yet on 23 July of that same year he was granted as a settler 200 acres of land on the first concession south of Point Traverse. However, it was later discovered that this was a clergy reserve and could not be willed to his descendants. It is most likely that William rented this property. At one time he was involved in a shoe-making business with Edward Ackerman in Kingston. The pioneer died in 1842 and was buried at South Bay.

As William Hudgins's farm in South Marysburg was a clergy reserve, he was unable to will it to any member of his family. Yet eight of his ten children whose residences are known stayed in the Quinte region, four remaining in South Marysburg. No mention is made in the property records of James, the oldest Hudgins, even though the Proctor genealogy indicates that he lived in South Marysburg until his death in 1861. The dates of birth for many of the Hudgins first generation are not listed and so discussion follows the order in which they appear in the genealogy. In June of 1846 William, the second son, purchased from the crown 50 acres of the east half of lot 9 in the concession west of Long Point in South Marysburg. Nine years earlier he had bought from Lewis Mouck 70 acres of the east half of lot 8 on the south side of Prince Edward Bay. No information exists for the third son, also named William, while no mention is made of the fourth son, Daniel, in the property records or manuscript censuses of Darlington Township, his residence according to Proctor's genealogy. Although married, Daniel and his wife apparently had no children.

The oldest girl, Hannah, married John Nixon and they lived in Ameliasburg. They also were childless. The fifth son, Lewis, never married and purchased 50 acres of lot E north of Point Traverse from Michael Mouck for £50 on 22 May 1848. Although his brother David is listed as living in South Marysburg, he is not mentioned in the property records. He is listed, however, in the 1861 manuscript census as a labourer living in South Marysburg. Apparently he died before 1871, as the census of that year designates his wife Phoebe as a widow and a tenant holding no acres on lot 8 in concession 2. Nelson, the seventh son, married Elizabeth Cole of Adolphustown, a daughter of a Loyalist and therefore entitled to a 200-acre grant. They moved to the Holloway area of Thurlow Township where the property records show that Nelson paid an undisclosed amount for 50 acres of the east quarter of lot 4 in the seventh concession from Hannah Abrams on 22 November 1851. He and his family do not appear in the 1861 manuscript census but they do show up ten years later. Nelson died in 1879.

The eighth son, Ezekiel, purchased lot 10 (200 acres) in the fourth concession of Richmond Township on 13 July 1852. Prior to this, he rented a clergy reserve in Richmond. The ninth son, Amos, first purchased 50 acres in the west quarter of lot 34 in the fifth concession of King Township in York County for a sum of $100 from John Grout in April of 1840. According to the census, he still lived on that property in 1851. In March of 1862 Amos sold this property to James McArthur for a total of $2,400 and then purchased for $1,200 30 acres of lot 1 in the third concession of the Gore of West Gwillumbury, remaining there until his death. The tenth son, Moses, is listed as living at one time in Sidney Township, although no reference is made of him in either the abstract records or the manuscript censuses. He does turn up in the 1871 manuscript census for Richmond Township, where he is listed as a toll-gate keeper with no land. He and his wife Margaret and their only child, Theresa, are also listed in the 1881 Richmond census.

THE RUTTAN FAMILY

In the spring and summer of 1784 Loyalists quartered and provisioned at Sorel were sent to Lachine, where they were loaded onto bateaux bound for the newly opened Cataraqui townships. Among those making the trip was William Ruttan, a lieutenant in the Associated Loyalists under the command of Major Peter van Alstine, and his wife Margaret who, along with ninety-one other men, forty-five women, 103 children, and seventeen servants, took up land in Adolphustown.[23] The Ruttan family hailed originally from St Mihiel in the Province of Lorraine in northeastern France. In the early seventeenth century Claude Ruttan converted to Protestantism and was forced to flee St Mihiel for nearby Metz. He was the first of the family to become a Huguenot and to experience religious persecution. Around 1670 Abraham Ruttan, Claude's grandson, joined thousands of other Huguenots fleeing into Germany and settled in the Palatinate for five years. In 1675 Abraham followed other Huguenots to Holland from where he accompanied Abraham Hasbrouck and his family as they sailed from Amsterdam to Boston and then on to New York City. The Hasbroucks were one of the "Douzaine" or twelve families that established New Paltz near Kingston, New York, on the west bank of the Hudson River in 1677. Abraham settled there and married Marie Pentilon.

By 1699 Abraham and his family had moved to New Barbadoes in Bergen County, New Jersey, later renamed Rutherford. Their second son, Paul, born in 1686, moved to Phillipsburgh, New York, now called Tarrytown, and in 1708 married Canadian-born Angela Davids. Their son William was baptised at the "Old Dutch Church of Sleepy Hollow" in 1710. Paul and a second wife moved to Schraalenburgh, New Jersey (Bergenfield), in 1725 and six years later William married Marie Demarest, the daughter of a prominent Huguenot landowner. They had at least ten children, of whom Elizabeth (married name Van Orden), born in 1733, Peter, born in 1742, Jacob, born in 1753, and William, our progenitor, born in 1759, went to Canada after the Revolution.

Peter was a captain in the New Jersey Volunteers and a close acquaintance of Chief Joseph Brant. William was a lieutenant in the same battalion, both men having joined the Loyalist cause in 1778. He married Margaret Steele in New York City in 1782. In the summer of 1783 the Loyalists were forced to flee New York City. Peter was in command of a group of eighty-six, including William and Margaret, who sailed on the ship *Hope*, one of a small fleet commanded by Captain Michael Grass, who would later head the party settling Kingston. They arrived in Quebec in August and shortly afterwards made their way to the winter encampment at Sorel. After a winter of severe hardships, Peter and his family, with William and Margaret, left for Adolphustown with the van Alstine party.

The Return of Disbanded Troops and Loyalists settled in Township 4 and mustered 6 October 1784 includes William Ruttan and his wife and it is recorded that his child had died since the last muster. William drew lot 18, concession 1 (200 acres) in Adolphustown for which he received a crown deed dated 22 February 1805. Peter lived nearby and they all survived the first year on milk from Peter's cow and four bushels of Indian corn, which they obtained by sending two men on a 200-mile trip in winter to Albany. Peter paid for this by selling his captain's commission.[24] According to Haldimand's instructions of 1784, William was entitled to 500 acres but land records show that he was granted another 650 acres in addition to the 200 mentioned above (100 acres of lot 43, concession

Bay of Quinte from Picton, 1847 (Public Archives Ontario/S15127)

1, Marysburgh, patented 17 May 1802; 100 acres of lot 41, concession 1, Marysburgh, patented 17 May 1802; 100 acres of lot 42, concession 1, Marysburgh, patented 17 May 1802; 100 acres of Bay Side concessions 10 and 34, Sophiasburgh, patented 14 November 1803; 50 acres southwest quarter of lot 23, concession 2, Camden Township, patented 22 February 1805; and 200 acres of lot 13, concession 2, southwest Green Point, Sophiasburgh, patented 22 February 1805). William and Margaret remained in Adolphustown for the rest of their days. The pioneer was buried at St Paul's Anglican Church on 10 October 1843.

William Ruttan acquired the most land among the five progenitors, receiving grants in Adolphustown, Sophiasburg, Marysburg, and Camden. There is no record of William leaving a will, but it seems that his children were able to secure property because of their status as direct descendants of a Loyalist. William's oldest son, Peter William, is said to have been the first white child born in Adolphustown. He married Fannie Roblin on 7 July 1807 and the next year received by order-in-council 200 acres in Camden Township (lot 41, concession 4) as a son of a Loyalist. Peter continued to live in Adolphustown and participated in the War of 1812, where he made his way up to the rank of colonel. For his efforts he was awarded a free grant (lot 25, concession 6) in Vespra Township, Simcoe County, in August of 1821. In 1827 he purchased lot 23, concession 1, west of Green Point in Sophiasburg from John Cartwright and lived there with his family until his death in 1861. There is reason to believe that he was also awarded a free grant in Verulam Township, Victoria County (lot 30, concession 9) by the Heir and Devisee Commission in 1847.

William's second child, Daniel, received his order-in-council as a son of a Loyalist on 25 February 1812 and was granted lot 20 in the third concession of Burgess Township of Lanark County. That same year he married Bathsheba Haight and they settled in Kingston. Next in line was Henry, who received his order-in-council on 15 March 1815. As a young man, Henry apprenticed in Kingston with John Kirby, a successful merchant. He advanced to be a partner and was entrusted to open a store near Grafton in Haldimand County. During this time Henry was credited with a number of inventions for ventilation of buildings. He saw service as a lieutenant during the War of 1812 and was wounded at Lundy's Lane. He was made a major of the militia in 1816 and in 1820 served as a member of the House of Assembly for Northumberland. In 1827 he was elected sheriff for Newcastle District and moved to Cobourg. In 1836 he was once again elected to the House of Assembly and in 1838 was appointed Speaker of the House. In 1816 Henry married Mary Jones, daughter of the prominent businessman and land speculator Elias Jones of Cobourg. During his lifetime, he managed to acquire a number of parcels of land, including lot 29, concession 1 of Cramahe Township (170 acres), lot 21, concession B of Haldimand Township (126 acres), lot 21, concession A of Haldimand

(200 acres), lot 19, concession 5 of Haldimand (200 acres), the north half of lot 35, concession 10 of Haldimand (100 acres), and lot 12, concession 7 of Haldimand (200 acres).

The fourth son, Abraham, received his order-in-council on 28 November 1821 and located in Adolphustown. Some time later Abraham drowned and no further information exists regarding his wife Mary or his son. Elizabeth, William's fifth child, received her order-in-council as a daughter of a Loyalist on 20 August 1817. She married Hugh Thompson, the editor and proprietor of the *Upper Canada Herald* of Kingston, in 1816. He died in 1834 and three years later she married Adam Townsley, an Anglican minister, and they moved to Paris, Ontario. Matthew Ruttan, William's fifth son, took over the original homestead (lot 18, concession 1 of Adolphustown) which had been given by William to all his children, who in turn transferred their share to Matthew in 1857 by way of quit claim (Peter, Henry, Jacob, Elizabeth, and Charles receiving £150, £90, discharge of all debts, £90, and £90 respectively). Matthew was granted his order-in-council (lot 28, concession 3 in Ops Township in Victoria County) on 25 June 1823. He stayed there until he sold the property in 1870 to John Stevenson for $1,000. He appears the following year in the manuscript census as a tenant residing on lot 13, concession 3 in South Fredericksburg. The Ruttan genealogy indicates that Matthew subsequently moved to Maidstone Township, Essex County, but no record of him exists in the 1881 or 1891 manuscript census.

Jacob, the sixth son, received his order-in-council on 24 March 1835 and was granted lot 26 in the seventeenth concession of Harvey Township in Peterborough County. He might have owned land in Murray Township (lot 16, concession 4) and Adelaide Township, Middlesex County (lot 9, concession 11). After his marriage to Margaret Clapp in 1841, Jacob continued to live in Adolphustown but by 1861 had moved to South Fredericksburg with his second wife Mary Ann (born McConkle) and his three children. He remained there until his death in 1867. The youngest child of William and Margaret, Charles, was born in 1808. He received his order-in-council in December of 1830 and was granted the south half of lot 1, concession 4 of Mariposa Township, Victoria County. Charles probably owned land in Ops Township (lot 27, concession 2) and on the basis of the listed birthplaces of his children, there is some reason to believe that he and his family lived in Hamilton Township, Ops Township, and Port Hope before moving to Iowa in 1864. The genealogy indicates that he died in Iowa in 1894.

INTER-GENERATIONAL MIGRATION PATTERNS

Migration theory suggests that the migration fields of successive generations during the nineteenth century became much wider and more random as mobility aspirations and opportunities increased, and the association with families, friends and familiar institutions weakened. The cumulative patterns of migration and persistence of the five family groups revealed in the maps included at the end of this chapter illustrate such an expansion but analysis may reveal that such patterns were anything but haphazard.

Persistence in the Quinte Region

The Mordens remained most strongly attached to the Quinte region followed by the Hudgins, Denyeses, Laughlins, and Ruttans. Proximity to family appears to have played a major role in determining persistence within the region. All three sons of Martin Denyes settled close to each other in Thurlow Township, breaking off ties with their father's homestead in order to acquire less expensive land in Hastings County. Thurlow would constitute the nucleus for the Denyes clan for the next two generations, with almost 25 percent of the second generation and over 10 percent of the third generation living in that township. Almost 44 percent of the second generation and 22 percent of the third generation remained within the Quinte region, excluding those who stayed in their parents' home for the rest of their lives.

The Mordens, a less peripatetic group than the Denyeses, displayed a much stronger attachment to the Quinte region over time. The four sons of Joseph (no information exists for his only daughter and so she is not considered in the analysis) settled in Sophiasburg and Ameliasburg townships, although the youngest would eventually disappear without a trace. Like the Denyes brothers who all settled within six miles of each other, the Morden boys lived close to each other. Prince Edward County, known affectionately as "the Island" among locals, would form the dominant core for this family for the rest of the century. Almost 66 percent of the second-generation Mordens, excluding those who lived at home for the rest of their lives, continued to live in the Quinte region.

Even more striking is the attachment to the Quinte region displayed by the third generation of the family, given the loss of population in the region and the changes occurring in agriculture. Examination of the published censuses reveals that Prince Edward County, the home county of many of the third-generation Mordens, lost 10.2 percent of its population during the 1881–91 period and a further 5.4 percent in the following decade. At the same time that the county was losing population, there was a substantial proportional increase in the number of small holdings. Average farm size decreased 29.9 percent during the 1880s alone, from 87 acres to 61 acres. The numbers of landowners and tenants were rising, from 2,348 landowners in 1881 to 3,104 in 1891, an increase of 32.2 percent, and from 394 tenants in 1881 to 763 in 1891, an increase of 93.7

percent.[25] Over 45 percent of the third-generation Mordens, again excluding those who never left their parents' homes, persisted within the region.

The Laughlins displayed mobility patterns more similar to the Denyeses
than the Mordens, although the trend to leave the Quinte region was
established as early as the first generation. One son remained in
Ernestown Township while the other two sons lived in Sheffield and Camden townships, also in Lennox and Addington County. One of Alexander
Laughlin's two daughters lived in Fredericksburg Township while the
other moved with her husband to Loughboro Township in Frontenac
County. Almost 26 percent of the second generation and 14 percent of the
third generation remained in Ernestown. Yet despite this attachment to
the pioneer homestead and to each other, the evidence clearly reveals a
widening of the kin network over time.

Eight of William Hudgins's ten children whose residences are known
stayed in the Quinte region, four remaining in South Marysburg. Of those
second-generation Hudgins whose locations are identified, almost 46 percent continued to live in the Quinte region, excluding those who never left
their parents' homes. Hudgins families continued to live in South Marysburg, Richmond, and Thurlow townships but some small movement into
the region's urban centres started to take place. Third-generation Hudgins
were more attached to the Quinte region than were the Laughlins and
Denyeses, although not as much as the Mordens.

Because of opportunities to acquire land and practise professions elsewhere, first-generation Ruttans displayed a greater propensity to leave the
Quinte region than the corresponding generations of the other family
groups. Only two of six sons and one daughter of William who left home
remained in the region. Of the second-generation Ruttans whose residential locations are known, only 16.7 percent last lived in the Quinte region,
excluding those who never left home. Those who remained scattered
throughout the region, with a handful moving to local urban centres. Only
10 percent of the third generation persisted in the region, again excluding those who never left home.

Composition of the Migrant Flow   Males tended to be the more frequent
movers than females for all the families with the exception of the Hudgins
(Table 19). For the most part, females were influenced by migration decisions made by parents or husbands. Only a handful of males were chronic
movers. Child-bearing and ordinal birth position (Table 20) did not seem
to have any bearing on the decision to move.

Following the example of Taylor, who tests the hypothesis of cumulative
mobility or what can be called the mobility legacy, second-generation and
third generation migration rates by parental migration frequency are
included in Table 21.[26] Chronic movers were rare in all families and thus
do not merit much attention. The correspondence of second-generation

Table 19   Generation Migration Rates by Sex: Quinte Families (%)[1]

Migration rates	DENYES		MORDEN		LAUGHLIN		HUDGINS		RUTTAN	
	Male	Female	Male	Female	Male	Female	Male	Female	Male	Female
1ST GENERATION										
0-1 (stayers)	33.3	100	100	0	33.3	100	0	0	71.4	0
2-5 (movers)	66.7	0	0	0	66.7	0	100	100	28.6	100
6+ (chronic movers)	0	0	0	0	0	0	0	0	0	0
2ND GENERATION										
0-1 (stayers)	46.7	50.0	63.2	87.5	58.8	68.8	96.0	77.8	31.6	72.7
2-5 (movers)	53.7	50.0	36.8	12.5	35.3	31.2	4.0	22.2	63.2	27.3
6+ (chronic movers)	0	0	0	0	5.9	0	0	0	5.2	0
3RD GENERATION										
0-1 (stayers)	57.4	54.7	63.8	76.9	61.0	59.3	75.0	73.7	73.2	92.3
2-5 (movers)	41.0	43.4	34.8	21.5	39.0	40.7	25.0	24.6	24.4	7.7
6+ (chronic movers)	1.6	1.9	1.4	1.6	0	0	0	1.8	2.4	0

Source: See table 18.

[1] Descendants living past the age of 20 and whose movements are known, not including place of retirement.

and third-generation grouped migration rates with parental migration frequency distribution shows that the stayers tended to follow the parental example more than the movers. Yet there is significant variation among the families. The Denyeses displayed the greatest tendency for children to mirror their parents' mobility habits, but the pattern among the other family groups is inconsistent. With the exception of the second-generation Mordens and Laughlins, the stayers proportionately decrease as their parents' migration rate increases. And again with the exception of the second generation Mordens and Laughlins, the movers proportionately increase as their parents' frequency of mobility rises. Yet these statistics alone do not provide sufficient evidence of any legacy of mobility or, for that fact, cumulative inertia.

Distance and Direction of Migration

Among the first-generation migrants, movement was predominantly rural-rural, with the exception of the Ruttans (Table 22). William Ruttan's children showed a greater tendency to leave the Quinte region and locate in urban centres than the other families. Subsequent generations of all families became more urban-oriented with time; this was more so for those emigrating to the United States and was most evident for the Ruttans.

The Morden lineage displayed the greatest tendency to relocate in rural areas in Canada while the other families fit somewhere between the Ruttans and the Mordens. Third-generation Laughlins were more likely than their counterparts in other families to move from urban to rural areas,

Table 20 Relationship between Father's Last Residence and Son's Last Residence, by Generation and Birth Order: Quinte Families[1]

Residential relationship between father and sons	DENYES				MORDEN				LAUGHLIN				HUDGINS				RUTTAN			
	First	Middle	Last	Total	First	Middle	Last	Total	First	Middle	Last	Total	First	Middle	Last	Total	First	Middle	Last	Total
PROGENITOR - FIRST GENERATION																				
within town/township	0	0	0	0		Not apply			0	33.3	0	33.3	11.1	33.3	0	44.4	0	14.3	0	14.3
outside town/township, but within county	0	0	0	0		Not apply			0	0	33.3	33.3	0	0	0	0	0	14.3	0	14.3
in adjacent counties	33.3	33.3	33.3	33.3		Not apply			0	0	0	0	0	22.2	11.1	33.3	14.3	14.3	0.0	28.6
elsewhere	0	0	0	0		Not apply			33.3	0	0	33.3	0	22.2	0	22.2	0	28.6	14.3	42.9
FIRST-SECOND GENERATION																				
within town/township	14.3	21.4	0	35.7	0	23.5	0	23.5	23.7	15.3	7.6	46.6	14.3	20.0	11.4	45.7	10.5	10.5	5.3	26.3
outside town/township, but within county	0	0	7.1	7.1	11.8	17.6	5.9	35.3	0	23.7	0	23.7	11.4	0	5.7	17.1	0	10.5	5.3	15.8
in adjacent counties	0	0	0	0	5.9	7.6	5.9	29.4	0	0	0	0	0	0	0	0	5.3	5.3	5.3	15.9
elsewhere	7.1	35.7	14.3	57.1	0	11.8	0	11.8	33.3	0	0	33.3	22.9	5.7	8.6	37.2	15.8	15.8	10.8	42.1

Table 20 (continued)

Residential relationship between father and sons	DENYES				MORDEN				LAUGHLIN				HUDGINS				RUTTAN			
	First	Middle	Last	Total	First	Middle	Last	Total	First	Middle	Last	Total	First	Middle	Last	Total	First	Middle	Last	Total
SECOND-THIRD GENERATION																				
within town/township	22.6	16.1	6.5	45.2	5.2	27.6	13.8	46.6	19.3	19.3	12.9	51.5	22.6	16.1	6.5	45.2	10.5	10.5	7.9	28.9
outside town / township, but within county	0	0	0	0	3.4	3.4	0	6.8	0	0	0	0	0	0	0	0	7.9	2.6	5.3	15.8
in adjacent counties	0	3.2	3.2	6.4	1.7	6.9	0	8.6	0	0	9.7	9.7	0	3.2	3.2	6.4	5.3	5.3	0	10.6
elsewhere	19.4	16.1	12.9	48.4	10.3	19.0	8.6	37.9	16.2	16.2	6.4	38.8	19.4	16.1	12.9	48.4	15.8	15.8	13.2	44.8

Source: See table 18

[1] Includes those who survived past the age of 20.

Table 21 Generation Migration Rates by Parental Migration Frequency: Quinte Families (%)[1]

1st Generation Migration Rates

2nd Generation Migration Rates	DENYES			MORDEN			LAUGHLIN			HUDGINS			RUTTAN		
	0 to 1	2 to 5	6+	0 to 1	2 to 5	6+	0 to 1	2 to 5	6+	0 to 1	2 to 5	6+	0 to 1	2 to 5	6+
0-1 (stayers)	70.0	38.5	0	57.1	81.8	0	55.6	69.2	0	100	70.0	0	52.4	40.0	0
2-5 (movers)	30.0	61.5	0	42.9	18.2	0	38.9	30.8	0	0	30.0	0	47.6	60.0	0
6+ (chronic movers)	0	0	0	0	0	0	5.5	0	0	0	0	0	0	0	0
N=	10	26	0	14	11	0	18	13	0	21	20	0	21	10	0

2nd Generation Migration Rates

3rd Generation Migration Rates	DENYES			MORDEN			LAUGHLIN			HUDGINS			RUTTAN		
	0 to 1	2 to 5	6+	0 to 1	2 to 5	6+	0 to 1	2 to 5	6+	0 to 1	2 to 5	6+	0 to 1	2 to 5	6+
0-1 (stayers)	73.1	32.9	0	78.6	48.2	0	64.4	56.4	33.3	74.7	47.4	0	88.9	59.1	0
2-5 (movers)	26.9	64.4	0	20	50	0	34.6	43.7	66.6	24.2	52.6	0	7.4	38.6	0
6+ (chronic movers)	0	2.7	0	1.4	1.8	0	0.9	0	0	1.1	0	0	3.7	2.3	0
N=	41	73	0	70	56	0	107	55	6	91	19	0	27	44	0

Source: See table 18.

[1] Descendants living past the age of 20 and whose movements are known, not including place of retirement.

Table 22 Migration Directions by Generation: Quinte Families[1]

Place of Birth	Canadian Destinations (%)					American Destinations (%)				
	DENYES Rural/Urban	MORDEN Rural/Urban	LAUGHLIN Rural/Urban	HUDGINS Rural/Urban	RUTTAN Rural/Urban	DENYES Rural/Urban	MORDEN Rural/Urban	LAUGHLIN Rural/Urban	HUDGINS Rural/Urban	RUTTAN Rural/Urban
1st Generation										
Rural	100/0	100/0	100/0	100/0	57.1/42.9	0/0	0/0	0/0	0/0	100/0
Urban	0/0	0/0	0/0	0/0	0/0	0/0	0/0	0/0	0/0	0/0
2nd Generation										
Rural	65.2/34.8	87.5/12.5	80.8/19.2	85.7/14.3	85.7/14.3	33.3/66.7	100/0	57.1/42.9	100/0	0/100
Urban	0/0	0/0	0/0	0/0	0/100	0/0	0/0	0/0	0/0	40.0/60.0
3rd Generation										
Rural	65.5/34.5	80.8/19.2	77.1/22.9	69.6/30.4	45.5/54.5	36.4/63.6	8.3/91.7	45.7/54.3	61.5/39.5	28.6/71.4
Urban	9.1/90.9	11.1/88.9	30.8/69.2	0/100	0/100	23.1/76.9	0/100	100/0	20.0/80.0	0/100

Source: See table 18.

[1] General direction of movement over the course of a lifetime.

Table 23   Generational Mobility by Type of Move over a Lifetime[a]: Quinte Families[b]

Generation	% Local (1)[c]	% Intra-Prov/ State (2)	% Inter-Prov/ State (3)	% (1) + (2)	% (1) + (3)	% (2) + (3)	% Not Move[d]	% Unknown [e]
DENYES								
First	75.0	0	0	0	0	0	0	25
Second	46.0	13.5	16.2	8.1	2.7	2.7	10.8	0
Third	26.6	16.4	21.9	3.9	3.9	7.8	10.2	9.3
Males								
First	100	0	0	0	0	0	0	0
Second	40.0	13.3	20.0	6.7	0	6.7	13.3	0
Third	17.7	22.6	27.4	4.8	3.2	3.2	14.5	6.5
Females								
First	0	0	0	0	0	0	0	100
Second	50.0	13.6	13.6	9.1	4.6	0	9.1	0
Third	34.9	10.6	16.7	3.0	4.6	12.2	6.1	12.1
MORDEN								
First	0	0	0	0	75.0	0	0	25
Second	65.5	6.9	0	3.5	6.9	0	13.8	3.5
Third	24.3	5.6	5.6	6.3	1.4	2.8	36.8	17.4
Males								
First	0	0	0	0	100	0	0	0
Second	65.0	10.0	0	5.0	5.0	0	15.0	0
Third	18.1	6.9	8.3	8.3	1.4	4.2	40.3	12.5
Females								
First	0	0	0	0	0	0	0	0
Second	66.7	0	0	0	11.1	0	11.1	11.1
Third	30.6	4.2	2.8	4.2	1.4	1.4	33.3	22.2
LAUGHLIN								
First	20.0	40.0	40.0	0	0	0	0	0
Second	5.9	17.6	20.6	5.9	0	2.9	47.1	0
Third	9.5	27.2	23.1	0.6	6.5	4.1	28.4	0
Males								
First	0	33.3	66.7	0	0	0	0	0
Second	5.9	23.5	23.5	5.9	0	0	41.2	0
Third	9.5	27.4	27.4	0	4.8	3.6	28.4	0
Females								
First	50.0	50.0	0	0	0	0	0	0
Second	5.9	11.8	17.6	5.9	0	5.9	52.9	0
Third	14.0	26.7	19.8	2.3	8.1	4.7	24.4	0

although they too were predominantly urban in their orientation. Interestingly, those third-generation Mordens born in rural areas and either moving to or moving within the United States were the most likely to settle in urban areas, a trend opposite that of their Canadian relatives.

Among the Denyeses, migration distance increased with each successive generation with the third generation most likely to move between

Table 23 (continued)

Generation	% Local (1)[c]	% Intra-Prov/ State (2)	% Inter-Prov/ State (3)	% (1) + (2)	% (1) + (3)	% (2) + (3)	% Not Move[d]	% Unknown [e]
HUDGINS								
First	45.5	9.1	0	0	0	0	36.4	9.1
Second	16.3	7.0	4.7	0	0	0	65.1	7.0
Third	17.4	7.8	17.4	1.7	5.2	2.6	34.8	13.0
Males								
First	40.0	10.0	0	0	0	0	40.0	10.0
Second	17.4	0	4.3	0	0	0	78.3	0
Third	15.4	11.5	13.5	1.9	7.7	0	40.4	9.6
Females								
First	100	0	0	0	0	0	0	0
Second	15.0	15.0	5.0	0	0	0	50.0	15.0
Third	19.0	4.8	20.6	1.6	3.2	4.8	30.2	15.9
RUTTAN								
First	25.0	50.0	0	0	0	12.5	12.5	0
Second	26.3	13.2	15.8	7.9	0	5.3	10.5	21.1
Third	8.4	15.3	21.4	1.5	1.5	0	10.7	41.2
Males								
First	28.6	42.9	0	0	0	14.3	14.3	0
Second	31.6	15.8	26.3	10.5	0	5.3	5.3	5.3
Third	9.7	19.4	25.0	2.8	2.8	0	0	34.7
Females								
First	0	100	0	0	0	0	0	0
Second	21.1	10.5	5.3	5.3	0	5.3	15.8	36.8
Third	6.9	10.3	15.5	0	0	0	17.2	50.0

Source: See table 18.

[a] Type of move descendant tended to make over the course of his/her lifetime.
[b] Includes descendants who lived past the age of 20.
[c] In county of birth, but outside township or urban centre of birth or in the case of those born in the Quinte region, outside of township or urban centre of birth within the region.
[d] Continue to reside in township or urban centre of birth.
[e] While exact locations may not be specified, the genealogies often indicate general direction of movement.

provinces and states (Table 23). Second-generation males were more inclined towards an inter-state or inter-province move than their female counterparts, but this was not the case for the third generation. Third-generation males were far more likely than females to move within the state or province of birth, while females were more disposed towards local movement.

The Mordens were far less inclined to move long distances, adhering for the most part to the areas in which they were born. Second-generation and third-generation males were slightly more likely to move greater distances than their female counterparts. The Laughlin families more closely mirrored the Denyes than the Mordens, although they displayed a greater tendency to move outside their township or urban centre of birth. Third-generation Laughlin females were less likely to locate within their township of birth or move between states and provinces than Laughlin males and more prone to move locally and within their state or province of birth.

The Hudgins displayed an unusual pattern. They ranked first among the second generation and second to the Mordens among the third generation in terms of their tendency to remain in their township or urban centre of birth, and yet they were the last among both generations in terms of moving within the local county or region. A notable percentage of third-generation males and females moved between provinces and states. Significant gaps in geographical information for the Ruttans muddle any interpretation, but enough evidence exists to suggest that the Ruttan males were more willing to travel greater distances to pursue opportunities.

Movement Elsewhere in Ontario

The Laughlins were by far the most likely to settle elsewhere in Ontario, followed by the Ruttans. Significantly less committed to living elsewhere in the province were the Denyeses, Hudgins, and Mordens. A significant number of Laughlins moved to northern townships in Lennox and Addington and Frontenac counties, showing evidence of kin connections, while others were dispersed throughout the rest of the province (Toronto, southwestern Ontario, Bruce, and Grey counties). The majority of second-generation Ruttans whose residences are known dispersed throughout the province, with one branch establishing itself in Cobourg and vicinity, and others locating in Toronto and Kingston. From the Quinte region, Toronto, Kingston, and Cobourg, Ruttans moved throughout the rest of the province, extending their migration fields to the southwestern and northwestern parts of Ontario.

Only a small number of second-generation Denyeses settled elsewhere in Ontario, locating in a number of areas. Yet they had a relatively large number of children who remained in the province, settling primarily in southwestern Ontario. Some of the second-generation Mordens did eventually leave the Quinte region and move elsewhere in Ontario, particularly Bruce and Grey counties, where newly opened land was selling cheaply. Third-generation Mordens eventually widened the migration fields to include the Shield townships, Manitoulin Island, and Northumberland County as well as Bruce and Grey counties. Settlement of second-generation Hudgins throughout the rest of Ontario was small and scattered, with the exception of a minor concentration in King Township, York County. From the Quinte region, York and Simcoe counties, third-generation Hudgins moved to other parts of Ontario, including Toronto and Collingwood.

The detailed life histories of the Denyeses and Mordens include several examples of transfers of aid among kin which, along with the natural desire to associate with family, explain patterns of locational clustering throughout the province.

Migration to the Prairies

Movement outside the province but still within the country was directed primarily towards the prairies, although some movement into Quebec did take place among a small number of third-generation migrants, the most notable being a few of the Ruttan males who practised their professions in Canada's largest city of the period, Montreal. It was also the Ruttans who showed the greatest inclination to move to the prairies, again with most of this group settling in Winnipeg, the largest city in the region, and practising professions or operating businesses. Next to the Ruttans, the Laughlins were most likely to move west but, unlike the former, they were involved for the most part in farming in Manitoba and Saskatchewan. But those who moved to the prairies were few in number. A far greater number took advantage of opportunities south of the border than in the Canadian west. This reflects in part the relatively late date of settlement expansion in this part of Canada, due in part to the delays in construction of a transcontinental railway, and the fact that many of the third-generation members of the chosen families had already reached adulthood and decided on location before the settlement boom in western Canada.

Emigration to the United States

The Denyeses showed the greatest propensity to move to the United States, followed by the Laughlins and then distantly by the Ruttans, Hudgins, and Mordens. Only two of the second-generation Denyeses initially left Canada for the United States, one taking up residence in New York State and the other in Michigan, where he was soon joined by five others who had previously lived in Ontario outside the Quinte region. This state became an important secondary nucleus of settlement for this family. Others made their way to North Dakota, Kansas, and California. The migration network was further extended as American-resident Denyeses propagated and Quinte-born migrants joined their relatives in Michigan and New York State. In addition, a number of Denyeses moved directly to the interior of the United States to take advantage of new agricultural and commercial opportunities.

The small group of six second-generation Denyeses who settled in various parts of Michigan expanded their numbers and branched into other parts of the state. From rural localities such as Caro and Greenbush, third-generation Denyeses moved into Detroit, Owosso, Saginaw and other growing cities, responding in part to increasing opportunities and influenced by the presence of kin in these same communities. Indeed, Michigan became a jumping-off point for the further expansion of the kin network west into the midwest and particularly into Missouri. Many of the branch of the family initially settling in that state subsequently left for Kansas and other states farther west. The attraction of expanding industrial centres in nearby New York State drew five Quinte-born Denyes families and created a new geographical branch of the family tree.

The movement of three second-generation Laughlins into nearby New York State was advanced by their children's moves into other parts of the state and into the midwest, particularly Michigan. Third-generation Laughlins extended the migration network as more and more Quinte- and Ontario-born migrants joined their relatives in New York, Michigan, Indiana, and other American states. Charles Stuart Ruttan, the youngest son of William, settled in Iowa. His children and a few of their Ontario-born cousins settled in New York State, Iowa, Kansas, and California. The third-generation American-based Ruttans continued to expand in New York State and throughout the midwest and the Great Plains states.

Only two second-generation Hudgins emigrated to the United States, both locating in New York State. A number of those born in New York continued to live there, while a handful eventually made their way to California and Washington. From Ontario, a number of third-generation Hudgins emigrated to Minnesota. Only one of the second generation moved to the United States, settling in New York State. Eventually six third-generation Mordens from Canada would settle in Michigan and others would scatter throughout the United States.

What do these patterns reflect? I think they say something about the flexibility of the family. Kinship relations survived the process of modernization, adapting to change through both mobility and persistence strategies. The nineteenth-century family did not operate in a void; it was not static, but dynamic, adapting to social and institutional transformation. This adaptation process was directed by many factors, including transfer of property, the sharing of residence, and the giving of various forms of aid such as care for the elderly, gifts or loans of money, inheritance of real estate and capital, the provision of employment, and the brokering of real estate. Yet tensions between individual and family interests, the latter often determined by the patriarch, meant that some members separated from their families in order to pursue their self-interests. The family can be also be seen as a dynamic collection of individual interests where decisions that affected the family unit as a whole are made either by individuals or the collective. In this sense, it is possible to infer family strategy from the behaviour of individuals and so, while the concept of family strategy is empirically convenient, it is theoretically ineffective.

PROPERTY TRANSFER AND MOBILITY

Providing for their children is a goal that most parents share; this was certainly true for the five Quinte families. For much of the nineteenth century, land was viewed as the most valuable legacy that could be transferred between generations. However, the vast majority of male descendants of the Quinte families did not inherit, receive, or buy land from their parents. First-generation males and females were awarded property because they were children of Loyalists and this may have discouraged any type of property transfer strategy. Yet differences do exist among the families. The majority of first-generation and second-generation male Denyeses acquired land from their fathers in one form or another, while an overwhelming majority of the third generation did not partake in any type of property transfer with their parent (Table 24 and Figure 1).[27] In total, 30.6 percent of the patrilineal Denyes males inherited, received, or purchased land from their parents. Only the first-generation Laughlin males demonstrated similar transfer figures, although Alexander Laughlin transmitted property through gift and sale rather than through inheritance, as was the case for Martin Denyes (Figure 2). Yet unlike the Denyeses, second-generation and third-generation Laughlin males, corresponding to the majority of all three generations from the other families, did not become involved in property transfer with their fathers. Only 23.5 percent, 17 percent, 10.5 percent, and 5.3 percent of the patrilineal Morden, Laughlin, Hudgins, and Ruttan males respectively inherited, received, or purchased land from their parents. Yet transmitted shares among the small number of Laughlins may have played a role in ensuring persistence, as seven out of eight of the Laughlin first-generation, second-generation, and third-generation males who received, inherited, or purchased property remained in the same township as their parents.

Yet while the Denyeses exhibited the greatest involvement in property transfer with their parents, they were among the most mobile of the five family groups and showed less attachment to the Quinte region than the Mordens and the Hudgins. Mobility, however, did not necessarily result in the disruption of the family network, as many relocated to where they had some family connection. The amount of land transferred between parent and child may explain the differences among the families. Following this assumption, we would expect larger amounts of property to be transferred among the Mordens and, thus, ensure their greater persistence. Yet over 82 percent of the properties transferred among the Mordens were less than 100 acres in size as compared to 58 percent for the Denyeses. Thus, size of property transferred between father and son would not seem to be a factor in explaining the greater persistence among the Mordens.

However, what is crucial is the fact that over 25 percent of the second-generation Morden males were involved in land transfers with their male

Table 24   Inter-generational Property Transmission within Ontario: Quinte Familes[1]

	Type of Transfer							
	Inheritance		Gift		Sale		No Transfer	
Generational Transfer [2]	No.	%	No.	%	No.	%	No.	%
a) DENYES								
Progenitor - first generation	2	66.7	0	0	0	0	1	33.3
first generation - second generation	6	40.0	1	6.7	1	6.7	7	46.7
second generation - third generation	1	3.2	0	0	4	12.9	26	83.9
b) MORDEN								
Progenitor - first generation	0	0	0	0	0	0	4	100
first generation - second generation	0	0	0	0	4	22.2	14	77.8
second generation - third generation	3	4.8	1	1.6	12	19.0	47	74.6
c) LAUGHLIN								
Progenitor - first generation	0	0	1	33.3	1	33.3	1	33.3
first generation - second generation	2	15.4	1	7.7	0	0	10	76.9
second generation - third generation	0	0	1	3.3	2	6.6	28	90.1
d) HUDGINS								
Progenitor - first generation	0	0	0	0	0	0	10	100
first generation - second generation	1	5.6	1	5.6	2	11.1	14	77.8
second generation - third generation	1	3.4	1	3.4	0	0	27	93.1
e) RUTTAN								
Progenitor - first generation	0	0	1	14.3	0	0	6	85.7
first generation - second generation	0	0	0	0	2	10.0	18	90.0
second generation - third generation	0	0	0	0	0	0	27	100

Source: See table 18.
[1] Patrilineal descent.
[2] Transfers between father and surviving sons.
Property information is obtained from the Abstract Index to Deeds, the Registrar of Deeds and Probate
Records all housed in the Public Archives of Ontario

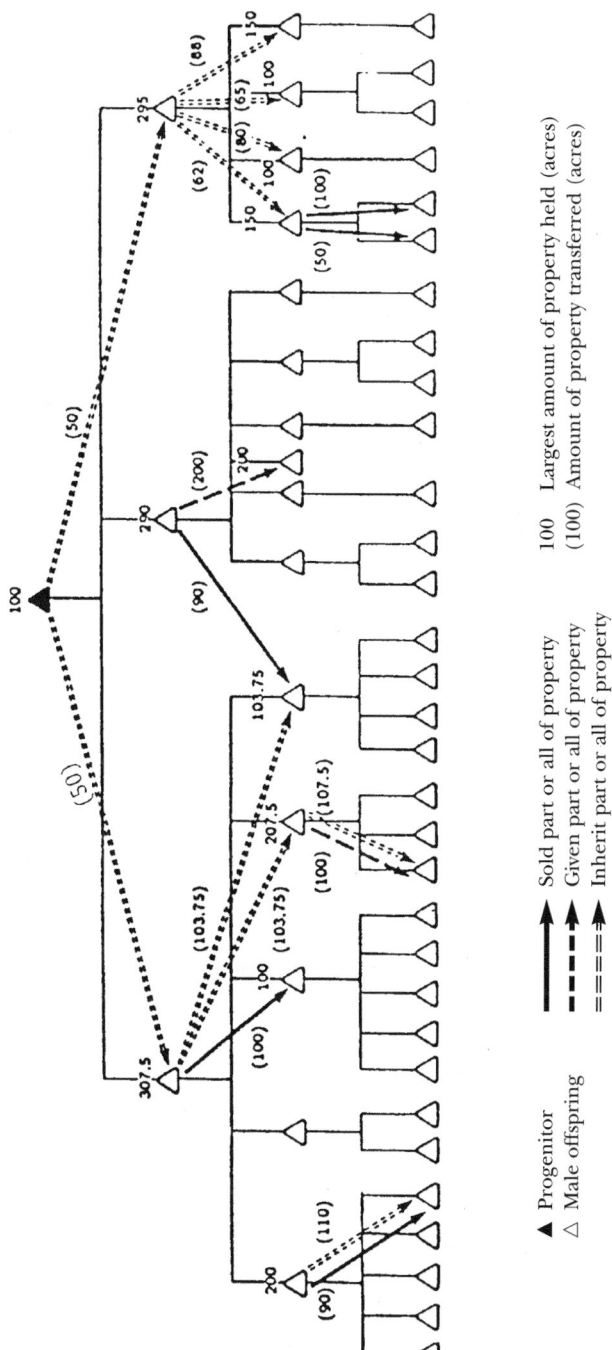

Figure 1: Patrilineal Property Transfer: Denyes Males

▲ Progenitor
△ Male offspring

→ Sold part or all of property
⇢ Given part or all of property
⇒ Inherit part or all of property

100 Largest amount of property held (acres)
(100) Amount of property transferred (acres)

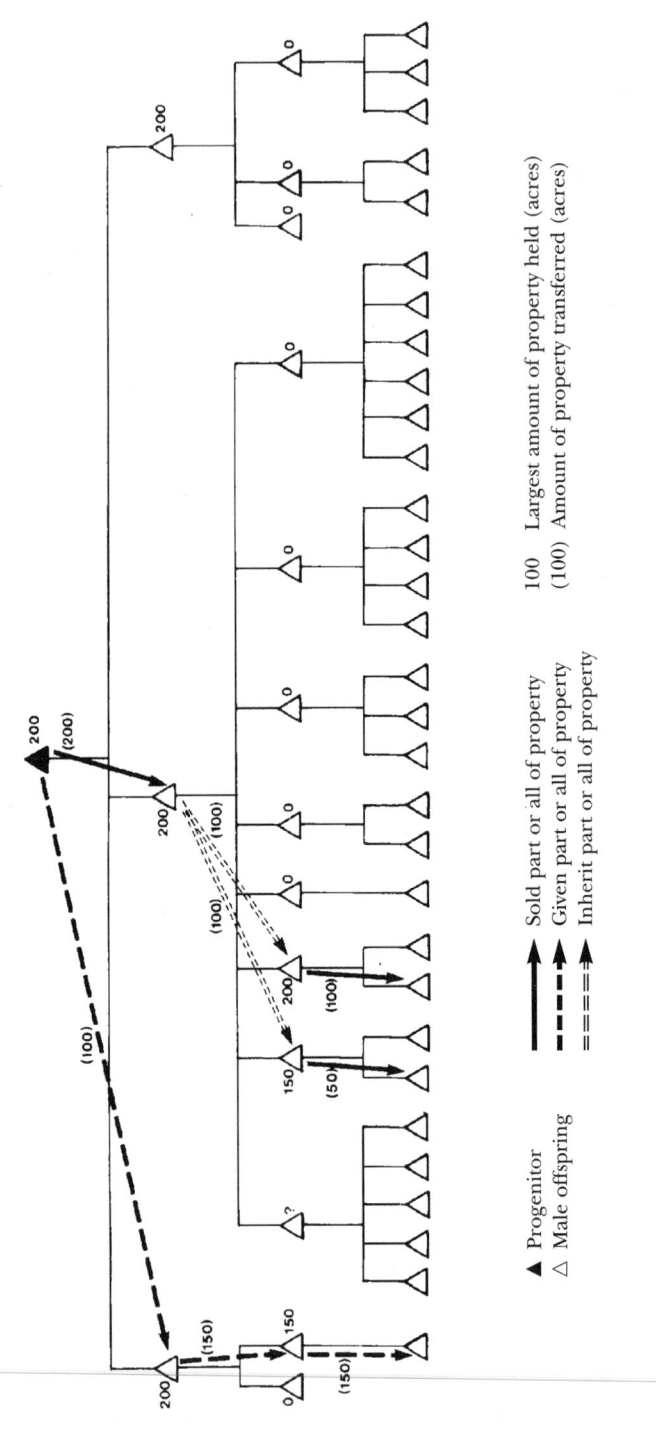

Figure 2: Patrilineal Property Transfer: Laughlin Family

▲ Progenitor
△ Male offspring

━━► Sold part or all of property
▄▄▄► Given part or all of property
===► Inherit part or all of property

100 Largest amount of property held (acres)
(100) Amount of property transferred (acres)

offspring as opposed to only 16.1 percent for their Denyes counterparts (Figure 3). This is attributed in part to the legacy of land entitlement experienced by the Mordens. While John Denyes was bestowed 200 acres as a son of a Loyalist, no mention is made in the records of his two younger brothers receiving similar grants. In contrast, James and Richard Morden received grants of 342 and 432 acres both as Loyalists and sons of a Loyalist. For some unknown reason their brother John, who was likely too young to have participated in the conflict, was not granted any land. Yet all the Morden second-generation descendants received property as children of Loyalists, even those of John, while none of the Denyes second generation were accorded the same privileges.

There were other types of kinship assistance besides the transfer of real estate which may have played a role in ensuring persistence. Kinship served many functions, such as providing aid, arranging employment, and furnishing accommodation, particularly during transitions in a relative's life-course. An examination of the probate records in the Ontario Archives revealed thirteen wills for the Morden families and seven wills for the Denyeses, the two family groups which displayed the greatest degree of inter-generational property transmission. In total, the Denyes wills included fifty-three transfers, while the Morden wills included eighty-one transfers. Besides inheritance of property, included in these documents were gifts of money, gifts of personal property, provision for education costs, and assignment of power to kin to dispose of property. Ten of the transfers included in the Denyes wills were between husbands and wives; of this number, four involved personal goods, two involved gifts of money, two involved inheritance of land and two included transfer of the right to dispose of property. Twenty of the transfers were between fathers and sons with eight involving transfer of property, seven involving inheritance of money, three including the right to dispose of property, one involving the provision of funds for education, and another involving the transfer of personal property. Fourteen of the transfers were between father and daughter; of this number, nine pertained to gifts of personal goods and five involved gifts of money. Only one of the Denyes transfers was between husband and wife and this related to the inheritance of property. Five of the transfers were between mother and daughter and all of these involved gifts of money. Finally, three of the Denyes transfers included those between grandmother and grandchildren and all of these involved gifts of money.

Ten of the Morden transfers were between husband and wife and four involved personal goods, four related to inheritance of property, and two involved transfer of power to dispose of land. Sixteen of the transfers were between fathers and sons; of this number, seven involved inheritance of land, four related to gifts of personal property, three involved money, and two included the power to dispose of property. Twenty-four of the Morden

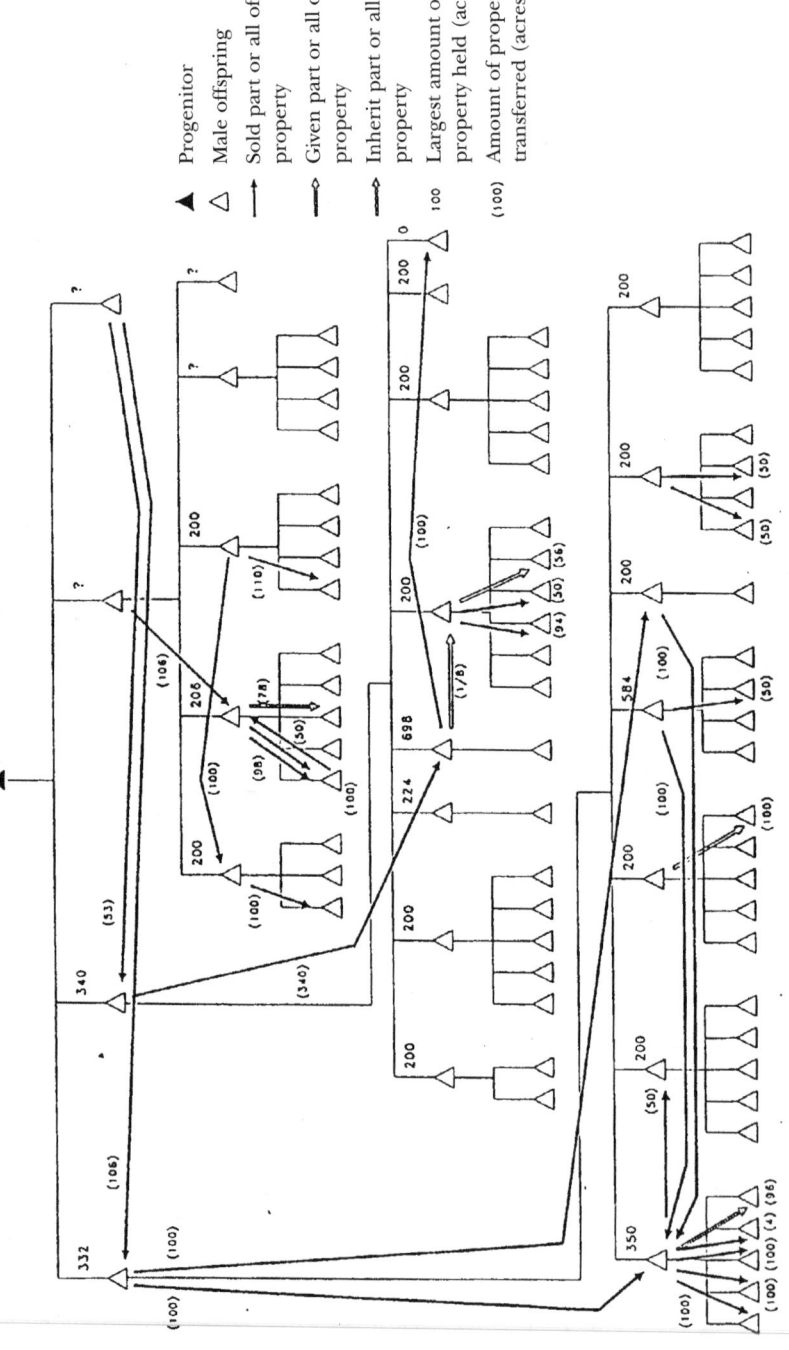

Figure 3: Patrilineal Property Transfer: Morden Family

Legend:

◀ Progenitor

◁ Male offspring

→ Sold part or all of property

⇒ Given part or all of property

⇔ Inherit part or all of property

100 Largest amount of property held (acres)

(100) Amount of property transferred (acres)

Table 25   Percent Buying and Selling Land by Second Generation Patrilineal Males: Quinte Families (%)

Kin Position	DENYES		MORDEN		LAUGHLIN		HUDGINS		RUTTAN	
	Sold	Bought	Sold	Bought	Sold	Bought	Sold	Bought	Sold	Bought
Parent	0	33.3	0	28.6	0	0	50.0	0	0	50.0
Sibling	20.0	33.3	36.8	50.0	0	0	50.0	16.7	100	50.0
Children	80.0	0	63.2	7.1	100	0	0	50.0	0	0
Grandparent	0	0	0	0	0	0	0	0	0	0
Aunt, Uncle	0	33.3	0	0	0	0	0	0	0	0
Niece, Nephew	0	0	0	0	0	0	0	0	0	0
Cousin	0	0	0	0	0	0	0	0	0	0
In-law	0	0	0	14.3	0	0	0	33.3	0	0
Grandchild	0	0	0	0	0	0	0	0	0	0
N=	5	3	19	14	2	0	2	6	1	2

Source: See table 18

transfers were between fathers and daughters; eleven involved personal goods, nine involved money, and four related to land. Eleven of the Morden transfers were between grandfather and grandchildren; six related to money, three involved personal goods, and two involved the provision of education costs. Eight of the transfers were between brother and brother; three related to money, another three involved the power to dispose of property, and two concerned the transfer of land. Five of the transfers were between brother and sister; three involved money and two pertained to land. Four of the transfers were between brother-in-law and sister-in-law; two related to money and one involved land. Three of the transfers were evenly split between brothers-in-law, uncle and niece, and son and mother, and they all involved the transfer of money.

Type and proportions of transfer associated with wills were almost identical for both families, but they differed in terms of the incidence of transfer among kin. Transfers among fathers and sons were more common among the Denyeses than the Mordens, but the latter showed a wider diversity of transfer of aid among kin. This pattern is further supported by the evidence in Table 25 which shows that the second-generation Mordens were more likely to buy and sell property from relatives than the other families, who were more involved in dealings with non-kin.

Why did the Mordens display a notable propensity to transfer real and personal property beyond the nuclear family, and did this play a role in their greater attachment to the Quinte region? The evidence presented from the analysis of wills and property records suggests that the Mordens experienced closer associations with members of their extended family, while the Denyeses provided as well as they could for their nuclear families. Analysis of the property records also shows that the Denyeses in the

Quinte region were over two hundred times more likely to sell parcels of land than the Mordens and it was the most active land dealers who were more likely to be geographically mobile. This was also true of the other families. Yet none of the Mordens or any of the other family groups, with the exception of a handful of the Ruttans, belonged to the landed upper class with vast amounts of property which they could place on the market. Instead, many of the families chose to play the great Upper Canadian land game, buying and selling land in order to either improve their farming effort or make enough capital to allow them to move on. The Mordens were more conservative in their land dealings and their mobility behaviour than the Denyeses, but they could afford to be given their cumulative legacy of property acquisition. This is especially noticeable by the time of the third generation when land was still being transferred between Morden parents and children to a significant degree and when many of the Morden patrilineal males were still farming in the Quinte region.

For all families, the good fortunes of the initial progenitors and their children were not always shared by their descendants, as land in the Quinte region became scarcer and more expensive. Tenancy was more common in the older settled areas of Canada West by the late 1850s. In fact, as many as 20 to 25 percent of the farms between Kingston and Napanee during this period were operated by tenants.[28] There was a slightly greater degree of tenancy among the designated families in the second generation, but the majority bypassed the agricultural ladder of tenancy to purchase property either within the region or elsewhere. Over time, families were less able to provide for their children by passing on property. One might argue that this in effect reduced the importance of property transmission as a prop supporting the maintenance of kinship ties; yet significant attachment to the home region and to the family continued in the face of change. And even among those who were mobile, notable kin clustering occurred, a testament to the continuing importance of the kinship network.

The reconstruction of the property and mobility histories of three generations of the Denyes and Morden patrilineal lines on a family-by-family basis (see note 17, chapter 4) reveals a tremendous range of experiences, an array that is complex and extremely difficult to understand, especially given the uneven quality of geographical and property data, missing information on income, and the non-existence of personal reflections. What is most obvious is the marked difference in mobility between the two family groups, a divergence attributed most directly to the legacy of Loyalist grants. Greater amounts of property granted to the first-generation and second-generation Mordens likely encouraged greater persistence in place than the Denyeses. Whether this landed legacy also resulted in greater occupational stability remains to be seen.

OCCUPATION AND MOBILITY

Farming continued to be the major occupation of the Morden, Denyes, and Hudgins males in Canada, although a considerable number of descendants, especially in the third generation, were employed in other fields. Our examination is limited to males, as well over 90 percent of females in all families worked within their own households and were directed in terms of migration by decisions made largely by husbands and fathers even though, in some cases, migrating families moved to join the wife's relations or maternal relations. The Ruttan and Laughlin families staying in Canada were more inclined to shift into other areas over time, the former moving most notably into the professions and the latter into urban-related trades and services. A considerable percentage of Ruttans did, however, remain in farming.

Males emigrating to the United States were more likely than those remaining in Canada to take up occupations other than farming, a reflection no doubt of the significant rural-to-urban character of Canadian emigration to the United States. Third-generation Denyes males in the United States owned businesses and worked in the trades and services. Their Morden counterparts, although considerably fewer in number, were more disposed to take up a profession. Because we know so little about the Ruttan occupations, any interpretation made about this family is subject to doubt; the information we do have suggests that the majority of the Ruttan males living in the United States practised some type of trade. Half of the small number of third-generation Hudgins in the United States remained in farming and the other half worked in some type of clerical or public service position.

What is most striking is the dichotomy between the third-generation Laughlin males in Canada and the United States. Those staying in Canada were more likely than any other family group to leave farming, even though more of them proportionately lived in rural areas, while those living in the United States were most inclined to continue in agriculture. It seems that it was a conscious decision made among members of this family that if they wanted to remain in farming they would have to emigrate. Why they made this decision is unknown, although an analysis similar to that of the Denyeses and Mordens might yield some insight into this mystery.

Again we focus on the Denyes and Morden families in order to probe more deeply the relationship between mobility and occupation. Did migration rates vary with major occupation? Should we expect stationary families to be most heavily committed to farming and frequent movers to display greater flexibility in occupation? This raises the question of whether mobility or occupation is the dependent variable. In other words, did one move to change jobs or change jobs in order to move?

Of Martin Denyes's three sons, all were farmers, moving away from Fredericksburg to take up land in Thurlow. Peter would spend the last few years of his life in nearby Sidney Township. Martin's only daughter, Anna, and her husband Jacob Young did not have any children. Martin had sixteen grandsons, of whom one died as a child. Of the remaining fifteen, nine continued to be farmers. Most of the others worked at a variety of jobs; the list includes three carpenters, one merchant, one clerk, and one broker. Of the nine farmers, five remained on farms in Thurlow Township, one in adjacent Sidney Township, one in nearby Ernestown Township, one in upstate New York, and one eventually moved to a fruit farm in California. Of the six non-farmers, all lived in more than one place, but if we consider the location in which they resided longest, then the list includes four in Michigan, one in Missouri, and one in nearby Belleville.

Five of Martin's granddaughters remained unmarried, three dying as children or young women, one remaining a spinster and living with her brother the rest of her life, and the other devoting her life to evangelical work. They all spent their lives in Thurlow Township. Of nineteen husbands of Martin's married granddaughters, nine were farmers, four were merchants, one a carpenter, one a railroad contractor, one a blacksmith, one a veterinarian, one a carriage painter, and one a clerk. Only two of the nine farmers occupied farms in Thurlow. Three farmed in Sidney, two in Ernestown, one in Kansas, and one in North Dakota. Only one of the non-farmers lived in Thurlow. Four had their primary residence in Belleville, two in Michigan, one in Ernestown Township, one in Toronto, and one in Claremont, Ontario.

For the second-generation Denyes males, farming appears to have promoted persistence more than non-agricultural occupations. Of the second generation who did not die as children or young adults, females were slightly more likely to remain in the Quinte region than their brothers, but their husbands were less apt to farm. Denyes males were also more tied to original homesteads in Thurlow, a reflection of transfers of property between themselves and their parents.

The third generation following Martin Denyes, impelled by economic and demographic pressures, tended to be more mobile as they searched for opportunity elsewhere. Of the thirty great-grandsons in the male line of the Denyes family, only twelve continued to farm. The primary occupations of the others included four merchants, two mechanics, two contractors, one cooper, one piano-maker, one confectioner, one missionary, one clerk, one real estate broker, one car dealer, one auto engineer, one real estate businessman, and one salesman. Of the thirty great-grandsons who did not die as children or young men and whose mothers were born into the Denyes family, the primary occupations of seven are unknown. Of the remaining twenty-three, nine were farmers, two were carpenters, two were merchants, two were labelled as businessmen in the genealogy, one owned a lumber business, one was a doctor, one was a minister, one owned a mail-delivery business, one was a civil servant, one was in management, one was a streetcar conductor, and one was a manufacturer. The percentage of third-generation males among both lines classified as farmers was virtually identical: 40 percent for the patrilineal line and 39 percent for the matrilineal line.

Of the twelve farmers following the patrilineal line, all farmed in the Quinte region, six in Ernestown, five in Thurlow, and one in Sidney. In contrast, of the nine farmers following the matrilineal line, only five remained in the Quinte region, three in Thurlow, one in Ernestown, and one in Rawdon Township. One moved to a farm in Wollaston Township in the north of Hastings County, one to Missouri, one to Manitoba, and one to Kansas. Again, property transfer among the patrilineal line seems to correlate with persistence in the Quinte region. Yet even among those sons who did not inherit, receive, or purchase property from their parents, there appears to be considerable attachment to place of birth.

Most of the third-generation sons from both patrilineal and matrilineal lines not farming moved away from the Quinte region, no doubt influenced by the lack of opportunities at home. Once they left the area, the kinship network weakened somewhat as a factor in their lives. But family members tended to follow each other, a fact that would be even more apparent if we considered the migration patterns of females in this analysis of the third generation but nonetheless is evident in the maps showing exact locations of the Denyes families. Of the seventeen non-farmers not dying as children or as young men following the patrilineal line, only one remained in the Quinte region, living in Belleville. Five relocated to Michigan, living in cities such as Detroit and Saginaw, three to Toronto, two to cities in New York State, and individual males moved to Fort William, Listowel, Indiana, Ohio, Minnesota (following his sister and her husband), and New Jersey. Of the twenty-two non-farmers following the matrilineal line, only three stayed in the Quinte region, two in Belleville and one in Ernestown. Three moved to Toronto, three to Michigan, two to Hamilton, and one each to Guelph, Vancouver, St Catharines, Madoc Township, New York State, Ohio, Illinois (Chicago), Missouri, Wisconsin, Oregon, and Washington State.

Of Joseph Morden's three sons for whom we have data, all were farmers living in Prince Edward County, one in Sophiasburg Township and the other two in Ameliasburg. Joseph had twenty grandsons following the male line, of whom one died as a child and one died as a young unmarried man still living at home. Of the remaining eighteen, sixteen continued to be farmers, one was a shoe-maker, and the other made a living as a tailor, bailiff, speculator, and agent of the crown. Of the sixteen farmers, twelve remained in the Quinte region, four in Sophiasburg, three in Amelias-burg, two in Tyendinaga, one in Sidney, one in Hallowell, and one in

Hillier. Two moved to Bruce County, eventually settling in Brant and Carrick townships. One settled in Percy Township in Northumberland County and another located in Bentnick Township in Grey County. Of the two non-farmers, one lived in Belleville and the other eventually settled in upstate New York.

One of Joseph's granddaughters died as a child in Ameliasburg. Of eight husbands of Joseph's married granddaughters, all were farmers except one, who was a carpenter. None of the women worked outside the home. All of the farmers lived in the Quinte region, two in Sophiasburg, two in Ameliasburg, and one each in Adolphustown, Hallowell, and Hillier. The carpenter and his family lived in Sophiasburg, Camden, and Ameliasburg townships but eventually settled in Utica, New York.

Nearly all the second-generation Mordens were tied to farming and the Quinte region. Their Loyalist grants certainly served as a forceful incentive to remain at home. Transfers of property between brothers and among extended family as well as between parents and offspring in greater numbers also fostered a greater persistence among the Morden males than their Denyes counterparts.

The third-generation Morden males continued to demonstrate a nota-ble loyalty to the Quinte region and farming. Of the fifty-two great-grandsons who did not die as children or young men following the male line of the Morden family, twenty-seven continued to farm. The primary occupations of the others included four doctors, two carriage-makers, two storeowners, two lawyers, one tailor, one cabinet-maker, one shoe-maker, one tailor, one hotel keeper, one labourer, one auctioneer, one agent, one carpenter, one ship captain, one teacher, and one owner of a canning factory. The primary occupations of three are unknown. Of the nine great-grandsons who did not die as children or young men and whose mothers were born into the Morden family, the primary occupations of three are unknown. Of the remaining six, five were farmers and one was a trader. Like the Denyeses, the percentage of third generation males among both lines classified as farmers was almost identical: 52 percent for the patrilineal line and 55.6 percent for the matrilineal line.

Of the twenty-seven farmers following the patrilineal line, seventeen farmed in the Quinte region, six in Tyendinaga, four in Sophiasburg, three in Hallowell, two in Hillier, and two in Sidney. All of the farmers following the matrilineal line remained in the Quinte region, two in Sophiasburg, one in Ameliasburg, one in Adolphustown, and one in Hillier. Of the twenty-five third generation sons following the patrilineal line not farming and not dying as children or young men, fourteen remained in the Quinte region, a proportion much greater than that of their Denyes counterparts. Four lived in Sophiasburg, three in Picton, two in Belleville, one in Hillier, one in Tyendinaga, one in Deseronto, one in Napanee, and one in Ameliasburg. Of the remaining eleven, four settled in Michigan, two in upstate New York, and one each in Chicago, the village of Marmora, Winnipeg, Toronto, and Brockville. One individual's location is not known. Of the four non-farmers in the matrilineal line, the locations of two are unknown, one settled in Hillier Township, and the other resided somewhere in Ohio.

Persister/stayer groups among the second generation were most tied to farming for both families, although the Denyes movers group was more prone to be employed in a trades position and just as likely to own a business or to be employed in a clerical position as to take up farming. The second-generation movers in both families were more likely to change occupations than persisters and stayers. This was particularly true for the more peripatetic Denyes group. A higher mobility rate meant a greater likelihood that an individual would be employed in more than one occupation.

Greater movement out of farming for both family groups is evident among third-generation males. This is especially noticeable for the Denyeses, where the mover group was much more likely to move into other occupations than the persisters and stayers. Of particular note was the tendency for the Denyes movers, especially those who went to Michigan, to take up semi-skilled and skilled occupations, not surprising given the development of that state's industrial base towards the end of the century. This group also showed some movement into business ownership and clerical occupations.

Third-generation Denyes persisters showed considerable movement into commercial dealings and private land dealings. Persistence in place, often afforded by land acquisition or some other basis, might have enabled some individuals to garner enough capital to enter into such ventures, although Quinte persisters faced a local economy struggling with sluggish growth and periods of real decline. Also significant is the fact that a considerable proportion of stayers as well as movers had three or more occupations, again perhaps a reflection of economic instability for those who remained in the Quinte region.

Third-generation Mordens were more tied to farming than their Denyes counterparts, especially those who persisted in place. Only a small percentage of Mordens inherited, received, or purchased land from their parents. But it was their legacy of Loyalist grants as well as their horizontal land dealings with other members of their nuclear and extended families which allowed many to persist in place and remain in farming. Almost one-half of the Morden stayers, who for the most part remained in the Quinte region after their one and only move, undertook a semi-skilled or skilled trade in nearby communities such as Picton, Deseronto, and Napanee. A considerable percentage of the movers entered the professions or started a business. Generally, the Mordens displayed occupational stability even among the more geographically mobile members.

Persisters were more likely in both families to carry on farming, while the more frequent movers were more likely to pursue other occupations and change jobs more often. Yet the Mordens were notably stable in terms of occupation. The positive association between frequency of migration and number of occupations for the Denyeses suggests a career instability among frequent movers and that the fundamental reason for moving was to change jobs. The very weak association between migration and occupational rates among the Mordens suggests that for this group, other factors besides the pursuit of another career may have played a role in migration. One might note here that the assumption of considerable occupational change in the last century is not supported in these two cases; Katz's diary writer, Wilson Benson, was not like most members of these two families.[29] Does this mean Benson was an exception, or that the occupational mobility experiences of the Denyeses and Mordens were unrepresentative? These data are too limited to bear wide generalizations, but their differences from the well-known Katz example conjure up a number of interesting questions.

The fact that over 30 percent of the third-generation Denyes males of the patrilineal line farmed after settling as compared to only 23 percent who farmed upon first leaving home indicates that, for some, migration and pursuing another occupation were temporary stages in their plans to eventually settle and resume farming. Of this group, ten last resided in the Quinte region while the remainder were scattered throughout the Canadian west and the American midwest.

Whether the positive association between migration and occupation rates reflects an upward socio-economic mobility or a socio-economic instability among more frequent movers is, as mentioned, a question that cannot be answered given the paucity of information on wealth, especially among those moving to the United States. Individual case studies of Denyes and Morden descendants indicate that wealth accrued to both persisters and movers, but no discernible trend emerges. Yet mention can be made of the second-generation and third-generation Mordens who continued to live in Ontario and farmed in 1861. The manuscript agricultural census of that year contains information on total cash values of farms and thus allows a comparison of farm value by migration frequency for the group who demonstrated greater persistence in both farming and residence within Ontario. The one second-generation Morden whose farm was worth over $10,000 in 1861 only moved once in his life. Fifty-four percent of the second-generation Mordens had farms valued at between $5,000 and $10,000, and of this group, 50 percent were persisters, 33.3 percent moved only once, and 16.7 percent moved between two and five times. Just over 27 percent had farms worth between $2,500 and $5,000, and of this group, 33.3 percent were persisters, 33.3 percent were stayers, and 33.3 percent were movers. The one farm that was valued under $2,500 was owned by a Morden who had moved four times during his lifetime.

Twenty percent of the third-generation Mordens who owned farms in 1861 were in the $5,000 to $10,000 category, and of this group, 33.3 percent were persisters and 66.7 percent were stayers. Of one-third in the $2,500 to $5,000 classification, 60 percent were persisters and 40 percent stayers. Almost 47 percent had farms valued between $500 and $2,500, and of this number, 14.3 percent were persisters, 57.1 percent were stayers, 14.3 percent were movers, and another 14.3 percent were chronic movers. This is evidence of a weak negative relationship between value of farm and frequency of movement, but the association is not significant. For some members of the third generation, the 1861 value only represents an assessment based on a limited time in farming; thus little of significance can be made of these statistics.

In summary, the Morden case shows neatly, although only illustratively, how a single genealogy raises questions about the selection of persistence and a landed legacy. Yet the tables also reveal the potentially idiosyncratic results of a handful of genealogies with respect to occupation, land transfer, migration, and settlement. The results can only show the variety of factors and patterns relating to the study of mobility at the micro-level and illustrate the richness of detail that can be achieved through a linkage strategy based on genealogies.

CONCLUSIONS

It should be emphasized that the genealogical approach to the study of rural transformation and migration is valuable only when placed in the larger context of change and continuity occurring in the region chosen for study. Yet representative genealogies, as defined previously, make it possible to reconstruct the spatial patterns for successive generations of migrants and persisters. Especially notable among migration patterns for the selected families were the interrelated aspects of chain migration and kin clustering, more frequent among certain family groups such as the Denyeses and Laughlins, and the remarkable persistence and attachment to the Bay of Quinte region displayed in particular by the Morden and Hudgins families.

The migration patterns demonstrated by the Quinte families are similar to those displayed by three generations of sons of the fourteen Adolphustown progenitors listed in *Pioneer Life on the Bay of Quinte*. For the most part, the first generation of Quinte migrants settled either in the same township as their parents or in adjacent townships. Second-generation sons moved farther afield as the pressure of competition for land and opportunities increased. They moved in larger numbers to other parts of Ontario, to the cities of the American northeast, and to the midwestern states. This trend continued in the third generation. The migration fields became even wider but some distinctive patterns emerge. Rural-urban migration increased, and there is evidence of greater numbers settling in the major Canadian cities (Toronto, Montreal, Ottawa), as well as prominent urban centres to the south (New York, Chicago, Boston, Buffalo). The increasing attraction of the American and newly-opened Canadian western frontiers is noticeable. Cheap and abundant land attracted Quinte natives intent on farming.

The study suggests that Quinte-born participated in the continental westward movement not only at the international and interprovincial levels, but also at the intra-provincial and local levels. The cumulative pattern of intra-regional flows exhibited by the first generations underlines the importance of short-distance moves in the frontier context. The short-distance nature of movement continued into the second and third generations among nuclear families, even though the span of the migration increased. This pattern can be described as a spread of the genealogical rather than the nuclear family. Over the course of the nineteenth century, these genealogical families crossed the continent along a number of routes well travelled by fellow Canadians. That many did so in a series of leaps following chains challenges the "successive wave" concept of migration associated with the frontier thesis.

Yet a closer investigation of these patterns raises a problem with the question of generations. Why study them? The important factors in migration appear to be specific to a place and time rather than generational. As disclosed in the analysis, the question of inheriting and subdividing land is much more pertinent, although it relates to the underlying question of the availability of land. The size of original grants was confirmed to be critical to subsequent migration patterns.

Migration has been viewed traditionally as a dramatic, disruptive experience with individuals either being uprooted or pulled from their homes by both exogenous and indigenous forces. Yet much recent work in social history and historical geography paints a very different picture of mobility. While the transition to capitalism was the central force in shaping group and individual behaviour, revisionist studies, such as John Bodnar's history of immigrants in nineteenth-century urban America, have emphasized the dimensions of individuals facing the processes of capitalism, industrialization, and urbanism, and view mobility not necessarily as a disruptive experience, but often as a response conditioned by the immediate goals of family-household welfare. The emphasis in this work is on the culture of everyday life, a culture which mediated between "the microscopic forces of daily life ... and the macroscopic world of economic change and urban growth."[30]

Hans Medick has argued that the determinant of family forms and processes among rural agriculturalists is inherited property. In such societies, much weight is placed upon patriarchal authority.[31] Yet what influence the frontier had on the continuity of the family in place is largely unknown. Also in question is the role that patterns of inter-vivos and post-mortem transfers of land played in ensuring the security of the family in a region undergoing transition from frontier to fully settled. Did the frontier threaten the maintenance of family ties, or were such bonds only jeopardized when land was settled and parents no longer had property to pass on to their children? Family strategies for property transmission, often linked to population density and growth, also may have played a role in ensuring persistence in place and maintenance of family ties. The dynamic of industrial capitalism, which proved to be more profound over time, produced a variety of options for individuals and decisions were made to ensure order and stability both for themselves and their families. For many, mobility was perceived as the best way to achieve stability, while for others, order was best attained by persistence in both place and occupation.

There is incomplete information on land ownership in *Pioneer Life on the Bay of Quinte*, but the evidence presented in Table 26 might seem to indicate that primogeniture was the exception rather than the rule. In fact, only when no will existed did a law enforcing some type of primogeniture come into effect in nineteenth-century Ontario. For families settling in Sidney, Adolphustown, and Sophiasburg townships, younger sons were almost as likely as older ones to settle in the same township as their parents. No really strong patterns emerge; the distances and directions involved in migration appear to be much the same for all three generations for all male descendants, regardless of their position within their family. Insofar as any pattern emerges, the practice seems to have been for the sons to have stayed with their fathers until they married, when they would leave and settle elsewhere. When the father retired or died, the farm may have passed to whichever son or sons remained on it at the time.

The kinship system promoted the interests of certain family members over others in order to ensure the persistence of the family in the community. As holding sizes decreased, the parcelling of land among all children became less practical. Once the Quinte region was settled, only improved homesteads were available for children and migrants. Start-up costs became too prohibitive in a region where productivity was already declining. The rationalization of farm operations in the light of the transformation from economic self-sufficiency to commercial production meant that farmers had to spend more capital on their farming operations or in purchasing land from less successful neighbours. Yet increasing land prices made the latter option more difficult for many families. As a consequence, more children moved away from home and the spatial and social ties between parent and offspring weakened.

In response to the changes taking place in rural Ontario, families adjusted their marriage and fertility practices. They also adopted certain land transfer and kinship assistance practices that protected the profitability of

Table 26   Inter-generational Migration: Aggregate Sample
(Sidney, Adolphustown, and Sophiasburgh Townships)

Original settlers=63

	First		Second		Third		Fourth		Fifth		
	No.	%	No.	%	No.	%	No.	%	No.	%	
a*	34	53.9	25	49.0	25	56.8	18	52.9	22	45.8	First-generation sons
b†	15	23.9	7	13.7	6	13.6	4	11.8	9	18.8	
c‡	8	12.7	11	21.6	10	22.8	7	20.6	10	20.8	
d§	1	1.6	0	0	0	0	1	2.9	0	0	
e**	5	7.9	8	15.7	3	6.8	4	11.8	7	14.6	
a	52	46.4	41	44.6	32	43.8	19	34.5	29	42.6	Second-generation sons
b	20	17.9	20	21.7	12	16.4	12	21.8	12	17.6	
c	26	23.2	15	16.3	15	20.5	12	21.8	12	17.6	
d	2	1.8	3	3.3	3	4.2	4	7.3	5	7.4	
e	12	10.7	13	14.1	11	15.1	8	14.6	10	14.7	
a	45	45.0	23	35.4	19	40.4	7	28.0	7	35.0	Third-generation sons
b	10	10.0	12	18.5	8	17.0	5	20.0	4	20.0	
c	23	23.0	9	13.8	12	25.5	5	20.0	3	15.0	
d	5	5.0	3	4.6	1	2.2	3	12.0	0	0	
e	17	17.0	17††	26.2	7	14.9	4††	16.0	6	30.0	

Source: Pioneer Life on the Bay of Quinte (Toronto: Rolph and Clark Ltd., 1904).

* Those who settled in the same township as their parents.

† Those who settled outside the township but in the same county.

‡ Those who settled elsewhere in Ontario.

§ Those who settled within Canada but outside Ontario.

** Those who settled in the United States.

†† The percentages do not add up to 100 in these cases as one second-born son and one fourth-born son settled in Europe.

the family farm and ensured persistence of at least some members of the family in the community. A variety of strategies were followed, ranging from placing the care for children and single children and for the elderly and widowed parents upon a single heir, to providing land and/or chattel for all the offspring in order to ensure the strength of kinship ties. Yet persistence through intergenerational transfer of land involved only males for the most part. As a result, females were more likely to leave home but, as Ravenstein noted, their mobility fields were more spatially restricted than males. Unfortunately, it is beyond the scope of this study to examine the social and economic roles of women in rural Quinte. Farm wives may have played a crucial part in determining whether the family would move or not, but such an investigation would require sources that would shed light on their participation in the decision-making process.

The longitudinal perspective afforded by the chosen genealogies revealed that the Mordens displayed a greater geographical and occupational persistence than the other families in spite of the lower degree of intergenerational property transfer through inheritance, gift, and sale than the Denyeses, the most mobile family group. The qualitative dimension of attachment to place is impossible to discern given the lack of appropriate sources such as letters, diaries, and so forth, but analysis of the property records suggests that the Mordens were more likely to transfer real and personal property beyond the nuclear family than the Denyeses. A legacy of Loyalist grants extending into the second generation and a greater degree of intra-generational property transfer played a major role in ensuring the persistence of the Mordens in place and in agriculture.

The intensive analysis of the patrilineal line also provides some insight into how families adapted to the changes occurring in the Quinte region and rural Ontario during the nineteenth century. Both the agricultural and personal manuscript censuses reveal that over time the genealogical families staying in the Quinte region or residing elsewhere in Ontario, and continuing to farm, decreased in size and reduced their dependence on wheat while responding to an increasing market for dairy production and cash crops such as barley. Upon examination of individual and family-specific factors for their possible influence on persistence and migration, only occupation and transfer of aid and property among kin in general played significant roles, although other factors such as sex, age, frequency of parental migration, and family size were influential determinants in individual cases. The land that made agriculture as a way of life possible was the common denominator for the majority of the Quinte families and played an important role in both persistence and migration decisions. A variety of strategies requiring capital investment were employed to meet the shifting demands of changing markets – delaying marriage, seasonal employment, reliance upon kin and kith, accumulating more land, speculative activity, and acquiring labour-saving machinery. Yet while land and agriculture was the foundation for most of the early generations, they eventually lessened in importance among subsequent generations who increasingly pursued opportunities in towns and cities.

The ultimate question of mobility research, that of whether persisters or movers were more successful, remains unanswered because of the lack of data on wealth and the absence of insight into the internal reflections of both groups, whether they lived in Canada or the United States. But some inferences can be made based on the limited information I do have. Persisters were more likely to carry on farming and work as unskilled labourers, while frequent movers were more likely to pursue other occupations and change jobs more often. Little of significance can be stated about the relationship between persisters and socio-economic mobility. While movement into the potentially higher-status professions was associated with more frequent movement among the Mordens, no such discernible relationship existed for the Denyes group.

Even if we had information on wealth, this would by no means ensure that we could identify those who were successful and those who failed. There are other criteria of success besides wealth that will forever remain hidden to the researcher's eyes. The numerous criteria which must be considered when assigning the label of success can only be ascertained at the individual level following the life-history approach. At the same time, individual life histories have to be placed in the context of the community and the society of which they are a part in order to more effectively identify success. While wealth and status information for some stayers and movers in different Canadian and, to a lesser degree, American settings is available, until enough individual and structural information is collected, any judgment of the meaning of success and failure in different places will be biased. To attempt such a study of the members of the chosen genealogical families, even if the kind of data needed to do such an analysis were available, would be inconceivable.

Yet the next section does attempt to examine the experiences of Anglo-Canadian migrants in different places, using a combination of longitudinal and cross-sectional strategies. The results yield greater insight into their experiences in different American and, because of our interest in the important dimension of return migration, Canadian settings.

APPENDIX TO CHAPTER 4

Patterns of Persistence and Immigration over Three Generations

Main Street, Picton, 1847
(Public Archives Ontario/S151127)

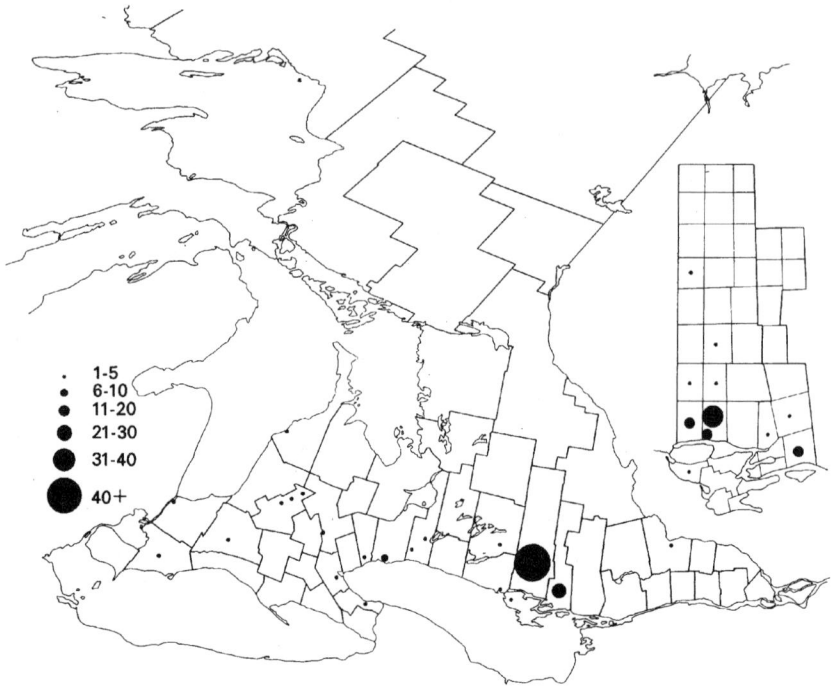

1-5
6-10
11-20
21-30
31-40
40+

Denyes Families: Destinations within Ontario

Unknown Locations in:
Michigan 5
New York 3
California 2
United States 2
Western Canada 2
Kansas 1
Nevada 1
North Dakota 1
Ohio 1
Oklahoma 1
Virginia 1
British Columbia 1
Manitoba 1

Denyes Family: Destinations elsewhere in North America

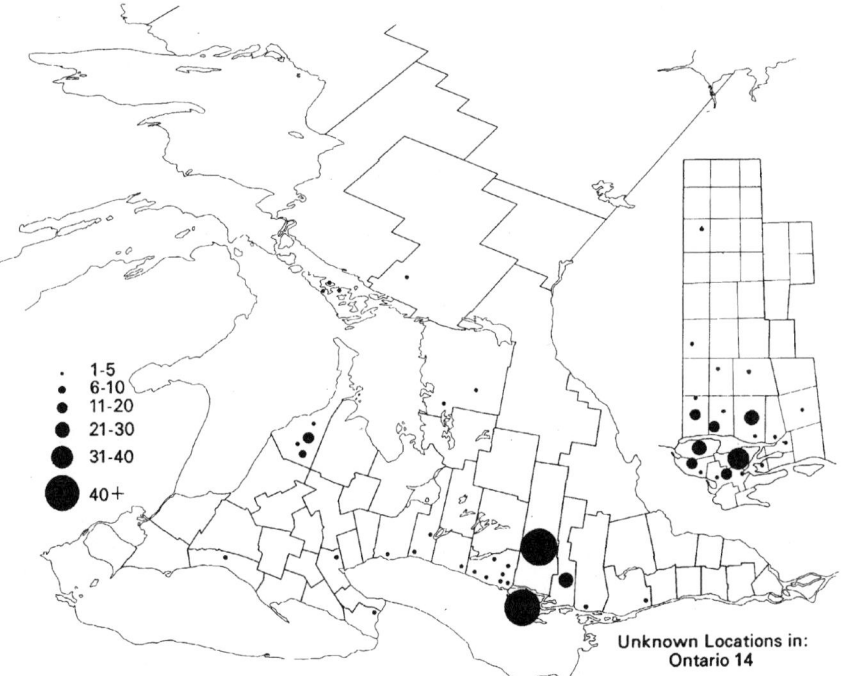

Unknown Locations in:
Ontario 14

Morden Families: Destinations within Ontario

Unknown Locations in:
Michigan 3
New York 1
Ohio 1
Pennsylvania 1
Washington 1
Alberta 1
Manitoba 1

Morden Families: Destinations elsewhere in North America

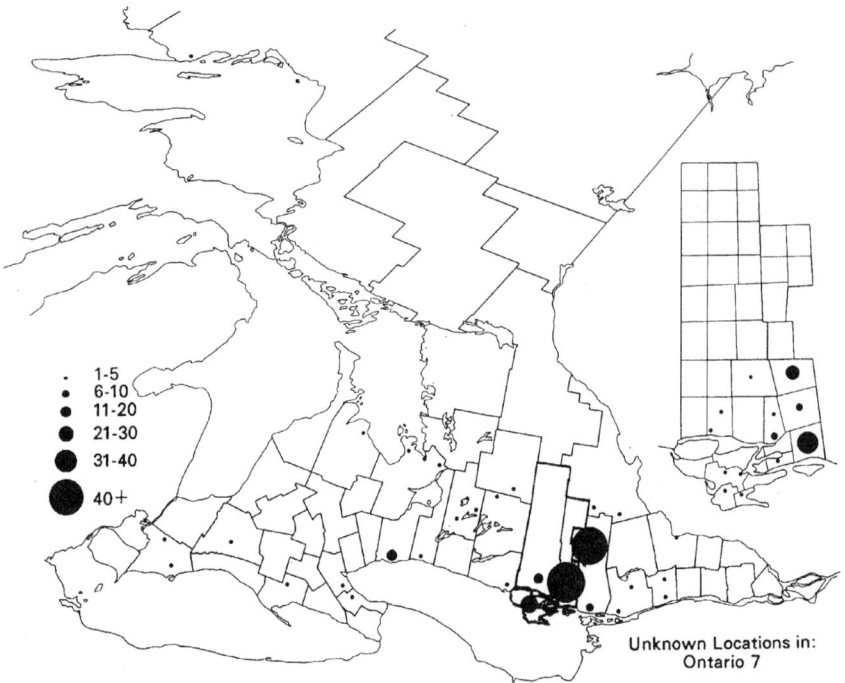

1-5
6-10
11-20
21-30
31-40
40+

Unknown Locations in:
Ontario 7

Laughlin Families: Destinations within Ontario

Unknown Locations in:
Michigan 2
New York 1
Wisconsin 1
Western U.S.A. 1
Alberta 1
Saskatchewan 1

Laughlin Families: Destinations elsewhere in North America

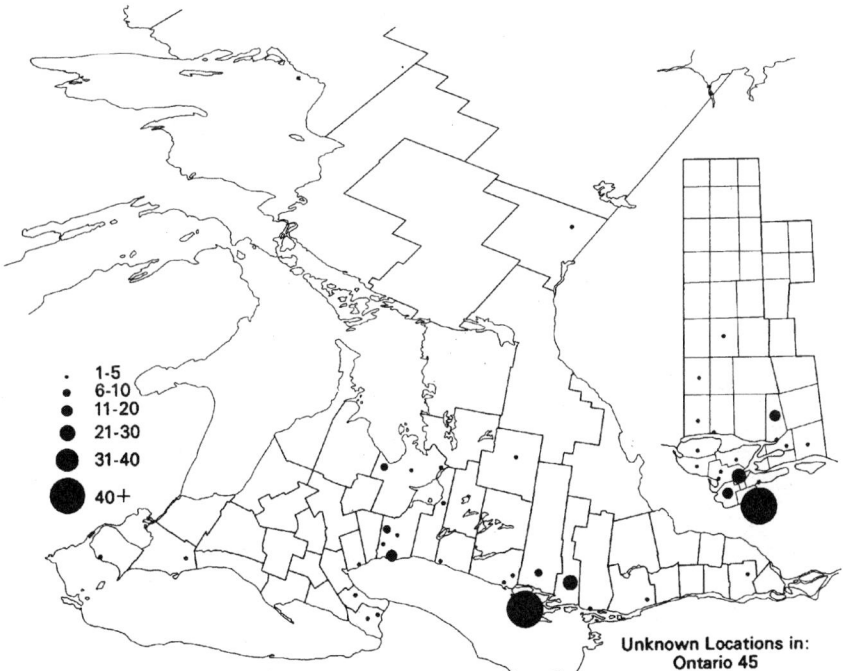

Hudgins Families: Destinations within Ontario

Hudgins Families: Destinations elsewhere in North America

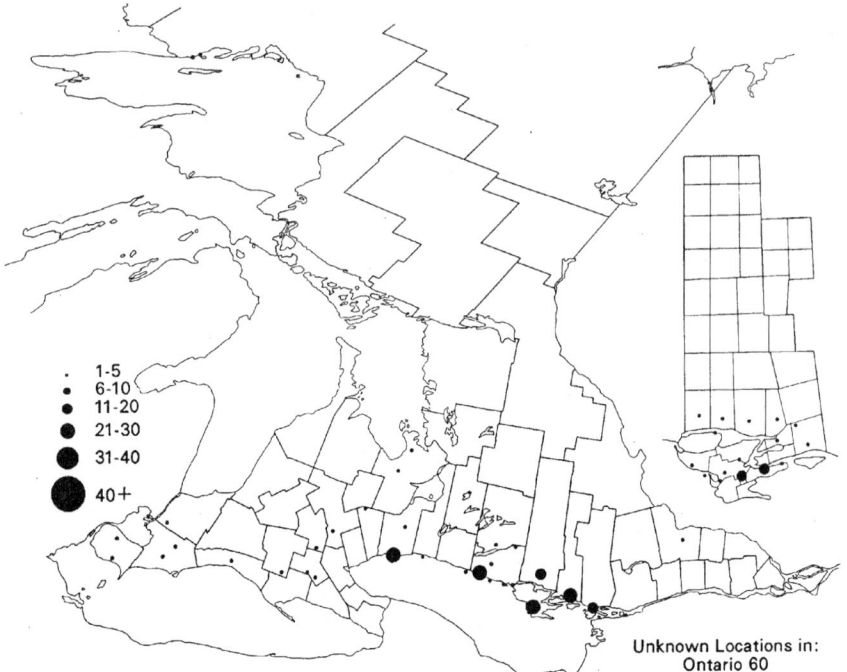

1-5
6-10
11-20
21-30
31-40
40+

Unknown Locations in:
Ontario 60

Ruttan Families: Destinations within Ontario

Unknown Locations in:
Iowa 4
California 2
Georgia 2
Manitoba 2
Quebec 1

Ruttan Families: Destinations elsewhere in North America

PART THREE

Destinations

First Home in Saskatchewan
(Saskatchewan Archives/R-A2336)

Introduction

> Canadians are generally indistinguishable from the Americans, and
> the surest way of telling the two apart is to make the observation to
> a Canadian.
> – Richard Starnes, quoted in *Between Friends*, NFB documentary

In the final part of our journey we follow the voyagers to two distinct reception areas beyond the edge of the map, one close and one distant, and to
another island in the archipelago, a location so unfamiliar and distant as
to be almost foreign. Understanding the process of adaptation in these
different settings is an almost impossible task. Piecing together the experiences of return and internal migrants is especially difficult given the
scarcity of records that follow such movements. As a consequence, my
investigation of return and internal migrants in Saskatchewan is less
insightful than the analysis of Anglo-Canadians in upstate New York and
the Red River Valley of North Dakota.

A number of historians have examined Canadians in the United States.
Berthoff contends that, like most native Americans, Anglo-Canadians were
more likely to seek land than any other immigrant group. On the other
hand, Percy shows that in both 1890 and 1900 a greater percentage of
native-born Canadians were semi-skilled and skilled workers while proportionately fewer were in farming and unskilled occupations than other
foreign-born.[1] To most emigrants, Hansen and Brebner maintain,
economic factors outweighed any political considerations. Canadians,
particularly from Ontario, were prominent in railway centres, many of
them trained in Canada by railways such as the Grand Trunk and the Great
Western. They were also prominent in lumbering and mining, business
departments, mechanical shops, telegraph offices, printing businesses,
mercantile firms, banking, and the medical profession.[2]

The 1890 US published census divided foreign-born from Canada into
English (i.e., Anglo-Celtic) and French origins. French Canadians, followed by the British, Germans, and English Canadians had the highest

concentrations among male workers in manufacturing and were lower than other groups in domestic and personal services. The British and English Canadians had the widest occupational distribution while French Canadians were most highly concentrated in certain occupations. Immigrant males from Canada employed in the United States grew in number from 290,000 in 1880 to 430,000 in 1890, with the greatest percentage increase in trade and transportation, followed by the professions, manufacturing, domestic services, and agriculture.

The 1900 census reveals further change. By this date, French Canadians had become one of the most highly industrialized groups, were numerous in domestic and personal services, and ranked very low in agriculture and the professions. English Canadians, on the other hand, were distributed widely among the different occupations. They were most numerous in manufacturing and a significant proportion were engaged in the professions. The census also shows that the sons of Canadian-born were more concentrated in trade and transportation and the professions. Such diversity may be reflective of the differences existing among this group as expressed by origin, occupation, religion, and other indicators.[3]

Gavit's analysis of the average interval between date of immigration and the filing of the final petition for naturalization of foreign-born applicants, 21 years of age and over, for the years 1913 and 1914 reveals that this interval was longest for Canadians (16.4 years). The average interval for all countries was 10.6 years. Gavit attributes the difference to democratic and economic conditions existing in the various countries, arguing that immigrants from more stable environments were more likely to retain their original citizenship.[4] Perhaps many Canadians hoped to return one day to Canada or maybe many were not willing to give up their Canadian citizenship despite deciding to live in the United States.

Because the Québécois carried with them to the United States a strong and visible subculture, the French-Canadian immigration experience has received considerably more attention than that of the Anglo-Canadian. The exodus from Quebec did not reach significant proportions until after 1840 when the shortage of desirable land and population pressure became too great for the outmoded agricultural technology and the maintenance of an inheritance system which had hitherto tied children to the family farm. At first, Québécois worked in the woods of Maine and New Hampshire and the mill towns of Massachusetts for various periods of time and then returned to Canada with cash in their pockets. They regarded it as an extended season away from home, as part of a cultural seasonal regime that transcended the border.

However, as time passed, more Québécois settled permanently in the United States, as conditions continued to deteriorate at home and as migrants acquired a taste for the benefits which a secure factory job could offer. Those who decided to stay in America still managed to retain their distinctive character. The attributes of language, faith, and family served to protect the interests and identity of the group, and both secular and religious institutions provided the mechanisms by which newcomers could seek aid and companionship. Societies such as the Association de Secours Mutuel des Canadiens Français Americans, the Union St Jean Baptiste d'Amerique, and the Société des Artisans Canadiens Français helped to maintain the traditional culture and facilitate the adjustment process. The emigré Québécois parish was perhaps even more important in the community, establishing newspapers, schools, and hospitals as well as social, athletic, and mutual benefit associations.[5]

Unlike the French Canadians, Anglo-Canadians rarely established formal ethnic institutions. Besides the *Canadian-American* (1898–1903) coming out of Minneapolis and Chicago and the *American-Canadian* (1873–6) published in Boston, very few publications served the Anglo-Canadian population in the United States. Almost every ethnic group in America was represented in the litany of newspapers published in New York City during the 1821–1936 period. Even the French Canadians briefly had their own newspaper, *Le Public Canadien* (1867–8). Significantly, no such paper served the Anglo-Canadian population in the country's largest city.[6] Most Anglo-Canadians joined established American Methodist, Episcopal, and Baptist congregations and so the church played virtually no role in preserving cultural heritage. Social institutions were also rare and those that existed, such as the Canadian Club of New York City, served particular groups such as businessmen and "gentlemen."[7] Few Canadians joined such institutions but of those who did, most moved into the clubs, societies, and church groups of the native-born Americans.

Post-migration experiences will be examined in the following chapters in terms of the family and the community. Apart from the individual migrant, the family constitutes the most important basic unit in analysing the migration experience. Migration and relocation in a new country were often carried out in a variety of familial forms, kinship being the most coherent factor. The process of migration, however, challenged traditional family patterns and various groups responded in different ways. The identification of kinship ties is crucial in ascertaining the importance of the family in the Canadian migration experience. Kinship ties both within and outside the household will be examined, as well as the role of kinship in supporting the migration of other relatives. The task of establishing such linkages outside the household, however, is especially difficult, because the most important source, the manuscript census, is arranged by household units.

The next important unit of migration is the community which, however defined, constitutes the context in which individual migrants adjust to their new environment. While spatial structure alone does not determine patterns of social dislocation, there are definite relationships between the two, the ecology of the place and settlement affecting the relationships between home, workplace, and community. It is important to distinguish between two senses of the term community. There is the ethnic community itself, which is a distinct spatial area inhabited largely by a particular ethnic group. It represents a set of social relationships manifested through formal and informal institutions, religion, social, and visiting patterns that serve to bring members of an ethnic group together and thereby create a sense of community. These sets of social relationships may occur within a locality or they may be strong enough to transcend distance and link individuals not clustered together. There is a need to examine residential patterns and the presence of institutions in order to see if this sense of community applied to Anglo-Canadians in the locales chosen for study.

The second level of community involves the idea that the size and structure of the receiving centre may not dictate but at least will affect immigrant behaviour. Thus, the distinct economic, demographic, and social composition of the chosen communities may in part explain any observed differences. Any attempt, however, to establish a connection between modes of behaviour and the context in which they exist is very difficult. Scholars have traditionally viewed ethnic groups as ascriptive groups sharing cultural traits derived by some common ancestry and historical experience. Ethnicity may be associated with the view of class as a collective experience shared by individuals who occupy a similar social and economic space. These human relations are embodied in traditions, value systems, and ideas which in turn are manifested in ethnic associations, specifically common occupational positions, residential clustering, interest groups, and kin networks. Ethnicity and class may thus be interchangeable and the result of such an intersection has been termed the "ethclass." Milton Gordon has suggested that the ethclass, in which people relate primarily to their own social class segment within their own ethnic group, is in most cases the group of participational identification, while the ascriptive group is most often the group of historical and psychological identification.[9] This study examines the relevance of both views in terms of the Anglo-Canadian experience.

5 "We Breathe the Same Air": Eastern Ontarian Migration to New York State[1]

Where we love is home,
Home that our feet may leave,
but not our hearts.
                    – Oliver Wendell Holmes, "Homesick in Heaven"

The following lament appeared on 30 January 1890 in the Brockville *Weekly Recorder*, a faithful Grit newspaper and therefore somewhat biased against the National Policy of the Conservative government.

At the meeting of the Grenville County farmers institute, held at Algonquin on the 13th and 14th, one of the speakers made the statement that he knew of at least thirty farms in that county which had been deserted. What is true of Grenville is no doubt true to a greater or lesser extent of every county in the older settled portions of the province. Furthermore, it is pretty safe to assert that the people who deserted these farms have moved into the States to avail themselves of the "sixty million market". There are thousands upon thousands of Canadian newspapers going into the United States each week, to people who should be living in Canada, and who would probably still be here but for the policy of the government.

Not all the newspapers put the blame on the National Policy, but all regretted the loss of human resources. A movement that had started as a trickle early in the century had turned into a raging flood during the decade of the 1880s and had every sign of continuing. This outflow of people affected every part of the province but was most noticeable in two regions: the lakefront counties east of Toronto and the longer-settled parts of eastern Ontario. While only three counties reported a net population loss during the 1870s, 178 townships, or 38.1 percent of the total number of townships in southern Ontario, lost population. This rate of depopulation for rural Ontario continued over the next thirty years: nineteen coun-

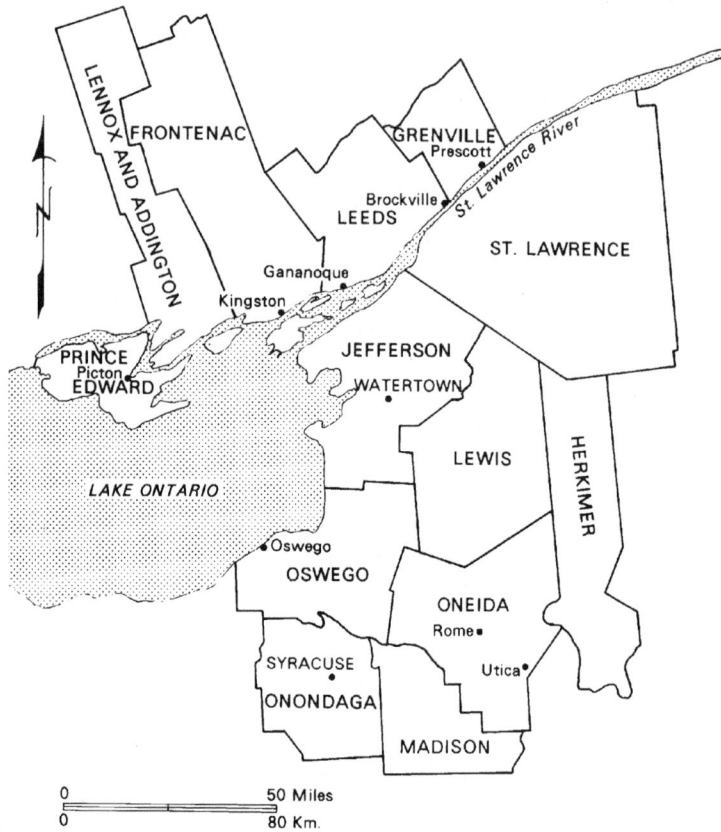

Map 5: Study Area: Eastern Ontario and Northern New York

ties lost population in the 1880s, twenty-one in the 1890s, and twenty-eight in the first decade of the new century.

Nowhere in Ontario were the effects of the changes in agriculture felt as much as in the eastern part of the province, including that region comprising the focus of this case study (Map 5).[2] With a few notable exceptions, eastern Ontario was burdened with relatively unproductive land and was the least able of all parts of the province to adapt to changing markets and new industrial opportunities. Even so, eastern Ontario had grown during the first half of the century, and the economy of the region developed as commercial interests in Kingston, Brockville, and Prescott tapped the agricultural hinterland.

The decline of the wheat market that wounded the central and southern parts of the province at mid-century had less effect in this region where farmers engaged in mixed agriculture.[3] However, a limited agricultural

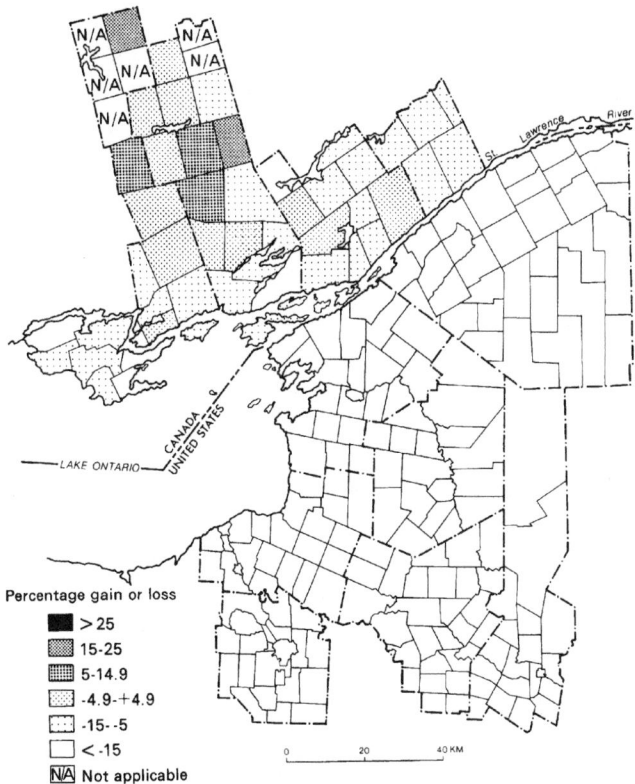

Percentage gain or loss

■ > 25
▓ 15-25
▦ 5-14.9
⬚ -4.9-+4.9
⬚ -15--5
☐ < -15
Ⓝ/Ⓐ Not applicable

Map 6: Population Changes in the Source Region

base, together with population pressure upon the land, reflected by changing farm sizes and number of farms, combined with changing markets to
create an environment for rural exodus. Map 6 illustrates very clearly the
widespread phenomenon of population loss during the last decade of the
nineteenth century. Almost all of the longer-settled southern townships
lost population through the period from 1871 to 1901. Many of the newly
settled northern townships, where the soils were only marginally fit for
agriculture, enjoyed modest growth for much of this period, but nearly all
were losing people by the turn of the century.

Yet the decline in the size of farms during the last few decades of the
century may also have been due to the pressure of a growing population.
In 1871, for example, one-year-old Henry Cox was living with his parents
James and Catherine, poor Irish immigrants, on a small farm of 18 acres
in Bastard Township in Leeds County. Cox was a tenant farmer with only 8
acres of improved land and 10 acres of pasture to support his wife and

Table 27   Average Size of Farm (acres) in the Origin Region, 1881–91

Census District[a] and Subdistrict	1881	1891	% Change
GRENVILLE, SOUTH	*80.6*	*72.3*	*-10.3*
Augusta	81.8	80.8	-1.2
Edwardsburg	82.1	78.4	-4.5
LEEDS AND GRENVILLE, NORTH	*103.5*	*63.2*	*-38.2*
Kitley	111.7	–	–
Elmsley	115.1	111.7	-3.0
Wolford	110.4	97.6	-11.6
Oxford	95.1	92.5	-2.7
Gower, South	103.7	97.1	-6.4
LEEDS, SOUTH	*99.9*	*89.8*	*-10.1*
Landsdowne, Front	98.7	–	–
Leeds, Front	95.7	92.6	-3.2
Landsdowne, Rear	120.1	103.3	-14.0
Leeds, Rear	90.2	–	–
Bastard, Burgess, South	115.6	111.7	-3.4
Yonge, Front	113.7	93.2	-9.2
Escott, Front	83.1	–	–
Yonge and Escott, Rear	79.5	92.6	16.5
Crosby, South	107.1	95.1	-11.2
Crosby, North	92.0	89.9	-1.1
FRONTENAC	*101.7*	*99.6*	*-11.2*
Kingston	98.0	90.0	-8.2
Wolfe Island	97.3	77.3	-20.6
Pittsburg	108.9	109.4	0.5
Howe Island	105.4	120.1	13.9
Storrington	103.7	127.3	22.8
LENNOX	*92.9*	*82.5*	*-11.2*
Amherst Island	103.0	119.3	15.8
Adolphustown	115.6	88.8	-23.2
Ernestown	100.5	77.4	-23.0
Fredericksburg, North	87.6	77.7	-11.3
Fredericksburg, South	108.4	94.5	-12.8
Richmond	97.4	92.6	-4.9
ADDINGTON	*132.0*	*124.6*	*-5.0*
Loughborough	124.2	100.0	-19.5
Portland	100.5	95.3	-5.2
Camden	118.7	98.0	-17.4
Sheffield	102.9	116.8	13.5
Denbeigh, Abinger, Ashby, Effingham	212.5	210.1	-2.7
Kaladar, Anglesea	151.0	130.9	-10.3
Hinchinbrooke	108.6	128.5	18.3
Olden	145.6	128.1	-12.0

Table 27 (continued)

Census District^a and Subdistrict	1881	1891	% Change
Bedford	153.8	166.5	8.3
Oso	193.4	151.6	-21.6
Barrie	128.0	118.4	-7.5
Kennebec	132.3	126.9	-4.1
Clarendon, Miller	182.3	189.1	3.7
Palmerston, Canonto	180.2	229.9	27.6
PRINCE EDWARD	*87.0*	*61.0*	*-29.9*
Athol	83.5	78.9	-5.5
Ameliasburg	92.1	76.0	-17.5
Hillier	98.9	82.4	-16.7
Marysborough, S.	77.9	69.1	-11.3
Marysborough, N.	90.7	79.7	-12.1
Sophiasburg	114.5	77.7	-32.1
Hallowell	69.5	57.4	-17.4

Sources: Census of Canada, 1880–81, vol. 3, table 22, 78–84. Census of Canada, 1890–91, vol. 2, table 16, 272–300.

^a Figures for districts include urban centres and townships.

their twelve children. Ten years later, the family was still farming the same lot. Two additional children had been born, but an older son and daughter had left. Four of the sons, aged between 16 and 29, were listed as farmers' sons in the 1881 census. Four daughters also still lived at home. Such a small farm could not support seven boys, and there was little affordable land left in the area. Faced with such miserable prospects, the 19-year-old Henry left home and took up farming in the town of Potsdam in St Lawrence County, New York.[4]

John Salsbury was another Canadian who found himself in such a situation. The youngest of four boys, John was unable to acquire enough capital to purchase a farm of his own in Camden Township, Lennox and Addington County. The demand for land pushed prices beyond the reach of people such as Salsbury. After marrying Alberta Edgar in 1890, he moved to Fulton, New York. The couple stayed there for a few years, and John worked in the factory where his cousin was employed. Yet unlike Henry, John did not become an American citizen. After a number of years, he saved enough money to return to Camden Township and buy a farm on the River Road.[5]

Table 27 shows the changing size of the average holding in the origin region during the 1880s. Sizes decreased throughout the region, but the greatest declines occurred in Prince Edward County and the northern parts of Leeds and Grenville. Nevertheless, sizes did increase or remain stable in certain northern townships where the Public Lands Act and the Free Grants and Homestead Act had recently distributed large blocks of lands to settlers.

These were difficult days for eastern Ontario and many people, both from the country and the town, chose to find a new life elsewhere. While most were young migrants from the countryside, they were diverse in terms of occupational, ethnic, and religious background. Those of British origin dominated but did not constitute a unified element. In 1881 the Irish formed the largest ethnic group (45.6 percent) followed by the English (23.6 percent), Germans (11.3 percent), Scottish (10.9 percent), French (3.8 percent), and others (4.8 percent).

Religious affiliation was similarly diversified. Methodists dominated in the rural districts, particularly in the western counties of Prince Edward (62.4 percent) and Lennox and Addington (57.9 percent), where superior numbers of English and native-born combined to give this group a numerical advantage. Presbyterians were better represented in Leeds and Grenville counties where more Scots and Scottish Canadians lived. Catholics, mostly of Irish origin and descent, were distributed relatively evenly throughout the region, although they were under-represented in predominantly rural Prince Edward and Lennox and Addington counties. Anglicans were best represented in Leeds (23.7 percent) and the towns of Kingston (27.1 percent) and Brockville (27.0 percent), both long-established Anglican and Loyalist strongholds.[6]

Religion and ethnicity served as differentiating forces throughout the region, particularly between Catholics and Protestants. With its relatively high percentage of Irish and French Catholic settlement, eastern Ontario was a locus for such antagonisms. The presence of Orangeism in this part of the province served to intensify religious and ethnic intolerance.[7] While this diversity had little to do with people leaving the region, it may have played a role in their subsequent adjustment in new communities.

In addition to religious and ethnic differentiation, eastern Ontario was characterized by an occupational stratification reflecting a predominantly rural society. Over 62 percent of the workers in the rural census districts were listed as farmers in 1881 and 25 percent were in labouring. A significant proportion (17.3 percent) of urban employment in Kingston and Brockville, the two largest centres in the region, involved labouring also.[8] As people left and the rural economy declined, some farming trades faced difficult prospects with diminishing demands for their products, and traditional artisan skills began to disappear in the face of new technologies. Some families chose to move to nearby centres while others decided to venture farther afield. However, the decline in growth of the region's major centres is an indication of the generally lower rate of development of this area compared to the rest of Ontario. The eastern region was failing to attract sufficient industry to stimulate the development required to maintain the position of its centres in the expanding urban hierarchy. Table 28 reveals significant declines or, at best, very slight increases in capital expenditures, wages, and value of products throughout the region. The failure to attract much development meant there were few jobs for urban residents and rural migrants entering the labour force.

However, the loss of rural population was a result not only of migration but of fertility decline as well. As discussed earlier, Upper Canada at mid-century had one of the highest birth rates in the world.[9] Yet all regions of the province experienced fertility declines during the last three decades of the century, particularly the older parts. Declining birth rates and family sizes may be interpreted as evidence of a conscious effort among farm families to trim the family unit. Other demographic characteristics reveal much about the population of this region. Rural census districts show that males generally outnumbered females among those between the ages of 15 and 45, which supports the theory that females outnumber males in out-migration. The predominance of females among the same age groups for Brockville, Kingston, and other urban centres in the region confirms females dominating short-distance moves to urban centres.

Lower has suggested that both the economic and social structure of the region were adversely affected by this loss of people:

Every year, young people, except the fortunate few or the one or two children of the family who could find something to do, had to go away. In the days of the large Victorian family, this emigration of the young, at their highest point of vitality, must have been like a constant bleeding. Some of the departing went to Toronto, others to Montreal. But Canada as a whole expanded slowly in the period 1861 to 1901, so the assumption can be made that most of them went "across the line". No doubt a town like Watertown, New York can find the origins of a majority of its people in our St. Lawrence river towns, Kingston, Brockville, Prescott, especially. It was a distinguished Kingstonian, Sir Richard Cartwright, who remarked of those bleak days that they "began in Exodus and ended in Lamentations." He was not far from wrong.[10]

Many eastern Ontarians did choose to move to nearby New York State. At several points along the border, trains and ferries crossed with scarcely any more delay than in passing state or provincial lines. Many decided to walk or drive their sleighs across the ice in winter. In physical terms the line was inconsequential, but the social and emotional consequences of crossing this line are much less clear.

While it is relatively simple to describe the context in which emigration from eastern Ontario took place at the end of the nineteenth century, the task of establishing the background in which immigration into northern New York took place is much more onerous. Like Ontario, New York was experiencing the same transformation from a rural to an urban-industrial

Table 28 Manufacturing Statistics for Selected Cities, Towns, and Villages, Ontario, 1891–1901

Centre	Year	Population	No. of establishments	Capital ($)	Employees	Salaries and wages ($)	Value of products ($)	Average wage per employee ($)	Average no. of employees per establishment
Cornwall	1891	6,805	108	2,905,572	1,755	537,971	2,193,877	306.54	6.3
	1901	6,704	32	3,067,677	1,619	500,849	2,159,809	309.36	50.6
Brockville	1891	8,791	135	1,207,107	1,161	374,630	1,404,638	322.68	8.6
	1901	8,940	23	1,536,485	1,130	439,423	1,551,590	388.87	49.1
Kingston	1891	19,263	401	1,645,381	2,671	786,198	3,113,573	294.35	6.7
	1901	17,961	42	1,703,909	1,495	527,700	2,045,173	352.98	35.6
Gananoque	1891	3,669	72	1,105,640	809	280,597	1,081,272	346.84	11.2
	1901	3,526	16	1,030,412	674	281,380	863,079	417.48	42.1
Napanee	1891	3,434	84	200,885	406	107,620	461,859	265.07	4.8
	1901	3,143	24	218,669	225	87,061	230,157	341.42	10.6
Prescott	1891	2,919	67	457,765	344	103,048	605,113	308.53	5.0
	1901	3,019	7	575,900	134	51,581	191,600	384.93	19.1
Picton	1891	3,287	105	390,900	617	141,564	597,722	229.44	5.9
	1901	3,696	11	145,575	599	83,460	368,157	139.33	54.5

Source: Census of Canada, 1911, vol. 3, 351–61.

Note: The data for 1901 only include those establishments with five employees or more.

society, albeit commencing earlier and proceeding at a more rapid pace. So while this transformation again featured some structural changes in agriculture, the upper New York region also experienced a concomitant growth in cities and large-scale industry.

Agriculture in New York enjoyed a period of relative stability and prosperity at mid-century, and the good times continued for another two decades. During this period, New York led the country in terms of number and value of farms; dairy, livestock, and orchard production; and the number of improved acres. However, a number of factors combined to bring about the end of these halcyon days. During the 1870s the agricultural sector began to feel the competition resulting from the expansion of western agriculture, a development ironically brought about with the assistance of New York capital and labour. In addition, little occupied farm land remained, and that already in production was beginning to be depleted following decades of constant, unrotated wheat production.[11]

While agriculture declined in relation to other sectors such as manufacturing, trade, and transportation compared to other states, New York still ranked high in agricultural production, particularly fruits, potatoes, dairy products, hay, and forage. By the turn of the century, dairying emerged as the main enterprise of most New York farmers, and in this activity the northern New York region was very prominent (Table 29). The area had a history of dairy specialization which helped farmers adjust to the rapid decline in the wheat market due to increasing competition from the west after 1860. Yet dairy specialization resulted in larger farms and fewer farmers. This, in turn, augmented the numbers of New Yorkers leaving the land. Though northern New York continued to attract Canadian migrants who could manage to acquire enough land and capital to operate a profitable dairy farm, for most eastern Ontarians, farming was too expensive a proposition, and so the majority who came to New York settled in towns or cities.

Whereas in 1870 Ontario was still primarily agricultural and rural, New York had already passed through the earlier stages of the transformation to an urban-industrial society. Manufacturing industries that had become well-established by mid-century had surpassed agriculture by 1870 in terms of value of products. Several factors combined to account for some of New York's industrial growth during the second half of the nineteenth century. First, there was an abundance of native and immigrant labour to work in the burgeoning factories. Secondly, financiers and entrepreneurs provided the capital and managerial expertise necessary to establish a system of large-scale enterprises. Thirdly, New York's proximity to raw materials, such as coal from Pennsylvania and iron ore from Michigan and Minnesota, favoured industrial development, and excellent transportation facilities eased the movement of these materials to New York's mills and factories. Lastly, the accessibility of the huge market in the northeast to New York's manufacturers provided a significant boost to development.[12]

Table 29 Number and Acreage of Farms, Classified by Tenure, with Averages and Percentages, and Dairy Products of Farms in 1899

Number and Percentage of Farms Operated by

Counties	Number	Average size in acres	Owner No.	Owner %	Part owner No.	Part owner %	Owners & Tenants No.	Owners & Tenants %	Managers No.	Managers %	Cash tenants No.	Cash tenants %	Share tenants No.	Share tenants %
Herkimer	3,227	118.7	2,049	63.5	146	4.5	24	0.8	49	1.5	324	10.0	635	19.7
Jefferson	6,052	123.1	3,740	61.8	334	5.5	38	0.6	51	0.9	528	8.7	1,361	22.5
Lewis	3,838	128.8	2,991	77.9	152	4.0	8	0.2	63	1.6	230	6.0	394	10.3
Oneida	7,232	90.9	5,057	69.9	328	4.5	26	0.4	130	1.8	999	13.8	692	9.6
Onondaga	6,305	72.0	3,975	63.1	505	8.0	84	1.3	97	1.5	709	11.3	935	14.8
Oswego	6,914	71.3	5,209	75.4	279	4.0	29	0.4	78	1.1	654	9.5	665	9.6
St Lawrence	8,353	128.0	5,649	67.6	410	4.9	73	0.9	76	0.9	1,323	15.8	822	9.9

Counties	Acres in Farms Total	Improved No.	Improved % of total	No. of farms reporting dairy products	Dairy farms as a % of total farms	Average value of dairy products per Farm ($)
Herkimer	383,180	272,158	71.0	2,882	89.3	474.51
Jefferson	745,093	526,288	70.6	5,393	89.1	391.67
Lewis	494,165	272,866	55.2	3,225	84.8	331.31
Oneida	657,748	447,359	68.0	6,731	93.0	322.38
Onondaga	453,934	383,621	84.5	5,269	83.6	275.48
Oswego	492,935	319,431	64.8	5,959	86.2	196.95
St Lawrence	1,068,798	550,010	51.5	7,738	92.6	432.06

Source: 12th Census of the United States, 1900: Agriculture part I, vol. V, table 10, pp. 106–9; table 19, p. 290; table 44, pp. 612–13.

The various counties in northern New York benefited disproportionately from this economic expansion and as a result presented different environments for the incoming migrant (Table 30). Agriculture-related products were still the most important manufactures in rural St Lawrence and Lewis counties. These small-scale enterprises generally paid low wages, held smaller amounts of capital, and employed fewer hands than the larger factories in the cities. Many of those who laboured in cheese- and butter-making establishments were farmers who chose to work part-time in order to supplement their incomes. Jefferson, Herkimer, and Oswego counties displayed a greater diversity in manufactures, with both agriculture-related products and industry-related products being turned out. Again the urban industries paid higher wages although there were a few exceptions such as the incomes of flour and grist mill workers in Oswego County. Certain industries emerged which were large in terms of size, hands employed, and capital invested. A worsted goods factory in the city of Oswego employed 939 people and the Remington gun and typewriter factory in Ilion employed 400 well-paid workers.[13] Pulp and paper mills along the Black River and foundries in Watertown were large-scale employers in Jefferson County.

However, the greatest industrial development took place in Oneida and Onondaga counties where industrial capitalism had reached an advanced stage. Large textile mills had emerged fifty years before in the Utica-Rome area and later in Syracuse. After the Erie Canal was completed in 1825, the production of salt in the Syracuse area reached its full eminence. Railroads complemented the canal and served to spur development in central New York. Iron and steel products were manufactured in Syracuse and the textile industry became more important in Utica. In terms of wages, this industry paid the least. A large inflow of immigrants produced an abundance of cheap labour for this business, with Germans and Irish predominating at mid-century and Jews and Italians taking over by the end of the century.[14]

Some fundamental changes in the industrial profile of the destination region occurred over the next twenty years (Table 31). Lewis and St Lawrence counties continued to be largely rural in nature, as reflected in the low number of earners per average firm and the generally low wages paid to workers in such towns as Ogdensburg, Canton, and Lowville. Traditional crafts, furniture-making, and construction were just a few enterprises rooted in the past which continued to operate. Pulp and paper, spurred by plentiful stands of spruce and balsam, developed into the major industry of St Lawrence County. In 1902 the Aluminum Company of America built a major plant in Massena.

The decline of the port of Oswego accounted for lessening development in Oswego County. Prior to 1873, Oswego, America's oldest freshwater port, enjoyed a lengthy period of growth. But the depression of

Table 30 Selected Statistics of Top Five Manufactures[1] by Counties, New York, 1880

Counties and industries	No. of establishments	Capital ($)	Average no. of hands employed	Total wages ($)	Value of products ($)	Employees per establishment	Average wages ($)
HERKIMER							
Cheese & butter (factory)	117	261,968	235	44,058	1,086,529	2.0	187.48
Firearms	1	700,000	400	350,000	700,000	400.0	875.00
Flour & grist mills	25	179,800	39	11,690	513,838	1.6	299.74
Hosiery & knit goods	3	260,000	440	83,785	498,336	146.7	190.42
Leather, tanned	10	222,750	102	53,466	494,097	10.2	524.17
JEFFERSON							
Flour & grist mills	53	471,850	99	27,921	1,232,993	1.9	282.03
Cheese & butter (factory)	161	239,325	273	44,562	814,370	1.7	163.23
Paper	7	373,400	206	72,814	677,150	29.4	353.46
Leather, tanned	14	225,500	134	42,781	624,621	9.6	319.26
Foundry & machine products	10	426,500	252	114,892	393,020	25.2	455.92
LEWIS							
Leather, tanned	13	629,900	375	123,909	1,550,160	28.8	330.42
Lumber, sawed	93	359,850	419	83,625	469,712	4.5	199.58
Cheese & butter (factory)	90	133,550	150	22,501	458,958	1.7	150.00
Flour & grist mills	17	149,400	39	9,206	258,026	2.3	236.05
Paper	3	40,000	49	15,000	90,330	16.3	306.12
ONEIDA							
Clothing, men's	27	948,520	2,489	455,855	2,284,550	92.2	183.15
Cotton goods	8	3,165,988	2,157	486,057	1,981,061	269.6	225.34
Woolen goods	8	1,272,000	895	290,302	1,624,006	111.9	324.36
Cheese & butter (factory)	132	257,452	264	46,429	1,124,196	2.0	175.87
Boots & shoes	5	560,000	747	239,369	1,066,056	149.4	320.44

Table 30 (continued)

Counties and industries	No. of establishments	Capital ($)	Average no. of hands employed	Total wages ($)	Value of products ($)	Employees per establishment	Average wages ($)
ONONDAGA							
Clothing, men's	28	924,300	2,776	488,671	2,552,483	99.1	458.85
Flour & grist mills	56	732,150	174	62,854	2,105,821	3.1	222.89
Iron & steel	5	1,360,000	735	271,487	1,268,852	147.0	332.56
Salt	69	2,286,081	1,012	274,087	1,107,760	14.7	379.82
Tobacco, cigars & cigarettes	69	303,230	835	280,443	962,923	12.1	433.83
OSWEGO							
Flour & grist mills	40	1,059,700	168	77,086	2,697,873	4.2	485.85
Worsted goods	1	938,157	939	209,291	1,356,741	939.0	222.89
Leather, tanned	21	627,050	302	100,433	1,128,904	14.4	332.56
Starch	2	480,000	468	177,754	996,759	234.0	379.82
Foundry & machine products	12	476,368	462	200,429	703,980	38.5	433.83
ST LAWRENCE							
Flour & grist mills	51	762,022	151	54,913	1,724,512	3.0	363.66
Cheese & butter (factory)	140	271,722	297	41,621	1,004,023	2.1	140.14
Lumber, sawed	120	1,050,160	912	182,939	831,793	7.6	200.59
Leather, tanned	23	299,100	119	45,184	628,427	5.2	379.70
Lumber, planed	3	51,000	63	29,110	564,618	21.0	462.06

Source: Department of the Interior, Report of the Manufactures of the United States, 1880, vol. 2, table 5, pp. 295–316.

[1] selected on the basis of value of products.

Table 31 Manufactures by Counties, 1900

Counties	No. of establishments	Capital ($)	Proprietors & firm members	Average No. of wage earners	Total wages ($)	Value of products ($)	Employees per establishment	Average wages ($)
Herkimer	529	11,201,221	562	7,908	3,416,735	12,430,060	14.9	432.06
Jefferson	903	12,773,758	974	5,436	2,514,606	13,738,196	6.0	462.58
Lewis	336	3,878,282	364	1,129	437,233	3,377,016	3.4	387.27
Oneida	1,521	33,079,437	1,684	18,860	7,045,825	35,197,339	12.4	373.64
Onondaga	1,863	43,551,892	2,021	20,085	9,011,848	42,162,691	10.8	448.69
Oswego	659	15,052,361	688	6,757	2,620,330	15,109,321	10.3	387.79
St Lawrence	861	15,039,790	961	3,585	1,462,751	10,822,930	4.2	408.02

Source: 12th Census of the United States, 1900, Census Bulletin No. 159 (25 April 1902), table 6, pp. 20–1.

1873 combined with increased competition from western milling centres and railroads and the McKinley tariff of 1891 brought about economic decline.

The higher average wages and larger firms in Herkimer and Jefferson counties are explained by the further expansion of large-scale enterprises in existence in 1880 (Table 32). While employees per establishment remained relatively low, due to the importance of rural-based enterprises, the development of industry in Watertown during the last two decades of the nineteenth century resulted in tremendous growth. Water power provided from the fast-flowing Black River and pulpwood supplied from the nearby Adirondacks spurred the growth of the pulp and paper industry. Other large manufacturing concerns provided employment and higher wages for a growing population.

Manufacturing in Onondaga County, particularly in Syracuse and its environs, continued to expand and wages similarly increased.[15] Syracuse's economic foundations were built upon salt-mining but by mid-century the city enjoyed a broad industrial base with a mixture of traditional manufactures of consumer goods and manufactures of producer goods.

Oneida County, dominated by the textile industry centred in Utica, had lower average wages than Onondaga. Utica developed rapidly as a textile centre after 1837 when the steam turbine was first introduced in the city.[16] Industrial development was also spurred by the introduction of the power loom in textile manufacturing; the forests and rivers which resulted in the founding of pulp and lumber mills and furniture, paper and box factories; the fur and cattle resources from which sprang the tanning and leather products industries; and the growing of hops and barley from which a significant brewing and distilling industry developed.[17]

The other major city in the county, Rome, by the end of the Civil War had become the largest cheese-producing centre in the world. But the next fifty years were to witness the development of iron and steel works, railroad shops, foundries, breweries, textile mills, soap factories, and brass and copper works in Rome.[18]

While conditions varied significantly within northern New York, most urban areas, with the possible exception of Oswego, were experiencing some degree of growth during the latter part of the nineteenth century. The same cannot be said for the major urban centres of eastern Ontario. Kingston, Gananoque, and Napanee actually lost population during the 1890s and Brockville, Prescott, and Picton experienced only marginal growth. Every significant urban centre in the New York destination region grew in population, with marked increases taking place in Syracuse, Utica, Ilion, Herkimer, Little Falls, Rome, and Watertown. The average wages ($414.29) paid in the destination region in 1900, both at the county and municipal levels, were higher than those paid in the origin region in 1901 ($319.76). Yet most rural towns in northern New York, just as their

Table 32   Urban Manufactures, Selected Cities, 1900

Counties	No. of establishments	Capital ($)	Proprietors & firm members	Average no. of wage earners	Total wages ($)	Value of products ($)	Employees per establishment	Average wages ($)
Herkimer	73	1,836,979	79	1,344	515,627	2,853,605	18.4	383.65
Ilion	47	2,172,209	57	1,946	1,185,975	2,944,655	41.4	609.44
Little Falls	124	4,020,573	147	3,112	1,125,777	4,364,994	25.1	361.75
Ogdensburg	197	1,855,116	207	1,052	404,955	2,668,952	5.3	384.94
Oswego	207	7,322,907	215	3,845	1,543,905	8,137,950	18.6	401.54
Rome	196	3,738,051	204	2,653	1,014,352	6,093,544	13.5	382.34
Syracuse	1,383	31,358,055	1,514	14,917	6,735,177	31,948,055	10.8	451.51
Utica	733	19,289,502	842	10,759	4,148,415	19,550,850	14.7	385.58
Watertown	289	8,281,845	302	3,760	1,821,477	7,881,977	13.0	484.44

Source: 12th Census of the United States, 1900, Census Bulletin No. 159 (25 April 1902), table 5, pp. 18–19.

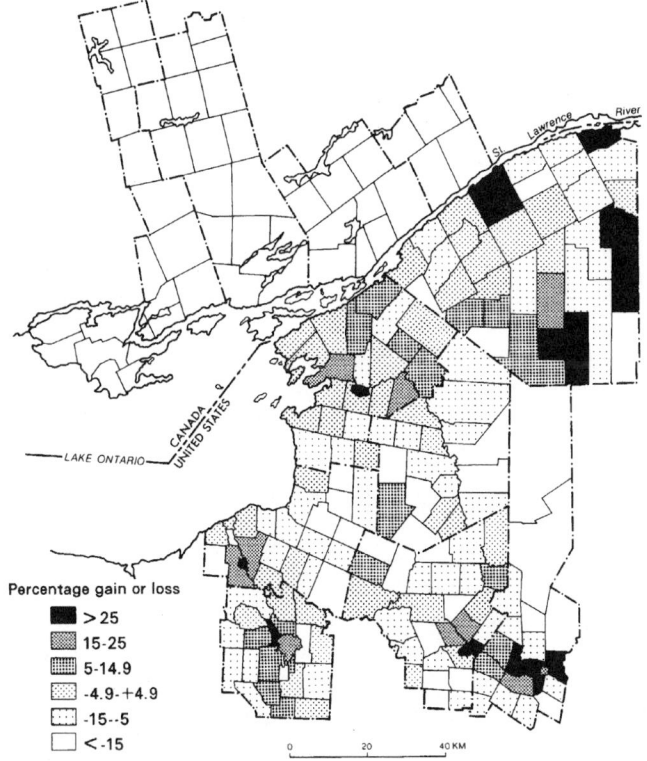

Percentage gain or loss
- ■ > 25
- ▨ 15-25
- ▦ 5-14.9
- ▩ -4.9-+4.9
- ▫ -15--5
- ☐ < -15

Map 7: Population Changes in the Destination Region

Canadian counterparts, also lost population towards the end of the century (Map 7).

Inevitably, many eastern Ontarians, attracted by the opportunities presented by New York's expanding economy, made the relatively short trip across the border and generally settled in adjacent border regions. Migrants from eastern Ontario and southwestern Quebec contributed most directly to the large Canadian population in the northern counties of Clinton, Franklin, St Lawrence, Jefferson, Essex, Oswego, Lewis, and Hamilton. Migrants from south-central Ontario constituted the largest percentage of Canadians living in Niagara, Monroe, and Erie counties. Nevertheless, a disproportionate number of this group settled in New York City, having yielded to the lure that this growing metropolis held out to all immigrant groups.

REGIONAL PATTERNS OF MIGRATION

The Petitions for Naturalization are used to map and analyse patterns of migration for the period 1880 to 1910. Table 33 shows the total number

Table 33   Petitions for Naturalization and the Study Region

Destination County	Total no. of petitions admitted and dismissed (1)	No. of petitions accepted from Eastern Ontario (2)	No. of petitions accepted from region (3)	$(3)/(2)$	$(2)/(1)$	$(3)/(1)$
Jefferson	970	402	284	70.6	41.4	29.3
Onondaga	2,982	155	91	58.7	5.2	3.1
Oswego	611	25	12	48.0	4.1	1.9
Oneida	2,251	47	32	68.1	2.1	1.4
Herkimer	986	21	6	28.6	2.2	0.6
St Lawrence	405	197	62	31.5	48.6	15.3
Lewis	149	50	25	52.0	33.6	17.4
Totals and Averages	8,336	897	512	56.8	10.8	6.1

Source: US Department of Immigration, Petitions for Naturalization, available in New York county courthouses.

of petitions admitted and dismissed in the northern New York destination region between 1906 and 1919 (pertaining to immigrants who came to the United States between 1880 and 1910); the number of petitions accepted from eastern Ontario (i.e., thirteen counties stretching from Hastings in the west to the Quebec border); the numbers of petitions accepted from the designated origin region; and various ratios involving these figures. Petitions from the origin region constituted a large proportion of the total number of foreign petitions in Jefferson, Lewis, and St Lawrence counties – 29.3, 17.4, and 15.3 percent respectively. The figures show that the petitions from eastern Ontario made up a significant proportion of the total numbers of petitions in these same three counties. The relative importance of this region as a source of immigrants is evident, for almost 60 percent of the total number of petitions submitted from eastern Ontario came from the five counties selected for study.

The distributions of the places of origin and final destinations claimed by the naturalization group settling in northern New York are illustrated in maps 8 and 9. Frontenac County was the most important source for these eastern Ontarians, followed by Lennox and Addington, Leeds, Grenville, and Prince Edward counties. The distribution within each county shows that the majority of emigrants were born in the longer-settled townships adjacent to the St Lawrence and the lake. A considerable proportion (15.4 percent) of the group were born either elsewhere in Canada or in Great Britain. In this sense, the region served as a stage in a larger migration process.[19]

This movement cannot be described simply as an exodus of rural people. Over one-third of the naturalization members born in the origin

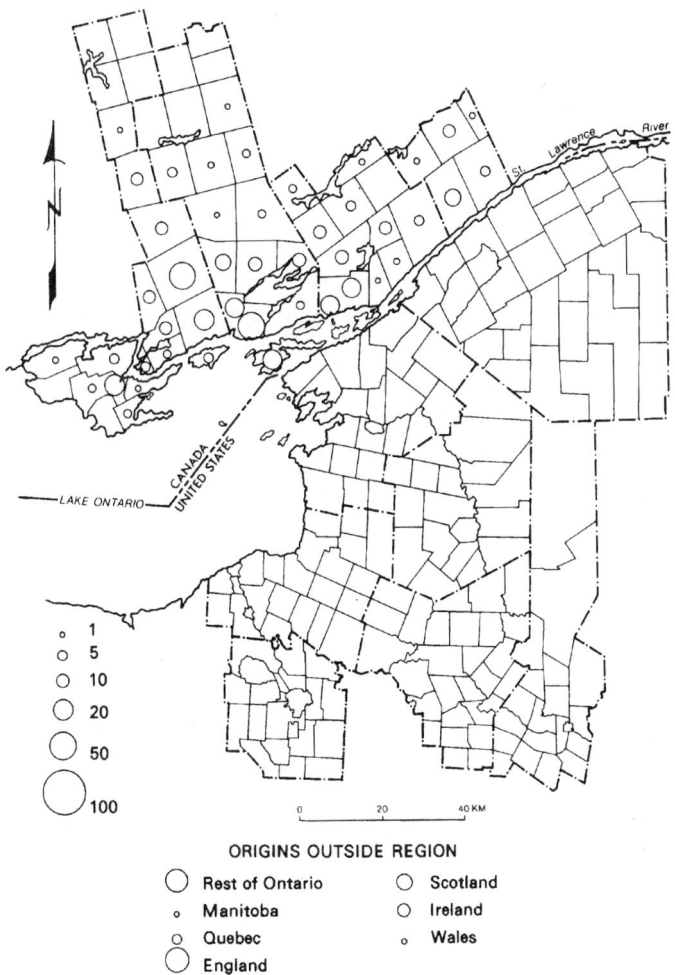

ORIGINS OUTSIDE REGION

○ Rest of Ontario	○ Scotland
○ Manitoba	○ Ireland
○ Quebec	○ Wales
○ England	

Map 8: Origins of Naturalization Group

region had last lived in towns or cities before they emigrated. Well over half of the migrants from Prince Edward County came from Picton, a town that experienced a significant turnover of people despite a general increase in population. In terms of sheer numbers, Kingston was the most important urban source, claiming 9.3 percent of the entire naturalization group. The fact that such a large percentage of the naturalization group was born in the region's urban centres reinforces the fact that these communities lacked the industrial base to accommodate the needs of both long-time residents and newcomers.

The naturalization group for the most part was predominantly young

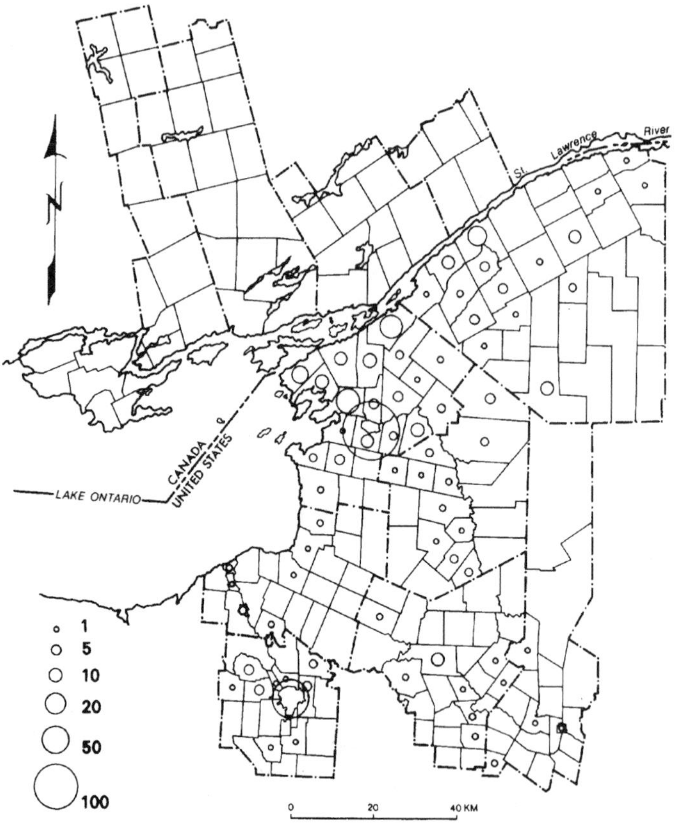

Map 9: Destinations of Naturalization Group

(85 percent less than 35 years of age), single, and male.[20] A significant number were children at the time of the move, from large households, and either Methodist or Anglican. Almost 60 percent were at least second-generation Ontarian while 22 percent and 10 percent came from families where the father was born in Ireland and England respectively. Of the ninety-one fathers of the naturalization members found in the census records, over 58 percent were farmers and almost 7 percent were farm labourers. Of the remaining 35 percent, the majority were engaged in a variety of traditional rural crafts.

The majority of this particular naturalization group settled close to their former homes. Almost 60 percent of the migrants settled within seventy kilometres of their place of origin, although one of the most distant areas of the region, Onondaga County, attracted close to 20 percent of this group, seventy-eight of them choosing to live in Syracuse-Solvay, the largest city of the region. Because the distances involved were so short, transportation was not very important. By far the most popular mode of travel was steamer or ferry. Several steamer services operated from each side of the border, the most notable being the Folger line of Kingston and its subsidiary, the Thousand Island Steamboat Company of Clayton and Gananoque.[21] Once emigrants disembarked at Cape Vincent, Clayton, or Ogdensburg, railroad connections could be made for points south.

The volume of trade carried across the river by several cargo-carrying steamers acquainted Ontarians with this northern part of New York. Lumber, barley, oats, and other foodstuffs connected the origin counties with such ports and markets as Oswego, Ogdensburg, and Watertown. By far the most popular point of arrival was Cape Vincent, a small river town that was directly connected by steamer to Kingston and its hinterland and was the terminus of the Rome, Watertown and Oswego Railroad. As such, it served as the jumping-off point for Canadians, many from Prince Edward, Lennox and Addington, and Frontenac counties, intending to travel to Watertown, Syracuse, and other locations south. The second most important point of arrival was Morristown in St Lawrence County, which attracted emigrants from Brockville and the eastern section of Leeds County. Clayton and Alexandria Bay were the primary points of arrival for Gananoque and Leeds County emigrants, whereas the vast majority of Prescott and Grenville County emigrants disembarked at Ogdensburg.

Both Canadians and Americans travelled across the border partly because of family connections, and this frequently explains this short-distance migration. As a result of the regular interchange of eastern Ontarians and northern New Yorkers, particularly those living near the border, many Canadians had direct links with their kin south of the border. For example, one of the Watertown migrants, Dr Edgar W. Lafontaine, was born in Maitland, Ontario, in 1890 shortly after his parents emigrated from Omar in Jefferson County. Edgar's father was a native of Canada who had moved to northern New York and married Alice Frazier of Fisher's Landing in Jefferson County. After their marriage the couple farmed near Omar, where their first two children were born. An opportunity to buy a large and prosperous farm near Maitland lured the Lafontaines back across the river, where Edgar, the third of five children, was born. Both parents died in Maitland and three of the five children, including Edgar, moved to Jefferson County, where they lived with relatives at different times and where two, Edgar and his oldest brother Oliver, practised medicine.[22] This example illustrates two of the basic principles of migration: the importance of kinship, and return migration, the latter occurring in this case in the next generation.

The rural-urban direction of this migration is illustrated by the fact that almost 64 percent of the naturalization sample took up residence in northern New York's urban centres. Forty percent chose to settle in one of the three largest communities in the region in 1910 – Syracuse, Utica, and

Watertown. The lure of better opportunities in growing industrial cities was the magnet drawing Ontarians to these places. One such migrant was Clarence Shangraw, a logger from Colebrook in Camden Township, who at 22 years of age moved to Glen Park, three miles west of Watertown on the Black River. The year was 1907, and Shangraw had heard from his brother who had moved to this area two years earlier that jobs were plentiful in the paper mill and wages were good. He settled between Brownville and Glen Park and the following year married the daughter of the couple with whom he boarded.[23] Again, chain migration as well as rural-urban orientation is evident in this example.

Yet this movement cannot be described simply as rural-urban migration, since 20 percent of the migrants moved from rural communities in Ontario to similar areas in northern New York, settling primarily in nearby Jefferson and St Lawrence counties. Considering the short distances involved, the low rail and ferry boat fares, and the importance of links to relatives and friends already living in the region, it is conceivable that many eastern Ontarians had travelled to Jefferson and St Lawrence before to assess the agricultural potential of these two dairy counties. As well, over 36 percent of this group settling in rural communities had last lived in one of Ontario's urban centres, reinforcing the fact that these communities lacked industrial and commercial opportunities for both long-time residents and newcomers.

The Wiley family of Storrington Township and Kingston, all relocating in Onondaga County, are representative of rural Ontarians who eventually acquired land in northern New York. In 1895, 16-year-old Bertram Wiley left the family farm in Storrington and moved to the town of Camillus in Onondaga County where he was employed as a farm labourer for a few years before acquiring land. In the meanwhile, his father and the rest of the family moved to Kingston. But by 1900 they had all joined Bertram in Onondaga. At the time of signing their petitions, William Howard, Bertram's younger brother, was farming in Camillus; Thomas, his other younger brother, was a cutter and living also in Camillus; and his older brothers, William Jr and John, were farming in Van Buren and working as a cutter respectively. William, the father, and the rest of the family also lived in Camillus where William worked as a farm labourer.[24]

Migration was seldom a one-step decision; rather, it was a multi-stage process, often spanning a considerable period of a person's life. The evidence shows that more migrants passed through stages than went directly to their final destinations, that is, the places where they signed their petitions. These steps often occurred on both the Canadian and American sides. The migration paths for Watertown and Syracuse migrants illustrated in maps 10 and 11 suggest different types of stage movements. This evidence shows that these centres lacked the economic opportunities to hold newcomers, but served merely as reservoirs or holding units of rural pop-

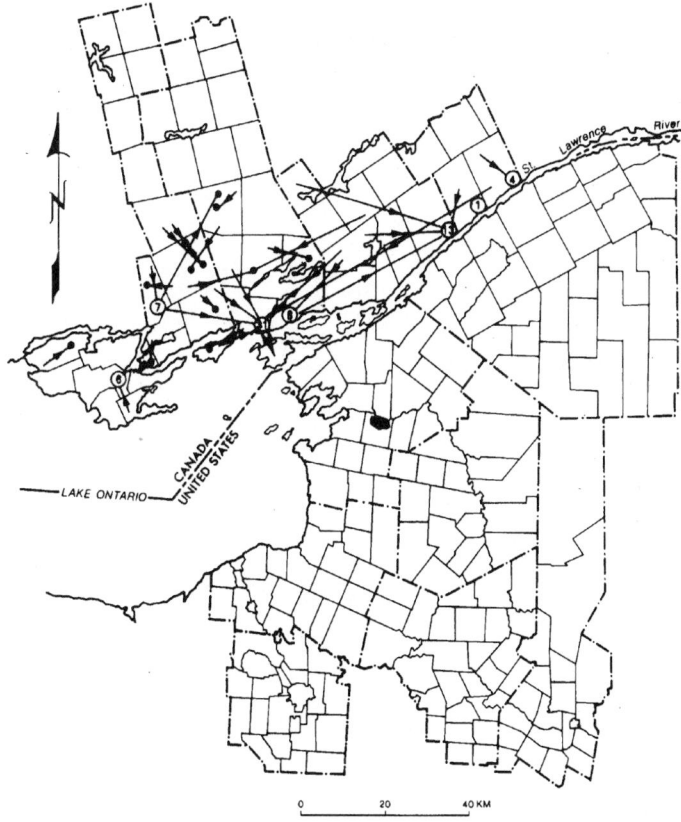

Map 10: Migration Paths: Watertown Sample

ulation. As a result, many left after only a brief sojourn and made the relatively easy move to nearby New York. Evidence also shows that some movement was taking place among townships.

    People who wanted to leave their immediate neighbourhoods had sev-
eral choices. First, they could move to another rural community and try to
farm or find employment, but opportunities to work or farm were becoming rare. Secondly, they could move to Kingston, Brockville, Prescott, Picton, Cardinal, or other towns of the region and try to find work. Finally,
those who chose to move to town but could not establish themselves or
meet their own expectations could either move elsewhere in Canada or go
to the United States. For many, this stage of movement up the urban hierarchy may have enabled them to acquire urban and industrial skills which
later helped their adjustment process.

    On the American side, the same migration in stages continued for many.
Examination of the time-lag between date of emigration and first appear-

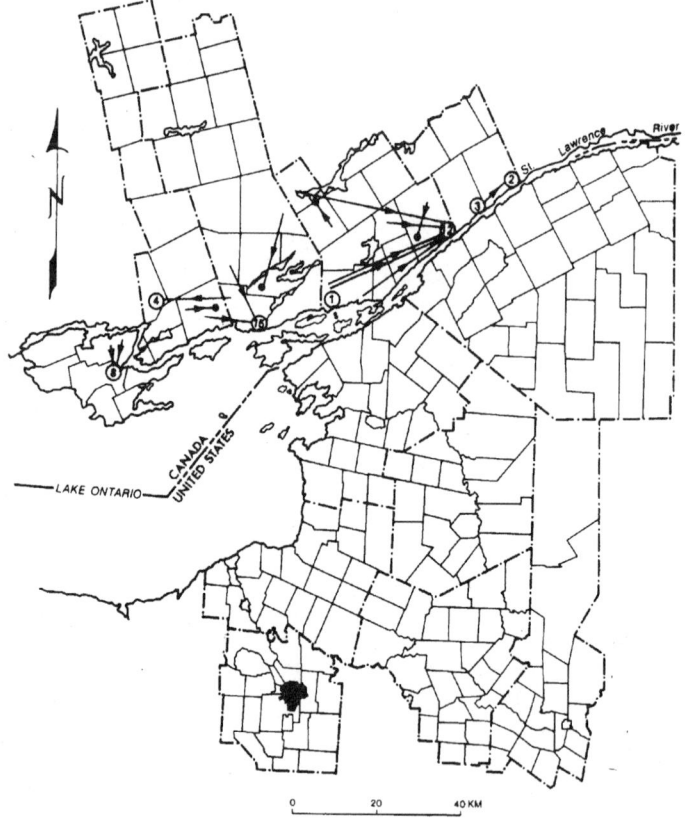

Map 11: Migration Paths: Syracuse Sample

ance in the Watertown city directories shows that only 19 percent of the Watertown group arrived within one or two years, 44 percent between two and five years, 17 percent between six and ten years, and 20 percent after ten years. The same analysis for Syracuse shows that 22.6 percent of the naturalization group arrived within one and two years, 23.9 percent between two and five years, 15.5 percent between six and ten years, and 38.1 percent after ten years.[25]

The following examples represent different types of stage processes that were occurring in this particular migration. Samuel Avery, his wife, and their six children left Lansdowne, in Leeds County, in 1899 and moved to Little Falls in Herkimer County. Samuel, a "shiftless, never-do-well, odd-job fellow," could not find work in Lansdowne but got a job working in the textile mill at Little Falls, where he was later joined by his son Elmer. In 1912 Samuel and Lillian took Elmer and his sister Ethel to Abbey, Saskatchewan, where they took up homesteading.[26]

Samuel Glenn was born on Amherst Island in Lennox and Addington County in 1877, one of seven children of William and Rachel Glenn, both of whom were farmers and Ontario-born. In 1909 Foster's *Kingston Directory* lists him as boarding at 307 Earl Street. The assessment records reveal that he was single, worked at the Locomotive Works, and owned no property. Kingston was a brief sojourn for Samuel; the next year he left for the United States and lived for a time in Dayton, Ohio, where he married an English woman named Gertrude and worked as an assembler. Seven years later he appeared in Watertown, where he was employed as a machine worker at the New York Air Brake factory. In June 1918 he signed his petition for naturalization, which shows that he had been promoted to foreman. Yet the 1919 city directory lists him as a labourer, and the 1920 directory states that he and his wife had moved to Detroit.

Another example is that of Alfred Pratt, who was born in London, England, in 1881. The Pratt family came to Canada in 1890 and took up residence in Napanee. On 20 February 1901, 19-year-old Alfred crossed the ice of the St Lawrence and travelled to Dexter, where he obtained a job with the Brownville Board Company. He was employed there as a stationary engineer for forty-nine years. In 1904 he married Jennie Steeles, a former Canadian living in Dexter and they had three children. In 1910 Pratt and his family moved the relatively short distance to Watertown, but he commuted to work, probably via electric trolley. Jennie died in 1914, and the following year Alfred married a Mrs Grace Riley. The Pratt family moved again in 1919, taking up residence in Brownville. Alfred retired in 1949, one year after the death of his second wife, and the following year he married Grace Laforest of Watertown. In 1951 he again moved to Watertown, where he died in 1958.[27]

These examples illustrate a diversity of step-wise movements both in scale and direction. The majority of Pratt's movements were confined within one community and its environs, and his migration history can properly be described as inter-urban in direction. Both Avery and Glenn hailed from rural communities, but the similarities between these two migrants end there. The urban phase for Avery was just one stage in his migration, which eventually took him back to a rural environment in another part of Canada.

Generally, the movement of the eastern Ontario naturalization group to Manhattan was more direct, with over 56 percent settling in the city within one to two years of leaving Canada. Over 43 percent of this group last lived in the place they were born, indicating that as a group they were less likely to be stage migrants than the northern New York migrants. The Manhattan Canadians also differed from their northern New York counterparts in that the majority (83.3 percent) had lived in urban centres before they emigrated.

The observed pattern of emigration from eastern Ontario to New York

State shows that partial displacement migrants – those who made short-distance moves – were in the majority. The primary direction was rural-urban; this movement often occurred in stages. Return migration was a significant factor among Canadians, although relying on the naturalization records makes it difficult to say much about specific chain migration processes. There is, however, little doubt that prospective immigrants learned of opportunities from friends and relatives who preceded them. The tracing procedure also supports the idea that this movement was channellized, with kinship networks strengthening existing connections between origins and destinations.

URBAN RECEPTION CENTRES:
WATERTOWN AND SYRACUSE

Economic and Social Profiles

The emigration of eastern Ontarians was primarily urban in orientation because northern New York's towns and cities, with few exceptions, were experiencing substantial industrial and urban growth after 1870. Two communities in particular, Watertown and Syracuse, benefited from this development and Canadians responded to the new opportunities emerging in these centres. The economies of both cities were developing from traditional craft and agricultural-based enterprises to large-scale manufacturing industry. Yet Watertown and Syracuse were also unlike in many ways and as a consequence presented different environments and opportunities to the immigrant.

Watertown   Watertown is an ideal setting for a study of the Anglo-Canadian experience in the United States. In 1900, 779 of Watertown's 5,083 households were headed by Anglo-Canadians, many of whom originated in eastern Ontario. They were the dominant immigrant group in the city, composing 52 percent of the foreign-born population.[28]

Why did so many decide on Watertown? The visitor who looks at the city today is struck by the juxtaposition of visible signs of past prosperity and present depression. The shells of once busy factories and mills flank the Black River. Large brick and stone mansions on tree-lined streets are impressive despite their dilapidated state in many cases. Many have been subdivided and some stand empty with boards where elegant windows once sparkled in the sun.

It is, however, the large public square, the centre of the city, which most dramatically underscores the contrast between the past and the present. One wonders why a small city in one of the most remote areas in New York possesses such an impressive central core. On the west side of the square sits the arcade, one of the first indoor shopping malls of its kind in the state. Just down the street is the Woolworth Building, the site of the first "5 and 10" cent store. Yet there are vacant stores in the next block, and on the north side of the square a large empty lot marks the site of the Woodruff House, for many years the largest hotel in the northern part of the state.

Watertown had originally been settled in 1800 by a group of New Englanders who recognized the site's potential for industrial and commercial activity. The village grew slowly as it established its position as an agricultural and milling centre. The first significant increase in population occurred when the Irish entered the area after the building of the Erie Canal in 1825. They came in even greater numbers in the late 1840s, "pushed" out of Ireland by the potato famine and "pulled" into the Watertown area with the extension of the railroad into Jefferson County. German migration was also greatest at mid-century, while Italians and other east Europeans came largely during the 1890s and the first decade of the twentieth century.[29]

Although the inflow of Canadians, both francophone and anglophone, had been constant through the years, they came in greater numbers after the depression of the 1870s. This flow increased as the extension of Watertown's industrial base attracted thousands of immigrants and rural migrants to the city. The population grew by almost 50 percent between 1890 (14,724) and 1900 (21,696). Although Watertown could hardly be classified as an immigrant city, by 1900 there were 5,119 foreign-born living there. It was estimated that nearly one-third of the population of Watertown was of Canadian origin or descent.

Watertown's situation along the Black, the second-longest river in the state, ensured the development of a power source that provided the spur to this growth. While the community had been slow to make use of this resource, the 1880s and 1890s witnessed the founding of certain industrial establishments that would produce the city's greatest period of development. In 1900, 289 manufacturing establishments employed 3,760 workers and they averaged a mere thirteen employees per firm (Table 34). Despite this diversity, three large-scale industries were dominant: foundries and machine products with six establishments; pulp and paper, also with six firms; and carriage and wagon makers with four companies. These were the major employers, with a workforce that averaged 224, 106, and 115 employees respectively. Together they employed nearly 71 percent of the city's wage earners.[30]

The foundry and machine products industry was by far the most prominent and the single most important establishment was the New York Air Brake Company. In 1900 the factory employed over 1,200 men, or about one-third of the total number of wage-earners in the city. Pulp and paper ranked second to foundry and machine products in Watertown, but it was the dominant industry in the region. Child's *Gazetteer of Jefferson County*,

Table 34 Manufactures in Watertown by Specified Industries, 1900

Industry	No. of establishments	Capital ($)	Proprietors	Average no. of wage earners	Average wage ($)	Average of wage earners per firm	Total wages ($)	Value of products ($)
Blacksmith	22	21,121	22	20	452.05	0.9	9,945	39,092
Bakery products	13	154,574	13	62	425.77	4.8	26,398	169,178
Carpentering	13	45,792	15	99	553.18	7.6	54,765	218,199
Carriages & wagons	4	1,236,480	–	463	499.24	115.8	231,150	985,400
Clothing, men's	20	45,128	20	88	350.11	4.4	30,150	111,938
Clothing, women's	22	19,865	23	79	207.44	3.6	16,388	85,184
Flour & grist								
Mill products	5	273,634	2	27	479.22	5.4	12,939	329,753
Foundry & machine products	6	3,594,582	3	1,347	553.02	224.5	744,924	2,352,945
Lumber, planing mill products	5	157,855	9	94	484.56	18.8	45,549	262,345
Masonry	4	28,521	6	58	620.40	14.5	35,983	119,258
Paper & pulp	6	1,458,304	–	640	479.53	106.7	306,901	1,870,282
Newspaper, printing & publishing	8	202,839	5	83	590.52	10.4	49,013	149,841
All industries	289	8,281,845	302	3,760	484.44	13.0	1,821,477	7,881,977

Source: 12th Census of the United States, Census Bulletin No. 159 (25 April, 1902), pp. 76–9.

published in 1890, lists thirteen paper and nine pulp mills along the Black River between Carthage and Dexter, a distance of some forty miles. Its importance to the economy of the city as well as the region is reflected in the fact that it was a group of Watertown businessmen who in 1898 organized what was to become one of the leading paper firms in the world, the St Regis Paper Company. The largest of the four carriage and wagon plants, the H.H. Babcock Company, employed 350 people in 1900 and occupied ten acres of floor space.[31]

The rapid pace of industrialization and urbanization during the last two decades of the nineteenth century changed the character of Watertown. The litany of social facilities enumerated at length in the city directory of 1900 testifies to the progress achieved during the industrial boom:

Twelve elementary schools, two private kindergartens, one business school, two hospitals, 54 physicians and surgeons, two orphanages, a bureau of charity, 21 churches, 24 blacksmith shops, eight horse and livery stables, seven harness shops, fourteen dealers in wagons and buggies, thirteen wood yards, eight coal dealers, twenty hotels, five commercial banks, two savings banks, sixteen restaurants, 31 saloons, 59 dressmakers, two large music halls, the City Opera House, 35 fraternal organizations, and a number of unaffiliated social clubs.[32]

In addition, the public transportation system, an electric trolley line which connected all parts of the city, and a telephone and electric service reflect the incorporation of modern technologies into the community. Many small businesses existed, but the jewel of the retail section was the Paddock Arcade, containing the post office, the telegraph office, ten stores, and a large saloon.

There existed a wide choice of facilities for entertainment and social affairs. Two large halls, the music hall in the American Block and Washington Hall, were used for public dances, concerts, lectures, and weekly band concerts.[33] The opera hall featured theatrical plays and vaudeville shows. But other types of social activities were less favoured in the expression of public opinion, if not in the popular use of them. The town gained a reputation for gambling and prostitution, and a prosperous red light and saloon district flourished next to the industrial section of town. The Watertown *Daily Times* often referred to labourers being cheated by "tinhorn gamblers and short-card men."[34] In 1915 there were eleven houses of prostitution along River Street alone.[35]

The editorials in the local newspaper were full of confidence, and they had good reason to be proud. The air brakes, carriages, paper-making machines, and portable steam engines made in Watertown were sold all over the world. In addition to its industries, the town was also noted for its citizens. Apart from the contribution of Frank W. Woolworth to the retail trade and Frederick Eames's development of the revolutionary air brake,

Watertown could also boast about one of its native sons, Roswell P. Flower, who was elected governor in 1891. Public Square (which was said to be the longest continuous block of buildings in the country in the 1890s), and stately mansions were visible signs of prosperity that gave support to this air of confidence and pride.

This prosperity, however, was to be short-lived. Watertown relied upon industries which, for one reason or another, were soon to disappear or decrease greatly in importance. With the overcutting of the Adirondack forests, the pulpwood supply practically ceased, signalling the demise of the paper mills along the Black River. With the mass production of the automobile came the decline and ultimate end of the carriage industry. The New York Air Brake factory experienced cutbacks as the railroad decreased in importance. And finally, Watertown's rather isolated location relative to other centres in the state reduced its attraction as a potential industrial site.

At the turn of the century, however, few people could envision the hardships that lay ahead as the city basked in its growing prosperity. Canadians, especially those from nearby eastern Ontario, were very much aware of the opportunities offered in the community. James Pappa certainly made the most of the opportunities presented to him and there is little doubt that other Canadians also achieved a comparable degree of success. In 1900, for example, the chief of the Watertown fire department, Fred Morrison, and the publisher of the *Daily Times*, Jeremiah Coughlin, were ex-Canadians. Yet their stories were not necessarily typical of the Canadian experience in Watertown.

Syracuse   Like Watertown, the juxtaposition of visible signs of past prosperity and present depression is evident in Syracuse, although not as striking. All of the old industrial communities of northern New York suffered greatly during the recent economic recession. However, Syracuse presents a much more varied environment than Watertown in terms of scale, industrial activity, and social geography. German bakeries, Italian restaurants, and Jewish delicatessens testify to the ethnic heterogeneity of the city, while chemical works, candle factories, and corporate headquarters are evidence of the economic diversity present.

Europeans and New England Yankees settled the Onondaga region after the American Revolution. Most took up farming but some were quick to realize the potential of the salt springs on the shores of Onondaga Lake. The state leased lots to salt-makers who took advantage of the large deposits, nearness to large markets, and access to wood and coal needed to boil the salt.[36] Several villages grew up near the salt deposits surrounding the lake – South Salina, Salina, Liverpool, Geddes. South Salina was renamed Syracuse and incorporated as a village in 1825, the same year that the Erie Canal was completed. The new transportation network provided easy access to markets for all the products produced in the region. Thousand of immigrants were attracted to the canal communities, first to work on the actual construction and later to gain employment made possible by realty development. During this period many Irish and Germans were attracted to the Syracuse area and the village grew rapidly. The population increased from 2,505 in 1830 to almost 20,000 by 1847, the year Syracuse merged with Salina and Lodi and was incorporated as a city.[37]

Growth remained steady throughout the mid-century period as Syracuse broadened its industrial base and continued to attract immigrants. But the tempo of development really increased towards the end of the century, particularly during the 1880s when population increased by over 70 percent from 52,000 to 88,000. Roughly 22 percent of the city's population was foreign-born, a figure almost identical to that of Watertown. But whereas Anglo-Canadians constituted the largest foreign element in Watertown, they were only the fourth-largest nativity group in Syracuse (2.8 percent). Of the 23,757 foreign-born residing in Syracuse in 1900, 7,865 or 33.3 percent of the immigrant total were born in Germany.[38]

In 1880, 724 establishments employed 10,996 wage-earners while twenty years later, 1,383 establishments employed 14,917 people. However, while the industrial base had expanded along with the population, there is some evidence of stagnation in the manufacturing sector during the 1890s. The average number of wage-earners per firm was less than that of Watertown, signifying both a greater range of manufacturing concerns and a lack of dominant large-scale firms such as the New York Air Brake Company in the smaller city. Average wages only increased 4.4 percent from $432.43 to $451.51 during the decade, a figure well below the state average of $481.70 and the Watertown average of $484.44.[39]

This lower wage average may be explained by the importance of textile and consumer industries in the central New York region. In 1880 Syracuse was the largest clothing centre in central New York and the industry traditionally paid low salaries to its workers. Almost 70 percent of the employees were women, who were generally paid less than males for the same work. Syracuse was built by the salt industry and the canal, but by 1900 both these elements of the city's economic structure had declined. Yet the development of durable manufacturing such as chemicals, iron and steel, and agricultural implements, served to offset the declining fortunes of various consumer nondurable industries and growth continued to be steady, if not spectacular, by the turn of the century.

With a population of 108,374, Syracuse in 1900 was the thirtieth largest city in the nation and it possessed all of the social facilities required by a growing population – thirty-five elementary schools, ninety-nine churches, nineteen missions, five major railroads, 266 physicians and surgeons, 101 bankers and brokers, 1,463 dressmakers, fourteen banks, 280 saloons, one central trade and assembly with sixty-five unions associated with it, seventeen different lodges with over one hundred chapters, and eleven Catholic societies. By 1860 the German and Irish populations were large enough to create distinctive ethnic areas. Both Irish and German immigrants settled on the western edge of the saltfields, a working-class area, although the Irish were more scattered around the city. The majority of this group in 1860 were unskilled labourers clustering in small pockets close to their places of employment.

In contrast, over half the Germans lived in Ward 2 where they constituted almost 90 percent of the population. Bigelow attributes this clustering to the fact that they were a linguistic minority, they possessed marketable skills so they could work for themselves, and they had enough capital to buy their own homes and not have to compete with other immigrants as renters in slum areas. Jews and black Americans formed a small segment of the population in 1860 but both were highly concentrated, the Jews in Ward 7 and the blacks in wards 4 and 8 near the canal. English-, Scottish- and Canadian-born, both francophone and anglophone, were spread throughout the city.[40]

The building of the West Shore Railroad between 1881 and 1883 and the expansion of industry in Syracuse attracted southern and eastern Europeans to the city, as well as Canadian and British immigrants. Italians tended to cluster on the north side while the Poles and Ukrainians settled in separate neighbourhoods on the west side. While most immigrants were working class, significant numbers of Italians and eastern Europeans operated small businesses catering to these immigrant neighbourhoods. As a result, Syracuse in 1900 was characterized by ethnic enclaves, both large and small, modest communities which served in some instances to support newcomers and in other cases to set them apart from the native community.

Attitudes Towards Immigrant Groups

Differences in attitudes held by the native-born population towards foreigners influenced ethnic solidarity and association, the integration process, and mobility decisions. Such differences are difficult to discern, although newspapers do serve as communicators of public opinion.

Watertown   Attitudes expressed in the Watertown *Daily Times* conformed to those widely held in the United States at this time. Local views were generally more favourable towards Anglo-Saxon Protestant groups coming from northern Europe and Anglo-Canada and less supportive of predominantly Catholic and Jewish non-English-speaking immigrants of eastern and southern Europe. An editorial from the *Daily Times* is typical:

The Irish, who when they first came in large numbers were dreaded and told they "need not apply", have proved to be the best mixing blood to produce a better race of Americans. The German, with his home loving instincts, his industry and frugality, has contributed a needed element to the life of the nation. The Swede and Norwegian, with a love of progress and education, have built up splendid communities and added to wealth and character. A later immigrant is the Italian. It will contribute an element of lightness which is perhaps necessary in our national character. At any rate he fills the need for common labour.[41]

Condescending and somewhat sectarian in tone, confidence is expressed in the American ability to assimilate and transform the array of foreign groups. The editorial subscribes to stereotype views: the German is "frugal," the Swede is "progressive," the Italian is "frivolous." The generally favourable attitudes towards the Germans and even towards the "dreaded" Irish reflected their long-standing presence in Watertown. But more recent immigrants from Italy and eastern Europe were thought of in different terms, even though there were few of them. The Italians are viewed as "menial," adding a bit of levity and supplying the need for labour, albeit "common" labour. But little else positive could be said about this group, the selective lexicon of "it" and "common" underscoring the contemporary judgement of this group.

Italians received the most focused commentary. A 1902 report made fun of Italians who during a minor smallpox epidemic mistook a doctor for a priest just because he spoke Italian. Several incidents of violence connected with this group were also reported in the *Daily Times*:

The barbarious custom of settling quarrels with the ever ready knife, which the horde of Italian labourers now domiciled in this city brought from their Calabrian homes, led a few days ago to a blood affray in which the deadly dirk was used freely ... The murderous affray apparently grew out of a trivial quarrel over a round of drinks, but those intimately acquainted with Italian ways and customs maintain that beneath the apparent motive was the racial hatred of the Calabrian and Sicilian for the Neapolitan and the Lombard.[42]

Not surprisingly, 42 percent of the Italian petitioners who arrived in the United States at some time between 1880 and 1910 and applied for naturalization in Watertown between 1906 and 1919 were denied citizenship. Ill-prepared for the naturalization process, unable to comprehend all the requirements that were necessary in order to attain citizenship, unfamiliar with the English language, and probably encountering considerable suspicion, if not hostility, the Italian performance in the citizenship courts was prejudiced from the outset.

Other immigrant groups received little attention. It would appear that Watertown at the turn of the century was primarily an American as opposed to an immigrant city. Indeed, the absence of a visible foreign element was commented on in the newspaper on more than one occasion. The 17 March 1900 edition of the *Daily Times* noted that Watertown was the only city in northern or central New York where St Patrick's Day was not celebrated in some fashion and concluded that this was evidence of either a lack of Irish in the city or a lack of Irish feeling. But there were 237 Irish-born household heads and many more first-generation and second-generation Irish in the city. Over one hundred French-Canadian households in the city warranted the selection of Watertown as the site of the Missionary of the Sacred Heart Order in America, and yet they too escaped much attention in the local newspaper.[43]

Anglo-Canadians were rarely mentioned in discussions of the city's foreign element, suggesting that this group was not thought of in the same terms as other foreigners, although Watertown residents were certainly aware of their neighbours to the north. Many were descended from Canadians who had made the short trip to the city years before and many continued to retain family, social, and business links with Ontario. News of major Canadian events appeared regularly in the *Daily Times* and mention was often made of friendly competition between local sports clubs and their Canadian counterparts. Indeed, some fifty-eight issues of the paper in 1900 included references to Canada, particularly Ontario. Issues also carried notices originally published in the Kingston *Whig-Standard*, most of them commenting on some type of interchange between the two communities.

The most focused discussion of Canadian character in the newspaper related to the success of Canadian soldiers in the Boer War: "No wonder Canadians are proud of them. They live much the same and breathe the same air which have made our Americans develop into such good soldiers. They have that strong individuality, power of taking the initiative, quickness of movement and readiness for an emergency which marks men of the west."[44]

It is clear that the approbation of the Canadian effort reflects an American ethos. They were an acceptable people, even admired, and they were looked upon as family rather than as strangers. Canadians were perceived as being part of a larger North American community and thus met the criteria for "good" Americans. The cultural-political context of this sense of community and common identity related more to continental expansion than to welcome accommodation. On a number of occasions, the *Daily Times* argued that it would be in Canada's best interest to join the United States, because the Canadian community was a mere reflection of the American one. One editorial commented on the visit of the noted Canadian continentalist Goldwin Smith, who suggested that Canada was a geographical absurdity: "Professor Goldwin Smith dislikes the word annexation as applied to the joining of Canada to this country, but prefers 'reunion', because the separation of English speaking people on the continent was only the result of an historical accident, and there is no natural line of separation. Everybody will agree to that. Continental reunion, let it be. Now let the ceremony proceed!"[45]

Syracuse   Attitudes towards certain immigrant groups in the Syracuse *Post-Standard* and *Herald-Journal*, as in Watertown, were often condescending. Of all the immigrant groups in the city, the Germans received the most attention and were looked upon favourably:

The German language is spoken here in Syracuse by at least 25,000 people, including immigrants and their children, although the latter prefer to speak English ... From the beginning they congregated in the northern part of the city, where for many years the German language reigned supreme in business and social life ... For more than fifty years they had their own churches, schools, societies, stores, saloons, artisans, tradesmen, doctors, druggists, etc., which relieved them from the necessity of learning English, but things have changed considerably. German churches and societies have hitherto been the main agencies in preserving the language. There are nine of the former and nearly forty of the latter to be found here.[46]

The same editorial also noted the increasing numbers of Italians in the city and their tendency to cluster in distinct neighbourhoods: "Since 1880 Italian immigration has assumed huge proportions ... Their living together in colonies and working in large gangs under 'bosses' of their nationality explains why they make so little progress in learning English ... There are comparatively few educated people among them." The Italians came primarily from poor agricultural regions where population growth combined with decreasing soil quality to spur migration. When they arrived in Syracuse, they were faced by labour unions unwilling to welcome them into their ranks because they represented a possible threat.[47] This hostile attitude combined with language difficulties, a strong sense of family, and an established institutional framework, served to separate Italians both residentially and socially from the larger community. As a consequence, Italians were viewed as they were in Watertown, as somewhat inferior but at the same time an important part of the "mundane and menial" workforce so necessary to the functioning of the city.[48]

The Irish did not garner as much notice as the Germans or the Italians and yet mention was always made of the St Patrick's Day celebrations. The Hibernians, in particular, were a powerful group. The state convention of Hibernians, held in July of 1890, attracted over 25,000 to the city.

Canadians received less attention in the Syracuse papers than they did in the Watertown *Daily Times*. A clue as to their invisibility is presented in one article which offered the view that Anglo-Canadians were "to a great extent Americanized before they even emigrated."[49] An examination of Syracuse's principle newspaper, the *Post-Standard*, failed to reveal any mention of Canadian festivals or events. Only eight issues of the paper for 1900 contained pieces which referred to Canada, including the familiar editorial opinions lauding the brave character of the Canadians in the Boer War, boasting that "Americans are justified in taking pride in this achievement across the border."[50]

Given such views of Canadians in Watertown and Syracuse, it is not surprising that Anglo-Canadians were seldom mentioned in the relatively limited discussions relating to the immigrant dimension of both cities. The fact that they did not establish ethnic boundaries to differentiate themselves further added to their invisibility.

Family and Kinship

Although they shared certain characteristics, Anglo-Canadian households in Watertown and Syracuse differed in some fundamental ways, including date of entry. There existed in Watertown an "old immigrant" category consisting of Germans, English, French-Canadians, and Irish, many who came as children and young adults at the mid-century period, and a "new immigrant" category of the Scots, Anglo-Canadians, eastern Europeans, and Italians, the majority coming to America during the 1880s and 1890s. Only 27 percent of the Anglo-Canadian household heads came before 1880 and 40 percent arrived at some time during the 1890s. Of the old immigrants present in Syracuse in 1900, over 65 percent of the Irish, 58 percent of the English, 57 percent of the French Canadian, and almost 55 percent of the German household heads arrived in America before 1880. Among the new immigrants present in 1900, almost 93 percent of the Italians, 73 percent of the Poles, and 55 percent of the "others" category came after 1880. Anglo-Canadians were generally an older group in Syracuse than in Watertown with 40 percent over the age of 45, reflecting the fact that many of this group arrived in the United States before 1880.[51]

An examination of tables 35 and 36 enforces the argument that Anglo-Canadians in Watertown adopted certain of the family and household traits of the so-called new immigrants – a stronger reliance on kin and boarders in the family economy, more living in multiple dwelling units, a greater frequency of extended households, and larger households – while the Anglo-Canadians in Syracuse were generally older, arrived at an earlier date, and were more likely to live in single dwelling units and in smaller households than more recent immigrants.

The differences between the two groups in 1900 are explained largely by the longer period of residence in America by the Syracuse migrants. Yet Anglo-Canadians in both communities were among the immigrant groups most likely to share their homes with relatives, regardless of length of res-

Table 35   The Composition and Role of Watertown's Families and Households, 1900

Characteristics	% of households headed by national groups[1]				
	1	2	3	4	5
A. COMPOSITION	(N=169)	(N=77)	(N=237)	(N=30)	(N=729)
Household size					
1–2	20.7	16.9	38.2	16.7	18.6
3–5	59.2	53.2	50.2	40.0	53.9
6–10	19.5	27.3	19.4	36.7	23.5
>10	0.6	2.6	2.1	6.7	2.7
No. of relatives in household					
0	81.7	81.8	78.9	76.7	75.5
1–2	17.2	15.6	17.7	16.7	22.1
3–5	1.2	2.6	2.5	3.3	2.4
>5	0	0	0.8	3.3	0
No. of families in the dwelling					
1	85.8	88.3	93.2	80.0	81.2
2	12.4	10.4	3.8	10.0	13.4
3–5	1.8	1.3	3.0	10.0	3.1
6–9	0	0	0	0	1.5
>9	0	0	0	0	0.8
B. ROLES					
No. of working members in nuclear family of household head					
0	4.1	0	11.8	0	2.4
1	64.6	70.1	44.3	76.7	74.5
2–5	31.3	29.9	42.2	23.3	22.7
>5	0	0	1.7	0	0.4
Household with boarders					
Not present	91.5	83.1	81.9	80.0	75.5
Present	9.5	16.9	18.1	20.0	24.5

Source: 1990 US Manuscript Census

[1] National groups: 1–English; 2–Germans; 3–Irish; 4–Italians; 5–Anglo-Canadians.

idence. For newcomers, kin connections were important in providing both accommodation and economic and social support, while for long-term residents such connections served to augment the household economy and to maintain familial connections. This was especially true for Canadians in Watertown where only Italians were more likely to share their homes with relatives.

Boarding was also a major institution of immigrant adjustment. Anglo-Canadians constituted only a small proportion of the total number of boarders living in Syracuse (9.6 percent) compared with a significant proportion in Watertown (21 percent), a difference explained in part by the proximity of Watertown to Canada and the fact that many boarders were

Table 36   The Composition and Role of Syracuse's Families and Households, 1900[1]

Characteristics	% of households headed by national groups[2]				
	1	2	3	4	5
A. COMPOSITION	(N=968)	(N=3464)	(N=2274)	(N=359)	(N=694)
Household size					
1–2	27.6	14.3	19.0	15.3	23.6
3–5	54.7	43.2	45.7	42.9	55.0
6–10	16.8	41.7	35.9	38.1	17.6
>10	0.9	0.8	8.4	3.7	3.8
No. of relatives in household					
0	77.7	87.9	87.8	87.6	79.6
1–2	19.4	9.4	8.4	16.2	27.3
3–5	2.9	2.8	1.9	4.5	3.1
>5	0	0	0	0	0
No. of families in the dwelling					
1	63.5	74.8	71.5	40.2	73.1
2	27.5	15.4	25.0	30.3	17.6
3–5	5.9	9.7	2.6	22.8	8.3
6–9	3.1	0	0.9	6.7	1.0
>9	0	0	0	0	0
B. ROLES					
No. of working members in nuclear family of household head					
0	3.8	3.6	3.8	0.3	2.0
1	69.5	46.1	41.6	82.6	72.3
2–5	17.6	58.3	50.9	17.4	25.7
>5	0	0	3.7	0	0
Household with boarders					
Not present	95.4	93.6	72.4	64.1	77.1
Present	4.6	6.4	22.6	35.9	22.9

Source: See table 35.
[1] Stratified sample compiled by weight factors.
[2] National Groups: 1–English; 2–German; 3–Irish; 4–Italians; 5–Anglo-Canadians

young single males seeking employment in the burgeoning factories of this community. In both cities, however, Anglo-Canadian households were more likely to have boarders than any other group except the "other Europeans" in Watertown and the Italians in Syracuse, signifying that boarding may have been perceived as a viable way of generating extra income. Yet it obviously meant more than economic gain in Watertown, where almost 65 percent of the Anglo-Canadian boarders in the city lived in non-related Anglo-Canadian households compared with only 8.6 percent of the Anglo-Canadian boarders in Syracuse living in Anglo-Canadian households.

Kinship connections, particularly in the Watertown context, may have been even more evident outside the household. Some examples may be illustrative of different types of connections, at least in the case of the Watertown migrants.[52] The Smith brothers, Frank, Melville, and George from Cataraqui, emigrated with their parents in 1896. The family did not appear in the Watertown city directories until 1900, suggesting that they lived somewhere else prior to coming to Watertown. In 1900 both Melville and George were listed as employees of a paper mill living with their parents at 54 Huntington Street. In 1904 George married a Watertown woman and moved just down the street. The following year Melville married and moved only a few blocks away.[53] This example reflects the fact that the nuclear family not only constituted the unit of migration for many Canadians but that it continued to be important during the first years of residence in the United States.

Migration often served to reunite nuclear families, as revealed in the following example. In 1898 the widow Charlotte Rendle and four of her eight children moved from Kingston to Watertown to join her daughter, Ada Ward, who had emigrated with her husband five years before. Another daughter, Blanche, died that same year and her three children went to Watertown when their father could no longer look after them. In 1900 Charlotte, her daughter Clara, and her grandson Frederick returned to Canada but a year later they emigrated for good to the United States. Charlotte and Frederick once again lived with Ada and her husband while Charlotte's other children soon married local residents and continued to live in Jefferson County.[54] This example shows that migration reunited families, and also demonstrates the importance of the nuclear family in accommodating newcomers.

Although many of the immigrants to Watertown came alone or in nuclear families, in many cases they either lived with or located near to previous migrants, taking advantage of the accommodation, information, and, in some instances, jobs which the latter provided. The small size of the city also meant that individuals who were neighbours back home were also close to each other in their new environment. In contrast, Anglo-Canadians in Syracuse were farther apart in both spatial and social terms. The larger size of the city enforced spatial separation, and both the wide range of opportunities available and the more varied profile of the Canadians present resulted in greater social separation among members of this group.

Community

Residential clustering is often seen as crucial to the maintenance of ethnic solidarity and identity. Such concentration may occur for reasons of congregation (forces bringing people of one group together) or segregation (forces keeping one group apart from others). The mapping of residential

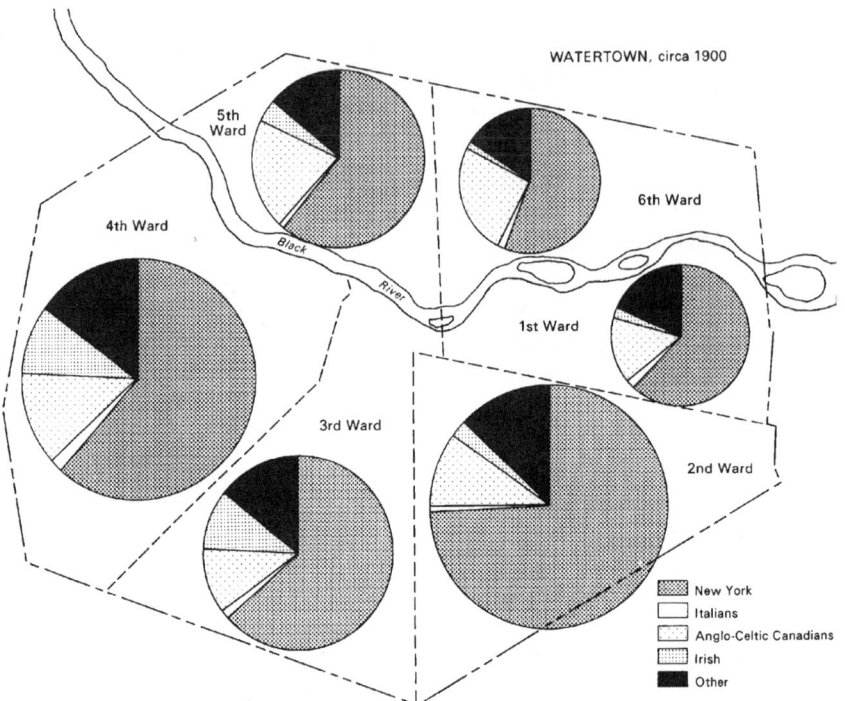

Map 12: Distribution of Watertown Nativity Groups among Wards, 1900

patterns at the ward level shows a relative lack of concentration among immigrant groups in Watertown in 1900 (Map 12). Even at the more specific scale of electoral districts, this same pattern is evident, although some notable patterns emerge. The index of dissimilarity among Watertown nativity groups for 1900 reveals that the Italians were the most segregated group residentially, coming close to only the "other" eastern Europeans in their location patterns (Table 37).[55] The small Italian group in 1900 was segregated in terms of residence with seventy percent living in wards 1 and 4 (Table 38). The well-noted Irish tendency to avoid residence among the Germans and vice versa is repeated in Watertown; in fact, the dissimilarity of the residential pattern of the Irish from all other groups except the New Yorkers is evident.[56]

Residential clustering was much more pronounced in terms of class where 50.7 percent, 36.2 percent, and 32.5 percent of the large capitalist, middle class, and petty capitalist groups respectively would have to move to be consistent with the residential locations of the unskilled (Table 39).[57] Eighty-four percent of the large capitalist group, composed primarily of American-born financiers and manufacturers, lived in the more

Table 37 Index of Dissimilarity among Watertown Nativity Groups, 1900
(12 Electoral Districts)

Nativity groups	New Yorkers	Other Americans	English	German	Scottish	Irish	Italian	French Canadian	Anglo-Celtic Canadian	Others
New Yorkers	–	9.9	25.0	23.4	18.7	21.3	57.5	22.6	19.5	34.7
Other Americans	9.9	–	26.5	27.6	24.8	26.0	52.3	23.7	16.6	29.4
English	25.0	26.5	–	37.8	21.2	37.7	49.7	18.9	15.3	31.1
German	23.4	27.6	37.8	–	29.9	44.8	53.6	29.9	16.4	27.4
Scottish	18.7	24.8	21.2	29.9	–	38.8	35.9	25.3	17.4	23.0
Irish	21.3	26.0	37.7	44.8	38.8	–	47.3	34.1	25.9	29.7
Italian	57.5	52.3	49.7	53.6	35.9	47.3	–	48.6	46.1	23.9
French Canadian	22.6	23.7	18.9	29.9	25.3	34.1	48.6	–	13.3	30.5
Anglo-Celtic Canadian	19.5	16.6	15.3	16.4	17.4	25.9	46.1	13.3	–	24.2
Others	34.7	29.4	31.1	27.4	23.0	29.7	23.9	30.5	24.2	–

Source: See table 35.

Table 38   Percentage Distribution of Watertown Nativity Groups among Wards, 1900

	Wards						
Nativity Group	1	2	3	4	5	6	Total
	% of each nativity within wards						
New Yorkers	60.8	74.4	69.3	60.0	61.5	56.8	64.6
Other Americans	5.5	5.6	6.3	4.6	4.5	6.1	5.4
English	2.8	1.5	2.8	3.6	5.2	5.9	3.3
German	3.4	1.5	0.9	1.2	1.1	1.0	1.5
Scottish	0.6	0.6	0.4	0.9	0.8	1.2	0.7
Irish	2.0	3.3	9.0	8.1	3.4	1.4	4.7
Italian	1.1	0.2	0.1	1.6	0.1	1.0	0.6
French Canadian	3.1	0.9	1.8	2.6	2.8	2.4	2.1
Anglo-Celtic							
Canadian	19.2	11.1	8.7	15.0	20.8	23.5	15.3
Others	1.4	0.8	0.6	2.4	1.0	2.0	1.2
	% of ward residents of each nativity						
New Yorkers	14.4	26.2	19.6	14.2	17.0	8.6	100.0
Other Americans	15.5	23.9	21.7	12.7	14.9	11.2	100.0
English	13.0	10.7	15.4	16.0	27.8	17.2	100.0
German	35.1	23.4	10.4	11.7	13.0	6.5	100.0
Scottish	13.9	19.4	11.1	19.4	19.4	16.7	100.0
Irish	6.8	16.0	35.4	25.7	13.0	3.0	100.0
Italian	30.0	6.7	3.3	40.0	3.3	11.0	100.0
French Canadian	22.0	10.1	15.6	18.3	22.9	11.0	100.0
Anglo-Celtic							
Canadian	19.4	16.6	10.4	14.5	24.3	14.9	100.0
Others	17.7	14.5	9.7	29.0	14.5	16.1	100.0
Total	15.6	23.1	18.5	15.0	18.0	9.8	100.0

Source: See table 35.

prestigious second and third wards (Table 40). People such as Hiram Remington, William Graves, and John Knowlton, all native-born Americans, lived in a four-block section in the thirty-sixth electoral district of the second ward. Petty capitalists were more widespread as the clientele for many of them, particularly such people as the the storekeepers and tavern owners, was restricted to small neighbourhoods, necessitating a location responsive to the economies of range and threshold. Nevertheless, the developing middle class tended to congregate in the second and third wards. The north side was more distinctively working-class (unskilled, semi-skilled and skilled) where they comprised 80.1 percent and 87.1 percent of the household heads in wards 5 and 6 with the largest percentage of unskilled labourers in the city (24.1 percent) living in the fifth ward. Wards 1 and 4 were decidedly more mixed in class and ethnic composition than wards 5 and 6 although all were predominantly working class. The

Table 39   Index of Dissimilarity among Watertown Class Groups, 1900
(12 Electoral Districts)

Class Groups	Class Groups					
	Unskilled	Semi-skilled and skilled	Petty capitalists	Large capitalists	Middle class	Private means
Unskilled	–	18.5	32.5	50.7	36.2	15.6
Semi-skilled and skilled	18.5	–	26.6	49.6	31.5	20.2
Petty capitalists	32.5	26.6	–	26.8	16.8	19.6
Large capitalists	50.7	49.6	26.8	–	28.2	34.4
Middle class	36.2	31.5	16.8	28.2	–.6	23.7
Private means	15.6	20.2	19.6	34.4	23.7	–

Source: 1900 US Manuscript Census.

Table 40   Percentage of Distribution of Watertown Class Groups by Wards, 1900

Class Groups	Wards						
	1	2	3	4	5	6	Total
% of each class group within wards							
Unskilled	22.3	11.2	23.1	26.4	27.5	13.5	21.1
Semi-skilled and skilled	54.1	48.6	36.0	44.5	52.8	73.6	49.7
Petty capitalist	7.8	11.6	11.0	10.9	6.7	4.7	9.1
Large capitalist	0.7	2.9	2.7	0.3	0.3	0	1.3
Middle class	5.1	12.2	9.6	3.9	4.4	1.6	6.7
Private means	10.0	13.5	17.5	14.0	8.4	6.7	12.1
Total	100.0	100.0	100.0	100.0	100.0	100.0	100.0
% of ward residents of each class group							
Unskilled	16.9	12.5	20.9	19.2	24.1	6.5	100.0
Semi-skilled and skilled	17.1	20.5	13.3	13.9	19.9	15.2	100.0
Petty capitalist	13.5	26.5	22.4	19.9	18.7	5.3	100.0
Large capitalist	8.1	45.2	38.7	3.2	4.8	0	100.0
Middle class	12.1	37.8	26.3	9.0	12.4	2.5	100.0
Private means	13.2	24.5	25.3	16.9	14.5	5.6	100.0
Total	15.6	23.1	18.5	15.0	18.0	9.8	100.0

Source: 1900 US Manuscript Census.

major industries were all located in the first ward, but the small size of the city and the availability of a good electric trolley service meant that workers did not need to live close to their place of work.

Residential clustering among immigrant groups at the ward level was

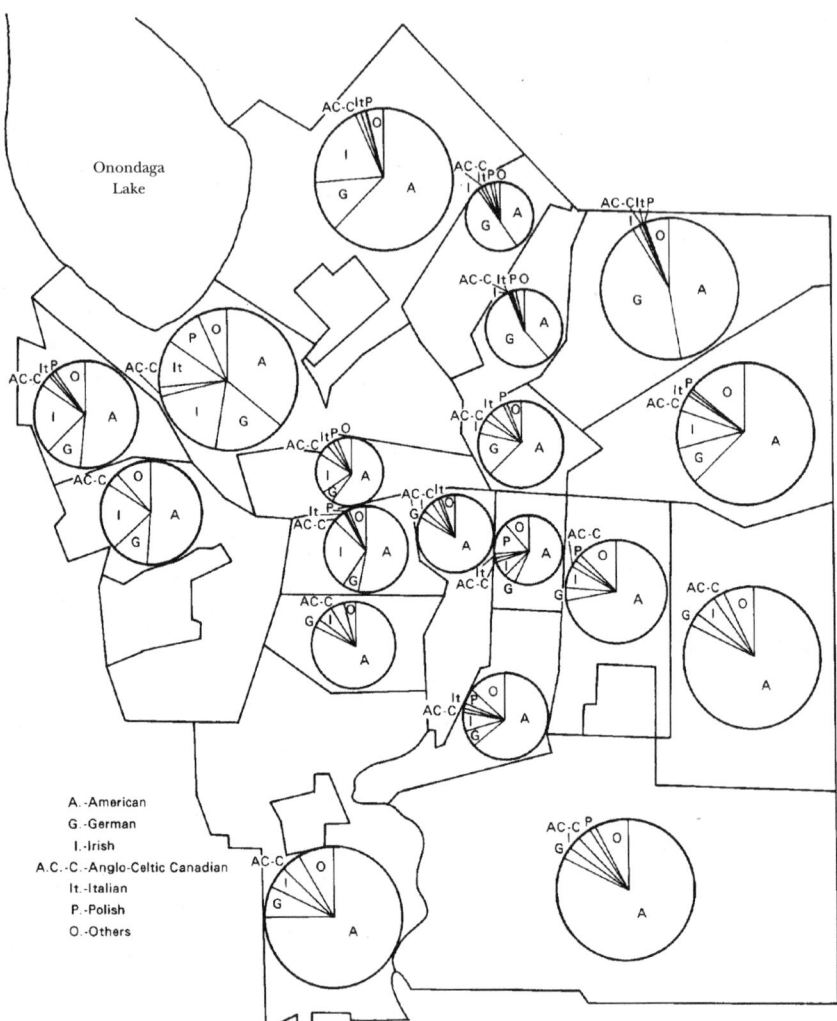

Map 13: Distribution of Syracuse Nativity Group among Wards, 1900

more notable for Syracuse (Map 13). Germans, Polish Jews, Italians, and, to a lesser extent, the Irish, formed distinctive communities near the corridors of industrial employment where the integration of immigrants was supported by the institutional completeness of the groups. The Germans in wards 2, 3, and 4, an area known as Germantown, the Irish residing in the western part of the city near the salt fields, the Poles in Ward 15, and the Italians in wards 6 and 7, all created communities within the city which were characterized by their own social organization and systems of stratification. The index of dissimilarity (Table 41) indicates that the Italians and the Poles were most segregated from others in terms of their residential patterns, followed by the Germans and the Irish. The significant segregation that took place among most immigrant groups and native-born shows that Syracuse families sorted themselves on the basis of national background. Anglo-Canadians and the English were most similar in residential location to each other and native Americans and were most segregated from the Polish, Italians, and Germans in that order.

In Syracuse, however, there is more evidence of a diversified class structure than in Watertown (Table 42). Although professionals tended to converge in wards 11, 14, 15, and 17, such clustering is less evident for business and clerical people and nearly non-existent for the working class. The existence of distinct ethnic communities among the Germans, Poles, Italians, and, to a lesser extent, among the Irish accounts to some extent for the lack of occupational segregation. The Germans, for instance, were of sufficient numbers and geographical proximity that their clustering can be explained by reasons of congregation. German-born doctors, dentists, and lawyers served German-born shoemakers and street labourers as well as German-Americans.

Anglo-Canadians in both Watertown and Syracuse did not establish neighbourhoods inhabited largely by their own members and distinguished by their own particular institutions, but were still affected by the spatial and economic structures in both these cities. Watertown was small enough that ethnic solidarity and identity was not so dependent upon residential congregation but more on formal and informal associations. "Neighbouring" was more a by-product of life itself. More direct relationships were possible in Watertown than in Syracuse.

Syracuse was a more open community with less likelihood of Canadians sharing activity fields. Because there was greater diversity of occupational opportunities, individuals were less likely to establish contact with fellow countrymen at their place of work. The economic and social differences among Anglo-Canadians, discussed in the next section, ensured that no such residential clustering would occur.

Ethclass and Assimilation

The ascriptive definition of ethnicity, which implies that individuals carry their values and traditions with migration, certainly applies to many of the immigrant groups in Syracuse, where German culture survived in the artisan shops and social clubs in Germantown, Irish culture was sustained in the factories and taverns near the canal, and Italian culture was manifested in the bakeries and restaurants of Butternut Street. While the immigrant community in Watertown was less obvious, visible manifestations of culture were evident in clubs, festivals, and churches. In both cities, St

Table 41 Index of Dissimilarity among Syracuse Nativity Groups, 1900 (79 Electoral Districts)*

					Nativity Groups					
Nativity groups	New Yorkers	Other Americans	English	Germans	Polish	Irish	Italian	French Canadians	Anglo-Celtic Canadians	Others
New Yorkers	–	18.3	23.4	65.7	79.9	44.3	72.6	41.4	22.1	35.9
Other Americans	18.3	–	24.5	63.6	82.4	49.7	75.3	39.9	30.0	42.9
English	23.4	24.5	–	61.0	78.9	39.2	77.2	38.5	24.8	38.6
Germans	65.7	63.6	61.0	–	85.3	61.1	72.3	65.5	62.0	58.7
Polish	79.9	82.4	78.9	85.3	–	84.3	91.4	78.2	83.9	69.1
Irish	44.3	49.7	39.2	61.1	84.3	–	71.7	47.0	37.6	45.3
Italian	72.6	75.3	77.2	72.3	91.4	71.7	–	74.6	71.9	68.6
French Canadians	41.4	39.9	38.5	65.5	78.2	47.0	74.6	–	38.9	51.7
Anglo-Celtic Canadians	22.1	30.0	24.8	62.0	83.9	37.6	71.9	38.9	–	40.5
Others	35.9	42.9	38.6	58.7	69.1	45.3	68.6	51.7	40.5	–

Source: 1900 US Manuscript Census

* based on actual figures.

Table 42 Percentage Distribution of Syracuse Occupational Status Groups among Wards, 1900[1]

Status Groups	1	2	3	4	5	6	7	8	9	10	11	12	13	14	15	16	17	18	19	Total
									% of Each Status Group Within Wards											
Unskilled	26.9	23.3	29.2	35.7	21.8	23.2	53.1	23.2	39.5	30.2	22.8	8.2	15.0	3.7	28.4	14.0	26.5	16.9	4.5	21.8
Semi-skilled	19.1	13.9	25.3	20.9	24.0	15.6	11.4	12.0	3.6	31.5	10.5	25.5	7.5	20.3	3.5	22.9	14.6	19.1	4.8	16.9
Skilled	4.3	20.9	18.1	21.4	15.1	6.1	2.7	16.5	5.1	22.0	10.1	14.3	29.0	17.1	10.4	6.3	2.8	14.1	4.0	13.5
Clerical	1.5	10.6	0.8	8.5	9.5	4.5	22.2	25.2	7.8	6.6	32.7	16.1	24.3	10.0	14.3	21.4	16.9	5.2	43.0	19.6
Business	26.7	15.0	9.1	10.0	12.8	48.4	1.9	22.3	4.6	3.0	6.7	29.1	21.4	30.2	18.4	19.4	24.5	40.7	12.6	19.5
Professional	0	0.5	0	0	1.0	2.2	0	0	1.1	0	9.8	1.9	0.7	16.9	9.1	4.9	13.2	2.1	0.2	3.5
Private means	21.6	15.8	17.5	3.6	15.9	0.6	8.7	0.7	38.3	6.6	7.5	5.0	2.2	1.8	15.9	11.2	1.5	1.9	30.8	10.1
Total	100.0	100.0	100.0	100.0	100.0	100.0	100.0	100.0	100.0	100.0	100.0	100.0	100.0	100.0	100.0	100.0	100.0	100.0	100.0	100.0
									% of Ward Residences of Each Status Group											
Unskilled	5.1	5.9	8.5	7.7	5.9	5.0	8.3	4.5	6.0	8.1	4.9	2.7	4.2	1.2	6.9	3.5	5.7	4.8	1.1	100.0
Semi-skilled	4.7	4.5	9.4	5.8	8.3	4.4	2.3	3.0	0.7	10.9	2.9	10.8	2.7	8.3	1.1	7.4	4.0	6.9	1.6	100.0
Skilled	1.3	8.5	8.5	7.5	6.6	2.1	0.7	5.2	1.3	9.5	3.5	7.6	13.3	8.8	4.0	2.5	1.0	6.4	1.7	100.0
Clerical	0.4	3.9	0.3	2.7	3.8	1.4	5.2	7.3	1.8	2.7	10.5	7.9	10.3	4.8	5.1	8.0	5.4	2.2	16.3	100.0
Business	5.7	4.2	3.0	2.4	3.8	11.7	0.3	4.9	0.8	0.9	1.6	10.7	6.8	10.7	5.0	5.47	5.8	12.8	3.6	100.0
Professional	0	0.7	0	0	1.6	2.9	0	0	1.0	0	12.9	3.8	1.2	33.2	13.5	7.6	17.4	3.7	0.31	100.0
Private means	8.8	8.5	10.9	1.7	9.3	0	2.9	0.3	12.5	3.8	3.5	3.5	1.3	1.3	8.2	6.0	0.7	3.2	16.8	100.0
Total	4.1	5.5	6.3	4.7	5.9	4.7	3.4	4.2	3.3	5.8	4.7	7.2	6.2	7.0	5.3	5.5	4.7	6.1	5.5	100.0

Source: 1900 US Manuscript Census

[1] Stratified sample computed by weight factors.

Patrick's Day and Columbus Day were celebrated by the Irish and the Italians respectively. Benefit associations such as the Ancient Order of the Hibernians and the Italian Benefit Society served immigrants in both cities. The Jews in Syracuse were assisted by the Young Men's Hebrew Society. A greater number of ethnic clubs existed in Syracuse; the Germans alone had thirty-nine different societies in 1899, the most important being the Turn Verein, an organization intent on fostering the use of the German language.

In addition to such formal associations, other organizations, while not primarily ethnic in orientation, also served the needs of newcomers. Workers' clubs in both Watertown and Syracuse allowed working people from different occupational and ethnic backgrounds to develop lines of communication, thereby strengthening support and creating worker consciousness.[58] Several fraternal orders and friendly societies existed in both cities which were designed to support the unions and provide a forum for workers of all backgrounds to share ideas and information. Prominent in terms of worker cohesion were groups such as the Order of the Odd Fellows and the Independent Order of Foresters. The objectives of the Odd Fellows, which began in England, "was the development and strengthening of brotherhood and union." The lodges provided information to newcomers about jobs and housing and also offered an opportunity for workers of all national backgrounds to meet.

The workers' clubs also supported the goals of the individual unions of which thirty-five and nineteen were present in Syracuse and Watertown respectively in 1900. The immigrant presence was very prominent in the unions in both cities, especially Syracuse; of the 35 percent of the total number of officers in 1896 who were foreign-born, 69 percent were born in Germany, 14.3 percent in Ireland, 12 percent in Poland and Russia, 7 percent in Canada and England, and only 2.4 percent (one person) in Italy.

While it is difficult to assess the importance that fraternities played in the adaptation experience of the immigrant, many would argue that the church served as a very important institution in meeting the needs of the newcomers. There were thirty-one churches of various denominations in Watertown in 1900 but only two were created with a specific immigrant group in mind. The first group to erect their own church was the Irish who constructed St Mary's Roman Catholic Church on Factory Street in the 1830s. In 1857 this group moved to the new St Patrick's Church on Massey Street and St Mary's was purchased by the French Canadians. Further, because of the considerable number of Québécois in the city, situated primarily on the north side, the Missionaries of the Sacred Heart Order in America erected the Church of Our Lady of the Sacred Heart in 1906.

The influx of Italians was small until the turn of the century, but during the next ten years upwards of one hundred families settled in the city. They congregated in the west Sand Flats area in the fourth ward. By 1910 there were over one thousand Italians in the city and plans were made to erect a church at the corner of Massey Avenue and Stone Street.[59] In 1910 the Polish of Jefferson County erected St Stanislaus Church to meet their spiritual needs. Protestants of Irish, German, British, and Canadian backgrounds attended various churches throughout the city. For these groups, the church played a relatively minor role in the adjustment process. But it certainly was an important institution for the Catholic immigrant groups, particularly given the anti-Catholic sentiment in the city at this time.

In Syracuse the church played an important role in group interaction. Each of the German, Italian, Polish, Russian, and Italian groups had their own churches; the Germans alone had nine churches in 1899. In many of these churches, sermons were delivered in the native language of the group.

The Italians in Syracuse were served by four different newspapers at different times during the period; yet, surprisingly, the two largest immigrant groups in the city, the Germans and the Irish, were not represented by their own newspaper. Only one foreign-language newspaper, *La Phare des Lacs* (1859) was published in Watertown between 1821 and 1936.[60] This lack of ethnic newspapers in both cities, with the exception of the Italian journals in Syracuse, suggests that the newspaper was not an important institution in serving the needs of the immigrants.

When the ascriptive definition of ethnicity is applied to the Anglo-Canadian immigrant experience in Watertown and Syracuse, no ethnicity is evident. There is little difference in traits such as dress, language, and ethnic clubs or distinctive values such as religious or political beliefs. Anglo-Canadians did not derive any sense of distinctiveness from social organizations and institutions peculiar to them; in most cases they joined established churches and social clubs of American or British origin. Only one fraternal organization, the Orange Order in Watertown, had special attraction for some Canadians, but the local lodge's membership was small, and it disappeared before the Second World War.[61] Cultural differences based on ethnicity, religion, and length of residence in Canada separated Canadians both at home and in the United States.

Because Anglo-Canadians possessed no visible culture of their own, it is easy to assume that they were not an ethnic group with any sense of group identity and, as a consequence, readily adopted American values and institutions. There existed little attachment to group symbols in both of these communities because there were few distinctively Canadian symbols to be grasped by the immigrant consciousness and, given the receptive attitudes of the host society, there was little need for such symbols.

But the idea of Anglo-Canadians as one of the most assimilative groups in America requires a reinterpretation based on their experience in Water-

Table 43   Membership in Class Groups by Nativity, Watertown, 1900[1]

	Class %						
Class Groups	Unskilled	Semi-skilled and skilled	Petty capitalists	Large capitalists	Business middle class	Private means	N
New York	17.6	47.4	12.1	1.7	7.4	11.6	3,311
Other American	6.6	42.9	11.9	1.1	13.1	15.3	273
English	20.1	58.6	5.3	0	4.1	10.7	169
German	16.9	59.7	10.4	1.3	2.6	9.1	77
Scottish	13.9	63.9	8.3	0	5.6	8.3	36
Irish	30.0	22.4	9.4	0	2.5	31.6	237
Italian	46.7	30.0	16.7	0	0	3.3	30
French Canadian	28.4	57.8	2.8	0	0.9	10.1	109
Anglo-Celtic Canadian	25.2	56.4	6.9	0.5	2.6	7.8	779
Others	14.5	54.8	21.0	0	3.2	4.8	62

Sources: Petitions for Naturalization; City Directories.
[1] Figures do not add up to 100% because of missing values.

town and Syracuse – an experience interpreted in terms of their household, occupational, class, marriage, and citizenship characteristics. While they were not segregated residentially from native Americans, the rigid class division in Watertown – where native-born composed 84 percent, 82 percent, and 88 percent of the clerical, business, and professional occupations respectively – ensured that most Anglo-Canadians would be congregated in a separate social and economic space. Although they made up over 15 percent of the total number of heads of household, only 7 percent of the Anglo-Canadian household heads present in 1900 owned a business, only 1 percent were employed in a clerical position, and only 0.5 percent engaged in a profession. They moved to Watertown to find work, and many acquired jobs in occupations for which their prior experience may have given them an advantage over others. For example, 6.7 percent of this group were employed as carpenters in 1900, and another 5.3 percent were blacksmiths.

The rural background of many of the Canadian migrants, most coming from eastern Ontario, may explain to a large degree their occupational profile in Watertown. Most farm boys learned to use a saw and shoe a horse and were thus prepared to take up carpentry and blacksmithing. In fact, almost 35 percent of the Watertown blacksmiths and over 24 percent of the carpenters who also headed households were Anglo-Canadians. As Table 43 indicates, Anglo-Canadians more closely approximated the structure of a recent immigrant group, with the majority doing manual labour and a large percentage employed as unskilled labour. In this respect, the difference between the predominantly northern European groups that came largely before 1880 and later immigrants was not that significant. Only the Irish diverged from this pattern, a difference attributed to the abnormally large percentage of household heads included in the private means category. The Irish heads in this grouping were predominantly widowed females.

The large representation of the Irish and the Italians in the unskilled occupations supports the traditional argument that both these groups arrived in America lacking industry-related skills. However, both French Canadians and Anglo-Canadians were over-represented in this category. Over 25 percent were employed as unskilled labourers, and Anglo-Canadians, because of their superior numbers, constituted 52.5 percent of the immigrant household head unskilled labour population. They dominated certain occupations; for example, as teamsters, where 5 percent of the Anglo-Celtic heads made up 28.5 percent of all household heads in that position.

It is difficult to make concrete conclusions about these statistics, as the trades and skills involved in both semi-skilled and skilled categories varied considerably in terms of expertise and income. Both Canadian groups along with the Germans and the Scots, were heavily involved in semi-skilled trades and industrial occupations. Many of the Germans were especially prevalent in such traditional trades as baking and butchering, while the other groups were involved in industrial occupations such as paper-making and carriage manufacture. The British groups, the English and the Scottish, were well represented in factory occupations, particularly the better-paying skilled positions, applying knowledge many of them had acquired prior to their arrival in Watertown. Again the large number of Anglo-Canadians meant that while only 17.7 percent of this group were involved in skilled occupations, they constituted 16.1 percent of Watertown's household heads employed as skilled workers and 51.5 percent of the immigrant household heads employed in that category.

Native-born Americans were clearly differentiated from the immigrants in terms of representation in capitalist and petty capitalist categories. While certain foreign groups ranked with or even surpassed American-born in terms of representation in the petty capitalist group, the latter controlled large capitalist positions. Anglo-Canadians in this respect more closely resembled the old immigrant groups in their limited involvement in business, although ranking ahead of the English and French Canadians. While only 7.1 percent of Anglo-Canadian household heads owned a business in 1900, they comprised over 45 percent of the immigrant business community, a fact related to their superior numbers.

Americans also dominated proportionately the clerical, managerial, and professional positions belonging to the middle-class occupation category. New Yorkers dominated among the professional and clerical categories, while other Americans were similarly over-represented in the professional and clerical categories. Anglo-Canadians along with the "other" Europeans were the most involved in clerical positions among immigrant groups, the former constituting almost 60 percent of the immigrant clerical population.

The over-representation of Anglo-Canadians in unskilled and semi-skilled positions might indicate that they were assigned to the lower levels of the socio-economic hierarchy in Watertown but we must be careful not to confuse prestige with economic status. Any interpretation of occupational data within the context of late-nineteenth century society is problematic because we lack a thorough understanding of the nature of many of the occupations and the impact of changing techniques on the nature of the different types of work. Some positions categorized as semi-skilled may have been more economically lucrative than skilled or clerical positions. Thus it is critical to try and determine the level of income associated with particular occupations.

Watertown   The 1900 United States Census of Manufactures is not available for Watertown, but we can infer income from the average hours and earnings statistics available in the published census. Correlations of average weekly earnings in selected industries representing the major sources of employment in Watertown and located in the middle states, including New York, for 1890 and 1900 are presented in Table 44. At this level of aggregation, the statistics are not representative of the specific wages paid in the city but at least they provide some idea of variations of income both between and within industries. For instance, carriage workers were better off than their counterparts in the paper mills and foundries. The largest single employer in Watertown, the New York Air Brake Company, paid its labourers $6.25 per week, much less than the average wage for foundry labourers in the middle states in general ($8.00). Generally, however, labourers occupied the lowest end of the scale both in status and real income. As almost 26 percent of the Anglo-Canadians were classified as unskilled and made up 19.4 percent of all household heads in that group, many Canadians were relegated to the lower end of the occupational and income hierarchy.

Yet other Canadians did very well within the working class. Some positions classified as semi-skilled and skilled paid more than those classified as clerical which contained a significant number of women who were underpaid for the work they did. For example, salespeople averaged $12 a week in Watertown in 1900 while carriage trimmers in the middle states averaged $13.50 a week.[62] In both the foundries and carriage plants, blacksmiths, carpenters, machinists, and moulders were better rewarded than most of the other occupations. A significant percentage of Anglo-Canadians were employed in these occupations and so enjoyed higher than average earnings. However, many of the Canadian blacksmiths and carpenters

Table 44   Average Weekly Wages for Selected Industries, 1890 and 1900

	Wages	
Industry	1890	1900
WAGONS AND CARRIAGES		
blacksmiths	$16.00	$15.00
painters	13.50	13.50
finishers	9.50	10.00
foremen	25.00	21.00
labourers	10.00	10.00
trimmers	13.00	13.50
All occupations	13.00	13.50
FOUNDRIES AND METAL WORKING		
apprentice machinists	5.00	4.00
blacksmiths	17.50	15.00
boiler makers	13.00	12.00
buffers	10.50	9.00
carpenters	13.50	13.00
core-makers	10.50	12.00
engineers	12.50	12.00
foremen	21.00	22.50
labourers	8.00	8.00
machine tenders	11.00	9.50
machinists	15.00	14.00
moulders	18.00	17.00
paintes	12.50	12.00
sheet metal workers	14.50	13.00
All occupations	10.00	10.00
PAPER MILLS		
back tenders	9.50	9.50
labourers	8.50	9.00
paper machine tenders	16.50	16.50
All occupations	9.00	9.00

Source: US Census Office, *Twelfth Census of the United States, 1900. Special Reports, Employees and Wages* (Washington, 1903), pp. xxxiii–lxxxvii.

worked in the small carpentry and blacksmith establishments existing in the city, where the wages were much less.

The pulp and paper industry, which attracted many Anglo-Canadians (21.4 percent of all heads categorized as paper-makers were Anglo-Canadians), generally paid a wage slightly less than the city annual average of $479.53. Yet many of this group also occupied the better paying, skilled positions within this and other industries. Over 7 percent of the Anglo-Canadian household heads were classified as machinists and they constituted almost 18 percent of all heads employed in that occupation. Three percent of the Anglo-Canadian heads were classified as moulders and they comprised almost 22 percent of all heads employed in that position. Table 44 shows that these two positions in the middle states were among the best paid of all non-managerial jobs. Yet at the same time, Anglo-Canadians were poorly represented in prestigious and well-paying managerial and clerical positions such as foremen and bookkeepers. Bookkeepers averaged $25 a week in Watertown but only eight Canadian heads were employed in that occupation in 1900.[63] Thus, while Anglo-Canadians were largely working-class in composition, they demonstrated a considerable diversity in terms of occupations filled and wages received.

An investigation of occupational mobility of this and other immigrant groups afforded by the 1900 manuscript census, and a trace of the eastern Ontarians who chose to file for naturalization in Watertown, reveals that Anglo-Canadians did not experience demonstrably greater success than most other groups despite their supposed cultural advantages. Some, such as James Pappa and Michael Kelly, attained considerable success and remained in the community for the rest of their lives. Kelly, who was born in Enterprise, Ontario, in 1888 and left that small village with his family in 1903, did not appear in the Watertown directories until 1906. He began his working life in Watertown as a moulder. By the time of his death in 1960, he had managed to become a successful business owner. By 1919, Kelly was president and owner of the firm of O'Connor-Kelly and Company which dealt in furniture and carpets. A decline in fortune must have occurred during the depression because by 1940 he was listed as a salesman for the Kamango Furniture Company, a position he held for five years. The year 1946 found him in control of his own business, the Kelly Roofing Company, which he ran until his death.[64]

Others, like Joseph Cassidy, stayed only a brief time in the "Garland City." Cassidy who was born in Scotland and came to Canada as a young child, emigrated to the United States at the age of twenty. He did not turn up in the Watertown directories until 1907 when he was a 30-year-old bachelor. He stayed less than two years, first employed as a motion-picture operator and then working as a marine engineer. After this brief stay, he left for Pittsburgh.[65] These are two somewhat extreme examples and so we turn to the census to acquire some understanding of Anglo-Canadian experiences as a group.

The relatively high percentage of unskilled among the longest-term Anglo-Canadian residents implies that progress was not possible for all. Comparison of this group with other immigrants reveals that they did not experience significantly higher rates of mobility (Table 45). Anglo-Canadian representation within the semi-skilled and skilled class categories remained high, most of the decrease being accounted for by increasing retirement among older immigrants. This suggests that many of the Canadians who arrived earlier settled into occupations, many of them familiar,

Table 45 Membership in Class Groups by Nativity and Length of Residence, Immigrant Groups, Watertown, 1900[1]

Length of residence (years)	Class group	Nativity Groups (%)							
		English	German	Scottish	Irish	Italian	French Canadian	Anglo-Celtic Canadian	Others
<1–2	unskilled	16.7	0	0	0	0	100	32.3	20.0
	semi-skilled and skilled	50.0	0	0	0	100	0	49.2	80.0
	petty capitalist	0	0	0	0	0	0	1.7	0
	large capitalist	0	0	0	0	0	0	3.4	0
	middle class	0	0	100	0	0	0	5.1	0
	private means	33.3	0	0	0	0	0	8.1	0
3–5	unskilled	0	0	0	80.0	0	42.9	31.9	50.0
	semi-skilled and skilled	90.0	100	100	0	0	57.1	53.6	50.0
	petty capitalist	0	0	0	0	0	0	1.0	0
	large capitalist	0	0	0	0	0	0	0	0
	middle class	10.0	0	0	0	0	0	1.4	0
	private means	0	0	0	20.0	0	0	13.0	0
6–10	unskilled	42.9	0	0	14.3	62.5	33.3	25.4	8.3
	semi-skilled and skilled	47.6	0	87.5	28.6	12.5	66.7	64.4	66.7
	petty capitalist	0	0	12.5	0	12.5	0	2.8	16.7
	large capitalist	0	0	0	0	0	0	0	0
	middle class	0	0	0	0	0	0	0.6	0
	private means	4.8	0	0	57.1	0	0	6.8	0

Table 45 (continued)

Length of residence (years)	Class group	Nativity Groups (%)							
		English	German	Scottish	Irish	Italian	French Canadian	Anglo-Celtic Canadian	Others
11–20	unskilled	25.4	19.2	21.4	41.7	56.3	15.4	23.8	15.8
	semi-skilled and skilled	66.1	76.9	51.2	25.0	25.0	69.2	59.6	42.1
	petty capitalist	3.4	3.8	14.3	13.9	18.8	7.7	9.2	26.3
	large capitalist	0	0	0	0	0	0	0	0
	middle class	5.1	0	7.1	5.6	0	7.7	3.2	10.5
	private means	0	0	0	13.9	0	0	3.5	0
>20	unskilled	12.3	86.7	20.0	27.0	0	27.4	22.3	8.7
	semi-skilled and skilled	2.12	47.9	50.0	22.2	60.0	54.8	49.3	52.2
	petty capitalist	9.6	14.6	0	11.8	20.0	2.7	11.4	26.1
	large capitalist	0	2.1	0	0	0	0	0.9	0
	middle class	4.1	4.2	10.0	2.1	0	0	3.3	0
	private means	20.5	14.6	20.0	54.9	20.0	15.1	12.3	13.0

Source: 1900 US Manuscript Census

[1] Figures may not add up to 100% because of missing values.

and continued to work in these jobs despite any new opportunities that may have arisen with Watertown's growth. Anglo-Canadians who arrived before 1880 continued to be over-represented in the unskilled and semi-skilled categories. They lagged behind the Italians, Germans, and the Irish in participation in the petty capitalist category, and trailed the Scots, Germans, and the English in middle-class occupations. Their fellow countrymen of French origin similarly were concentrated among semi-skilled positions regardless of length of residence, many of them, like the Anglo-Canadians, coming from a rural background.

Table 46 shows the relationship between first and last occupational categories of transient eastern Ontarians according to length of residence.[66] Among those transients who first held an unskilled position, the majority continued to hold the same or similar job when they left, regardless of how much time they spent in the city. Some movement into more prestigious manual occupations did take place, particularly among those who stayed in the city long but only two people moved from unskilled positions to a business and professional position respectively by the time of their departure. The greatest movement among the unskilled was into the clerical category.

The majority of semi-skilled transients remained in that category except for those who stayed in Watertown for over thirty years, a group strongly suspected of being persisters despite the fact that their deaths are not recorded in the directories. There is some evidence of a very small movement from the ranks of the semi-skilled to the skilled, clerical, and business sectors, but there is also evidence of movement to the ranks of the unskilled among both those transients staying the least amount of time and those staying the greatest amount of time. This downward movement took place after the First World War, when Watertown entered into a long period of decline as the carriage industry died and the pulp and paper industry moved elsewhere.

It appears that among the transients the skilled and clerical workers stayed longer than the unskilled and semi-skilled and displayed less downward movement than the semi-skilled. Only one of the eastern Ontarians owned a business when first coming to Watertown and not one person was engaged in a professional position upon arriving in the city. Movement of manual and clerical workers into the ranks of business and the professions was virtually non-existent. What is most striking is the relatively large number of families leaving the city who had lived there for considerable periods of time.

The degree of residential stability and vertical mobility was somewhat greater among those eastern Ontarians who remained in the city. Although 60 percent of those who entered the workforce as unskilled labourers finished their working careers in that category, 20 percent moved up to a skilled position and another 20 percent finished their work-

Table 46 First and Last Occupations of Transient Eastern Ontarians[1] Recorded in the Watertown Directories by Length of Residence

Original occupation	Length of residence (years)	Last-Occupation Recorded[2]											
		Unskilled		Semi-skilled		Skilled		Clerical		Business		Professional	
		Row %	Col %	Row %	Col %	Row %	Col %	Row %	Col %	Row %	Col %	Row %	Col %
unskilled	1–5	100	15.4	0	0	0	0	0	0	0	0	0	0
	6–10	57.1	30.7	14.3	50.0	14.3	33.3	14.3	16.7	0	0	0	0
	11–20	33.3	15.4	0	0	33.3	66.7	33.3	33.3	0	0	0	0
	21–30	40.0	15.4	0	0	0	0	40.0	33.3	0	0	20.0	100
	>30	50.0	23.1	16.7	50.0	0	0	16.7	16.7	16.7	100	0	0
semi-skilled	1–5	33.3	14.3	66.7	18.2	0	0	0	0	0	0	0	0
	6–10	0	0	100	9.1	0	0	0	0	0	0	0	0
	11–20	0	0	50.0	45.4	20.0	50.0	20.0	40.0	10.0	33.3	0	0
	21–30	0	0	66.7	18.2	0	0	0	0	33.3	33.3	0	0
	>30	46.2	85.7	7.7	9.1	15.4	50.0	23.1	60.0	7.7	33.3	0	0
skilled	1–5	0	0	0	0	0	0	0	0	0	0	0	0
	6–10	0	0	0	0	100	42.8	0	0	0	0	0	0
	11–20	16.7	100	16.7	100	33.3	28.6	16.7	100	16.7	100	0	0
	21–30	0	0	0	0	100	14.3	0	0	0	0	0	0
	>30	0	0	0	0	100	14.3	0	0	0	0	0	0
clerical	1–5	0	0	50.0	33.3	0	0	50.0	12.5	0	0	0	0
	6–10	0	0	100	33.3	0	0	0	0	0	0	0	0
	11–20	0	0	0	0	0	0	75.0	37.5	0	0	25.0	100
	21–30	0	0	20.0	33.3	0	0	60.0	37.5	20.0	100	0	0
	>30	0	0	0	0	0	0	100	12.5	0	0	0	0

Table 46 (continued)

Original occupation	Length of residence (years)	Unskilled		Semi-skilled		Skilled		Clerical		Business		Professional	
		Row %	Col %	Row %	Col %	Row %	Col %	Row %	Col %	Row %	Col %	Row %	Col %
business	1–5	0	0	0	0	0	0	0	0	0	0	0	0
	6–10	0	0	0	0	0	0	0	0	100	100	0	0
	11–20	0	0	0	0	0	0	0	0	0	0	0	0
	21–30	100	100	0	0	0	0	0	0	0	0	0	0
	>30	0	0	0	0	0	0	0	0	0	0	0	0
professional	1–5	0	0	0	0	0	0	0	0	0	0	0	0
	6–10	0	0	0	0	0	0	0	0	0	0	0	0
	11–20	0	0	0	0	0	0	0	0	0	0	0	0
	21–30	0	0	0	0	0	0	0	0	0	0	0	0
	>30	0	0	0	0	0	0	0	0	0	0	0	0

Last-Occupation Recorded[2]

Sources: Petitions for Naturalization; City Directories

[1] transients include those disappearing from the directories without any indication of their deaths.

[2] not include private means which for the mast part were retirees.

Table 47   Index of Dissimilarity among Anglo-Celtic Canadians for Class by
Electoral District, Watertown, 1900

	1	2	3	4	5	6
1	–	21.8	30.2	35.2	35.3	19.3
2	21.8	–	32.0	54.0	34.6	26.4
3	30.2	32.0	–	47.4	21.9	27.0
4	35.2	54.0	47.4	–	61.5	41.7
5	35.3	34.6	21.9	61.5	–	32.0
6	19.3	26.4	27.0	41.7	32.0	–

Source: 1900 US Manuscript Census

Note: 1–unskilled; 2–semi-skilled; 3–petty capitalists; 4–large capitalists; 5–middle class
(new business); 6–private means.

ing lives in a clerical occupation. There was some downward movement –
one skilled worker finished as an unskilled labourer – but more ended
their careers as managers and foremen.

When we trace the moves of each occupational category for eastern
Ontarians, it is apparent that the most transient were the unskilled. Many
of these individuals moved more than ten times during their often short
stay in Watertown. What upward mobility did occur among the working
class only took place after a series of moves. The eastern Ontarians displayed notable change in terms of occupations and residence, but most of
the occupational movement did not transcend class lines.

Both the 1900 manuscript census and the naturalization records allow
us greater insight into the specifics of residential mobility among Anglo-
Canadians. Table 47 reveals a sharp dissimilarity between the residential
patterns of the working class and both the capitalist class and the middle
class. There even existed a notable dissimilarity in residential locations
among the petty capitalists, middle class, and the capitalists. The latter
group was the most segregated from the others.

The census-based analysis reveals that Anglo-Canadians were predominantly working-class regardless of length of residence or stage of life. Yet
the specifics of mobility remain hidden. A deeper insight into mobility
among this group, at least among those who decided to apply for American citizenship, is made possible through the longitudinal approach using
the naturalization records. The majority of the eastern Ontarian naturalization migrants were unskilled, semi-skilled, and skilled workers (76.7
percent) and clerical workers (15 percent). Job stability was rare for this
group. Almost 49 percent of the naturalization members changed their
occupations (types of occupations and not number of jobs) three to five
times, while 24.8 percent changed their occupations once or twice, and
4.5 percent changed their occupations more than five times. Only 21.8
percent of this group retained their same occupation throughout their res-

idence in Watertown and this figure includes several individuals who are only recorded for a very brief time in the city.

A considerable degree of residential mobility existed within Watertown for the naturalization group. Just over 1 percent of the eastern Ontarians were in the city for such a short time that they were never listed in a city directory, while 7 percent stayed between one and five years, 10 percent between six and ten years, 20 percent between eleven and twenty years, 16 percent between twenty-one and twenty-nine years, and 45 percent for thirty or more years. Just over 30 percent were traced until the time of their deaths.

Tenure is another indicator of stratification which often differentiates people and poses the question of the variation in ownership among different nativity groups. Fifty-five percent of the 5,029 housing units in Watertown were rented in 1901, 22 percent were encumbered with a mortgage, and only 28 percent were owned free of title. Table 48 shows the relationship between tenure, nativity, and length of residence in the United States. The Irish and the Germans were more likely to own their homes than any other group, including the native-born. The French Canadians and English resembled the American pattern. By contrast the newer immigrants, the Anglo-Canadians, Scottish, Italians, and "other" Europeans, were more likely to rent. The difference between old and new immigrant groups establishes the importance of length of residence in home ownership, as the longest-established groups enjoyed the highest ownership rates. The relatively high tenancy rates among New Yorkers and other Americans may be explained by the fact that many of their members were recent migrants to the city, and, like the newer immigrants, did not have enough time to amass enough capital to purchase their homes. Of particular interest is the fact that Anglo-Canadians were least likely of all groups to own a home.

A possible indication of assimilation is intermarriage among immigrant groups and marriage with the native population. The argument is often advanced that a high frequency of intermarriage with the national group may be taken as a clear sign of Americanization.[67] While the majority of Watertown immigrants, regardless of place of origin, were unmarried at the time of departure, they did not display significant differences in terms of marriage within and outside their respective group. Just over 32 percent of the Anglo-Canadian household heads were married to New Yorkers in 1900 as opposed to 35.1 percent for the Germans, 33.9 percent for the French Canadians, and 30 percent for the Italians. Only the English (26 percent), the Irish (20.7 percent), and the Scottish (19.4 percent) displayed significantly lower patterns, all characterized by a higher incidence of marriage to Anglo-Canadians which, combined with data on place of marriage, indicates that many of them lived in Canada for some time before coming to Watertown. What is most interesting is that Anglo-

Table 48 Members of Tenure Groups by Nativity and Length of Residence, Immigrant Groups, Watertown, 1900

Length of residence (years)	Tenure group	English	German	Scottish	Irish	Italian	French Canadian	Anglo-Celtic Canadian	Others
<1–2	rent	100	0	100	0	100	100	96.8	100
	own encumbered	0	0	0	0	0	0	1.6	0
	own free	0	0	0	0	0	0	1.6	0
3–5	rent	100	100	100	80.0	0	100	89.9	100
	own encumbered	0	0	0	0	0	0	10.1	0
	own free	0	0	0	20.0	0	0	0	0
6–10	rent	85.7	50.0	85.7	38.5	100	86.7	83.5	75.0
	own encumbered	9.5	50.0	14.3	7.7	0	13.3	13.1	25.0
	own free	4.8	0	0	53.8	0	0	3.4	0
11–20	rent	64.4	34.6	78.6	63.9	87.5	69.2	69.4	78.9
	own encumbered	16.9	34.6	21.4	22.2	6.3	30.8	20.8	15.8
	own free	18.6	30.8	0	13.9	6.3	0	9.7	5.3
>20	rent	41.1	23.4	40.0	25.5	50.0	53.4	55.2	65.2
	own encumbered	19.2	23.4	30.0	21.8	0	21.9	24.8	13.0
	own free	39.7	53.2	30.0	52.7	50.0	24.7	20.0	21.7

Source: 1900 us Manuscript Census.

Canadians displayed a marked tendency towards endogamy (54.7 percent), a rate exceeded only by the Italians (63.3 percent). By contrast, the rates for the other immigrant groups ranged from 25 percent to 48 percent.

Over 80 percent of the Anglo-Canadians who arrived between 1898 and 1900 were married to fellow Canadians by 1900. This figure decreased to 73.5 percent for those who had lived three to five years in America, 66.7 percent for those who had resided there from six to ten years, 56.6 percent for those who had come during the 1880s, and 32.7 percent for those who had arrived before 1880. As the percentage of marriage within the group declined with length of residence, so marriage to native Americans increased. Yet only those who had lived for more than twenty years in the United States, many of them emigrating as young children, were more likely to be married to Americans (55.5 percent) than fellow Anglo-Canadians (32.9 percent).

This high frequency of intermarriage may be explained by the fact that Anglo-Canadians constituted the dominant foreign element in the city and thus contacts with members of the opposite sex of the same ethnic background were easier. Literacy and religious background may be two other factors, but the high frequency of intermarriage among Anglo-Canadians in Watertown suggests that many chose to share their lives in their new home with fellow Canadians.

Citizenship is an important measure of integration, representing the final decision to remain permanently in the United States and to renounce a former allegiance. Of all immigrant groups, Anglo-Canadians were the least likely to give up their former citizenship. Over 40 percent in 1900 were classified as aliens or aliens who had merely declared the intention to become American citizens, followed by the "others" category (30.6 percent), the Italians (30 percent), the English (28.4 percent), the Scottish (25 percent), the French Canadians (18.3 percent), the Irish (8.4 percent), and the Germans (7.8 percent). A strong connection existed between length of residence and citizenship, but the relationship was not as evident for Anglo-Canadians as it was for other immigrant groups. Reluctance to give up their Canadian citizenship suggests that many retained the idea that one day they would return home.

The low rates of home ownership, the lack of representation in the more prestigious parts of the city, the almost annual residential and occupational changes, and the departure of many from the city all reflect an environment of structural inequality. Anglo-Canadians were situated below native-born Americans on the economic and social ladder because many started out poor, with less in the way of capital, connections, education, and other requirements that would have permitted their rise. Anglo-Canadians did not establish ethnic boundaries to differentiate themselves from others but they, as well as other first-generation immigrants, were confronted by a class barrier which served to separate both foreign groups and Americans alike from a certain sector of the population.

It is in this context that the concept of ethclass has some relevance. Evidence suggests that first-generation Anglo-Canadians in Watertown continued to associate with each other within their own class segment, the ethclass. Relatives served to assist the newcomer establish a base in the community and, after this initial stage, Anglo-Canadians were likely to establish attachments to other Canadians with whom they interacted on the job, in the tavern, or in the union.

Syracuse Anglo-Canadians in Syracuse were less likely to identify with their ethclass for two reasons. First, they were a different group from their counterparts in Watertown; more had lived in other Ontario and New York communities, and Syracuse for many was a step up the migration hierarchy. In addition, they were an older group, over 40 percent emigrating to the United States before 1880 when the city was experiencing rapid development. Some of this group had acquired skills, experience, education, and savings that allowed them to enter the professions or start a business. Secondly, Syracuse presented a much different setting from Watertown. It was a larger and more open city characterized by industrial and tertiary diversity, a wider variety of occupations and, consequently, more avenues of mobility.

Most immigrant groups were better represented in the middle class, petty capitalist, and large capitalist groups than those in Watertown (Table 49). While the majority of capitalists in town, in terms of absolute numbers, were native Americans, the percentages of certain immigrant groups belonging to that class were comparable to that of Americans. And while only 54.4 percent and 61.7 percent of the other American and New York groups respectively belonged to the blue-collar segment of the working class, the figures were comparable for the English, Germans, Poles, "others," Irish, and Anglo-Canadians. Only the French Canadians and the Italians had more than 70 percent of their household heads classified as manual workers.

The division between old and new immigrants in terms of representation within manual labour was less obvious in Syracuse than Watertown. Both French Canadians and Anglo-Canadians were still concentrated in the semi-skilled positions, but a significantly smaller percentage of Anglo-Canadians were employed as unskilled labourers. Generally, the Anglo-Canadians in Syracuse were more evenly distributed among the different class groups, although their representation among the large capitalist group was non-existent.[68] Americans also dominated the petty capitalist occupations but in terms of relative representation, New Yorkers and other Americans ranked behind the Poles and the "others." Russian, Hungarian, and Polish Jews placed high priority on running their own businesses and

Table 49   Membership in Class Groups by Nativity, Syracuse, 1900[1]

			Class %				
Nativity Group	Unskilled	Semi-skilled and skilled	Petty capitalists	Large capitalists	Business middle class	Private means	N
New York	17.1	44.6	18.4	1.8	9.3	8.7	13,827
Other American	13.9	40.6	10.3	4.7	21.9	8.7	1,548
English	13.8	47.9	8.7	2.0	16.6	10.1	968
German	25.1	38.3	15.8	2.0	3.5	14.6	3,464
Polish	24.7	35.0	29.3	0	5.3	5.1	474
Irish	42.6	25.2	13.9	1.0	2.7	13.9	2,274
Italian	74.1	9.3	14.6	0	0	1.3	359
French Canadian	28.8	53.6	5.4	0	6.3	5.1	224
Anglo-Celtic Canadian	16.9	45.8	8.9	0	12.6	15.3	694
Others	20.5	45.4	21.0	1.0	4.0	7.9	780

Source: 1900 US Manuscript Census.

[1] stratified sample computed by weight factors;

[2] figures do not add up to 100% because of missing values.

did so within a close-knit and spatially concentrated community. Considerable percentages of Germans, Italians, and Irish owned small businesses, particularly serving the large ethnic population on the city's north side. Both Canadian groups and the English showed the least inclination to operate a small business.

Anglo-Canadians and the English were closest to native Americans in middle-class representation, the former well represented among clerical and professional occupations. The Germans, Irish, and Anglo-Canadians were most represented in the private means category, the majority being widows and retirees. This reflects the earlier date of arrival of the majority of these groups.

In the Syracuse of 1900, the largest proportion of males in manufacturing and mechanical occupations reflects the rapid growth in secondary manufacturing during this period. Americans, Irish, and Italians were under-represented in this category; Poles, Britons, and Anglo-Canadians were slightly above average while the French Canadians and Germans in particular were concentrated in these semi-skilled and skilled positions. Anglo-Canadians displayed the greatest relative concentration among blacksmiths, machinists, painters, and varnishers and were second to French Canadians in the numbers employed as carpenters and joiners.

In the trade and transportation category, every national group was under-represented with the exception of the Poles and the Americans, the former dominant as hucksters, peddlers, and merchants. Americans dominated proportionately the positions of banker, broker, clerk, and salesman. A considerable number of Anglo-Canadians were employed in sales and clerical posts. Anglo-Canadians, Americans, Britons, and the Poles were under-represented in the domestic and personal service occupations, while almost 70 percent of the Italians were employed as labourers. The fact that such a large percentage of the Italians and the Irish were labourers supports the argument that both these groups arrived in America lacking industrial-related skills. Anglo-Canadians and Americans ranked the highest in the professional service category. The former were greatest in terms of relative percentage employed as electricians and ranked second to the latter in terms of percentage working as physicians and surgeons.

Most opportunities for females were found in the domestic and personal service category. Anglo-Canadians as well as the Irish, Italians, and Britons were over-represented in servant and waitress positions. Anglo-Canadian females ranked below the average in every manufacturing and mechanical job except milliner, where they comprised the highest relative percentage. Like their male counterparts, they displayed a tendency to become clerks and salespersons. Not one Anglo-Canadian woman was a merchant or a dealer. Anglo-Canadian women were also under-represented among the professional services, although they ranked well above the aggregate average (5.6 percent) for immigrant groups.

Certainly Syracuse was a more open community in terms of economic opportunities than Watertown. Business played a greater role with almost 20 percent of the total household head population included in that category as opposed to 12.7 percent in Watertown. Capital may have flowed much more freely in the larger city with first-generation and second-generation immigrants having a greater role in handling money. Certainly the relative proportion of foreign-born bankers and moneylenders was much greater in Syracuse than in Watertown.

Occupational mobility was more evident among most groups in Syracuse than in Watertown (Table 50). Patterns of progress among Anglo-Canadians were more dramatic, particularly among the working class. Movement of this group into the middle class and petty capitalist class correlates generally with length of residence. Significant declines occurred among the proportions engaged in unskilled and semi-skilled occupations with the exception of the pre-1880 group who remained largely working class in orientation. Anglo-Canadians who arrived prior to 1880 differed somewhat from those who followed them, as more were employed in unskilled positions despite their longer residence. Retired persons constituted the largest number among this group. However, they were the least involved in owning a business, which perhaps may be seen as resulting from a lack of the kind of support provided by other ethnic communities.

Length of residence was far more important than age in discriminating among occupational groups in Syracuse. Whereas Watertown's Anglo-Canadians between the ages of 15 and 60 were concentrated within the

Table 50   Membership in Class Groups by Length of Residence, Anglo-
Canadians in Syracuse, 1900[1]

Length of residence (years)	Class Groups[2]					
	1	2	3	4	5	6
<1–2	25.0	75.0	0	0	0	0
3–5	29.2	65.6	0	0	5.2	0
6–10	5.9	68.2	12.6	0	8.4	5.9
11–20	9.6	52.4	19.3	0	15.5	3.2
>20	23.2	24.3	7.6	0	13.9	31.0

Source: 1900 US Manuscript Census.
[1] Stratified sample computed by weight factors.
[2] Class Groups: 1–unskilled; 2–semi-skilled and skilled; 3–petty capitalist;
   4–large capitalist; 5–middle class; 6–private means.

unskilled and semi-skilled categories, regardless of their date of arrival, Syracuse's Anglo-Canadians showed a much more diverse occupational profile with age. While younger immigrants (15–30) were more concentrated in the unskilled category in Watertown, a significant percentage (42.7 percent) of their Syracuse counterparts were employed in semi-skilled jobs. Most of those classified as unskilled came either after 1895 or before 1880 when they were, for the most part, children or young adults.

While the majority of Watertown's Anglo-Canadians between the ages of 31 and 45 were employed in semi-skilled positions (40.7 percent), the Syracuse Anglo-Canadians of this age category displayed a greater diversity, with more employed in skilled (20.1 percent), clerical (14.7 percent), and business (10.1 percent) occupations and less in semi-skilled positions (25.2 percent). Of this group, those arriving between 1895 and 1900 were for the most part semi-skilled and a minority were clerical workers. Those who came between 1890 and 1894 were just as likely to be skilled workers in 1900 as semi-skilled workers, while those who came during the 1880s, when they were teens or young adults, showed a greater tendency to be clerks or business owners. Those who came prior to 1880 again displayed a predilection for occupying unskilled positions (34.1 percent).

Among the 46–60 age group, the majority coming before 1880, there was a much greater propensity to operate a business and practise a profession. Many came to Syracuse as young or middle-aged men and women and had either continued their business and professional careers or had acquired capital and the abilities that allowed them to enter or carry on such occupations. Among this group, the recent immigrants who arrived between 1895 and 1900 and thus were of mature age at the time of emigration, were concentrated among clerical and unskilled positions. Those who came between 1890 and 1894 were divided among semi-skilled (28.6 percent), skilled (33.3 percent), and professional positions (38.1 percent). Of those who came during the 1880s, a large number owned businesses (30.4 percent) or occupied clerical positions (30.4 percent), while many of those Anglo-Canadians who came prior to 1880 were employed in unskilled (17.9 percent) and semi-skilled (18.8 percent) occupations.

Whereas the Watertown naturalization group closely resembled all Anglo-Canadian heads of household in that city in occupation, their Syracuse counterparts differed somewhat. They were far more concentrated both in blue-collar jobs (70.4 percent as compared to 52.8 percent for all Anglo-Canadian heads of household) and in clerical positions (28.2 percent as compared to 15.3 percent) and were much less represented in the business (none as compared to 11.2 percent), professional (1.4 percent as compared to 5.2 percent), and private means (none as compared to 15.5 percent) categories.

Job stability was also unusual for the Syracuse eastern Ontarians, although they changed occupations less than their Watertown counterparts. In Syracuse only 23.9 percent of the group kept their same occupation throughout their stay, whereas 46.5 percent changed their occupations once or twice, 25.4 percent changed three to five times, and 4.2 percent changed more than five times.

Table 51 shows the relationship between the first and last occupational changes of transient Canadians according to length of residence in Syracuse. Among those transients who first held an unskilled position, we see some movement into more prestigious and better-paying occupations as time passed. It is suspected that many of the 40 percent of this group who stayed for more than thirty years and managed to acquire their own businesses either retired elsewhere or their deaths were not recorded in the directories. Of the semi-skilled transients, the majority remained in that category except for those who stayed in Syracuse for over thirty years. They moved into clerical and business positions and it is suspected that many of them too were persisters whose deaths were not recorded in the directories.

In Syracuse length of residence showed little association with occupational category. Skilled workers displayed the greatest downward movement as 50 percent of those who had lived in the city for eleven to twenty years moved into the unskilled category. Similarly, all of those who stayed between twenty-one and thirty years moved into the ranks of the unskilled. Syracuse experienced a slower pace of growth during the first few decades of the twentieth century but certainly did not experience the drastic decline in fortune that Watertown encountered after the First World War. Yet, while a few individuals experienced downward movement and eventually left the city, in general the Syracuse group was more persistent than its Watertown counterparts.

Table 51 First and Last Occupations of Transient Eastern Ontarians[1] Recorded in the Syracuse Directories by Length of Residence

Original occupation	Length of residence (years)	Unskilled Row %	Unskilled Col %	Semi-skilled Row %	Semi-skilled Col %	Skilled Row %	Skilled Col %	Clerical Row %	Clerical Col %	Business Row %	Business Col %	Professional Row %	Professional Col %
unskilled	1–5	100	15.4	0	0	0	0	100	0	0	0	0	0
	6–10	57.1	30.7	14.3	50.0	14.3	33.3	14.3	2.0	0	0	0	0
	11–20	33.3	15.4	0	0	33.3	66.7	33.3	40.0	0	0	0	0
	21–30	40.0	15.4	0	0	0	0	40.0	40.0	0	0	20.0	100
	>30	50.0	23.1	16.7	50.0	0	0	16.7	20.0	16.7	100	0	0
semi-skilled	1–5	33.3	14.3	66.7	18.2	0	0	0	0	0	0	0	0
	6–10	0	0	100	9.1	0	0	0	0	0	0	0	0
	11–20	0	0	50.0	45.4	20.0	50.0	20.0	40.0	10.0	33.3	0	0
	21–30	0	0	66.7	18.2	0	0	0	0	33.3	33.3	0	0
	>30	46.2	85.7	7.7	9.1	15.4	50.0	23.1	60.0	7.7	3.3	0	0
skilled	1–5	0	0	0	0	0	0	0	0	0	0	0	0
	6–10	0	0	0	0	100	42.8	0	0	0	0	0	0
	11–20	16.7	100	16.7	100	33.3	28.6	16.7	100	16.7	100	0	0
	21–30	0	0	0	0	100	14.3	0	0	0	0	0	0
	>30	0	0	0	0	100	14.3	0	0	0	0	0	0
clerical	1–5	0	0	50.0	33.3	0	0	50.0	12.5	0	0	0	0
	6–10	0	0	100	33.3	0	0	0	0	0	0	0	0
	11–20	0	0	0	0	0	0	75.0	37.5	0	0	25.0	100
	21–30	0	0	20.0	33.3	0	0	40.0	37.5	20.0	100	0	0
	>30	0	0	0	0	0	0	100	12.5	0	0	0	0

Last-Occupation Recorded[2]

Table 51 (continued)

Original occupation	Length of residence (years)	Unskilled		Semi-skilled		Skilled		Clerical		Business		Professional	
		Row %	Col %	Row %	Col %	Row %	Col %	Row %	Col %	Row %	Col %	Row %	Col %
business	1–5	0	0	0	0	0	0	0	0	100	0	0	0
	6–10	0	0	0	0	0	0	0	0	0	100	0	0
	11–20	0	0	0	0	0	0	0	0	0	0	0	0
	21–30	100	100	0	0	0	0	0	0	0	0	0	0
	>30	0	0	0	0	0	0	0	0	0	0	0	0
professional	1–5	0	0	0	0	0	0	0	0	0	0	0	0
	6–10	0	0	0	0	0	0	0	0	0	0	0	0
	11–20	0	0	0	0	0	0	0	0	0	0	0	0
	21–30	0	0	0	0	0	0	0	0	0	0	0	0
	>30	0	0	0	0	0	0	0	0	0	0	0	0

Last-Occupation Recorded[2]

Sources: Petitions for Naturalization; City Directories

[1] transients include those disappearing from the directories without any indication of their deaths.

[2] not include private means which for the most part were retirees.

The degree of residential stability and upward movement was somewhat greater for eastern Ontarians who remained in the city (Table 52). While 60 percent of those who entered the Watertown workforce as unskilled labourers finished their working careers in that category, only 20 percent of those who entered the Syracuse labour force finished their careers as unskilled labourers. There was notable movement among both the unskilled and semi-skilled into all other categories. Most of those who first occupied a skilled position continued to do so, although some moved into clerical positions and others operated their own businesses. There was no movement down the hierarchy among either semi-skilled or skilled eastern Ontarians. The majority of the Syracuse group who first held a clerical position continued to do so.

When we trace the moves of each occupational category, it is apparent that those who first occupied an unskilled position were not much more likely to be transient than others who occupied higher skilled or business positions. While upward mobility among the working-class Anglo-Canadians in Watertown was shown to be achieved only after a series of many moves, mobility among this same group in Syracuse was usually achieved much more quickly, sometimes within the first ten years of residence and after only one or two residential moves. There were apparently more avenues of opportunity in the larger city.

An examination of initial and final residences of the Watertown transients and persisters shows that the former group tended to live in the more working-class and ethnically mixed northern half of the city, while the latter group were inclined to move over time to the wealthier and more American south side. Such clear patterns do not emerge for the Syracuse study. The initial and last residences for both transients and persisters were dispersed throughout the city. The only notable clustering took place among persisters where almost 27 percent of this group last resided in Ward 13 near the university.

Anglo-Canadian household heads also displayed little evidence of clustering according to length of residence, with the exception of those arriving between 1896 and 1900 and living in Ward 12 and those arriving between 1890 and 1895 and living in Ward 18. They shared with the host American group and the English a dispersed residential pattern although few of them lived in the same neighbourhoods as the upper-class Americans.

As in the Watertown sample, the rate of turnover of the Syracuse naturalization group reinforces the idea that the host community was many things to Canadian immigrants. Just over 4 percent stayed between one and five years, and another 4.2 percent remained between six and ten years. Over 15 percent lived in the city between eleven and twenty years, 16.9 percent between twenty-one and twenty-nine years, and almost 60 percent lived in the city for more than thirty years. Over 57 percent of the

Table 52   First and Last Occupations of Persistent Eastern Ontarians[1] Recorded in the Syracuse Directories

| | Last-Occupation Recorded[2] | | | | | | | | | | | |
| | Unskilled | | Semi-skilled | | Skilled | | Clerical | | Business | | Professional | |
Original Occupation	Row %	Col. %	Row %	Col. %	Row %	Col. %	Row %	Col. %	Row %	Col. %	Row %	Col. %
unskilled	20.0	100.0	20.0	16.7	10.0	16.7	30.0	23.1	10.0	16.7	10.0	33.3
semi-skilled	0	0	60.0	75.0	5.0	16.7	10.0	15.4	20.0	66.7	5.0	33.3
skilled	0	0	0	0	66.7	66.7	16.7	7.7	16.7	16.7	0	0
clerical	0	0	12.5	8.3	0	0	87.5	53.8	0	0	0	0
business	0	0	0	0	0	0	0	0	0	0	0	0
professional	0	0	0	0	0	0	0	0	0	0	100	33.3

Sources: Petitions for Naturalization; City Directories.

[1] persisters refer to those who remained in Syracuse until their deaths, including persons remaining in the city for the rest of their lives and the percentage who left the city but returned.

[2] not include private means which for the most part were retirees.

group were traced in Syracuse until the time of their deaths. Thus Syracuse Ontarians were more persistent than the Watertown Ontarians. This may be explained in part by the older age composition of the Syracuse group and the greater opportunities the larger city provided. While Watertown was a brief sojourn for many Canadians, Syracuse may have represented the final stage of migration for these same people.

Only two eastern Ontarian households remained in the same residence during their stay. The seventy-one households made a total of 401 residence changes during their lives in Syracuse, an average of 5.6 moves per household. Anglo-Canadians were generally more geographically mobile in Watertown and more occupationally mobile in Syracuse. Yet a surprisingly high proportion of Canadians remained in the lower ranks of the occupational hierarchy despite increasing length of residence, although they were less concentrated in the working class than Canadians in Watertown.

Syracuse was even more a city of renters than Watertown (Table 53) and yet tenure varied somewhat with nativity. As in Watertown, the Irish and the Germans were more likely to own their homes than other groups, and the newer immigrant groups were predominantly renters. Yet both the French- and Anglo-Canadians, more correctly identified with the old immigrant category, mirrored the tenure patterns of southern and eastern Europeans.

Length of residence in the United States played a much greater role in home ownership than class, and the older European groups enjoyed higher rates of home ownership. Yet the Anglo-Canadians experienced higher rental rates among the pre-1880 immigrants than any other group with the exception of the small Polish group. Surprisingly, among this group of Canadians, the unskilled, next to the private means category, were most likely to own their homes, while the semi-skilled and skilled and middle class were most likely to rent.

While Anglo-Canadians in Watertown were highly endogamous and least likely to give up their citizenship, the same was not true for their Syracuse counterparts. Of the foreign groups, the French Canadians (43.4 percent), English (41.9 percent), and Anglo-Canadians (38.6 percent) showed the greatest tendency to marry New Yorkers and other Americans. Anglo-Canadians displayed a much weaker tendency to marry within their own group (35.1 percent) than they did in Watertown (54.7 percent). Only the French Canadians (29.4 percent) and the English (35.8 percent) displayed similar low endogamy rates. As the percentage of marriage within the Anglo-Canadian group declined with length of residence, marriage to native Americans increased. The difference in endogamy between the Watertown and Syracuse Anglo-Canadians may reflect the fact that in Watertown they made up the dominant foreign element but were insignificant in Syracuse. The small size of Watertown and the dominance of a few

Table 53   Members of Tenure Groups by Nativity and Length of Residence, Immigrant Groups, Syracuse 1900[1]

Length of residence (years)	Tenure group	Nativity Groups (%)							
		English	Germans	Polish	Irish	Italians	French Canadian	Anglo-Celtic Canadians	Others
<1–2	rent	100	100	100	100	100	0	100	0
	own encumbered	0	0	0	0	0	0	0	0
	own free	0	0	0	0	0	0	0	0
3–5	rent	100	100	100	100	90.2	100	100	100
	own encumbered	0	0	0	0	0	0	0	0
	own free	0	0	0	0	9.8	0	0	0
6–10	rent	65.4	74.5	94.9	90.6	100	89.6	81.5	100
	own encumbered	0	16.1	5.1	0	0	10.4	18.5	0
	own free	34.6	9.4	0	9.4	0	0	0	0
11–20	rent	83.7	38.4	76.3	72.9	85.5	69.0	67.7	77.5
	own encumbered	9.8	41.1	13.6	20.5	11.5	20.9	18.6	19.1
	own free	6.6	20.5	10.1	6.5	3.0	10.1	13.6	3.3
>20	rent	44.2	22.6	80.1	43.7	50.5	57.9	61.5	54.3
	own encumbered	30.3	22.5	19.9	19.2	33.1	21.2	21.1	26.1
	own free	25.6	54.9	0	37.1	16.4	20.9	17.4	19.6

Source: 1900 US Manuscript Census.

[1] stratified samples computed by weight samples.

Table 54   Occupational Profile of Anglo-Canadian Household Heads in
Watertown, Syracuse, and Manhattan, 1900

	Watertown		Syracuse		Manhattan	
Occupational Group	N	%	N	%	N	%
Unskilled	201	25.8	111	16.2	106	13.6
Semi-skilled	254	32.6	168	24.5	113	14.5
Skilled	138	17.7	83	12.1	102	13.1
Clerical	55	7.1	105	15.3	170	21.8
Business	55	7.1	77	11.2	123	15.7
Professional	10	1.2	36	5.2	61	7.8
Private Means[1]	66	8.5	106	15.5	106	13.5
Totals	779	100.0	686	100.0	781	100.0

Source: 1900 US Manuscript Censuses

[1] including no occupation.

industries in the city meant that former neighbours in Canada could also
be neighbours and co-workers in America. But the larger scale and greater
variety of job opportunities in Syracuse meant that affinal connections outside the household were less likely.

Length of residence played a greater role in obtaining American citizenship among this group in Syracuse than in Watertown. Whereas almost
30 percent of the Watertown migrants who came during the 1880s
remained as aliens in 1900, only 19.1 percent of the Syracuse migrants
who emigrated during that decade had not acquired citizenship. Almost
40 percent of the entire alien Anglo-Canadian household head population
in Syracuse arrived between 1896 and 1900 while another 35 percent emigrated at some time between 1890 and 1895.

Occupational profiles of Anglo-Canadian household heads in Watertown and Syracuse in 1900 are compared with that of the Manhattan
Anglo-Canadian household heads in order to examine the occupational
and mobility profiles of this group in three different levels of the urban
hierarchy in New York State: the small industrial city, the larger regional
city, and the most populous borough in the largest metropolis in the country. The data in Table 54 provide evidence that different types of Canadians were attracted to these three different communities, suggesting that an
occupational as well as an age and sex selectivity characterized the migration flow. While the Syracuse Anglo-Canadians showed a greater range of
occupations than their Watertown counterparts, the Manhattan group was
even more diverse in their vocations. New York City, which was much larger and more diversified, offered more avenues of mobility, especially for
those qualified to take advantage of such opportunities. It was this promise

that inspired some eastern Ontarians to make the longer trip, especially those who practised a profession, such as physicians.

Unfortunately, it is impossible to complete a longitudinal study based on the eastern Ontarians naturalized in Manhattan because the 1925–30 Manhattan directories are missing and only telephone directories are available after 1933. Yet the initial occupations of the thirty Ontarians from the origin area naturalized in Manhattan reflect the fact that a greater proportion of Canadians practising a profession or holding a white-collar occupation were attracted to this metropolis. Eleven members were professionals, eight held clerical positions, four held skilled positions, three worked in semi-skilled occupations, two owned businesses, and another two were unskilled workers. Three of the eastern Ontarians were physicians, a figure which resembles the twenty-seven Anglo-Canadian household heads who practised that profession in Manhattan in 1900.

CONCLUSION

It is important to realize that for many eastern Ontarians, migration to the United States and movement to other regions of Canada were closely linked. The young men and women who left the economic stagnation of a marginal farm or the St Lawrence River town may have gone to work in the factories and offices of nearby Watertown, Syracuse, or Toronto, or they may have decided to travel a greater distance and go to New York City, Chicago, or some other American metropolis. The lure of newly opened agricultural land in the Dakotas and later the Canadian west may have persuaded them to travel even farther afield. The choice depended on circumstances and desire, but what mattered most was that they felt they had to go somewhere. Anglo-Canadians seeking land joined the westward flow of Americans settling free homestead land in the American Great Plains. It is to this particular region that we now turn.

6 Red River Bound: Canadian Migration to Eastern North Dakota

Vos rivières coulent sur notre territoire, nos rivières coulent sur le votre.

– Wilfrid Laurier, quoted in *Between Friends*, NFB documentary

THE CONTEXT OF MIGRATION

In 1659 the French explorers Radisson and Groseilliers first laid eyes on the Red River valley of southern Manitoba and the Dakotas. That they were impressed by what they saw is evident in the observations of Radisson: "The country was so pleasant, so beautiful and so fruitful that it grieved me to see that the world could not discover such enticing countries to live in ... I can say that in all my lifetime I have never seen such a finer country."[1] Later-arriving Canadians, both francophone and anglophone, coming first to trade for furs and afterwards to take up farming, shared the adventurers' appreciation of this region. Indeed, Canadians would come to play an important role in the settlement of the valley on the American side.

Long before the great "Dakota Boom" of 1879 to 1886, Canadians settled in the northeastern part of the present state of North Dakota. Prior to 1800, several fur-trading posts run by the Hudson's Bay and North West companies had established operations in the northern Red River valley. In 1812 the first permanent settlement was made in Pembina by Scottish and Irish settlers sent to this area by Lord Selkirk under the leadership of Miles MacDonnell. This colony proved to be short-lived as six years later an agreement was reached by Britain and the United States to establish the forty-ninth parallel as the international boundary. The settlers withdrew north of the line leaving the valley to a small group of traders and Indians. In 1823 the Hudson's Bay Company retired to Fort Garry and it was not until the 1840s that Americans began to establish fur-trading posts in the region.[2]

Pembina became the centre of a vast trade territory whose main commerce was furs taken from the Dakota side of the Red River and western

Canada. Beginning in 1843, ox carts operated by the Hudson's Bay Company travelled from Fort Garry and Pembina to St Paul carrying furs east and finished products west. But the days of the cart trade were numbered with the appearance of the first steamboat on the river in 1859. Anglo-Ontarians along with native-born Americans became involved in the development of the steamboat trade in the 1860s and played a major role in the establishment of the first river towns.[3]

Agricultural settlers, many from Canada, slowly made their way into the Pembina District of the Minnesota Territory. By 1850 there were 1,134 people in this area farming 2,145 acres of land. Over 64 percent of this population was born in Canada.[4] Yet settlement of the region proceeded at a sluggish pace even after the Homestead Act was passed in 1862. Only thirty-three homesteads were granted in the Dakotas in 1871.[5] Mobility among Americans was slowed considerably by the Civil War. But soil exhaustion back east, an increase in foreign migration, the building of railroads connecting the Dakotas to eastern markets, and high wheat prices triggered the Dakota Boom in 1879. While the population of the North Dakota portion of the territory was only 2,000 in 1870, by 1890 it had increased to 183,000.[6] Extensive advertising in Europe by the railroad companies and the state and the phenomenon of chain migration were important factors in this population growth.

Before the construction of the Canadian Pacific Railway in 1883, the lack of a transportation route through the Canadian Shield meant that those Canadians intent on settling in Manitoba travelled through the United States, usually by train to St Paul, at which point they transferred to wagons carrying them to lower Red River ports where they connected with stages and steamboats to Fort Garry. As Sherman states, "the Red River could, in some respects, have been called a Canadian waterway during the several decades preceding American homestead settlement."[7] Yet many of those Canadians intent on taking up land in Manitoba following the passing of Canada's Homestead Act in 1872 were attracted by intervening opportunities in the Dakotas and as a consequence changed their travel plans. They were soon joined by many of their countrymen who were well aware of the area because of its significance as a "Canadian" route to the west. In addition, American railroad agents actively recruited Ontarians to settle in Dakota and preyed on Canadian land seekers along the route.

The well-publicized Dakota Boom only served to augment the flow of Canadians into the Red River valley, many of them deciding on the Dakotas before leaving their homes. It has been said that by 1879 Canadians, many of Scottish descent, settling along the northern part of the Red River were so numerous that more Canadian than American money circulated there.[8] Norrie estimates that between 1870 and 1890 over 120,000 Canadian-born chose the American prairies over Canada, many of them settling in North Dakota.[9] The valley, with its flat surface, sand and clay

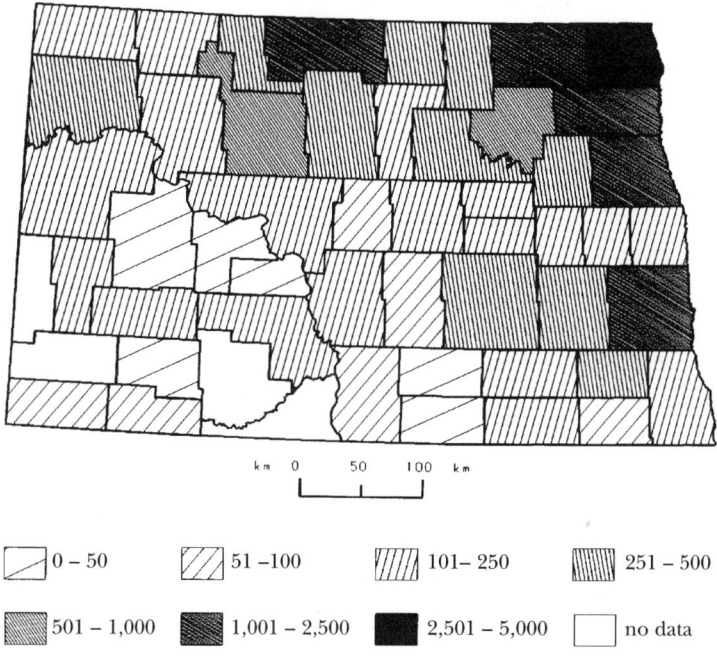

km 0   50   100   km

| ⬜ 0 – 50 | ▨ 51 –100 | ▨ 101– 250 | ▨ 251 – 500 |
| ▨ 501 – 1,000 | ◼ 1,001 – 2,500 | ■ 2,501 – 5,000 | ⬜ no data |

* designated as non-French in the US census

Map 14: Anglo-Canadians* by North Dakota County, 1910

loams, long hot summers and cool dry winters, quickly acquired a reputation
as an excellent region for cereal production and thus was viewed favourably
by eastern Canadians intent on pursuing agricultural opportunities.

REGIONAL PATTERNS OF MIGRATION
AND SETTLEMENT

Elwyn B. Robinson, the noted Plains historian, divides the original settlement of North Dakota into two periods: the Great Dakota Boom
(1879–86) and the Second Boom (1898–1915).[10] During the first period,
the eastern two-thirds of the state was settled by Americans, largely from
the midwest, Norwegians, Canadians, Germans, and others, most concentrating along or near the Red River. In 1890 Norwegians composed the
largest foreign-born group, comprising 14.1 percent of the total population of the state, followed closely by Canadian-born (12.6 percent) and
then distantly by Germans, Swedes, Russians of German descent, English,
Irish, and the Danes.[11] Canadians settled along the Red and the northern
border, a pattern which still dominated in 1910 (maps 14, 15). Towards

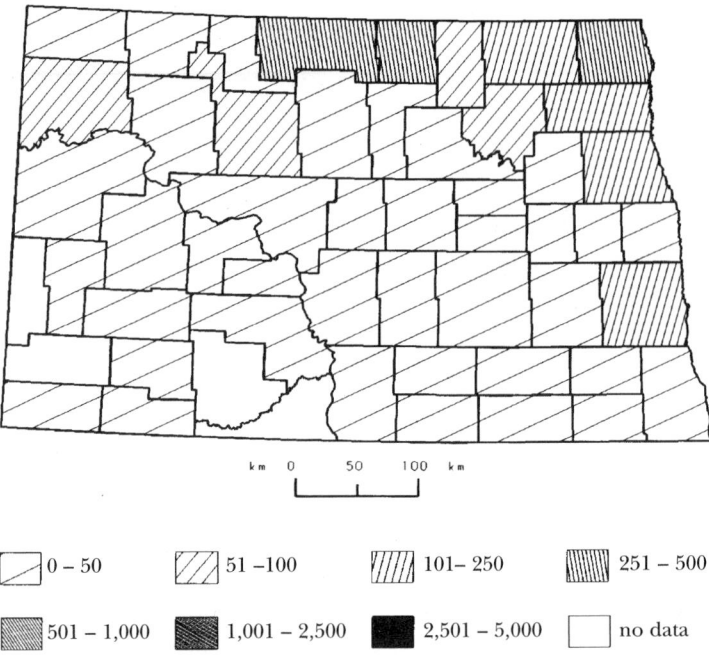

km   0   50   100   km

☐ 0 – 50   ▨ 51 –100   ▨ 101– 250   ▨ 251 – 500

▨ 501 – 1,000   ▨ 1,001 – 2,500   ■ 2,501 – 5,000   ☐ no data

Map 15: French Canadians by North Dakota County, 1910

the end of the 1880s, Russian-Germans moved to the Bismarck area, signalling the first phase of western expansion in the state. Yet settlement of
the western part would not take take place in earnest until after 1900, by
which time little available land was left in the more fertile and humid lands
of the east. Settlement of the Dakotas proceeded at a snail's pace until the
railroad made its appearance: the Northern Pacific reached Fargo in 1872,
Bismarck in 1873, and the Little Missouri in 1880; the Great Northern
reached Grand Forks in 1880, Minot in 1886, and the Montana border a
year later; and the Soo Line crossed the border into Saskatchewan by
1893. Railroad companies promoted immigration by sending special
agents abroad to establish land and immigration departments and by producing promotional literature in foreign languages in these countries.
They also offered free transportation to purchasers of railroad land which
ranged from $2.50 to $8 an acre with a down payment of 10 percent and
seven years to pay the remainder.[12] Yet most immigrants were more interested in obtaining free homestead, tree claim, and pre-emption lands.

The mechanisms for obtaining homestead land were well established by
the early 1880s. Most newcomers got off the train at Fargo, Grand Forks,
or other points and set out across the prairie searching for a good piece of

land. Many looked for land near family and friends. After finding and marking the chosen site, they would continue to the nearest federal land office to file their claim. Family heads, widows, and single people 21 years and over could apply for free land provided they were a citizen or had signed their declaration of intention. After filing at the land office, homesteaders had six months to move on to their property, plough ten acres, plant a crop, and establish some sort of residence. After five years of residence and improving the land, homesteaders could then pay a proving-up fee of $4 and receive their patent. They were allowed seven years after filing to fulfil these conditions, and many immigrants waited out this seven-year period before fulfilling all the required duties.[13]

The same group of settlers could also purchase a quarter-section at $1.25 an acre after paying a settlement fee of two dollars and living on the land for one year. Pre-emptors paid $2.50 an acre for land lying within the Northern Pacific land grant. Proof of residence and improvements had to be submitted at any time after six months but before a year. Again, the same group could obtain a tree claim of up to 160 acres provided that the parcel was completely devoid of timber. The same qualifications regarding duties and time as under the homestead and pre-emption claims were enforced. Settlers could not own a pre-emption and homestead claim at the same time but they could take either one along with a tree claim.

In the eastern half of the state, largely settled by 1890, many settlers obtained three quarter-sections of land under homestead, pre-emption, and tree claim provisions. Yet because of extensive land fraud and speculation, both the pre-emption and tree claim laws were repealed in 1890 and from that date until 1909, homesteaders were only allowed one quarter-section. At that time, the amount was increased to two quarters because of the lower productivity of available land in the western half of the state.[14]

During the 1880s settlers flooded the Red River valley and then spread along the railroad lines into the interior. By 1890 the six counties along the Red River accounted for 47 percent of the state's population.[15] The drop in grain prices caused by the drought in 1889 signalled a decade of sluggish economic growth. Yet settlement remained steady and was revived by the development of the western part of the state at the end of the 1890s.[16]

Scandinavians and Canadians dominated the influx of immigrants during the first boom. They were soon joined by thousands more of Scandinavian origin. In his groundbreaking study, Hudson paints a picture of westward movement into North Dakota "accomplished through successive concentrations and scatterings of the foreign-born and first-generation groups and through what appears to have been a haphazard series of trial and error approaches by the native-born."[17] Many Canadians also migrated in a series of steps that carried them farther west, although Hudson's small sample of Ontarians migrated directly to North Dakota with no intervening place of residence. His analysis identified three major source areas: the Huron Tract north of London; a colony from Glengarry County settling near Pembina; and Bruce and Grey counties, a part of Ontario experiencing recent and significant population/land pressure.

Although foreign-born were distributed widely among the counties of the valley, clustering did occur. As maps 14 and 15 make clear, Canadians, both French- and English-speaking, settled predominantly in the northern counties and along the border west of the Red River. They were the most numerous among the foreign-born in Pembina and Walsh counties and ranked second in Grand Forks, Cass, and Traill counties in 1890. Ten years later, Canadians continued to dominate in Pembina County but their numbers were significantly reduced in Walsh County. A loss of almost 72 percent of the population of this county was almost surely the result of extensive out-migration to western North Dakota and points elsewhere, including western Canada. Canadians continued to rank second in Grand Forks, Cass and Traill counties. French Canadians were more apt to locate in forested areas while their English-speaking counterparts found the urban environment and open prairie more congenial.

Many of the first settlers in the northern towns and townships were Ontarians who named their settlements after the Ontario communities from which they originated. For example, Drayton in Pembina County was founded by a group of settlers from Drayton, Ontario, in 1878.[18] In 1880 Antoine Gerard from Acton, Ontario, founded and named the town of Acton in a section of Pembina County, and Norton Township, Walsh County, was originally named Galt after Galt, Ontario. Because Norwegians who settled in the northern half of the township wanted to call it Nordland after a town in Norway, and because Canadians wanted to retain the name of Galt, the residents agreed to simplify the name Nordford and call the township Norton.[19]

A deeper insight into Canadian migrants to the Red River valley is afforded by the Historical Data Project files used by Hudson in his study of migration to North Dakota.[20] Examination of the files for the most populous Canadian counties – Pembina, Walsh, Grand Forks, and Cass – shows that the overwhelming majority of Canadians came from the major source regions of Ontario identified by Hudson and that most moved directly to North Dakota from their home province (Table 55). They were generally young, some coming as children but the majority being single and either travelling alone or with friends or accompanying their family. A small percentage were married and had their own families. What is quite striking is the relatively high rate of endogamy among this group, particularly among those marrying in North Dakota. Hudson shows that Canadians were more likely to marry outside their national group than Germans, German Russians, Swedes and Norwegians. Yet the high degree of endogamy is significant nonetheless.

Table 55   Canadian Migration Characteristics, Historical Data Project Files, North Dakota County of Destination

Characteristics of migrants	Pembina (N = 53) Row %	Pembina Col %	Walsh (N = 42) Row %	Walsh Col %	Grand Forks (N = 42) Row %	Grand Forks Col %	Trail (N = 5) Row %	Trail Col %	Cass (N = 21) Row %	Cass Col %	Richland (N = 4) Row %	Richland Col %	Total (N = 167) Row %	Total Col %
Province of birth:														
Ontario	28.6	79.2	25.9	90.5	25.9	90.5	2.7	80.0	14.3	100	2.7	100	100	88.0
Quebec	57.1	15.1	28.6	9.5	14.3	4.8	0	0	0	0	0	0	100	8.4
New Brunswick	0	0	0	0	0	0	100	20.0	0	0	0	0	100	0.6
Nova Scotia	50.0	1.9	0	0	50.0	2.4	0	0	0	0	0	0	100	1.2
Manitoba	100	1.9	0	0	0	0	0	0	0	0	0	0	100	0.6
PEI	50.0	1.9	0	0	50.0	2.4	0	0	0	0	0	0	100	1.2
Last province / state of residence:														
Ontario	30.8	75.5	23.8	73.8	27.7	85.7	0.8	20.0	16.2	100	1.5	50.0	100	77.8
Quebec	50.0	9.4	40.0	9.5	10.0	2.4	0	0	0	0	0	0	100	6.0
Manitoba	75.0	5.7	0	0	25.0	2.4	0	0	0	0	0	0	100	2.4
Nova Scotia	50.0	1.9	0	0	50.0	2.4	0	0	0	0	0	0	100	1.2
PEI	50.0	1.9	0	0	50.0	2.4	0	0	0	0	0	0	100	1.2
Michigan	0	0	66.7	4.8	0	0	33.3	20.0	0	0	0	0	100	1.8
New York	0	0	0	0	0	0	100	20.0	0	0	0	0	100	0.6
Minnesota	0	0	50.0	4.8	25.0	2.4	0	0	0	0	25.0	25.0	100	2.4
Missouri	50.0	1.9	0	0	0	0	50.0	20.0	0	0	0	0	100	1.8
Illinois	0	0	0	0	0	0	50.0	20.0	0	0	25.0	25.0	100	1.2
Wisconsin	0	0	100	4.8	0	0	0	0	0	0	0	0	100	0.6
Iowa	0	0	100	2.4	0	0	0	0	0	0	0	0	100	0.6
Kansas	0	0	0	0	100	2.4	0	0	0	0	0	0	100	0.6
Massachusetts	100	1.9	0	0	0	0	0	0	0	0	0	0	100	0.6
New hampshire	100	1.9	0	0	0	0	0	0	0	0	0	0	100	0.6

Table 55 (continued)

Characteristics of migrants	Pembina (N = 53)		Walsh (N = 42)		Grand Forks (N = 42)		Trail (N = 5)		Cass (N = 21)		Richland (N = 4)		Total (N = 167)	
	Row %	Col. %	Row %	Col. %	Row %	Col. %	Row %	Col. %	Row %	Col. %	Row %	Col. %	Row %	Col. %
Average number of moves before settling	0.56		0.9		0.33		1.8		0.05		0.25		0.65	
Travel with family:														
Alone or with friends	34.7	32.1	30.6	35.7	24.5	28.6	0	0	4.1	9.5	2.0	25.0	100	29.3
As an adult with some or all of family	17.3	26.4	24.7	47.6	22.2	42.9	6.2	100	8.6	33.3	0	0	100	48.5
As a child (<16)	59.5	41.5	18.9	16.7	32.4	28.6	0	0	32.4	57.1	8.1	75.0	100	22.2
Average age at emigration	20.7		20.7		19.0		24.4		21.7		20.3		21.1	
Marriage to Canadian:														
Not apply	34.7	32.1	20.4	23.8	34.7	40.5	4.1	40.0	4.1	9.5	2.0	25.0	100	29.3
In Canada	31.8	26.4	34.1	35.7	13.6	14.3	4.5	40.0	15.9	33.3	0	0	100	26.3
In U.S.	29.7	41.5	23.0	40.5	25.7	45.2	1.4	20.0	16.2	57.1	4.1	75.0	100	44.3
Married Canadians as a % of total	67.9		76.2		59.5		60.0		90.5		75.0		70.6	

Source: North Dakota Historical Data Project Files

The files reveal much about the motives and modes of migration and provide evidence of the importance of social associations in this movement. For example, James Abercrombie, the eldest of nine children, was born in Burgess Township, Lanark County, Ontario, in 1858. When he was 5, his family moved to a 200-acre timber farm near Perth. In 1878 his friends, the four McGilvery boys from an adjoining farm, Thomas McCulloch, who worked on the Abercrombie farm, and a number of other young men from the district travelled together to Dakota Territory where they settled on land near Ardoch in Walsh County. Ardoch was named by the brothers George, John, James, and Will Stevenson who had come from Ardoch, Ontario. James wanted to accompany his friends but his father needed him at home. Four years later, James finally made it to Ardoch, and stayed with Bill and Alex McGilvery on Alex's quarter. Thomas McCulloch, who had filed on the northwest quarter of the adjacent section, was busy buying and selling lots in the village and building a large hotel and livery stable on Main Street. Bill McGilvery was discouraged by the early June frost that year and wanted to sell his land and go to the Klondike. In July of 1882, James bought McGilvery's quarter with its standing crop, small barn, a granary, well, three horses, and a number of implements for $4,000. He received the money from his father in Canada, $2,000 as a gift and the other $2,000 to be paid back at a rate of $300 a year or as crop returns permitted. Abercrombie lived with Alex for two years before building his own house.

John Martyn was born in 1862 in Huron County, Ontario. At the age of 20 he decided to emigrate to the Dakota Territory "for the reason that a new country offered better opportunities for a young man and because many of his acquaintances had emigrated to D.T. before him." John and his friend Louis Ritter arrived in Grand Forks in the spring of 1882. Shortly after, he and another Canadian, William Widdes, took an emigrant train to Minto in Walsh County. The next six years Martyn hired out to three different men, two Canadian-born, in the Kensington district. Eventually John rented a number of farms in the Park River area.

James McDonald was born in Westmeath Township, Ontario, in 1847. When he turned 20, he left the family farm and went to work in the woods. For seventeen years he worked for lumber companies bringing rafts down to Ottawa and on the St Lawrence to Quebec City for export to England. It was largely by accident that McDonald came to Dakota:

A friend, William Tierny, was bringing horses to Manitoba. Another friend, Tim Haley and Mr. McDonald decided to go along to get a view of the country. That was in 1882. They met Tierny in Grand Forks. The Manitoba branch of the Great Northern was being laid at that time, so Mr. Haley and Mr. McDonald decided to take the construction train north. Two hotels were for sale in Grafton that year. Mr. Haley bought the Oriental and Mr. McDonald bought the other which he called the Ottawa House. The next year, Mr. McDonald returned to Pembroke, Ontario to marry Mary Elizabeth Kennedy, bringing his wife back to Grafton.

Henry Warnington, born on 12 August 1864 near Fergus, Ontario, was inspired to emigrate by the success of another local, James J. Hill, who had gone to St Paul, Minnesota, became prominent as a railroad builder, and later participated in the development of agriculture in the Dakota Territory. Stories of Mr Hill's success in the United States came back to his native Wellington County, Ontario. These impelled young Warnington, not yet 19 years old, to go to Dakota Territory to seek his fortune. In 1883 Henry and his cousin John Keys, who paid his rail fare, left for Fargo. Immediately upon their arrival, Henry began working on the farm of his cousin, David Keys, for $18 a month for eight months and $10 a month for four months. Eventually, Warnington bought two different quarter-sections, sold them and moved into Fargo where he got into the apartment renting business.

N.G. Benner, born in December of 1865 near Port Colborne, Ontario, was another young man influenced by the success of a local in the Dakota Territory. As a teenager, Benner moved to Port Colborne to work as a clerk in the store run by R.B. Griffith. In 1888 he moved to Grand Forks to work as a clerk for Griffith who had preceded him and opened the Ontario Store. Eventually, Benner left R.B. Griffith and went into partnership with another Canadian, W.S. Beggs, in the department store business.

These few examples reflect a predominantly rural-rural migration with individuals for the most part moving directly from their place of birth to Dakota. The primary motive for migration among this young group was the desire to acquire cheap land. Older migrants viewed Dakota as an opportunity for them and their children to acquire land and live close together, thus ensuring the continuity of the family unit. Many immigrants followed family members or friends west and many came with a number of other families from their Canadian homes. The transplantation of Ontario communities was made possible by the processes of chain and cluster migration, and it had a significant impact on their settlement experience in their new Dakota homes.

MIGRATION EXPERIENCES:
GRAND FORKS COUNTY

Economic and Social Profiles

Although Pembina County was home to the largest number of Canadian-born at the turn of the century, Grand Forks County with a large rural Canadian population and Grand Forks City with the largest urban Canadian population in the Red River valley are the subjects of this case study. Canadians would prove to be important players in the development of both the county and the city.

French-Canadian fur explorers named the junction of the Red River and the Red Lake River "Les Grandes Fourches," which would later be anglicized and applied to the village developing at that site and the county which was created in 1875. Alexander Henry the Younger of the North West Company out of Montreal erected a fur-trading post at the junction in 1801 but it was short-lived. Over the next few decades a number of posts were built in the vicinity by both the North West and Hudson's Bay companies and the junction became a stopping-off point for the Red River carts carrying goods between St Paul and Fort Garry. In 1870 a post office was established, and Grand Forks became a regular stagecoach stop when a new stage route was opened between Moorhead and Winnipeg in September of 1871.[21]

With the establishment of a post office, the small settlement began to develop. Thomas Walsh, who built the stagecoach station, also established a saw mill; John Ferry ran a ferry across the river; D.P. Reeves constructed a boatyard; and Frank Viets opened a blacksmith shop. While there were only thirty-three living there in 1871, within a year the village supported a boarding house, hotel, a steamboat warehouse, and four saloons.[22] In 1872 the Canadian-born St Paul capitalist James J. Hill joined forces with a Mississippi steamboat captain, Alexander Griggs, and Norman Kittson to form the Red River Transportation Line. Griggs built a log cabin in the small settlement and took possession of a quarter section in which 9 acres were set aside and planned as an official townsite after the county of Grand Forks was created in 1875. The Red River steamboats stimulated the growth of Grand Forks, Fargo and other towns along the river, bringing in people and goods necessary for development. The movement of the Hudson's Bay Company from Caledonia in Traill County to Grand Forks in 1873 further encouraged the growth of the young settlement.

Towards the end of the decade, thousands of immigrants and eastern Americans flooded into the area and both the village and the county grew (Table 56). In 1880 the populations of the county and town were 6,248 and 1,705 respectively. Over 56 percent of the population of the town was foreign-born, with the largest number coming from Canada.[23] The coming of the railroad in the early 1880s signalled the demise of the steamboat era and ushered in the next stage in the growth of Grand Forks. Both the Great Northern and the Northern Pacific Railroad crossed the Red at Grand Forks, bringing immigrants into the region and spurring trade throughout the valley. Farmers could deliver grain to steam stops located every six miles along the track.

As early as 1880 the community and the surrounding countryside were

Table 56   Foreign-born Population, Grand Forks County, 1880–1900

	Years		
Foreign-born population	*1880*	*1890*	*1900*
Canada[1]	1980	2648	2986
England[2]	139	258	248
Ireland	188	362	312
Scotland	80	127	125
Germany	149	418	469
Norway[3]	1214	3518	3308
Sweden		398	535
Total all groups	3852	7971	8483

Sources: Department of the Interior, *Statistics of the Population of the U.S. at the 10th Census* (Washington: Government Printing Office, 1883); *Statistics of the Population of the U.S. and the 11th Census* (Washington: Government Printing Office, 1893), 648–9; *Statistics of the Population of the U.S. at the 12th Census,* Vol. 1 (Washington: Government Printing Office, 1903), 775.

[1] both English and French Canada and including Newfoundland.
[2] including Wales in 1880.
[3] including Sweden in 1880.

being promoted and praised outside the region. With obvious pride, the 22 April 1880 edition of the Grand Forks *Herald* reprinted the following report that had appeared in the St Paul *Globe:*

In this famous Red River Valley, the garden of the Northwest, whose wonderful productions and unsurpassed fertility has become so generally celebrated, no fairer spot by nature for the location of a large commercial and manufacturing center can be found than the "Northern Jewel" occupies. The effect upon newcomers is magical. One glance and they become enraptured with the place, and hunt up a real estate dealer without delay ... For commercial advantages, being practically at the head of navigation on Red River and at the confluence of the Red Lake River, only the advent of the road which reached it last fall was necessary to put our jewel in the front rank. As a manufacturing point, in addition to flouring mills already springing up and which are to be found anywhere in a great wheat region like this as soon as it becomes developed, there is a fine prospect at no distant day for a great lumbering business ... In the city over two hundred buildings are now under contract and over two miles of sidewalks are ordered built. During the last month, 468 foreign citizens have been naturalized, which represents but a small portion of the newcomers.

Despite the hyperbole of this immodest piece of boosterism, the article rightly emphasized the potential of Grand Fork's site and situation. Rich soils combined with good drainage, a gentle east-west rise in elevation, and a sub-humid climate with sufficient rainfall during the growing season to produce a region deemed ideal for growing wheat. The city's situation in the middle of the valley and at the junction of two rivers and two railroads made it an ideal gateway for immigrants coming to Dakota.

Rapid growth in the county and city only increased the confidence of residents. In 1885 the populations of the county and the city reached 20,000 and just under 5,000 respectively. Larimore, the second-largest centre in the county, had a population of 1,100. Over 564,300 acres in Grand Forks County were farmed in 1884 and Number One hard wheat was fetching a high price on the market. Grand Forks City had two newspapers, one brewery, three brickyards, four sawmills, and three flour mills in 1885. But it was most proud of being the home of the University of North Dakota, created by an act of the Territorial Assembly in 1883.[24]

A drop in wheat prices, frost and drought in the late 1880s slowed growth to some extent. The 1890 census shows the population of the county as 18,357 but the decrease was due primarily to parts of Grand Forks being taken by the newly created counties of Walsh and Nelson. Yet the city had not grown very much, with a population of 4,984, of which 55 percent were native-born. Norwegians now surpassed Canadians as the largest immigrant group in the county. Lagging far behind these two groups were the Germans, the Swedes, the Irish, the English, the Scots, and a variety of other European groups.[25]

Considering the large amount of wheat grown in the immediate hinterland, the milling industry was surprisingly small in Grand Forks during the 1880s and 1890s. Competition from Minneapolis millers did much to discourage this industry in North Dakota. Nevertheless, Grand Forks was the original home of what was to become an American breakfast staple, Cream of Wheat cereal. Thomas Anderson, head miller of Grand Fork's Diamond Mill, persuaded the principal partners to try his idea for a new porridge using the middlings which were the whitest and best part of the wheat. They were, in Anderson's terms, the "cream" of the wheat. The mill started production in 1893 and it became an instant success. But in 1897 operations were transferred to Minneapolis, and Grand Forks once again suffered because of its hinterland position relative to Minneapolis–St Paul.[26]

Grand Fork's only brewery during the 1880s was closed after prohibition was put into effect in North Dakota in 1889. Not surprisingly, twelve days later, fourteen new saloons opened across the river in the much smaller East Grand Forks.[27] The principal non-agricultural industry of the 1880s was the railroad. Grand Forks was a division headquarters for two railroads whose switching yards, foundries, and shops provided the greatest opportunities for employment in the city. By the mid-1890s a number of mills, grain elevators, and factories sprang up along the tracks. In addition, a number of agricultural implement dealerships and related wholesale businesses began to operate. North Third Street became a wholesale district with the Northern Pacific rail spur running behind the businesses on the east side of the street. A smaller wholesale district also developed along De Mers Avenue during this period. The influx of railroad workers, boilermakers, machinists, and mechanics attracted to the city needed houses and services and this in turn promoted development and inflated property values (Map 16).[28]

As a consequence of this development, Grand Forks experienced steady growth during the 1890s, reaching a population of 7,682 in 1900, an increase of 54 percent over the 1890 figure. The city also benefited from the opening of the White Pine lands near Red Lake, Minnesota, in 1896. This stimulated the development of a number of sawmills in Grand Forks and East Grand Forks. Likewise, the county experienced modest growth, reaching a population of 24,459 (including Grand Forks City), an increase of 33 percent over the 1890 decade. Unfavourable weather and declining wheat prices acted to slow the pace of agriculture in the Red River region during much of this decade. In addition, land prices increased significantly as most available land was taken up. Settlers intent on farming were heading for the newly opened western tier of counties.

Yet Grand Forks City would enjoy an accelerated rate of growth during the 1900–1910 decade as the population increased 63 percent from 7,652 to 12,478. Even though the city was tied to the agricultural economy of the region, the railroads and sawmilling industry helped sustain a steady growth during this period. Such development was manifested in the entertainment facilities, transportation, and social affairs. Two opera houses were built in 1890, and residents could choose from two newspapers, the *Plaindealer*, a Democratic paper established in 1879, and the *Herald*, a Republican paper founded one year later. Some of the oldest professions were carried out on North Third Street, a neighbourhood of mills and factories and a notorious reputation for its saloons (after the repeal of prohibition), brothels, and gambling houses.

An electric street railway system was built in 1904. Eighteen years earlier, gaslight first came to Grand Forks, followed by electric lights in 1887. That same year, Western Union telegraph lines connected Grand Forks to Fargo and three years later a local telephone exchange was started. The prosperity of the period was reflected most visibly in the city's elegant mansions along Reeves Drive, Belmont Avenue, and South 6th Street. Reeves Drive was particularly renowned for its spacious houses built with Victorian towers and neo-classical pillars, the domiciles of six bankers, four lawyers, three businessmen, and a host of other professionals in 1900.[29]

Yet the Gilded Age splendour of Reeves Drive would diminish as both the city and the county experienced declining growth. The removal of the Cream of Wheat owners to Minneapolis and California, the over-cutting of the northern Minnesota white pine forests which brought about the demise of the sawmill industry, and the decline of agriculture in the region

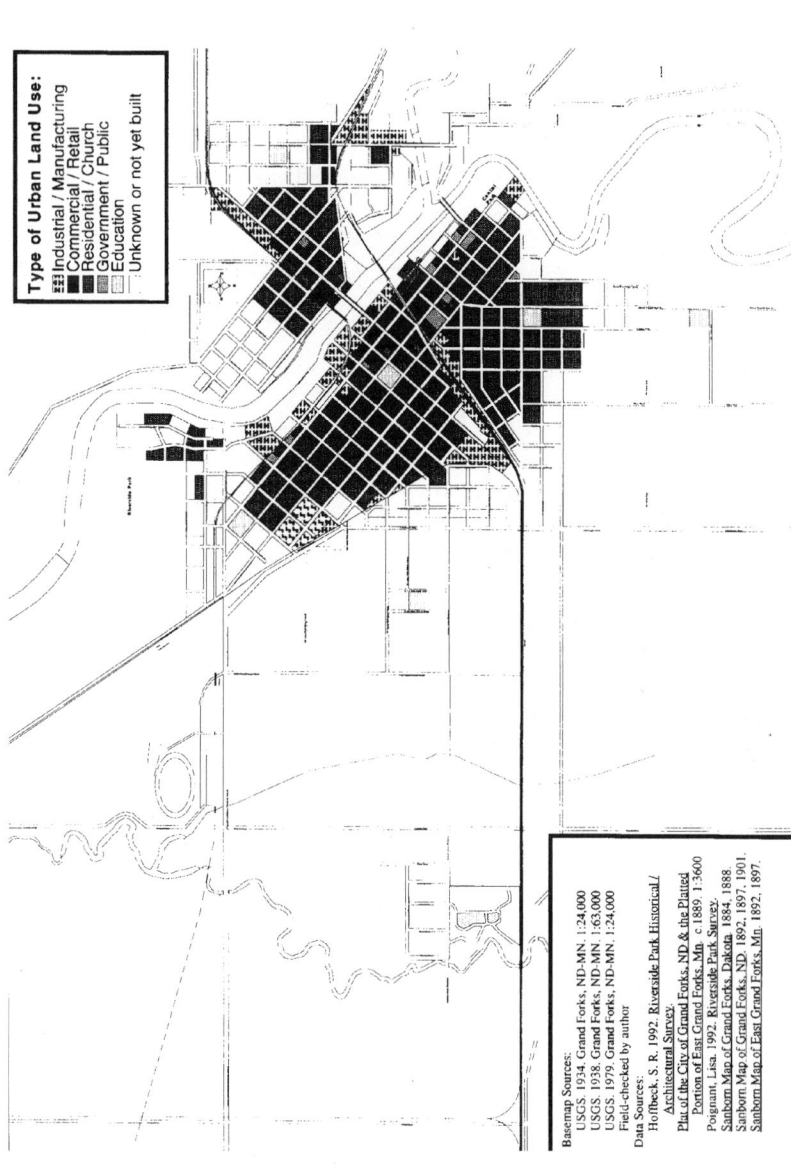

Type of Urban Land Use:
- Industrial / Manufacturing
- Commercial / Retail
- Residential / Church
- Government / Public
- Education
- Unknown or not yet built

Basemap Sources:
USGS. 1934. Grand Forks, ND-MN. 1:24,000
USGS. 1958. Grand Forks, ND-MN. 1:63,000
USGS. 1979. Grand Forks, ND-MN. 1:24,000
Field-checked by author

Data Sources:
Hoffbeck, S. R. 1992. Riverside Park Historical /
    Architectural Survey.
Plat of the City of Grand Forks, ND & the Platted
    Portion of East Grand Forks, Mn. c.1889. 1:3600
Poignant, Lisa. 1992. Riverside Park Survey.
Sanborn Map of Grand Forks, Dakota. 1884. 1888.
Sanborn Map of Grand Forks, ND. 1892. 1897. 1901.
Sanborn Map of East Grand Forks, Mn. 1892. 1897.

Map 16: Urban Land Use in Grand Forks, North Dakota, and East Grand Forks, Minnesota, 1901

contributed to a slower rate of development. The population of the county (including city) in 1913 remained at its 1910 total of 27,888.[30] Grand Forks City would continue to grow but at a slower pace, consolidating its position as a regional trade centre. The construction of the North Dakota State Mill and Elevator at Grand Forks in 1920, still the only state-owned flour mill in the United States, and the outcome of the efforts of the radical Nonpartisan League, enabled North Dakota farmers to bypass Minneapolis-based railroads and milling monopolies, thus ensuring that more capital generated by grain production would stay in the state.[31]

Attitudes Towards Immigrant Groups

Attitudes of the native population towards foreigners are almost impossible to discern and thus attention is directed towards those views expressed in local newspapers. Relatively few critical comments were directed towards any foreign groups in the various papers of the Red River counties, a reflection perhaps of the fact that this was a region of immigrants and newcomers and perhaps more accepting of differences. Unlike the Watertown and Syracuse newspapers, the Grand Forks *Herald*, the Fargo *Record*, the Grafton *Herald News and Times*, and other papers in the region did not display any overly condescending or prejudicial attitudes towards non-English-speaking groups.

Canadians, or to be more precise, Canadian affairs, both at home and in association with Canadian-American relations, received considerable attention, both favourable and negative. Regional papers reprinted stories from Winnipeg and such Ontario points as London, Ottawa, and Toronto, as well as the Canadian financial reports. They included many reports on events and affairs such as the Manitoba Schools Question, the Riel Rebellions, and the Boer War that deeply affected Canada and would be of interest to their considerable Canadian readership. The Grand Forks *Herald* included a column entitled "Canadian Comment" from time to time with notices on Canadian events such as Orange Lodge meetings in Manitoba centres.

Several issues of the regional papers reported on excursions made by local citizens to Manitoba and Ontario. One such trip was made by over six hundred people from Grand Forks and vicinity to take part in the Dominion Day celebrations held in Winnipeg in 1885. On that occasion, the Reverend H.G. Mendenhall reflected on the similarities of Canadians and Americans:

Surely the prominence on these grounds and on your public and private buildings of the American flag, which gets along so harmoniously with that flag on which the sun never sets, is indicative of the mutual sympathy and cordial feelings which should exist between these two English-speaking countries. Alike in language, in religions, in a common birthright, in fair play, in amelioration of the wronged and the suffering, so should we ever strive to be helpful and beneficial to each other. For this reason the American people sympathize with you and your countrymen across the sea in the troubled times that have recently come upon you [the Riel Rebellion]; but we know that English pluck and Scottish grit and Irish valour will calm the stormy sea.[32]

Such comments indicate that local views were most favourable towards Anglo-Saxon, Protestant groups, but there were few blatantly critical diatribes against foreigners not belonging to this category. On the contrary, several pieces reflected favourably on the character of Scandinavians and Germans, the other significant immigrant groups in the region. Canadians were perceived as being part of a larger North American community and thus Canadians met the criteria for being good Americans. Indeed, from time to time, North Dakota papers looked to Canada for guidance. as was the case when the 10 December 1909 edition of the Fargo *Forum and Weekly Republican* advocated the adoption of the Canadian law of compulsory arbitration to settle its strike of railroad switchmen. An editorial appearing in the 31 December 1909 edition of the Hillsboro *Banner* claimed: "Canada has an admirable federal government, superior in some respects to our own, and the late development of the country's institutions has permitted the rulers of the Dominion to heed many a lesson taught by the American experience." Yet no mention is made in any of these comments of a Canadian identity; the people to the north were associated with their British roots, not their Canadian character. Admiration was expressed for the "British-ness" of the Canadian people but, as we shall see, comments on the Canadian character were usually negative in tone.

During the boom period of Dakota settlement, several items in the papers detailed the large-scale emigration of Canadians to the Dakotas, such as the following report appearing in the 1 April 1880 edition of the Grand Forks *Herald*: "A second party for the Northwest left this section [Ottawa] by special train today. There were about two hundred persons, with ten car loads of freight. Two-thirds of them go to settle in Dakota, less than fifty being bound for Manitoba. The policy of the government has undoubtedly injured emigration to the Canadian Northwest, and as national poverty seems to be coming, they do not desire to be in this land."

The papers seemed to take special delight in comparing the slower rate of development in adjacent Manitoba. Grand Fork residents venturing to Winnipeg for the Dominion Day celebrations had some critical comments to make on Manitoba agriculture: "On the way north to the boundary line it was a matter of general congratulation to behold the vast fields of waving grain ... Much of the land, however, between Gretna and Winnipeg, on the line of the C.P., is waste and wild and one could not avoid observing the contrast."

Patronizing attitudes were presented from time to time in editorials commenting on the financial difficulties that Canada was experiencing in the 1880s. An editorial in the *Herald* of 19 February 1885 commented: "In spite of the financial straits of our young neighboring cousin, she objects to annexation to the United States, as if it meant her everlasting perdition. The United States, if it adopted such a careless child into its national family, would in a short time inculcate some rigid business doctrines and would see that she cut her coat according to her cloth."

The newspapers paid close attention to any Canadian reports that were at all negative towards North Dakota. Typical is the reaction to the report delivered to the Committee on Agriculture and Colonization by the Dominion Immigration Agent, W.A. Webster, of his trip through North Dakota in the fall of 1889:

He drew a vivid picture of the destitution and woe which he witnessed in travelling through the state. Great distress prevailed everywhere except in the Red River Valley. In the most flourishing districts only half a crop prevailed, which was most about five bushels to the acre, whilst in Manitoba it was 15 bushels ... He met with many Canadians, all of whom said it was no use trying to farm there; the land was not suited for agricultural purposes. In many cases the Canadian settler had been induced to go there by immigration agents in Chicago when on their way before the C.P.R. was built to the Canadian northwest ... He went on to say that he had agents at work to bring many Canadians back to Canada.

To this report, the Grafton *Herald News and Times* responded:

Is there any county in Manitoba which can show up with this county in public and private buildings, schools, churches, areas of cultivated ground, farm implements and the thousand things which go to make life comfortable? Webster and others are unhappy because so many Canadians have made good homes for themselves in Dakota, and because every one of these is an immigration agent of a hundred fold more value than any government can secure. And still they come. They wish to attract Canadians from Dakota. Well, some few have gone and, as a rule, Manitoba is welcome to all she got. Walsh County is still getting a good class of Canadians who are paying fair prices for good improved farms. To such men a welcome is extended. Come on boys, there is still room. To Mr. Walsh, farewell.[33]

Tariff barriers and disputes between the two countries were commonly noted in the newspapers and sometimes their critical reactions towards Canadian policy resulted in vitriolic attacks on the Canadian character, as is evidenced in the following editorial criticizing Nova Scotia's protestations of American actions towards the fishery following the end of the Treaty of Washington:

The growl set up by the aquatic Bluenoses from the rocky reefs of Nova Scotia may possibly portend a more than ordinary international squall if carried into effect when the Treaty of Washington ceases, as it will with the present month. Should complications arise, however, our government will not be responsible, for it made proper efforts some time since to be on terms of reciprocity with our arctic neighbour which by declining, showed its proverbial hostility to progress, whether from blindness or vapidity it matters little now... Some intense admirers of the exclusive policy of the Canadas, who in becoming American citizens probably foreswore their fealty to the Union Jack, with a very big broad H. of a reservation, profess to believe our government will have a very ugly question on its hands ... One is amused at the tender solicitude these "good Americans" with a foreign accent display for the future of this government, if it does not humiliate itself on all fours and with lamb-like meekness beg of the Lions whelps on the rock-bound shores, to have mercy upon us. They will, however, have to be horrified, it is to be feared. For, in all probability, our government has never dreamed of renewing a treaty on Fisheries by which it paid a useless privilege to a piratical province.[34]

The editorial is revealing not only for its critical judgment of Canadian character but also for its suggestion that former Canadians are to be questioned about their loyalty to their new country.

Yet there were times when regional interests transcended the border and newspapers applauded Canadian actions against the United States not because they served the best interests of Canada but because Dakotans stood to gain from such measures. For example, an editorial appearing in the 22 January 1885 issue of the *Herald* lauded Canadian efforts to increase the duty on American flour:

The Minneapolis millers by unhallowed alliances with the railroads have not only been permitted to skin the Northwest farmer alive through arbitrary control of the market and grade of wheat, but also have under the liberal import law of Canada been enabled to fill the provinces with flour at prices that ruined the local manufacturers and caused the milling industry to become panicky. While this foreign competition has been damaging to Canada, it has been in no way helped the farmers of the Northwest, but has rather been a detriment to them. It is therefore to be hailed with delight that the coming Canadian policy proposes to share a double blow at this steel hearted monopoly; first, by increasing the duty of American flour so that it will be prohibitory, and second by taking off the duty on American wheat so that it may be marketed either in bulk or manufactured in transit in Canada ... By a counteraction on the part of Canada, of the porcine alliance at Minneapolis and St. Paul, the whole crop can be diverted via the Red River through Canada to the markets of the world. To this end let them take off the duty on wheat and put a prohibitive tariff on flour. That will cook the monopoly goose.

As North Dakota began to experience a downturn in agriculture and as settlement accelerated in the Canadian west, the papers published more editorials and articles critical of Canada. An editorial appearing in the 20

January 1895 edition of the Grand Forks *Herald*, commenting on the desire of more than twenty American families in Indian Head, Northwest Territories, to return home without paying duty on their stock and effects, included a letter sent by one of this group to the American consul in which the writer cried: "For God's sake, help us all you can to get out of this god-forsaken country." To this incident, the editorial commented: "This is another warning, so often repeated by the press. It seems to us that it is a self-evident proposition that, granting that the northwest country is equal in soil in climate to this; that the fact that it is hundreds of miles further from the market where the farmer must sell and buy, proves a great financial disadvantage over this country."

Even favourable assessments of Canada sometimes revealed an attitude that can only be described as patronizing. An 1899 report by the editor of the *Record*, a weekly paper coming out of Fargo, on his trip to Rat Portage, Ontario, extolled the potential of this region for development. According to the editor, "the universal Yankee is found everywhere in this region, dipping into everything that there is either money or excitement in, awakening, of course, the jealousy, the ire and some times the emulation of the slow going Canadian."[35] Yet on balance it can be said that Canadians, indeed most groups, faced an environment that welcomed them with open arms, or at least expressed little dissatisfaction with their presence.

Family and Kinship

While Anglo-Canadians in Watertown, New York, showed a significant reliance on kin and boarders in the family economy, a tendency to live in multiple dwelling units, a greater frequency of extended households, and larger households, the same cannot be said for their counterparts in Grand Forks, at least in 1900. There were few evident differences among all nativity groups in terms of household composition and household roles in both the county and the city. In the county, Anglo-Canadians were more likely to live in smaller households than Germans, French Canadians, and Norwegians and showed less reliance on other members of their families for economic support than the Irish, Russians, and Norwegians, but again the differences are not that striking. Household size was generally smaller for all groups in Grand Forks City, with the exception of the French Canadians and the Austro-Hungarians. The Irish and Russian households were most likely to have children contributing to the family economy, with other groups relying predominantly on the household head. Length of residence played little importance in determining differences among households of various groups.

In the county, Anglo-Canadians were most likely to share their homes with relatives, regardless of length of residence. For newcomers, kin and kith connections were especially important during the first few months of settlement in this frontier region where the isolation and unfamiliar nature of this flat, largely treeless area presented difficulties to the individual migrant. The longer distance and greater expense associated with moving to North Dakota combined with the prospect of acquiring land cheaply for all members of the family, or at least the sons, meant that family migration was more the norm for this Canadian migration than the movement of Canadians to nearby New York State. And because many Anglo-Canadians came from areas experiencing the same unfavourable human/land ratios and expensive land values, decisions were made to travel and settle together in North Dakota and take advantage of the assistance that they could provide to each other.

Community

Just as was the case for Watertown and Syracuse, indices of dissimilarity were calculated to give a composite score of relative residential concentration among Grand Forks City wards according to nationality, class, tenure, and length of residence.[36] Residential clustering was more strongly related to national origin than any of the other factors (Table 57).[37] Immigrants were generally widespread throughout the city, although almost 55 percent of the Norwegian households and 54 percent of the Russian households were located in Ward 2, a working-class area housing 66.4 percent of the blue-collar household heads (Table 58). The neighbourhood was largely a Scandinavian community and was designated by the townspeople as Little Norway. A small community of eastern Romanian Jews settled on the south side of the Great Northern tracks, but many owned shops downtown or peddled wares to surrounding communities.[38]

Anglo-Canadians were slightly more represented in Wards 5 and 6 in the northern part of the city (Map 16). But Grand Forks was small enough that ethnic solidarity and identity were not so dependent upon residential congregation as on formal and informal associations.

Only the large capitalist group was segregated residentially in Grand Forks City in 1900 (Table 59); almost 70 percent were located in Ward 4, an area of grand avenues and large homes near the university (Table 60). A smaller cluster of capitalists were located in Ward 1, particularly along Reeves Drive, the most fashionable neighbourhood in the city. Many of the more prosperous merchants and businessmen, included in the petty capitalist group, also lived in this area. Because most of the population were recent migrants, length of residence played little importance in residential patterns.

A significant degree of residential concentration took place in the rural townships of Grand Forks County (maps 17 and 18). Almost 50 percent of the Anglo-Canadian household heads resided in seven townships north of Grand Forks City. They constituted the dominant group, including native-

Table 57 Index of Dissimilarity among Grand Forks City Nativity Groups, 1900 (6 wards)

	Nativity groups[1]											
Nativity groups	1	2	3	4	5	6	7	8	9	10	11	12
1	0	25.0	37.9	33.6	30.4	42.6	27.3	20.8	34.8	38.8	45.5	42.0
2	25.0	0	18.2	10.3	33.5	15.8	33.2	27.9	15.1	34.5	33.3	17.8
3	37.5	18.2	0	15.5	35.1	14.6	42.9	23.8	8.7	41.6	34.8	24.7
4	33.6	10.3	15.4	0	26.8	26.6	32.4	38.2	12.5	33.4	23.0	22.6
5	30.4	33.5	35.1	26.8	0	38.4	27.2	29.2	27.5	32.5	22.4	44.1
6	42.6	15.8	14.6	26.6	38.4	0	44.2	25.2	14.5	42.4	36.0	27.6
7	27.3	33.2	42.9	32.4	27.2	44.2	0	25.5	37.3	12.5	40.0	40.3
8	20.8	27.9	23.8	38.2	29.2	25.2	25.5	0	35.0	31.0	37.7	41.5
9	34.8	15.1	8.7	12.5	27.5	14.5	37.3	35.0	0	38.4	28.6	22.6
10	38.8	34.5	41.6	33.4	32.5	42.4	12.5	31.0	38.4	0	24.5	40.0
11	45.5	33.3	34.8	23.0	22.4	36.0	40.0	37.7	28.6	24.5	0	38.9
12	42.0	17.8	24.7	22.6	44.1	27.6	40.3	41.5	22.6	40.0	38.9	0

Source: 1900 US Manuscript Census

[1] 1–North Dakotans; 2–Other Americans; 3–English; 4–Germans; 5–Swedes; 6–Irish; 7–Russians; 8–French Canadians; 9–Anglo-Canadians; 10–Norwegians; 11–Austro-Hungarians; 12–Others

Table 58   Percentage Distribution of Nativity Groups among Wards,
Grand Forks City, 1900

	Wards (% of each nativity within wards)					
Nativity Group	1	2	3	4	5	6
North Dakotans	20.0	40.0	0	20.0	20.0	0
Other Americans	18.9	20.6	11.7	20.8	15.5	12.5
English	17.8	13.3	15.6	11.1	26.7	15.6
Germans	7.1	21.4	16.1	17.9	23.2	14.3
Swedish	1.8	35.7	3.6	12.5	19.6	26.8
Irish	29.2	12.5	14.6	10.4	14.6	18.8
Russian	5.8	53.8	7.7	13.5	13.5	5.8
French Canadian	29.6	37.0	0	7.4	14.8	11.1
Anglo-Canadian	15.2	16.4	14.2	13.6	21.9	18.6
Norwegian	6.3	54.8	12.0	7.7	7.2	12.0
Austro-Hungarian	9.1	27.3	9.1	0	18.2	36.4
Other Europeans	18.0	20.0	26.0	18.0	2.0	16.0

	Wards (% of ward residents of each nativity)					
Nativity Group	1	2	3	4	5	6
North Dakotans	0.4	0.5	0	0.4	0.4	0
Other Americans	50.6	32.5	38.4	54.4	39.4	34.9
English	3.4	1.5	3.7	2.1	4.9	3.1
Germans	1.7	3.0	4.7	4.2	5.3	3.5
Swedish	0.4	5.0	1.1	2.9	4.5	6.6
Irish	6.0	1.5	3.7	2.1	2.8	3.9
Russian	1.3	7.1	2.1	2.9	2.8	1.3
French Canadian	3.4	2.5	0	0.8	1.6	1.3
Anglo-Canadian	22.7	14.4	25.8	19.7	31.0	29.3
Norwegian	5.6	28.7	13.2	6.7	6.1	10.9
Austro-Hungarian	0.4	0.8	0.5	0	0.8	1.7
Other Europeans	3.9	2.5	6.8	3.8	0.4	3.5

Source: 1900 US Manuscript Census.

born Americans, in Elkmount, Falconer, Gilby, Grand Forks, Johnston, Levant, Perry, Rye, Strabane, Turtle River, and Wheatfield townships, such clustering being the result of chain and group migration. American-born, the vast majority coming from outside the state, ranked second in number in all but one of these townships. In those eight Grand Forks townships in which Anglo-Canadians ranked second in population, the dominant group in all but two were native-born Americans. Thus, the evidence indicates that Anglo-Canadians were most like native-born Americans in their settlement patterns in Grand Forks County.

Table 59   Index of Dissimilarity among Grand Forks City Class Groups, 1900 (6 wards)

		Class Group				
Class Group	Unskilled	Semi-skilled and skilled	Petty capitalist	Large capitalist	Middle class	Private means
Unskilled	0	20.7	21.2	50.9	26.4	19.8
Semi-skilled & unskilled	20.7	0	22.2	70.4	25.4	33.0
Petty capitalist	21.2	22.2	0	58.4	29.0	22.4
Large capitalist	50.9	70.4	58.4	0	48.5	43.7
Middle class	26.4	25.4	29.0	48.5	0	32.9
Private means	19.8	33.0	22.4	43.7	32.9	0

Source: 1900 US Manuscript Census.

Anglo-Canadians composed the largest foreign element in the predominantly rural Walsh and Pembina counties located north of Grand Forks, so this collection of Canadians in the northern townships may be interpreted as a southern extension of this significant rural ethnic island. Again, kinship forces and group migration played important parts in this concentration. Norwegians, the largest foreign group in the county, were more widespread than the Anglo-Canadians, although 15 percent of the household heads of this group resided in Northwood Township.

Ethclass and Assimilation

Drache argues that the high percentage of foreign-born in the counties of the Red River Valley and the presence of the American-born bonanza farmer "tended to delay making the area a real melting pot. Generally, the immigrant had the smallest farm; the transplanted American had the next largest operation; and the well educated and well financed American operated the bonanza. There were exceptions, but it was not until uniformly hard times hit local agriculture, or when the second generation grew up, that nationality and class lines broke down."[39] There is considerable evidence that many of the rural immigrant groups were slow to learn English, had high rates of endogamy, and were very attached to their church. The use of their own language in church services and sermons continued until the 1980s for the Ukrainians, the 1950s for the German-Russian Catholics, the 1940s for the Bohemian Czechs and Poles, the 1930s for the German-Russian Protestants, German-Hungarians, Finns, Norwegians, and French, the 1920s for the Swedes, and the 1910s for the German-Catholics and German-Protestants.[40]

Hudson's sample of historical data files shows that pioneer German-Russian men in North Dakota married within their ethnic group 97.5 per-

Table 60 Percentage Distribution of Grand Forks City Class Groups among Wards, 1900

Class Groups	Wards % of each class group within wards					
	1	2	3	4	5	6
Unskilled	13.3	26.5	12.6	17.5	16.6	13.6
Semi-skilled/skilled	6.2	39.9	13.1	3.9	20.0	16.9
Petty capitalist	7.4	45.1	4.9	19.7	17.2	5.7
Large capitalist	12.2	4.9	6.1	68.3	7.3	1.2
Middle class	29.3	13.6	18.1	11.3	21.4	6.3
Private means	14.5	15.1	4.4	25.2	16.4	24.4

Class Groups	Wards % of ward residents of each class group					
	1	2	3	4	5	6
Unskilled	17.6	20.7	20.5	22.6	17.9	22.5
Semi-skilled/skilled	11.6	43.9	30.0	7.1	31.1	39.2
Petty capitalist	3.9	13.9	3.2	10.0	7.5	3.8
Large capitalist	4.3	1.0	2.6	23.4	2.1	0.5
Middle class	52.8	14.4	40.0	19.7	32.1	14.0
Private means	9.8	6.1	3.7	16.7	9.3	19.9

Source: 1900 US Manuscript Census

cent of the time, Norwegians 93.2 percent, Germans 78.5 percent, Swedes 62.2 percent, and Ontarians 55.4 percent.[41] No doubt the high degree of endogamy among these groups was partly a result of propinquity as well as cultural affinity and so these data must be interpreted with this fact in mind. The tradition of marriage-brokering among German-Russians as well as the survival of the custom of giving each son a quarter-section of land and farm equipment upon marriage and dowries for daughters contributed to the clannishness of this group.

Norwegian language and culture were preserved in newspapers such as the *Tidende* and the *Normanden,* the latter being the largest immigrant paper in the state having a circulation of over nine thousand in 1910. German-born pioneers in Richland County met regularly at least every Sunday. Icelandic-born settlers from Gimli, Manitoba, settled close together in Pembina County and carried on their culture through reading societies, subscribing to Icelandic papers from both Canada and the United States, and by attending the Lutheran church where services were carried on in their native language.[42]

In Grand Forks City, immigrant cultures were sustained in clubs, festivals, and churches. Norwegians celebrated Norwegian national Indepen-

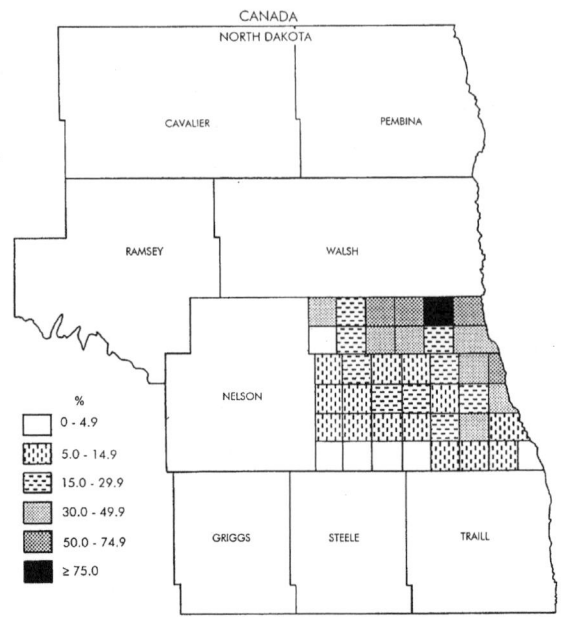

Map 17: Anglo-Canadian as a Percentage of Total Production of Townships, Grand Forks County, 1900

Source: 1900 US Manuscript Census

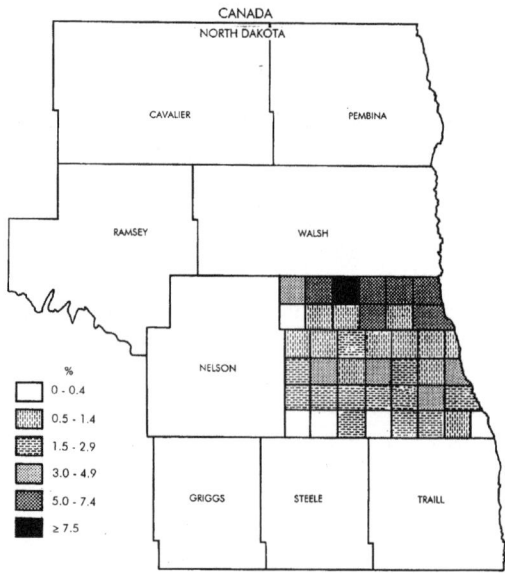

Map 18: Percentage of Grand Forks County Anglo-Canadian Population by Township, 1900

Source: 1900 US Manuscript Census

Table 61   Membership in Class Group by Nativity, Grand Forks County, 1900[1]

Nativity Group			Class %				
	Unskilled	Semi-skilled & skilled	Petty capitalist	Large capitalist	Business middle class	Private means	N
North Dakota	12.5	12.5	75.0	0	0	0	16
Other American	9.1	13.9	69.0	1.6	3.6	2.8	1017
English	10.7	16.1	64.3	0	0	8.9	56
German	5.2	6.9	84.5	0	0.9	2.6	116
Swedish	10.7	7.8	76.7	0	2.9	1.9	103
Irish	5.2	6.5	76.6	0	2.6	9.1	77
Russian	14.3	0	85.7	0	0	0	7
French Canadian	10.4	10.4	72.9	2.1	2.1	2.1	48
Anglo-Canadian	7.1	9.0	78.1	0.2	3.2	2.4	590
Norwegian	8.0	7.0	82.1	0.2	0.5	2.2	967
Austro-Hungarian	14.3	0	85.7	0	0	0	7
Other European	13.0	8.7	70.7	0	3.3	4.3	92

Source: 1900 US Manuscript Census.

[1] figures do not add up to 100% because of missing values – not included Grand Forks City.

dence Day in the Scandia Club. The Irish celebrated St. Patrick's Day usually under the auspices of St. Michael's Church. The Scots observed Robbie Burns Day. No ethnicity is evident for the Anglo-Canadians. They did not derive any sense of distinctiveness from dress or from social institutions and organizations peculiar to them. Not only did the host society associate Anglo-Canadians with their British roots, but many of the Canadians did themselves. A handful of Scots and a larger number of Canadians in the 1890s organized the Caledonia Curling Club of Grand Forks and soon Canadians in other towns followed suit.[43] There was little attachment to group symbols or institutions because there were few distinctively Canadian symbols or institutions to be grasped. And given the receptive attitudes of the host society, there was little need for such symbols. One notable exception was the Canadian celebration of Dominion Day. Even though Anglo-Canadians in Grand Forks made little fuss over this event in North Dakota, many of them travelled to nearby Winnipeg to celebrate their former country's birthday. To this the satirist might say: how typically Canadian.

Without any doubt, Anglo-Canadians were one of the most assimilative groups in this particular American destination but this statement needs some qualification. Most immigrants in the county were farmers, classified as petty capitalists in Table 61. Their membership in farming and other working class occupations was generally representative of their percentage of the population, although they were slightly over-represented among skilled positions (Table 62). Anglo-Canadians were slightly under-

Table 62   Occupational Profile of Anglo-Canadians in Grand Forks County in 1900: Occupational Groups and Specific Occupations

Occupational groups	No. of Anglo-Canadian household heads	% of Anglo-Canadian household heads	Anglo-Canadians as a % of all heads employed in that position
Unskilled	460	78.0	19.5
Semi-skilled	32	5.4	18.0
Skilled	12	2.0	24.5
Clerical	12	2.0	11.5
Business	44	7.5	17.0
Professional	18	3.1	29.5
Private Means	11	1.9	13.3

Specific occupations[1]	No. of Anglo-Canadian household heads	% of Anglo-Canadian household heads
Farmer	430	72.9
Labourer	25	4.2
Carpenter	13	2.2
Merchant shopkeeper	12	2.0
Blacksmith	10	1.7
Wheat buyer	7	1.2
Landlord/landlady	6	1.0
Minister/priest	4	0.7
Doctor/physician	4	0.7
Teacher	4	0.7

Source: 1900 US Manuscript Census.

% of Total heads who are Anglo-Canadian – 19.1

[1] Occupations with greatest number of employees.

represented in business and notably so in the clerical and private means categories, the latter perhaps indicating the relatively young age of the average migrant. They were considerably over-represented in the professional category, reflecting the fact that a newly opened agricultural region also attracted people other than farmers. The fact that Anglo-Canadians in seven townships comprised the largest nativity group, even including American-born, means that they interacted at both social and economic levels. And kinship and kith connections ensured that a sense of community survived at least to some degree among Ontario immigrants in North Dakota, particularly in Grand Forks, Walsh, and Pembina counties. Anglo-Canadians interacted with each other at the curling club, in the general store, and at church. A high endogamy rate of almost 60 percent is testimony to this interconnection.

In Grand Forks City, Anglo-Canadians entered politics, engaged in business, and joined the various lodges and churches of Anglo-American origin. They differed from their fellow countrymen in northern New York.

Table 63   Membership in Class Group by Nativity, Grand Forks City, 1900[1]

			Class %				
Nativity group	Unskilled	Semi-skilled and skilled	Petty capitalist	Large capitalist	Business middle class	Private means	N
North Dakota	20.0	40.0	0	20.0	20.0	0	5
Other American	15.2	25.8	7.7	7.2	34.4	9.8	625
English	11.1	28.9	8.9	0	37.8	13.5	45
German	19.6	33.9	10.7	0	17.9	17.8	56
Swedish	28.6	44.6	5.4	3.6	8.9	9.0	56
Irish	27.1	18.8	8.3	4.2	25.0	16.7	48
Russian	46.2	11.5	9.6	3.8	21.2	7.6	52
French Canadian	44.4	25.9	0	0	18.5	11.1	27
Anglo-Canadian	19.6	26.8	7.2	6.6	28.0	11.9	347
Norwegian	23.6	39.4	10.1	1.9	16.3	8.6	208
Austro-Hungarian	27.3	54.5	9.1	0	9.1	0	11
Other European	28.6	26.5	10.2	6.1	24.5	6.1	50

Source: 1900 US Manuscript Census.

[1] figures do not add up to 100% because of missing values.

Table 63 shows that Anglo-Canadians ranked first among immigrant groups in the large capitalist class, although they were far less represented amongst this group than native-born Americans, and ranked just behind Americans born outside North Dakota and the English in the business/middle class category. Anglo-Canadians constituted a considerable proportion of the professional, clerical, and business occupational groups in the city (Table 64). Grand Forks appeared to be especially attractive for Canadian-born doctors and merchants.

Many Anglo-Canadians came to the Dakotas to take advantage of the business opportunities accompanying the opening of a new frontier. It was much easier for the Canadian to adopt to an Anglo-American way of life where Yankee traditions shaped the banks, businesses, schools, and politics. One such individual was John Dinnie, who was born in 1853 on a farm in Dundas County, Ontario, one of three sons and six daughters. Seeing little opportunity to acquire land, Dinnie learned the trade of mason and in 1881 he, his wife, and two children followed his two brothers to Grand Forks. John worked as a mason for a few years, saving enough money to start a brick manufacturing business in 1889. He served four years as an alderman for Ward 5 and was twice elected mayor of Grand Forks.

Another Canadian success story is that of Robert Griffith. In 1881 the 25-year-old Griffith, who had previously operated a store in Port Colborne, Ontario, came to Grand Forks and opened the Ontario Store, selling hardware, dry goods, materials, and books. By 1891 he was doing $361,000 in business. Americans and Canadians dominated commerce in Grand Forks.

Table 64   Occupational Profile of Anglo-Canadians in Grand Forks City in 1900: Occupational Groups and Specific Occupations

Occupational groups	No. of Anglo-Canadian household heads	% of Anglo-Canadian household heads	Anglo-Canadians as a % of all foreign-born heads employed in that position
Unskilled	75	21.6	33.3
Semi-skilled	44	12.6	23.7
Skilled	31	8.9	35.6
Clerical	60	17.2	49.2
Business	76	21.8	41.1
Professional	26	7.5	54.2
Private means	36	9.2	57.1

Specific occupations[1]	No. of Anglo-Canadian household heads	% of Anglo-Canadian household heads
Labourer	27	7.8
Carpenter	21	6.0
Farmer	14	4.0
Salesperson	12	3.4
Carter/teamster	11	3.2
Contractor	11	3.2
Agent-general & insurance	10	2.9
Doctor/physician	10	2.9
Merchant/shopkeeper	10	2.9
Dressmaker	8	2.3

Source: 1900 US Manuscript Census.
[1] Occupations with greatest number of employees:
  % of total heads who are Anglo-Canadian – 22.7;
  % of total foreign-born heads who are Anglo-Canadian –38.6.

The Pioneer Club, organized in 1883, was the city's most exclusive and
powerful organization and of the fifty-five charter members, all business-
men, only five were not descended from American and Canadian families.
The Commercial Club, incorporated in 1904, was an offshoot of the
Pioneer Club and "of the 174 members, the vast majority were old-stock
Americans and Canadians with only fifteen percent Scandinavian,
German, and Jewish immigrant businessmen."[45]

In *Plains Folks*, the most complete ethnic history of North Dakota,
Wilkins discusses how the state's politics were strongly influenced by
native-born Americans and people of British descent, including Canadian-
born. In particular, he tells how the Republicans, the dominant party
throughout the history of the state, had come under the influence of
Alexander McKenzie, Canadian-born and of Scottish descent, during the
1880s. Born near Barrie in 1850, McKenzie left for the United States as a
teenager and by the age of 18 had worked his way to the position of con-

struction foreman working on the Northern Pacific Railroad. Impressing his superiors with his ability to handle men and get things done, McKenzie became the Northern Pacific's liaison with the government of the Dakota Territory based in Bismarck, and in that position and as a dealer in real estate and securities, he managed to become rich. The extent of McKenzie's power is evident in the fact that some authorities attribute much of North Dakota's economic development during this period to his contacts with wealthy men in the eastern United States.[46]

An investigation of class categories by length of residence among immigrant groups not unexpectedly reveals that the longest-settled residents of all groups were more likely to be better represented in the more prestigious business and professional occupations (Table 65). And in this context, the Anglo-Canadian emerges as one of the more "successful" groups. Some Anglo-Canadians in Grand Forks City started out poor and continued that way because they had less in the way of capital, connections, education, and other requirements that would have permitted their rise. Others possessed those attributes and reached high levels of success. They, more than any other immigrant group, mirrored the native American occupational profile, leading the way among foreigners in terms of achieving large capitalist positions and lagging behind only the much smaller English group in their representation among the businesses. Grand Forks presented an environment more open to mobility and no rigid class barriers, so obvious in Watertown, served to separate foreign-born from native-born.

Again, the concept of ethclass has some relevance in the interpretation of the Anglo-Canadian experience. Because of their relatively large numbers, the small scale of the city, and their association with each other in the context of business, the professions, and labour, Anglo-Canadians were likely to establish attachments with their own class segment. As in other communities, relatives assisted the newcomer to get established. After this initial stage, Anglo-Canadians interacted with each other on the job, in the clubs, at church, or in the tavern.

In both the city and the county, figures for 1900 ranked Anglo-Canadians low among immigrant groups in terms of home and farm ownership, a characteristic they shared with their counterparts in northern New York. Interestingly, French Canadians had the highest ownership rates. More recent arrivals did not have sufficient time to amass enough capital to purchase homes and farms and so were more likely to be tenants. Yet the Dakota Boom had ended in the late 1880s, so most foreign-born had been present in the region for at least a decade. Therefore, the differences among these groups in Grand Forks is related to some other factor than length of residence. Analysis shows that home ownership among immigrant groups varied little with class and occupation and so it remains unclear why Anglo-Canadians experienced such low ownership rates.

Table 65   Membership in Class Groups by Nativity and Length of Residence, Immigrant Groups, Grand Forks City, 1900[1]

Length of residence (years)	Class Group	English	German	Swedish	Irish	Russian	French Canadian	Anglo-Canadian	Norwegian	Austro-Hungarian	Other Europeans
<1–2	Unskilled	0	0	0	100.0	50.0	100.0	50.0	0	0	0
	Semi-skilled and skilled	0	0	100.0	0	50.0	0	0	40.0	0	0
	Petty capitalist	0	0	0	0	0	0	0	0	0	0
	Large capitalist	0	0	0	0	0	0	0	0	0	0
	Middle class	100.0	0	0	0	0	0	12.5	20.0	0	100.0
	Private means	0	0	0	0	0	0	37.5	40.0	0	0
3–5	Unskilled	0	100.0	0	100	60.0	0	23.1	0	0	0
	Semi-skilled and skilled	50.0	0	0	0	20.0	0	38.5	100.0	100.0	0
	Petty capitalist	0	100.0	100.0	0	0	0	44.0	0	0	50.0
	Large capitalist	0	0	0	0	0	0	0	0	0	0
	Middle class	0	0	0	0	20.0	0	38.5	0	0	50.0
	Private means	50.0	0	0	0	0	0	0	0	0	0
6–10	Unskilled	0	33.3	42.9	25.0	61.1	100.0	14.6	35.7	66.7	11.1
	Semi-skilled and skilled	62.5	33.3	42.0	25.0	0	0	41.5	42.9	33.3	55.6
	Petty capitalist	0	16.7	14.3	0	11.1	0	7.3	7.1	0	0
	Large capitalist	0	0	0	25.0	0	0	9.8	0	0	0
	Middle class	12.5	0	0	25.0	16.7	0	17.1	3.6	0	11.1
	Private means	25.0	16.7	0	0	11.1	0	9.6	10.7	0	22.2

Nativity Groups

Table 65 (continued)

Length of residence (years)	Class Group	Nativity Groups									
		English	German	Swedish	Irish	Russian	French Canadian	Anglo-Canadian	Norwegian	Austro-Hungarian	Other Europeans
11–20	Unskilled	20.0	29.2	23.5	14.3	36.4	25.0	19.9	25.7	16.7	50.0
	Semi-skilled and skilled	25.0	25.0	50.0	28.6	13.6	33.3	26.9	43.8	66.7	11.1
	Petty capitalist	5.0	8.3	2.9	0	9.1	0	6.5	4.8	16.7	11.1
	Large capitalist	0	0	2.9	7.1	0	0	4.3	2.9	0	5.6
	Middle class	40.0	25.0	11.8	21.4	31.8	33.3	29.0	15.2	0	22.2
	Private means	10.0	13.8	8.8	28.6	9.1	8.3	13.0	7.6	0	0
>20	Unskilled	7.7	4.0	35.7	25.9	20.0	50.0	18.2	17.4	0	20.0
	Semi-skilled and skilled	15.4	44.0	28.6	14.8	20.0	25.0	21.2	30.4	0	30.0
	Petty capitalist	23.1	12.0	7.1	14.8	20.0	0	10.1	20.3	0	10.0
	Large capitalist	0	0	7.1	0	40.0	0	11.1	1.4	0	10.0
	Middle class	46.2	16.0	7.1	29.6	0	8.3	30.3	23.2	100.0	25.0
	Private means	7.6	20.0	14.2	14.8	0	16.7	9.1	7.2	0	5.0

Source: 1900 US Manuscript Census.

[1] figures do not add up to 100% because of missing values.

Depression, increasing land prices, and the occasional drought may have persuaded many of this group not to purchase homes and farms because they wanted the freedom to pursue opportunities elsewhere, either in the newly opened western part of the state or across the line in western Canada. It may be that they were waiting until they acquired the resources necessary to make such a move.

Anglo-Canadians did not cut all ties with Canada. As the newspapers and family histories make clear, many travelled back and forth across the line, either to visit relatives in Ontario or to make shopping or business excursions to Winnipeg. For instance, on 18 October 1896 the Casselton *Reporter* advised its readers that "once again the time of Canadian excursions is at hand [and] the old folks in Ontario and Quebec will feel better if you start upon your long trip over the Northern Pacific." According to an advertisement placed in the Drayton *Echo* of 10 August 1899, the cost of excursions to Canada during this period amounted to $40 per person. Information or editorials about Canada appeared in the papers on almost a daily basis. The newspapers were obviously aware that a substantial percentage of their readers were eager to receive information about their former home. The economic and social intercourse between this region and Manitoba ensured by proximity and competition for settlers and markets also guaranteed that considerable space be devoted to Canadian news in the local papers.

Canadians in both the county and city were not more likely to give up their Canadian citizenship than other immigrant groups; in North Dakota all immigrants acquired American citizenship at a rapid rate, a reflection of the fact that acquisition of a homestead required applicants to have signed their declaration of intent to become an American citizen. As we shall see, many of these same American-Canadians would reacquire their Canadian citizenship after leaving North Dakota.

CONCLUSION

For many Anglo-Canadians, Grand Forks, indeed North Dakota, would only be a temporary stage in their life-long migration, a fact substantiated in tracing the persistence of naturalization migrants and linking Canadians appearing in both the 1900 and 1910 manuscript censuses. Thirty of the fifty-seven Canadians who emigrated to the United States between 1880 and 1910 and signed their petitions for naturalization between 1906 and 1919 lived in Grand Forks City. These individuals comprised 11.2 percent of the total number of immigrants who signed petitions during this time period, and over 77 percent came from Ontario. Their average age at emigration was 21.7 years with over 36 percent coming between 1896 and 1900 and 32 percent arriving between 1901 and 1905. Of the Canadians who signed their petitions while living in Grand Forks City, six were presumably in the city for such a short period of time that they were never listed in a city directory, while one person was listed for one year only, three stayed between two and five years, eight between six and ten years, three between eleven and twenty years, and nine for over twenty years. Four individuals were traced until the time of their deaths as listed in the directories, while information as to where a person moved was only provided for one person.

The twenty-four naturalization members linked to the directories made a total of forty-seven residential changes during their lives in Grand Forks City. Such relative stability, particularly when compared to the Watertown and Syracuse migrants, is explained by the greater tendency of this group to leave the city after a brief period. The mobility of Anglo-Canadians becomes even more evident upon examination of the published and manuscript censuses. While Grand Forks County's population increased by 14 percent between 1900 and 1910, its Canadian-born population, including both anglophone and francophone and those born in Newfoundland, decreased by over 34 percent during that same decade. Canadians were leaving not just Grand Forks but the whole state over the 1900–1910 period.[47] And finally, a trace of Anglo-Canadian household heads between the 1900 and 1910 manuscript censuses shows that less than 20 percent of this group living in Grand Forks City in 1900 and less than 30 percent of their fellow countrymen living in the county in 1900 were present ten years later.

Between 1900 and 1910 North Dakota's population burgeoned as people from the eastern half of the state joined other Americans and immigrants moving to the newly opened region beyond the Missouri. Many Canadians joined this particular flow, prompted to move out of the Red River Valley region by increasing land prices and mortgage rates and a series of poor crops. Many tried their luck in the western part of the state, especially after 1904–5 when both the Soo and Great Northern railroads built lines between the Red River and northwestern North Dakota.

Yet the state's efforts to settle its western half met with strong competition from Canada. Given the extensive immigration propaganda program of the Canadian government and the lure of cheap homestead land in the Canadian west and the poorer quality of the generally drier land in the western part of the state, especially when compared to the Red River Valley, many Americans, including ex-Canadians and other foreign-born, crossed the border into Saskatchewan and Alberta. This tale of migration and the movement of eastern Canadians to the "Last Best West" are the subjects of the final part of our voyage.

7 The Last Best West? Return and Interprovincial Migration to Saskatchewan

By an odd chance, the forty-ninth parallel
Turned out to mean something.
                    – Stephen Leacock, *My Discovery of the West*

THE CONTEXT OF MIGRATION[1]

Most Canadian school children know that prairie settlement was shaped and directed by the combination of tariff, railway, land, and immigration policies developed in the post-Confederation period by the Conservative government of Sir John A. Macdonald and the Liberal government of Sir Wilfrid Laurier. The success of these policies has long been the subject of historical debate, discussion centring on the relative roles of Canadian government policies and external forces – such as falling transport costs for wheat exports, the resumption of international capital and labour flows, rising wheat prices as a result of industrialization in Europe and the United States, and the end of the American land frontier – in bringing about prairie settlement.[2] Both played significant roles in the settlement of western Canada.

Immigration Policy

As minister of the interior from 1896 to 1905, Clifford Sifton established the basic framework for immigration and settlement in what was termed "the Last Best West." Sifton deemed the United States the greatest source of first-class settlers because American immigrants had capital, goods, and experience in prairie farming and because Ottawa considered them ethnically desirable.[3] The Interior Department especially wanted to "tap the pool of discontented tenant farmers, ambitious established farmers and ex-Canadians, all of whom might be receptive to the promises of free homestead land in western Canada."⁴ Sifton expanded the number of immigration offices in the United States and began an intensive program of promotion through newspaper advertisements and displays at public exhibitions in those areas where experienced farmers lived.

The second most important source of immigration was Great Britain, a natural choice given Anglo-Canada's heritage and the commitment of the federal government to maintaining a steady flow of British stock into the west. The department employed many of the same publicity techniques in Great Britain as in the United States. Largely because restrictive laws made it difficult to promote emigration through government agents, the department did not emphasize recruitment in continental Europe, but Sifton awarded bonuses to steamship agents who sent immigrants to Canada. Emigrants who were agriculturalists received high bonuses if they possessed at least $100 upon arrival.⁵

The End of the American Land Frontier

Although western Canada's first Homestead Act was passed in 1872, the region failed to attract the hundreds of thousands of Europeans and North Americans moving westward. Between 1870 and 1896 adjacent American lands were filling up while the Canadian prairies remained largely empty of white settlement. The lack of rail connections to export points limited development before 1879, but the completion of the Canadian Pacific Railway in 1886 and the extension of its subsidiary, the Soo Line, to the Canadian border removed this barrier.⁶

Scattered settlement occurred throughout the North-West Territories during the 1870s and 1880s but the southern part of Saskatchewan and Alberta was viewed generally as a region to be avoided by the settler intent on wheat farming. This perception was due in part to the reports produced by early explorers and surveyors, such as David Thompson, John Palliser, Henry Hind, and John Macoun. Among this group, opinion was divided as to the suitability of this region for agriculture. All these explorers agreed that the great triangle comprising the northwest part of the United States and the southern part of western Canada is a semi-arid plain, but they disagreed as to its suitability for agriculture.⁷ The report of the Palliser Expedition of 1857–60 did much to dissuade those who were entertaining thoughts of settling in the Canadian west, for Palliser described much of southern Saskatchewan and southeastern Alberta, the "Palliser Triangle," as an extension of the Great American Desert and unsuited for cultivation. The closing of southwestern Manitoba to homestead entry in July 1882 redirected later migrants to the Dakota Territory. A process of land abandonment by settlers in Manitoba was the result of the farmers' anger with government land policy and its high import duties.[8] Only by 1896, when lands to the south had largely filled and the worldwide recession of the 1890s was ending, did significant numbers of settlers begin to flow into the region.

The repeal of the 1871 Distribution and Pre-Emption Act in 1891 reduced significantly the allotment of free and cheap public lands in the United States. As the supply of land decreased and the price increased, more and more American dryland farmers looked north.[9] Land in the Red River valley of Dakota that had sold for $5 to $10 an acre in the mid-1890s increased to $20 to $40 an acre by 1900. The rate of tenancy quadrupled between 1890 and 1920 and by 1910 more than half of the owner-operator farms in the state were mortgaged. The period from 1900 to 1906 saw excessive rainfall in both spring and summer during four of these years, delaying harvesting and planting, while there was drought in the other two years.[10]

Canada promised cheap land for wealthy American-born farmers and hyphenated Americans and their children, and continued religious and ethnic cohesion for the latter within group colonies. While some Canadians likely welcomed the opportunity to return home to Canada, there is no doubt that inexpensive land was the major attraction underlying their decision to move.

As a result of these developments and the opportunities associated with the branch plant industrialization of Ontario, hundreds of thousands of American-resident immigrants crossed the border into Canada between 1896 and 1914, and many of them settled in the prairie provinces. In 1901, 65 percent of American-born in Canada lived east of Manitoba; just ten years later that figure was reduced to 32 percent.[11] A significant, but unknown, number of the migrants crossing the forty-ninth parallel were Canadian-born. In 1905 the US Public Lands Commission reported: "Several hundreds of Canadians have crossed the border, declared their intention to become citizens of the United States, filed on land under the free homestead act, committed their entries, after a period of fourteen to eighteen months, and then returned to their former homes across the border, and became citizens once more of the Dominion of Canada."[12]

Land Policy

While the free homestead was the staple of western land policy, other devices played a major role in settlement. In 1872 the awarding of alternate sections of land in a belt twenty miles on each side of the main line ensured that the Canadian Pacific Railway was to become the largest single land holder in the West. Ten years later, homestead land was extended to all unalienated even-numbered sections, including those within the CPR belt. But under a second CPR bill, the company was granted a subsidy of

$25 million and a land grant of 25 million acres in a belt extending twenty-four miles on each side of the main line. Alternate sections were also set aside outside the railway belts until 1908.

The Conservative government passed regulations to provide for the creation of colonization companies in 1881. This legislation made provision for sale of odd-numbered sections situated twenty-four miles south of the CPR line at $2 an acre to any business satisfying the government of its capability and interests in promoting settlement. Companies were to receive $160 for every newly established bona fide settler, but few colonization companies successfully placed settlers on the land. The twenty-six colonization companies that finished their five-year contract in 1886 and 1887 had sponsored only 1,080 settlers. Crop failure in 1883, the outbreak of the Northwest Rebellion in 1885, competition to the south, speculative practices, and negative newspaper coverage of the railway monopoly, climate, and soil all contributed to the companies' lack of success.[13]

Land companies sprang up again after 1902 in response to the increasing influx of immigrants, particularly Americans. Although some seriously promoted settlement, most were simply speculators. They aggressively bought land from individual settlers and from railway companies and recruited immigrants coming into Canada by train. Smaller railway companies, more interested in quick profits than in incurring expenses associated with promotional advertising, were willing to sell to land companies that also provided advertising and real estate expertise for the larger companies like the CPR and Canadian National Railway (CNR) in return for land.[14] Most companies, however, were not very successful in either settling the land or reaping profits.

The Department of the Interior did not usually sell government lands to farmers desiring to enlarge their homesteads, but settlers could purchase homesteads on land that had been reserved for but never taken up by the railways and on property sold by the latter to land companies. When the government discontinued the Railway Land Grant in the late 1890s, thousands of acres intended for the railways lay idle until the Dominion Lands Act of 1908 freed up these sections and allowed settlers within travelling distance to pre-empt this land or purchase it as a homestead. Land grants to soldiers came out of these sections.

The salient features of Canadian land policy in the West – homesteads, sectional survey, railway land grants – were transplants from the United States. Some, including Norman Macdonald, argue that the federal government was too anxious to dispose of its western lands and as a consequence was too ready to adopt wasteful American policies, but others, including Chester Martin, believe that rapid settlement and railway development were necessary to counter American expansion into the region and so in the context of the time the policies adopted appeared successful.[15]

REGIONAL PATTERNS OF MIGRATION
AND SETTLEMENT

The Broad Picture

Indigenous policies and external events stimulated a flood of immigrants into western Canada after 1896. Before that date, only southern Manitoba had received a significant influx of migrants, primarily from Ontario. It has been estimated that just over 166,000 immigrants arrived in the North-West Territories (Assiniboia, Saskatchewan, Alberta) between 1881 and 1886.[16] Statistics from the Department of the Interior indicate that of 4,701 homesteaders registered for the year 1892, 54 percent were Canadian-born, almost 17 percent were from Great Britain, and another 11 percent were from the United States. Ninety-two or 18 percent of the American homesteaders were born in Canada and Ontarians comprised 64 percent of the Canadian-born. Ontarians and Americans dominated the purchase of CPR lands that same year with almost 42 percent and over 37 percent of the American purchasers coming from the Dakotas and Washington State respectively.[17]

The settlement pattern of the region was influenced by several factors, including soil quality, ethnic congregation, kinship and kith affiliation, land availability, and access to markets and railways. Settlers actively petitioned provincial governments to support the construction of branch lines in their respective areas.[18] The result was the creation of an extensive railway system within a relatively short time.

For large numbers of Europeans and migrants from the United States who began to establish ethno-religious bloc settlements across the prairies, settlement was shaped more by ethnicity than by distance to the market. Anderson outlines the three main processes by which these settlements came into being: organized group settlements founded by organized groups of political or religious refugees (e.g., Mennonites, Hutterites, Doukhobors); settlements that developed slowly as a result of chain migration whereby one or two pioneers established links with friends or family back home; and, finally, gravitational group settlements formed when individuals who had migrated independently were drawn together by forces such as common language and a common religion.[19] All three processes influenced the settlement of certain groups such as the German-Catholics, Ukrainians, and Poles.

The two most influential groups in terms of numbers, economic power, and cultural influence were native-born Canadians and Americans. By the turn of the century, Canadian- and American-born had an impact on western Canadian settlement that was out of proportion to their numbers. Harvest excursions first organized by the railways in 1890 and continuing until 1929 brought thousands of young men from eastern North America to the west. While many of these young men returned home, others stayed, using their earnings to support their homestead efforts. Canadian-born comprised well over 50 percent of all four census districts of the North-West Territories in 1901. Alberta was by far the most common destination among the census districts for American-born, with 54 percent of these migrants, including a significant number of Mormons from Utah, acquiring Canadian citizenship. Similarly, over half the American-born in Saskatchewan were Canadian citizens in 1901. The highest and lowest percentages of Canadians born in the North-West Territories lived in Saskatchewan and Assiniboia West respectively. Ontario was the most important source province for internal migrants except for Saskatchewan, where a greater number of Manitoba-born lived. In fact, more Ontarians were present in Assiniboia West than Canadians born in the North-West Territories.

Europeans often emigrated in large groups and were encouraged by government to settle in blocs, but Americans and Canadians for the most part travelled alone or with friends or immediate family and were dealt with individually. The Department of the Interior consulted with ethno-religious groups as to what type of land they preferred and then directed them to areas best suited to their desires (e.g., Ukrainians locating in the wooded parkbelt). Canadians and Americans, on the other hand, often preferred open prairie. Early in the period, Ontarians tended to settle in wooded areas as they associated well-developed woodland with good soil and they depended on the wood for fuel. Yet by the late 1880s, they followed the American example and moved onto the open prairie where barbed wire for fencing, tools for deep-well drilling, and dryland farming techniques made it possible to break land quickly and get a wheat crop in right away.[20]

Immigration increased dramatically after 1896.[21] The British were the largest immigrant group (N=562,054) between 1900 and 1910 although the numbers of Americans (N=497,249) and, to a lesser extent, continental Europeans (N=394,088) increased dramatically at the end of the decade. While many of the British were attracted to the developing industrial heartland of Ontario and Quebec, Americans and continental Europeans were more responsive to the opportunities presented by settlement in the west. Between 1897 and 1910, 32 percent of arrivals from continental Europe and 42 percent of arrivals from the United States made homestead entry in western Canada. By contrast, only 22 percent of the English, 22 percent of the Scots, and 26 percent of the Irish filed for homesteads. In the last five years of the decade the Americans and continental Europeans comprised 28.5 percent and 16.3 percent of the homestead entries respectively while the English, Scots, and Irish made up only 14.2 percent, 3.5 percent, and 1.3 percent of the total respectively.

Yet it was the Canadian-born that made the most homestead entries during this period, 35.6 percent of the total, although the statistics do not

Table 66   US and Canadian-born by Census District, 1911

Province and district	No. of US-born	% of total population	No. of Can.-born	% of total population	Total population
MANITOBA	16326	3.6	264828	58.1	455614
Brandon	983	2.5	24625	62.0	39734
Dauphin	1735	3.9	26905	61.1	44000
Lisgar	527	2.2	17381	74.0	23501
Macdonald	1920	5.4	23392	65.3	35841
Marquette	1016	3.0	20766	61.8	33598
Portage la Prairie	784	2.8	19643	70.3	27950
Provencher	1863	4.6	27076	66.5	40693
Selkirk	1111	2.1	27206	51.2	53091
Souris	751	2.6	20845	71.8	29049
Winnipeg	5636	4.4	56989	44.5	128157
SASKATCHEWAN	69628	14.1	248751	50.5	492432
Assiniboia	7049	16.6	24336	57.2	42556
Battleford	7284	15.5	24588	52.2	47075
Humboldt	9679	18.5	22100	42.3	52195
Mackenzie	2861	7.0	16764	41.3	40588
Moose Jaw	18712	21.3	41886	47.7	87725
Prince Albert	3939	10.8	21191	58.3	36319
Qu'Appelle	1842	5.2	21747	61.1	35608
Regina	9232	13.0	35011	49.6	70556
Saltcoats	1492	5.2	14708	51.3	28695
Saskatoon	7538	14.7	26420	51.7	51145
ALBERTA	81357	21.7	162237	43.3	374663
Calgary	7657	12.6	26115	43.1	60502
Edmonton	8126	14.2	29173	51.1	57045
Macleod	7625	22.1	15900	46.1	34504
Medicine Hat	23615	33.4	23492	33.3	70606
Red Deer	18725	30.5	24346	39.7	61372
Strathcona	11788	23.8	21098	42.6	49473
Victoria	3821	9.3	22113	53.7	41161

Source: Fifth Census of Canada, 1911, Vol. 11 (Ottawa: 1913) Table XVI, pp 376, 377, 379–381, 422–424

differentiate between Canadian internal migrants and returning Canadians. Based on a average of 2.5 persons per entry, one can calculate that 254,125 Canadians and 209,370 Americans had homesteaded in western Canada by 1910. Together they comprised 65 percent of the total of 714,260 homesteaders. In Saskatchewan alone, the preferred destination at the turn of the century, the population increased 1,124.7 percent between 1891 and 1911.[22]

The peak years of migration from the United States into Canada were 1910 and 1911 when 93,798 and 121,451 immigrants respectively registered with border officials.[23] A boom in wheat prices resulted in an

Table 67   Immigrant Arrivals in Canada and Saskatchewan, 1905–22

Dominion fiscal year ending 31 Mar.	Immigrant arrivals from					Immigrants to Saskatchewan	% of total
	United Kingdom	United States	% of total U.S.A.	Other countries	Total		
1905–6	86,796	57,796	30.5	44,472	189,064	28,728	15.1
1906–7	55,791	34,659	27.8	34217.0	124,667	15,307	12.2
1907–8	120,182	58,312	22.2	83,975	262,469	30,590	11.6
1908–9	52,901	59,832	40.7	34175.0	146,908	22,146	15.0
1909–10	59,790	103,798	49.7	45,206	208,794	29,218	13.1
1910–11	123,013	121,451	39.0	66,620	311,084	40,763	13.1
1911–12	138,121	133,710	37.7	82,406	354,237	46,158	13.0
1912–13	150,542	139,009	34.5	112,881	402,432	45,147	11.2
1913–14	142,622	107,530	27.8	384,878	384,878	40,999	10.6
1914–15	43,276	59,779	41.2	41,734	144,789	16,173	11.1
1915–16	8,664	36,937	76.1	2,936	48,537	6,001	12.3
1916–17	8,282	61,389	81.4	5,703	75,374	9,874	13.1
1917–18	3,178	71,314	90.1	4582.0	79,074	12,382	15.6
1918–19	9,914	40,715	70.5	7,073	57,702	8,552	14.8
1919–20	59,603	49,656	42.3	8079.0	117,336	14,287	12.1
1920–21	74,262	48,059	32.3	26,156	148,477	13,392	9.0
1921–22	39,020	29,345	32.5	21,634	89,999	9,894	10.8

Source: Department of Agriculture, *Arrival Report 1923* (Ottawa; 1924), 251.

increased influx of Americans into the region between 1906 and 1911. Prairie census districts with the highest number of American-born were primarily rural in 1911, the crest of the land boom (Table 66). While few Americans chose the longer settled Manitoba, many settled along the railway lines in Saskatchewan and Alberta. In 1916 American-born comprised 35.9 percent, 29.8 percent, and 8.2 percent of the foreign-born populations of Alberta, Saskatchewan, and Manitoba respectively.[24] A general impression of the contribution of native-born, British-born, and American-born to the growth of population in Canada is afforded by Table 67 which clearly shows a growing American presence, particularly in the prairie provinces, between 1901 and 1921. After the First World War began, immigration of Americans into Canada dropped considerably.

For most of the period from 1880 to 1930, it is unclear how many of the American migrants were returning Canadians. Certainly, Canadian officials made a conscious effort to attract their former countrymen by concentrating "their attention in areas where former Canadians were numerous, and the difficulty of their task was lessened by the fact that many of the ex-Canadians were a 'border people' who were easily persuaded to return to the Dominion. These Canadian repatriates [from North Dakota] came principally from Pembina, Cavalier, Walsh, and Grand Fork Counties." [26]

298 With Scarcely a Ripple

A Closer View

While many Americans and returning Canadians did come to the west as clients of various land companies, the majority operated independently, making decisions as to where to settle entirely on their own. It is this individual nature of the migration process that makes the examination of American and Canadian settlement of western Canada so difficult. However, records do exist which permit one to reconstruct the migration patterns of these groups during the pioneering period of settlement.

Border Crossing Record Sample   The two major border crossing points for Americans and returning Canadians entering the prairies were at Emerson, Manitoba, and North Portal, Saskatchewan, with the Canadian National, Soo Line, and Burlington Northern railways meeting at the former and the Soo Line crossing the latter in 1894 and joining the CPR main line near Moose Jaw. A brief empirical analysis of migrants crossing at North Portal between 1 December 1909 and 1 January 1911 allows us to compare the characteristics of the various groups involved in this movement from the United States to Canada.

During this thirteen-month period, 7,353 migrants were admitted into Canada by the immigration inspectors at North Portal and of this number, 414 were Canadian-born heads of families or individuals over the age of 17. Returning Canadians ranked third behind American-born and Norwegian-born. The Canadian-born were a varied lot. Most entries stated Canada as place of birth but there is good reason to believe, based on the information collected on province of birth and last place of residence for Canadians coming from Canada, that the majority were born in Ontario. Almost 88 percent of the group had acquired American citizenship and over 50 percent of those retaining their Canadian citizenship last resided in the United States.

North Dakota was by far the most common place of origin among returning Canadians at 46.8 percent, followed by Minnesota (9.4 percent), Ontario (referring to people from this province who chose to travel to Saskatchewan through the United States) (8.9 percent), Michigan (6.8 percent), Iowa (4.9 percent), Wisconsin (4.7 percent), Illinois (4.2 percent), South Dakota (3.7 percent), Montana (1.6 percent), and Kansas (1.4 percent). The migration field funnelling into western Canada via North Portal was significantly wide, demonstrating the pulling force of this new agricultural frontier. The availability of train transportation reduced the importance of distance as a factor in migration, yet it was largely a movement within the transborder region of the Great Plains. North Dakota was the major place of origin for Saskatchewan- and Alberta-bound migrants while considerable numbers to both provinces came from the midwestern region of the United States and the province of Ontario. Considerable numbers of Ontarians continued the tradition of travelling through the United States to western Canada despite the presence of the CPR. Ontario was the most important place of origin for British Columbia-bound migrants.

Saskatchewan (48.2 percent) and Alberta (47.8 percent) were by far the preferred destinations, reflecting the fact that the migration was composed mainly of farmers attracted to the cheap land available in these new provinces. Yet while the vast majority listed their occupation as farming (78.1 percent), many were of such a young age that it is reasonable to believe that they were farm labourers prior to their move. This reflects the fact that the vast majority of migrants from the United States came from nearby states and regions where agriculture dominated the local economies. Forty-six percent of the Canadian-born migrating to British Columbia were not farmers, reflecting the fact that many of this group disembarked in Vancouver, where some of them might have chosen to live.

The majority of migrants were males, and of the female migrants, over 74 percent indicated that they were travelling to join their husbands in their new homes. This suggests that many of the men went ahead with their stock and equipment and started the homestead before sending for their families. Canadians proved among the most disinclined among immigrant groups to give up their citizenship, although in this case the requirement of American citizenship in order to obtain homestead land in the United States played a major role in such high percentages of naturalization.

The average age of the returning Canadian-born migrant was 37.5 years, which might lead us to believe that this migration was atypical. Over 71 percent of native-born Americans were under the age of 35 as compared to only 50.9 percent of the Canadian-born. The fact that almost 50 percent of the migrants were over the age of 34 reflects the strong lure of free homestead land in western Canada. For many Canadians, movement to western Canada represented a later or even last stage in their mobility life-cycle, while this movement was for many Americans the first step in this same cycle. Perhaps this also supports to some extent the claim that ex-Canadians were a border people, easily persuaded, particularly in light of conditions in North Dakota and elsewhere, to return to Canada.

Western Canada appealed to Canadian-born and American resident alike but capital certainly facilitated the migrant's adaptation. The average amount carried by the Canadian-born was $4,058, a considerable sum given the availability of homesteads and cheap lands, but necessary to cover the costs of farm-making. The considerable deviation around this mean indicates that while some had very large amounts of capital which they may have used in speculative ventures, others had very little money and probably had to work as labourers before they could afford to start a farm of their own. Canadian-born ranked highest in terms of cash on

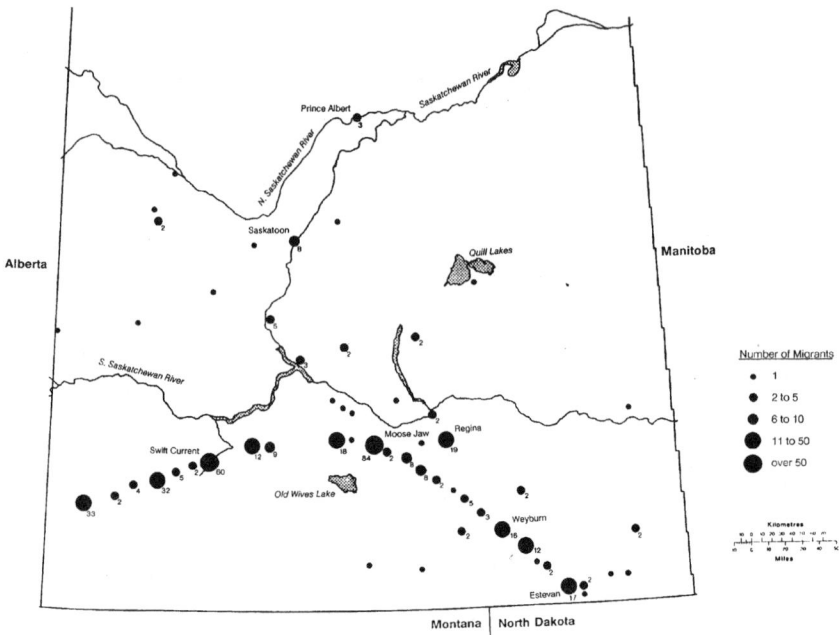

Map 19: Places of Disembarkation for Saskatchewan-bound Migrants

hand, with 32.9 percent reporting they had more than $2,500 on their person. They were followed by the Germans (26.7 percent), the Norwegians (24.1 percent), the English (22.0 percent), the Russians (19.1 percent), and the Americans (17.4 percent). Wealth closely correlated with age and life cycle.

Canadian-born from North Dakota dominated the migration to areas surrounding small rural communities in Saskatchewan and Alberta, including Maple Creek, Gull Lake, Mortlach, Herbert, and Morse in the former and Taber and Seven Persons in the latter. The larger destinations such as Regina, Moose Jaw, Swift Current, Medicine Hat, Calgary, Edmonton, and Vancouver experienced wider migration fields. Places of disembarkation for Saskatchewan-bound Canadian-born migrants are shown in Map 19. What is most striking about this map is the linearity of the destination pattern. The majority of the places of disembarkation were along the main CPR line and the Soo line.

Access to rail transportation and the market was obviously a major factor in the decision-making process. But because the destinations given to immigration officers were simply the places migrants planned to disembark, the border crossing records are of little use in tracing the migration experiences of American-born and returning Canadian-born.

Local Histories Samples   A more useful source for reconstructing migration patterns is the local history. As revealed in the last chapter, Hudson has used county histories and information from the North Dakota Historical Data Project to map migration to North Dakota during the nineteenth century. While the migration patterns derived from these histories are illuminating, the limitations are significant, as Hudson himself admits. Most county histories were paid for by those whose biographical sketches were included, thus introducing a socioeconomic bias to the sample; and many of these sketches omit places of intermediate residence, thus making a full understanding of the migration process impossible. The local histories housed in the Regina Public Library are, for reasons described in the Appendix, less problematic than the histories used by Hudson for his work.

Birthplaces and last places of residence were identified for all 1,265 migrants born in Canada and the United States before 1900 and settling before 1920 in seven rural municipalities chosen for study.[27] Over 54 percent of the migrants were born in Ontario and they comprised over 91 percent of the entire Canadian-born group. Just less than half of this group had foreign-born parents, with Irish, Scottish, and English ancestry predominating. Next in line, but considerably less significant in terms of size, were migrants born in England, followed by Scotland, Quebec, Ireland, Germany, Russia, Sweden, Norway, Northern Ireland, Iowa, and Minnesota. Ontario-born migrants settling in these seven rural municipalities came from all over the province, with the greatest percentage coming from Bruce and Grey counties, where rapid population growth between 1850 and 1880 created an unfavourable population/land ratio. The St Lawrence Valley and Eastern Townships of Quebec comprised a secondary Canadian source region but the majority of Québécois who left these areas moved to New England. Only 6.2 percent of the sample migrants were born in the United States.

More important, perhaps, for many migrants was last place of residence before settling, because it was here that strong kin and kith relations shaping future migration experiences in western Canada may have developed. Over 30 percent of the migrants moved more than once before settling in Saskatchewan. Many Ontarians moved directly from their rural Ontario homes to Saskatchewan, although there was some internal movement in the province, primarily to urban centres among the young and to newer agricultural regions among those born earlier in the century. A considerable number had also moved to Manitoba before settling in Saskatchewan. While Ontario continued to be most important as a source region (46.7 percent), Manitoba, Minnesota, North Dakota, and South Dakota formed important secondary source regions. Many of the Scandinavian, German, and other eastern European groups settling in Saskatchewan previously resided in Manitoba, the Dakotas, Minnesota, and other states in the midwest region. Many of the English-, Scottish-, and Irish-born last resided in Ontario, Manitoba, and the upper midwest.

Canadian birthplaces and American last places of residence were identified for Canadian-born migrants (N=174) returning to twenty-seven Saskatchewan rural municipalities.[28] The majority of Canadian-born came from Ontario with a significant number hailing from the eastern townships and the St Lawrence Valley of Quebec. Again, as Hudson found in his study, the two most important Ontario source areas were the Huron Tract north of London and Bruce and Grey counties.

Most of the returning Canadians last resided in North Dakota, clustering very close to the international border. About half of this group moved directly from their Ontario homes to North Dakota while the other half moved westward in either one of two general patterns – that is, either a succession of usually blue-collar, non-farm occupations in or near midwestern cities (Detroit, Duluth, Minneapolis–St Paul), or movement from one or two farms located elsewhere throughout the midwest and Great Plains states. Few returning Canadians last resided in states not approximate to Saskatchewan although some, primarily Québécois-born, came from industrial centres in New England.

While these patterns are illuminating, they only capture three points in the migration histories of Saskatchewan-bound settlers: their origins, last place of residence, and destinations. For some, these locations reflect their entire migration story, but for most, they tell only part of the tale. The community histories also include intermediate places of residence and so a decision was made to examine the migration histories of North American-born settling in the rural municipality of Estevan before 1920.[29] A slight majority (50.9 percent) of the North American migrants were born in Canada, with the majority of this group hailing from Ontario (Table 68). The Huron Tract, Peterborough region, Bay of Quinte, and Ottawa Valley were important Canadian source areas while the majority of American-born came from Minnesota, Iowa, Wisconsin, and North Dakota. While the majority of Britons emigrated directly to Saskatchewan, many of the eastern Europeans had previously resided throughout the midwest and Great Plains states before coming to Canada.

The accumulated intermediary locations show that many of the Ontario-born resided in Manitoba and elsewhere in Saskatchewan before settling in the rural municipality of Estevan. While twenty-seven of the American-born moved directly from their place of birth to Estevan, only seven Ontarians mirrored this pattern. Many of these direct migrants were children accompanying their parents. Thirteen Ontarians moved to Manitoba before settling in Saskatchewan; five lived elsewhere in Saskatchewan before locating in their last place of residence; eleven made intermediary moves within their home province; two experienced intermediary moves in North Dakota; one made an intermediary move in South Dakota; and

Table 68   Last Places of Residence (Country/State/Province) of Estevan
R.M. Migrants

Last place of residence	No.	% of all countries	% of country only
Canadian total	59	28.5	–
Ontario	44	21.3	74.6
Quebec	10	4.8	16.9
Nova Scotia	3	1.4	5.1
Manitoba	1	0.5	1.7
New Brunswick	1	0.5	1.7
United States total	57	27.5	
Minnesota	17	8.2	29.8
Iowa	10	4.8	17.5
North Dakota	9	4.3	15.8
Wisconsin	8	3.9	14.0
Pennsylvania	3	1.4	5.3
Maine	2	1	3.5
New York	2	1	3.5
Illinois	2	1	3.5
Michigan	1	0.5	1.8
South Dakota	1	0.5	1.8
Indiana	1	0.5	1.8
Massachussetts	1	0.5	1.8
England	37	17.9	–
Russia	10	4.8	–
Scotland	9	4.3	–
Sweden	8	3.9	–
Norway	7	3.4	–
Northern Ireland	4	1.9	–
Ireland	3	1.4	–
Romania	3	1.4	–
Wales	2	1.0	–
Denmark	2	1.0	–
Germany	2	1.0	–
France	1	0.5	–
Poland	1	0.5	–
Hungary	1	0.5	–
Ukraine	1	0.5	–
Total	201		

Source: Estevan Book committee, *A Tale that is Told* (Estevan, 1981).

one lived in Iowa before locating in his last place of residence. The majority of Québécois moved directly to Saskatchewan, 40 percent to Estevan. Two of this group made intermediary moves in Wisconsin, North Dakota, and Michigan. American-born relocated elsewhere in the midwest region, often close to their place of birth, and elsewhere in Saskatchewan. Six American-born migrants made their intermediary moves within

Minnesota. Four American-born made intermediary moves in Saskatchewan, and one each in Ontario and Manitoba.

Many Canadian- and American-born last resided in Saskatchewan before making their move to Estevan. Some of the Ontarians and other settlers actually farmed in adjacent rural municipalities and retired in Estevan, while others worked in agricultural-related occupations and other jobs before either purchasing land or taking up homesteads in this particular study area. Five American-born last resided in North Dakota, two each in Minnesota, Iowa, and Nebraska, and one each in Wisconsin and South Dakota. Thirteen American-born last resided in Saskatchewan before moving to Estevan, two in Manitoba, and one in British Columbia.

Kinship linkages played a major role in the pattern of chain and step migration revealed in the Estevan case study. The importance of kinship is revealed in the next section which explores the migration experiences of Saskatchewan-bound migrants.

MIGRATION EXPERIENCES

The Canadian prairies are often perceived as simple and amorphous but the area is a more enigmatic region evoking many different images. Viewed from the outside, the prairies seems a vast, featureless region, offering little more than hockey players, wheat for the world, and boredom for the traveller heading to more exotic points east and west. Yet those familiar with the region have a more compelling view.[30] The prairies actually constitutes a huge region with numerous distinct and interacting ecological elements and processes. And just as distinct physical processes ensure heterogeneity in the environments encountered, so the peopling of these divergent areas by disparate ethnic groups at different times results in variable settlement experiences. Such diversity in physical and historical contexts complicates the analysis of migration and settlement experiences. This section pursues a number of strategies to provide a limited understanding of internal and return Canadian migration. As well, attention is focused on the experiences of American-born migrants who were the immigrant group that arguably made the greatest impact on settlement of the Canadian west.

Attitudes Towards Immigrant Groups

Newspapers contain vital information to discern attitudes towards Canadian-born migrants and immigrant groups, particularly Americans. As was the norm throughout North America, local views were generally more favourable towards Anglo-Saxon Protestant groups coming from eastern Canada, Great Britain, and the United States and less supportive of predominantly Catholic and Jewish non-English-speaking immigrants of southern and eastern Europe. Anglo-conformity was stressed in many editorials, including that published in the 16 September 1890 edition of the Moose Jaw *Times*: "Canada is now in a position to extend a hearty welcome to the people of every land who are willing to drop old world prejudices, and unite as Canadians in building up and developing a nation on the broad lines of Anglo-Saxon institutions."

Another editorial from the *Times*, while arguing that the northwest needed immigrants to augment the qualities brought to the region by native-born Canadians, mentioned only what the English, Scots, and Irish could contribute to western Canadian society:

That unity of aim, sentiment and destiny should characterize the inhabitants of the British Northwest is the wish of every loyal and patriotic citizen. That a composite people welded into one, drawn together by common interests and prompted by common motives should be cemented by enduring bonds is logical and rational ... A speaker [in the House of Commons] states "that one true Canadian is worth any half dozen of imported immigrants". The [Canadian] possesses inherent qualities of the highest value. The representative Canadian has the conservative tenacity of the Saxon-Englishman. The Canadian is, as a rule, energetic, orderly, amenable to duty, quick-witted, level-headed, insisting upon his own rights but respecting the rights of others. These are valuable qualities, but they are partially neutralized by serious deficiencies. The average Canadian is, as regards mental and social culture, raw, crude, and ill informed on matters outside his own immediate sphere ... We ask, then, whether it is all true that one such person is worth any half dozen of "imported immigrants" as material out of which to form communities such as ours must necessarily be? On the contrary, there are whole classes of immigrants as valuable as the very best specimens and they are so, not because they resemble the average Canadian best but because they differ from him. The educated Englishmen, for example, who has been to Eaton or Harrow, and also to Cambridge or Oxford, contributes to our national makeup the very qualities conspicuously lacking in the native Canadian ... The canny Scotchmen too has approved himself able to live and thrive while many native Canadians have failed ... we are prepared to welcome as well the mind and muscle of Ireland and Scotia, confident that when these are united to the qualities characteristic of the native Canadians our country shall boast a race second to none.

Subscribing to stereotypical views of Anglo-Saxons, the editorialist ignores other immigrants and most likely did not consider those Canadians of French descent in his characterization of native-born. With the passing of time, Saskatchewan newspapers showed greater concern over the ethnic make-up of western Canada. Earlier issues, while favouring British immigrants, recognized the need for migrants from less favoured countries to fill the need for labour, as is evidenced in the Regina *Leader* of 19 July 1910:

There are people who condemn the Government for having encouraged Galicians, Doukhobors, and other peoples of foreign nationality to come to Canada. These critics lose sight of the fact that in very large measure the rapid development of this Western country during the past ten or twelve years has largely been made because of these hardworking people ... Are we to do without these works necessary to our continuing progress and prosperity or shall we welcome those people who are ready and willing having brought into our midst what some people are pleased to regard as an undesirable class? Of the two evils which is greater – the stopping or rather retarding of our growth as a nation ... or the influx of some tens of thousands of labourers from other lands, lower in the plane of civilization, uneducated and possibly not quite so moral as ourselves but who, with our boasted superiority, we should be able to educate and uplift?

Condescending and somewhat racist in tone, the editorial nonetheless advocates some kind of tolerance in the same year that a restrictive Immigration Act was passed in Parliament.

At the turn of the century the dominant culture in the Canadian west was Anglo-Canadian, which in effect was Ontarian, and there was considerable pressure for ethnic groups to assimilate as rapidly as possible. In this respect, the school system was regarded as one of the major institutions of assimilation. Yet government encouragement of bloc settlement actually fostered an ethnic cohesiveness. Such a contradiction between policy and attitude during this period reflects the uncertain nature of the country itself. A new country with few transcendent ideals serving as guideposts for non-British immigrants, Canada "was a setting better suited to the transplanting of old worlds than to the making of new ones."[31]

The prairies were, in many ways, as foreign to native-born Canadians as they were to Europeans and Americans from the eastern United States. How different the prairie landscape must have seemed to migrants as the tall trees and shimmering lakes of northern Ontario and Minnesota, viewed by train windows, gave way to empty plains and a limitless sky. The earliest settlers faced isolation, blizzards, stifling heat, and an uncertain market and thus depended heavily on one another. In such an environment people were arguably more tolerant of each other. It was only later as lands were filled and institutions had more of an impact on people's lives that the pressure increased to conform to an ill-defined hybrid Anglo-culture, partly North American and partly British, Canadian in name but regional in disposition.

While editorials were somewhat condescending towards non-Anglo-Saxon groups, they were unanimous in their judgment of eastern Canadians as being the most desirable group of migrants, as is evident in this quote from an 17 August 1899 edition of the Regina *Leader*. "And while Western Canada extends a welcome to the people from all lands, yet the glad hand is most easily extended to the people of the eastern Canadian provinces." Yet while the papers praised the Canadian-born migrant, their considerable annoyance and, at times, intolerance of French Canadians, coupled with the admiration of Anglo-Saxon institutions, leads one to believe that the individual they had in mind was not representative of all those citizens born in the eastern provinces.

The views expressed towards American immigrants in Saskatchewan newspapers were certainly mixed. While the American was generally perceived in favourable terms, less enthusiastic opinions were directed towards American society and government. In many ways, the American migration to Canada at the turn-of-the-century period was international in character. Many of the participants were European-born and first-generation Americans.

Like their Anglo-Canadian counterparts in the United States, Anglo-Americans in western Canada were generally inconspicuous, even in areas of relatively high concentration such as southeastern and southwestern Saskatchewan. Yet despite their low profile, Americans made a significant impression in the Canadian west, a contribution embellished somewhat by Arthur Morton in the following statement: "As a large proportion of the American settlers were dry farmers, and many settled in the semi-arid areas, egs. between Estevan and Regina, between Regina and Saskatoon, and in southwestern Saskatchewan and southern Alberta, and in most cases made those areas blossom as the rose, they may be said to have contributed more than any other nationality to increase the productivity of the Canadian northwest."[32] While having a major impact on the development of the region, Americans, just as the British, were not lumped with other "foreign" groups. Hansen and Brebner picture the American migration to the Canadian west as part of a continental westward movement, apolitical but individualistically motivated, and representing a shared sense of participation in a larger frontier dynamic among anglophones on both sides of a relatively meaningless border.[33]

The newspapers valued American immigrants for their wealth and experience even though those listed in the Border Crossing sample were generally younger and had less cash than other immigrant groups. An analysis of farming operations of 70,703 individuals presented in a 1906 census bulletin entitled *Immigrants of the Agricultural Class in the Northwest* pictured Americans as having a wealth of farming experience and exceeding their proportion of the total sample of immigrants in terms of possession of occupied acreage, acres in crops, and livestock owned. They were described in a 31 March 1893 edition of the Moose Jaw *Times* as

a more than valuable class, because, in addition to the equipment for the pursuit of agriculture which so many of them bring into the country with them – that is their cattle, horses and implements – and which enable them at once to commence the cultivation of their lands, they bring also an experience of the climate and soil characteristic of the great prairie regions of the west, of the most approved methods of agriculture ... which it takes the immigrant from Britain or continental Europe some years to acquire.

Mention was also made, although often secondarily, of the bonds of unity fostered by immigration and family ties. An editorial appearing in the Swift Current *Sun* on 2 April 1910 welcoming North Dakota settlers to Saskatchewan stresses the close relationship between Canadians and Americans: "We welcome them, help them, and wish them God speed in the work they are doing for the upholding of this, their new country and home ... This feeling is natural to people of the same blood and we ought to find on either side of the line a reciprocal kindly spirit."

While generally positive about the individual American immigrant, Saskatchewan papers were often critical about American society. They took particular exception to what they perceived as ignorant attitudes taken towards Canada by their neighbours to the south. The Moose Jaw *Times* was livid over the following vitriolic comments made about Canada by the Rock Island *Blade*:

While there are a great number of enterprising and worthy citizens in Canada the majority are ignorant, illiterate and superstitious ... you find a majority of the people to be Chinamen, Swashes (or low class Indians), Indians, renegades, European foreigners, low Dutch, Canucks, ignorant French Canadians, simple unenterprising Canadians and lastly villains of all descriptions and from all parts of the globe. Are these the people we want within the realms of the "Land of the Free and the Home of the Brave"?

To this diatribe, the indignant *Times* responded:

For pure and unadulterated gall and cheek, the above clipping ... takes the cake, and should prove to the Canadian people that in certain quarters of the United States there is not much sympathy for them ... The editor of the *Blade* will find more ignorance and superstition in one city of the United States than he would in the whole Dominion of Canada. Americans need not lose any sleep over this question as it will be a very long time before they are asked to accept Canada within the realms of the "land of the free and the home of the Brave". But, perhaps such rot is not worth comment.[34]

American Manifest Destiny and the threat of political annexation generated the most passion among Saskatchewan commentators. On 4 December 1891 the Moose Jaw *Times* offered these comments on the threat of annexation:

Annexation with the American republic finds no place in the political belief of the people of Canada ... We do not think that the people of any part of the Dominion take any stock in the theory that annexation is the manifest and ultimate destiny of Canada. On the contrary, an increasing faith in the development of the unlimited resources of the country, a desire to fashion our institutions after the pattern of those grand old British institutions from which we draw our best inspirations is the characteristic of the Canadian people at present ... Politically, we could lose our identity.

To partly allay fears about annexation, the Qu'Appelle *Vidette* published a number of excerpts from articles noting a growing sense of Canadian unity. A 24 January 1899 issue included the following passage written by Watson Griffin, a Canadian, in the *Magazine of American History*:

It may be asked, will not this multitude of American [immigrants] so control public sentiment as to bring about annexation? I do not think so. Had the rush of Americans begun ten years ago that would probably have been the result, but the pioneers are Canadians, Canadian laws and Canadian customs are established, Americans cannot vote until they have become naturalized, and the extraordinary development of the country will excite Canadian pride and intensify the present opposition to annexation ... Moreover, it is probable that the majority of those who come from the United States to Canada will not be very enthusiastic Americans. These will stay at home, while millions of Canadians, Scotchmen, and Englishmen now residing in the United States, will cross the boundary, bringing with them, of course, a great many who are American by birth ... Mr. Goldwin Smith, who was a professor of history, ought to know that, in guessing the future of nations, history as well as geography must be taken into account ... there is a great deal of British sentiment in the Dominion; but stronger than that, more general than that, is the sentiment of Canadianism, the love of Canada. We like the Americans, we imitate them in many ways ... but we will never listen to any proposition involving the disintegration of "this Canada of ours", which we all love so well.

On 13 March 1900, the *Vidette* printed an excerpt of an article written by Charles Dudley Warner, an American, published in the March 1899 edition of *Harper's Magazine*:

In Canada today there is a growing sense of independence; very little, taking the whole mass, for annexation ... Among the minor causes of reluctance to a union are distrust of the Government of the United States; ... dislike of our quadrennial elections; the want of a system of civil service; ... [and] dislike of our sensational and irresponsible journalism ... The railway development, the Canadian Pacific alone, has ... given a new impulse to the sentiment of nationality. It has produced a sort of unity which no Act of Parliament could ever create.

While appreciating American capital and labour, Saskatchewan papers also expressed some regret about the weakening of the British connection, in economic as well as social terms. A July 1910 article appearing in the

Regina *Leader* entitled "Wake Up England" argued that Britain must be more aggressive in marketing British products in Canada:

If British manufacturers are to secure a fair trade in Canada they must take heed to the warning addressed to them by His Majesty, King George V, when, as Prince of Wales, on his return from his famous trip around the world during which he travelled across Canada, uttered ... "the Old Country must wake up, if she intends to maintain her old position of pre-eminence in her colonial trade against foreign competitors".[35]

The newspapers were also aware of the significant numbers of ex-Canadians returning to the land of their birth. Several editorials included reports of such return migrants. On 7 April 1893 the Moose Jaw *Times* included a note from the Toronto *Empire* about their interview with a Thomas Loughead, who with his family moved from a farm in the neighbourhood of Meaford, Ontario, to South Dakota five years previously, but who returned to Ontario and was on his way to settle in the Canadian west. The promise of a great future in Dakota induced Loughead to leave his prosperous farm in Ontario, but his venture resulted only in a great loss of capital: "I wish the American railway land agent who some years ago drew a glowing picture of Dakota to me, and with them induced me to leave Canada, would go with me today to that God forsaken region today, I would show him miles and miles of abandoned land, farm after farm." By printing such accounts, Saskatchewan papers were serving as a propaganda tool for western settlement.

What effects any unfavourable opinions held by western Canadians regarding American society and government had in terms of attitudes directed toward American immigrants are largely unknown but there is little evidence, at least in the Saskatchewan newspapers, of any significant anti-Americanism among native Canadians or European migrants. The sheer number of Americans by the end of the first decade of the twentieth century ensured that they would play a major role in developing the province. After 1911, American immigrants were more likely to go to other regions of Canada, responding to changing economic conditions.

Assiniboia School Districts Study

The flood of immigrants into western Canada began in earnest after 1896. Unfortunately, only the recently released 1901 manuscript census is available for research into this period, thus restricting any effort to trace migrants' experiences over time. Yet this source does include much valuable information about various immigrant groups.

Before its establishment in 1905, Saskatchewan was composed of the two administrative districts of Assiniboia and Saskatchewan. The former incor-

porated the southern-most part of the present province and is characterized mostly by flat and rolling prairie. Settlement in the southeastern section of Assiniboia was stimulated by the completion of the Souris branch
(the Soo Line) of the CPR in 1894, but drought and crop failure over the
next three years resulted in many abandoning their homesteads. Yet the
introduction of summer fallow, the end of depression, and a higher price
for wheat towards the end of the decade stimulated migration into this
region. Among these migrants were those settling eight school districts in
the Assiniboia Electoral District, including Alameda, Alma, Balcarres,
Beaverdale, Bellegarde, Estevan, Grenville North, and Indian Head. A
complete survey of 1901 manuscript census schedules for these school districts produced a cross-section of 974 households. Canadian-born dominated the settlement of these school districts (55.9 percent of the household heads) with the largest number coming from Ontario (48.8 percent
of the total and 87.3 percent of Canadian-born). English-born constituted
the largest immigrant group in the chosen school districts (15.9 percent
of the total and 36 percent of foreign-born), followed by the Scots,
Americans, the Irish, Austrians, French, Belgians, Hungarians, Swedes,
Germans, and Russians.

Only one of the Canadian-born living in the eight school districts was an
American citizen, suggesting that for this study area, return migration
among Canadians was virtually non-existent, or that those returning from
the United States reacquired their Canadian citizenship prior to 1901. In
any case, the vast majority of Canadians either moved directly from
Ontario or lived elsewhere in Manitoba or the North-West Territories
before settling in the Assiniboia district.

The majority of Americans and Austrians were recent arrivals, that is,
had immigrated after 1895, and had not yet completed the naturalization
procedure required for aliens applying for homesteads. The bulk of other
nativity groups, with 50 to 65 percent of their household heads receiving
Canadian citizenship, arrived in Canada during the 1890s. Those with the
highest naturalization rates – the English, Scottish, and Irish – came to
Canada at some time during the decade of the 1880s.

Canadian-born were spread throughout the eight school districts
although a certain degree of clustering did take place (Table 69). Significant percentages of Canadian-born designated as coming from rural
Ontario settled in Alameda, Indian Head, and Alma school districts. Fifty
percent of urban Ontarians located in the Indian Head school district,
with many settling in the town which to this day is distinguished for its
Ontario architecture and brick construction. Almost 50 percent of the
American-born, the majority from North Dakota, lived in the Beaverdale
school district. Most of the Scots settling in the Indian Head school district
worked in non-farm occupations in the town. English-born were distributed widely, while significant numbers of Irish-born lived in Grenville

Table 69 Nativity by Electoral District, Assiniboia Study Area, 1901 (%)

Electoral districts

Nativity[1]	Alameda Row %	Alameda Col %	Alma Row %	Alma Col %	Balcarres Row %	Balcarres Col %	Beaverdale Row %	Beaverdale Col %	Bellegarde Row %	Bellegarde Col %	Estevan Row %	Estevan Col %	Grenville North Row %	Grenville North Col %	Indian Head Row %	Indian Head Col %
Ontario (rural)	29.8	66.9	15.0	55.6	4.8	46.3	3.8	12.7	9.8	33.9	6.8	27.3	9.3	34.9	21.0	35.6
Ontario (urban)	0	0	10.3	7.4	0	0	3.8	2.5	5.1	3.5	15.4	12.1	15.4	11.3	50.0	16.5
Rest of Canada	0	0	2.9	1.9	7.2	12.2	4.3	2.5	37.7	22.6	26.1	18.2	2.9	1.9	18.8	5.5
United States	19.4	3.9	11.1	3.7	0	0	38.9	11.9	2.8	0.9	11.1	4.0	0	0	16.7	2.5
England	13.5	11.8	1.9	2.8	3.2	12.2	14.2	18.6	11.0	14.8	9.0	14.1	16.8	24.5	5.3	2.8
Scotland	19.3	6.2	3.5	1.9	8.8	12.2	19.3	9.3	0	0	16.7	2.5	30.3	19.9	29.8	7.2
Ireland	2.9	0.6	14.3	4.6	5.7	4.9	8.6	2.5	8.6	2.8	11.4	4.0	25.7	8.5	22.9	3.4
Germany	21.4	1.7	0	0	7.1	2.4	21.4	2.5	7.1	0.9	14.3	2.0	7.1	0.9	21.4	1.3
Russia	63.6	3.9	0	0	0	0	18.2	1.7	0	0	0	0	9.1	0.9	9.1	0.4
Hungary	18.2	2.2	0	0	0	0	36.4	6.8	0	0	0	0	0	0	45.5	4.2
France	0	0.0	53.3	14.8	8.8	7.3	6.7	1.7	26.7	7.0	0	0	0	0	13.3	1.7
Austria	0	0.0	0	0	0	0	50.0	14.4	0	0	0	0	38.2	12.3	2.9	0.4
Sweden	0	0.0	0	0	0	0	28.6	3.4	0	0	71.4	10.1	0	0	0	0
Belgium	4.3	0.6	30.4	6.5	0	0	0	0	65.2	13.0	0	0	0	0	0	0

Source: 1901 Manuscript Census.

[1] countries with more than ten thousand heads in study area.

North and Indian Head school districts respectively. The Germans settled for the most part in Alameda, Beaverdale, and Indian Head school districts. Other notable clusters included the Russians in Alameda, the Hungarians in Indian Head and Beaverdale, the French in Alma and Bellegarde, the Austrians in Beaverdale and Grenville North, the Swedes in Estevan and Beaverdale, and the Belgians in Bellegarde and Alma school districts. Table 70 shows a notable clustering among nativity groups, a segregation related to ethnic congregation, kinship affiliation, and recency of migration. Even among those who had been in Canada for some time or had previously lived in the United States, there was notable congregation.

The majority of household heads for most nativity groups were in the 31 to 35 age category, the only exceptions being the Russians with over 45 percent under 31, and the Belgians, with 35 percent under 31 and 35 percent over 45. Almost 28 percent of the Canadian-born household heads were under 31 and over 21 percent were over 45, emphasizing the fact that the west attracted both young and old alike. The older group consisted of many types of migrants, including those who were perhaps finishing the last leg of a history of movement back and forth across the border or within Ontario and Manitoba, and those who left their homes back east in hopes of acquiring homestead land for family members. The thirty-six American-born were younger on average than their Canadian-born counterparts, with over 33 percent under 31. Yet almost 28 percent of this group were over 45, again testifying to the drawing power of this new frontier.

Time of arrival had little relationship with household size, as is evidenced by the generally larger households of the Irish, who came to Canada primarily in the 1880s, and the Austrians, who for the most part, were recent immigrants (Table 71). The presence of relatives in the household and relatively large numbers of children account for the large household sizes of the Irish and Austrians respectively. Canadian- and American-born did not stand out in terms of household composition in any category. Nor did they distinguish themselves in terms of household roles, as a remarkable degree of similarity was displayed by all groups as regards dependence on nuclear and extended family members for labour.

Ontario-born, along with the Irish and Swedes, were the groups most likely to have boarders, but the differences are not that significant. The relative ease of land acquisition in this new agricultural frontier meant that newly arrived settlers could move quickly on to their homesteads. Many of those boarding either worked in the villages or were employed as farm labourers. In fact, as Table 72 makes clear, these three groups had the largest percentages of their household heads employed in non-farming occupations. Urban Ontario household heads dominated both absolutely and relatively the semi-skilled, skilled, clerical, business, and professional categories, the only exceptions being the relative dominance of the Swedes

Table 70 Index of Dissimilarity among Assiniboia Study Area Nativity Groups, 1901 (8 electoral districts)

Nativity groups[1]	Ontario rural	Ontario urban	Rest of Canada	United States	England	Scotland	Ireland	Germany	Russia	Hungary	France	Austria	Sweden	Belgium
Ontario (rural)	–	43.9	50.7	40.4	31.4	36.5	43.0	28.9	47.5	56.4	57.4	78.5	90.4	70.1
Ontario (urban)	43.9	–	51.1	55.3	34.5	43.6	31.2	48.0	78.0	50.8	67.5	77.9	80.8	84.6
Rest of Canada	50.7	51.1	–	62.2	48.8	49.9	45.4	45.4	83.7	76.9	52.8	82.6	69.6	59.3
United States	40.4	55.3	62.2	–	41.9	30.1	46.9	28.5	53.3	28.8	75.8	58.2	60.3	81.8
England	31.4	34.5	48.8	41.9	–	23.1	26.1	24.4	54.1	42.0	67.2	62.8	76.8	82.7
Scotland	36.5	43.6	49.9	30.1	23.1	–	39.8	13.5	48.1	32.8	76.5	64.2	66.7	92.2
Ireland	43.0	31.2	45.4	46.9	26.1	39.8	–	35.8	70.4	65.7	56.7	57.1	80.1	79.2
Germany	28.9	48.2	45.4	28.5	24.4	13.5	35.8	–	44.1	39.0	72.8	61.4	64.2	88.5
Russia	47.5	78.0	83.7	53.3	54.1	48.1	70.4	44.1	–	54.6	77.3	69.8	81.8	95.7
Hungary	56.4	50.8	76.9	28.8	42.0	32.8	65.7	39.0	54.6	–	80.1	60.7	71.5	95.9
France	57.4	67.5	52.8	75.8	67.2	76.5	56.7	72.8	77.3	80.1	–	90.4	93.3	37.9
Austria	78.5	77.9	82.6	58.2	62.8	64.2	57.1	61.4	69.8	60.7	90.4	–	71.4	99.2
Sweden	90.4	80.8	69.6	60.3	76.8	66.7	80.1	64.2	81.8	71.5	93.3	71.4	–	99.9
Belgium	70.1	84.6	59.3	81.8	82.7	92.2	79.2	88.5	95.7	95.9	37.9	99.2	99.9	–

Source: 1901 Manuscript Census.
[1] countries with more than ten thousand household heads in study area.

Table 71 The Composition and Role of Saskatchewan Families and Households, Assiniboia Study Area, 1901

Characteristics A. Composition	Ontario rural (N=397)	Ontario urban (N=78)	Rest of Canada (N=69)	United States (N=36)	England (N=155)	Scotland (N=57)	Ireland (N=35)	Germany (N=14)	Russia (N=11)	Hungary (N=22)	France (N=30)	Austria (N=33)	Sweden (N=14)	Belgium (N=23)
1. Household size														
1	22.0	14.1	21.7	16.7	24.0	28.1	17.1	14.3	0	4.5	26.7	0.0	28.6	17.4
2	12.8	17.9	4.3	16.7	14.9	10.5	22.9	14.3	27.3	9.1	13.3	5.9	14.3	17.4
3 to 5	36.8	35.9	33.3	33.3	27.9	45.6	17.1	28.6	63.6	45.5	36.7	41.2	35.7	26.1
6 to 10	26.0	28.2	29.0	30.6	30.5	15.8	40.0	35.7	9.1	36.4	23.3	47.1	14.3	34.8
>10	2.5	3.2	11.6	2.8	2.6	0	2.9	7.1	0	4.5	0.0	5.9	7.1	4.3
2. No. of children in household														
0	41.5	35.9	36.2	30.6	44.5	54.4	51.4	28.6	27.3	18.2	40.0	5.9	50.0	47.8
1	15.3	23.1	6.7	19.4	9.0	8.8	0	0	27.3	9.1	16.7	17.6	14.3	13.0
2	12.3	11.5	10.1	11.1	11.0	10.5	8.6	14.3	27.3	18.2	16.7	18	14.3	0
3 to 5	23.5	20.5	24.6	33.3	25.2	21.1	25.7	50	18.2	45.5	20.0	44.1	14.3	26.1
>5	7.5	9.0	20.3	5.6	10.3	5.3	14.3	7.1	0	9.1	6.7	14.7	7.1	13.0
3. No. of relatives in household														
0	87.0	84.6	91.3	88.9	93.5	84.2	74.3	92.9	72.7	81.8	86.7	91.2	85.7	87.0
1	8.8	9.0	7.2	8.3	4.5	10.5	20.0	7.1	18.2	4.5	13.3	2.9	14.3	0
2	3.3	5.1	0	2.8	1.3	1.8	5.7	0	9.1	9.1	0	0	0	4.3
3 to 5	0.8	1.3	1.4	0	0.6	3.5	0	0	0	4.5	0	5.9	0	4.3
>5	0.3	0	0	0	0	0	0	0	0	0	0	0	0	4.3
4. No. of families in the dwelling														
1	98.4	97.3	94.2	100	98.0	100	100	100	100	94.7	100	96.7	92.3	100
2 to 5	1.6	2.7	5.8	0	2.0	0	0	0	0	5.3	0	3.3	7.7	0
>5	0	0	0	0	0	0	0	0	0	0	0	0	0	0

Table 71 (continued)

Characteristics B. Roles	Ontario rural (N=397)	Ontario urban (N=78)	Rest of Canada (N=69)	United States (N=36)	England (N=155)	Scotland (N=57)	Ireland (N=35)	Germany (N=14)	Russia (N=11)	Hungary (N=22)	France (N=30)	Austria (N=33)	Sweden (N=14)	Belgium (N=23)
5. No. of working members in the nuclear family of the head														
0	1.5	0	1.4	0	0	0	0	0	0	0	3.3	0	7.1	0.0
1	61.3	65.4	60.9	75.0	61.9	66.7	60.0	64.3	63.6	68.2	70.0	64.7	78.6	60.9
2	21.3	14.1	20.3	8.3	24.5	12.3	20.0	21.4	9.1	22.7	20.0	20.6	7.1	17.4
3 to 5	15.0	17.9	15.9	16.7	11	21.1	20.0	14.3	27.3	9.1	3.3	14.7	7.1	21.7
>5	1.0	2.6	1.4	0	2.6	0	0	0	0	0	3.3	0	0.0	0
6. No. of relatives in the household who are working														
0	93.8	97.4	97.1	97.2	98.1	91.2	91.4	100	90.9	90.9	100	97.1	92.9	95.7
1	4.8	1.3	2.9	2.8	1.3	3.5	8.6	0	0	4.5	0	2.9	7.1	4.3
2	1.5	1.3	0	0	0.6	5.3	0	0	9.1	0	0	0	0	0
3 to 5	0	0	0	0	0	0	0	0	0	4.5	0	0	0	0.0
7. No. of children >14 and working														
0	88.8	91	73.9	86.1	84.5	86	77.1	85.7	81.8	86.4	80.0	76.5	92.9	73.9
1	7.0	2.6	17.4	5.6	9.0	3.5	11.4	7.1	0	9.1	16.7	11.8	7.1	4.3
2	2.0	3.8	5.8	2.8	2.6	5.3	2.9	7.1	18.2	4.5	0	5.9	0	4.3
>2	2.3	2.6	2.9	5.6	3.9	5.3	8.6	0	0	0	2.9	5.9	0	17.4
8. Households with boarders														
not present	81.3	76.9	85.5	83.3	84.5	91.2	80.0	92.9	90.9	90.9	90.0	97.1	78.6	95.7
present	18.7	23.1	14.5	16.7	15.5	8.8	20.0	7.1	9.1	9.1	10.0	2.9	21.4	4.3

Table 72   Membership in Occupation Groups by Nativity, Assiniboia Study Area, 1901

	Occupation Groups						
Nativity group[1]	Unskilled[2]	semi-skilled	skilled	clerical	business	professsional	unknown
Ontario (rural)	77.3	3.0	0.8	3.8	8.5	4.0	2.8
Ontario (urban)	39.7	12.8	6.4	15.4	14.1	9.0	2.6
rest of Canada	66.7	4.3	1.4	7.2	5.8	7.2	7.2
United States	75.0	0	2.8	2.8	5.6	6.2	7.7
England	75.5	5.8	1.9	3.2	4.5	3.2	5.8
Scotland	73.7	10.5	1.8	5.3	5.3	3.5	0
Ireland	65.7	2.9	0	14.3	5.7	8.6	2.9
Germany	78.6	7.1	0	0	7.1	0	7.1
Russia	100	0	0	0	0	0	0
Hungary	100	0	0	0	0	0	0
France	80.0	3.3	0	0	3.3	7	6.7
Austria	88.2	0	0	12	0	0	0
Sweden	71.4	0	0	28.6	0	0	0
Belgium	87.0	0	0	0	0	0	13.0

Source: 1901 Manuscript Census.
[1] countries with more than ten thousand heads in study area.
[2] well over 90% of the household heads employed in this category were either farmers or farm labourers.

in clerical positions and the significant proportion of the Scottish-born in the semi-skilled occupations. The Irish ranked next to Canadian-born and Germans in the business category. Americans were represented in every category, taking advantage of opportunities present in a newly settled frontier. The major influx of Americans into Saskatchewan took place after 1901 and so one might surmise that an occupational profile of the 1911 manuscript census might reveal a pattern closer to that of the Canadian-born group.

The relative ease and cheapness of land acquisition meant that few found it necessary to rent property. Nine percent of urban Ontarians rented, many of this group doing so in the communities included in the eight school districts. Likewise, other groups with relatively more of their members living in urban centres and employed in non-farm positions – the Swedes, Irish, Germans, and Scots – had proportionately greater rental rates. Yet the number of renters was so small as to be almost significant.

Although most homestead and pre-emption grants were 160 acres, settlers from all nativity groups living in settlements often held much smaller amounts of land. Yet the majority of all household heads in every nativity group held a full or half a quarter-section. Irish-born were the most likely to hold one or more quarter-sections (54.3 percent), followed by rural Ontarians (44.1 percent), Americans (33.4 percent), English (31.6 percent), Germans (28.5 percent), Scottish (28.1 percent), French (26.7 percent), urban Ontarians (25.6 percent), Austrians (20.6 percent), Belgians (17.3 percent), other Canadians, primarily from Quebec (12.9 percent), Russians (9.1 percent), Hungarians (9.1 percent), and Swedes (7.1 percent). Longer-settled groups were more likely to acquire more land and eastern Europeans, either because of their recent arrival or lack of capital, or both, had smaller holdings. The majority of Swedes were urban-oriented and thus did not acquire much property. Native North Americans and those from Britain also were more likely to have more farm buildings than eastern Europeans. Very few employed farm labourers and few owned more than one dwelling house. The majority of all nativity groups reported more than $2,500 in earnings although less than thirty percent of the household heads volunteered such information, thus making any conclusions on relative income among nativity groups uncertain.

Despite some differences among nativity groups, especially in regards to time of arrival and location and to a much lesser degree in terms of occupation and holding size, a notable measure of similarity characterized the households chosen for study. Perhaps this can be attributed to the opportunities open to all in this place at this particular time. Yet we must be careful not to make too much of this rather restricted study area, population, and time period.

Local History Analysis of Returning Canadians

By linking information on families contained in Saskatchewan local histories to the US manuscript censuses and Canadian homestead records, an informative, although limited, family, migration, and settlement profile of 117 returning Canadian-born can be constructed. Of this number, only sixteen (13.7 percent) could be linked backwards to either one or both of the 1900 and 1910 US manuscript censuses and forwards through the homestead records; seventeen (14.5 percent) could be traced backwards through one or both of the 1900 and 1910 manuscript censuses; thirty-eight (32.5 percent) could not be linked to any of the Canadian or American records; and only forty-six (39.3 percent) could be traced forwards through the homestead records.[36] Yet even though a large percentage of this group could be followed in only one temporal direction and a significant percentage could not be linked to any of the records, the family histories for the most part include information on persistence and mobility.

Only one of the returning migrants came to Saskatchewan before 1890; one between 1890 and 1894, four between 1895 and 1900, thirty between 1901 and 1905, fifty-three between 1906 and 1910, seventeen between 1911 and 1915, and eight after 1915. The first decade of the twentieth century witnessed the greatest influx of immigrants from the United States, consisting of both native-born Americans and those from other countries, Canadian-born included. In many ways, this group of returning

Canadians resembled the border-crossing sample analysed earlier in this chapter. The majority of the local history migrants were male, older than the typical migrant, and last resided in nearby North Dakota.

This was by and large a family migration as 76 (68.5 percent) of those marrying did so before coming to Saskatchewan. Almost half of the sample returned to Canada with their spouses and children, while sixteen travelled alone and unmarried. Seventy percent of the married members had first marriages to other Canadian-born, 23.4 percent married American-born, and 6.3 percent married European-born. Just over 60 percent of the returning Canadians lived in only one American location before coming to Saskatchewan, 28.2 percent moved twice before their arrival, 8.5 percent lived in three or four different places, and 2.6 percent moved five or more times before settling in Saskatchewan. Only twenty-two family histories indicated that individuals followed family members to the province and another fifteen revealed that people were trailing friends. It is very likely that many of the others in this group were also following kin and kith but failed to mention this.

The local histories supplemented with census and homestead information reveal much about the particulars of this migration, as demonstrated in the following examples. Occasionally, family histories reveal that return migrants possessed a strong affection for Canada, a sentiment that would play a role in their decision to leave the United States. One such person was Myres Davidson Carey, who was born on a farm near Florence, Ontario, in 1868. He was the youngest of five boys and two girls. Myres and his next older brother Arthur decided that there was little chance to acquire a farm around home and proceeded to search for opportunities elsewhere. They heard about a scheme in the Dakotas whereby one could get free homestead land and free trees to plant on their farms from the government. The boys resolved to leave immediately but their father, George Carey, decided that he couldn't let them make the trip alone. So he sold his farm and loaded a railcar with equipment, animals, household effects, and some hardwood lumber and together father and two sons left for the Dakotas in the summer of 1886. They took up land three miles from Bradley which is located in what was to become South Dakota. They were soon joined by their mother and two sisters.

Before they could erect a house, Myres and Arthur contracted typhoid fever from drinking impure water. Their mother nursed them back to health and eventually the family home was finished. Myres' parents always regretted the move; they hated the hot, dry winds that seemed to blow continuously and they missed their old home and friends. George died after four years in South Dakota and left the property to Myres with the understanding that he would take care of his mother and sisters. In 1889 Myres married Mary Ellen Day, who had come to the Bradley area from Wisconsin some years before. A few years later, Arthur was killed in an accident.

At this point Myres took over his brother's spread in addition to working his sister Mary's homestead and the original family farm. Despite drought, scanty crops, and scarce fuel, Myres managed to build a house in Bradley so his children could get schooling. The manuscript census indicates that in 1900 Myres still retained his Canadian citizenship and that he and Mary had three girls and one boy. His mother had either died or was living with one of his sisters.

"Myres was always nostalgic about his Ontario home, so he sold the idea of returning to Canada to his family by telling them that it would mean they could live near a lake, sit under shade trees and especially burn wood instead of buffalo chips."[37] In 1906 Myres and his family moved to Saskatchewan where they took up a homestead three miles south of the village of Foam Lake where someone else had filed but not proved up. To their delight, a house was already erected on the property. Their good fortune continued that first year as the crop proved to be excellent. Myres was relatively successful in his Saskatchewan home and was instrumental in getting the school started in the rural municipality of Foam Lake. He died in 1928 at the age of sixty and Mary passed away in 1954.

Quite a few of the returning migrants first moved to Manitoba before taking up residence in Saskatchewan. One such migrant was William McCartney who was born in Ethel, Ontario, in 1874. After finishing school, he worked on his father's farm for a few years and then emigrated to Michigan where he continued to toil as a farm labourer. Michigan was just a brief sojourn for this young man as he continued moving west, working once again as a farm labourer outside Portage La Prairie, Manitoba. In 1900, William came on an excursion to Moose Jaw to visit his sister. He stayed in the Moose Jaw area for a couple of years labouring on various farms and then in 1902 filed on the northwest quarter of 28-11-19 near Milestone. William worked for Angus Brady and Archie Johnson while proving up his land. That first year he managed to break 10 acres but none were cropped. In 1904 and 1905 he broke another 10 acres each year and managed to crop it all. Twenty more acres were broken in 1906 and the full 50 acres were cropped. That year William received his patent and his house was valued at $140 and his stable, granary, hen house, and well were worth another $250. In the next few years he purchased the remaining three-quarters of section 28 and in 1910 married Bertha Wilkinson. Together they had four children before Bertha died while on vacation in California in 1919. For many years William received weekly papers from his home town in Ontario and his connection with Ethel continued with the migration of friends from the Ethel area to the rural municipality of Caledonia. His neighbour Charles Ames was born on the farm next to that of his father back in Ontario. William lived until 1959, passing away at the age of 86.[38]

Another return migrant who lived in Manitoba before settling in

Saskatchewan was Charles Gillies who was born in Lucknow, Ontario, in 1867. He emigrated as a young man, to Hanna, North Dakota, a community with many ex-Canadians. There he met and married Annie Hunking who came to North Dakota from Toronto and together they had four girls and two boys while in the United States. During that time Charles acquired American citizenship. He worked as a dairyman and owned his own home free of mortgage in 1900. Yet for some unknown reason, Charles and his family left Hanna in 1904 and moved to Winnipegosis in northern Manitoba where he worked on the railway.

In 1910 Charles went to visit his brother George who was living in Wawota, Saskatchewan, and together they decided to file for homestead land in the rural municipality of Happy Valley. He homesteaded on the northeast quarter of 18-1-24 while George filed on the southeast quarter of 19-1-24. Charles's homestead statement of December 1913 indicates that he had once again become a Canadian citizen and that he had left his land for some weeks at a time to labour in Winnipegosis. He and his four children took up permanent residence in April 1912. In 1911, Charles managed to break 18 acres but didn't crop any. The following year he broke 10 acres and cropped 18 and in 1913 he broke 10 more acres and cropped 23. His house that year was valued at $200 and his stable and well were assessed at $100 and $15 respectively. One hundred acres were fenced and valued at $125. Charles received his patent in February 1914 and lived on his homestead until his death in the mid-1920s.[39]

For some, such as William McIntosh, both the United States and Saskatchewan served as stages in a peripatetic migration history which ultimately resulted in a return to the province of his birth. McIntosh was born in Bentick Township, Grey County, Ontario in 1879. In his early twenties he emigrated to Sarles, North Dakota, where he farmed with his stepbrother Peter for eight years. Both Peter and William were followed by their younger brother Fred, who, like William, would eventually return to Ontario. William travelled back to Ontario in 1909 to marry Sarah Elizabeth Orr and then he and his bride moved back to North Dakota. For some unknown reason, they decided to return to Ontario the following year.

In 1913 William and Sarah followed William's oldest brother Jim to Bestville, Saskatchewan, where they filed for homestead on the northeast quarter of 36-17-22 W3. By 2 December 1916, the date of William's statement, they had managed to break 135 acres and clear 80. Their house, barn, two granaries, well, and ten acres that were fenced were valued at $350, $100, $150, $20, and $30 respectively. The patent for the Bestville holding was approved on 2 March 1917. Yet things didn't work out at this location as evidenced by the fact that William and Sarah homesteaded at three different sites over the next six years. In the winter of 1923, they returned to Ontario and lived in Fraserburg for two years before taking up

322 With Scarcely a Ripple

a farm in the Barrie area. In the fall of 1935 they retired from farming and moved into Barrie where Sarah died in 1953 and William died five years later.[40] The local history upon which this vignette is based reveals that six Ontario-born migrants moving to the Hazlet area last lived in the Sarles vicinity before returning to Canada, evidence once again of the importance of community and kinship links in migration.

Several of the Canadian-born moving to the Prairies from the United States learned of their new home prior to their migration by travelling west on a harvest excursion. One such migrant was Francis Cummings, who was born in Kemptville in 1882 and as a young man left for Syracuse, New York, where he worked in a typewriter plant, a watch factory, and as a carpenter. From 1902 to 1909, Cummings made frequent trips west with a group of surveyors. He worked seasonally as a farm labourer near Roleau, Saskatchewan, between 1905 and 1912, and was also was employed by a Regina paving company. Francis filed for a homestead in the rural municipality of Newcombe in 1909 which he sold immediately after proving it up. In 1913 he travelled by rail from Regina to Swift Current and filed on another homestead, the southwest quarter of 6-25-21 W3. His brothers from Ontario often came to visit and joined him in the winters working in logging camps in British Columbia. In January of 1920 Francis married Mary Lavigne of Aylmer, Quebec, and together they had five boys and three girls. Frank died in 1965.[41]

The opportunity to own land was a major factor in the decision to return to Canada. Twenty-four year-old William Hislop of Ontario came to Lakeville Township, Grand Forks County, North Dakota, with his bride Catherine Stewart in 1888. There they had one girl and five boys. After twenty years of farming in North Dakota, William was still unable to garner enough money to purchase his own farm, so in 1909 he travelled to Saskatchewan and filed for homestead entry in the Alsask area. That winter he returned to North Dakota and the following spring he shipped his horses and machinery to his new homestead. He built a house that year and the following spring was joined by his family. By June of 1913, the year he signed his statement, William had broken and cleared 160 acres of his combined homestead and pre-emption, the eastern half of 34-27-29 W3. The statement shows that his house, barn, granary, well, and fencing for 60 acres were worth $500, $200, $100, $20, and $75 respectively. William eventually retired from farming and moved into Alsask.[42]

Many of the returning Canadian-born migrants had several occupations before coming to Saskatchewan. Only 32 percent of the sample who could be traced, a group who for the most part were older and living in adjacent Great Plains states, farmed prior to coming to Saskatchewan. They were followed in descending order by farm labourers, cotton factory workers, lumberjacks, blacksmiths, carpenters, sugar factory labourers, textile mill workers, flour mill workers, and merchants. A wide variety of occupations held by only one of the members in the United States include mechanic, cheese-maker, shipping clerk, land surveyor, tailor, doctor, bank teller, jeweller, lumber business owner, tinsmith, mason, and lawyer. Upon arrival in Saskatchewan, most of the migrants took up farming. A handful continued to practise the occupation they held in the United States.

For the majority of these returning Canadians, the move to their home-stead was the last one they made in their lifetime (Table 73). This was as true for those who had a history of movement as for those who had only made one move to the United States before coming to Saskatchewan. This is somewhat surprising considering the fact that many of them were living in the province during the drought and depression years of the 1930s. Yet many of this group were no longer young by this time and were either reluctant or unable to pick up and start again elsewhere. Those who did leave their homesteads were more likely to move elsewhere in the province than travel outside. Whether this group was typical of all returning Cana-dians is hard to say, especially in light of the bias inherent in local histories towards those who persist over time.

The Migrant Experience in the Rural Municipality of Estevan

A final case study focuses more closely on the experiences of Canadian and American migrants in the rural municipality of Estevan. The city of Este-van is situated approximately ten miles north of the international border, seventy miles west of the Manitoba boundary, and 130 miles southeast of Regina. During the Cretaceous Period, a continental sea covered Saskatch-ewan. Most of the rocks deposited by this sea were marine shales although shales of shoreline origin and sands, clays and coal seams of alluvial plains and swamps were also included in this deposition. At the beginning of the Tertiary Period, a continual uplifting of the Rocky Mountains and the Plains basin deposited sedimentary material that formed the basis of the Ravenscrag Series, the dominant geological formation of southeastern Sas-katchewan. These materials were formed under an alluvial plain which accounts for the existence of clays, sands, and coal seams. The coal deposits are best developed in the area surrounding the present-day city of Estevan. Glacial advances and retreats resulted in deposition of extensive areas of glacial till. As a result, southeastern Saskatchewan is flat to gently undulating and traversed in a northwest-southeast direction by the Souris river valley which occupies a former glacial drainage channel.[43] Although agriculture would become the economic activity around which the region would develop, it was the coal which first attracted white settlers to this area.

That Estevan is a product of the railways is evident from its name, which was formed by the selection of letters from the names of two men promi-nent in the building of the CPR, George Stephen and William Van

Table 73 Persistence Characteristics of Returning Canadians according to their Number of Moves before Settling on their Homesteads

Persistance/mover category[1]	1 Move			2 Moves			3–4 Moves			5 Moves			Totals		
	No.	Row %	Col. %	No.	Row %	Col. %	No.	Row %	Col. %	No.	Row %	Col. %	No.	Row %	Col. %
on homestead or within R.M. for rest of working life	51	62.2	70.8	21	25.6	67.7	6	7.3	60.0	4	4.9	100	82	100	100
moved elsewhere in province	14	70.0	19.4	4	20.0	12.9	2	10.0	20.0	0	0	0	20	100	100
moved elsewhere in Canada	2	28.6	2.8	3	42.9	9.7	2	28.6	20.0	0	0	0	7	100	100
moved to the United States	3	75.0	4.2	1	25.0	3.2	0	0	0	0	0	0	4	100	100
moved to the United States but again returned to Canada	2	50.0	2.8	2	50.0	6.5	0	0	0	0	0	0	4	100	100
Totals	72	100	100	31	100	100	10	100	100	4	100	100	117	100	100

Source: Homestead Records, Local Histories.

[1] not including retirement moves.

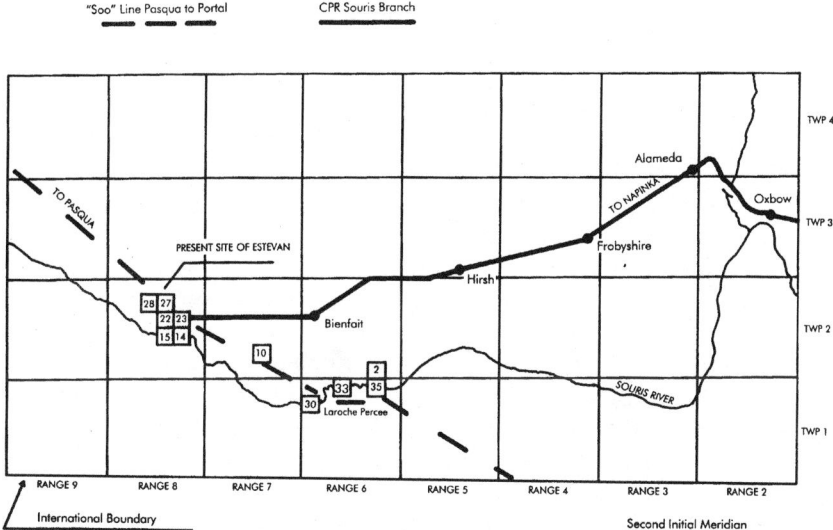

Map 20: Railway routes to Souris Coalfield

Source: Corporate Archives, Canadian National Railway

Horne.[44] Yet well before the community was founded, a number of individuals expressed interest in developing the lignite coal reserves in the area. During the 1880s settlers, many originally from Ontario, moved west from the Manitoba border along the so-called Coalfields Trail, the anticipated rail route for the Manitoba Southwest Colonization Railway. This company received its charter in 1879 and the following year was granted permission to extend its service from Manitoba to the coalfield. Many farmers in the Roche Percee vicinity operated their own coal mines, waiting eagerly for the arrival of the railway. Yet this line, which subsequently was purchased by the CPR, was not completed until 1892 (Map 20).[45]

It was in that year that Estevan was founded. The major players in the establishment of the community were involved in the Dominion Coal Company, who opened a mine on the west side of town. They envisioned the development of an industrial centre based on the coal reserves but their dreams were quickly shattered. The development of the coal industry around Estevan was retarded because the sub-bituminous coal shipped from Alberta and the United States was favoured by the railways and settlers over the lower grade local coal. Development was also restricted because the bulk of coal-burning equipment was adapted only for higher-ranking coals.[46]

The closing of the Dominion mine and a combination of drought and poor markets slowed development in the early 1890s, but growth was again stimulated with the completion of the Soo Line in 1894. Estevan benefited as the junction site for the Soo and Souris branch lines as the capital generated by the railways stimulated business and the coal industry. Good growing seasons and the end of the global depression encouraged agriculture in the region and Estevan profited as the major service centre for the expanding hinterland. The clay soil of the area provided the raw material for the development of the town's brick industry. Free homesteads, agricultural prosperity, and the accessibility afforded by the railways attracted immigrants, particularly Americans and returning Canadians coming from North Dakota, Minnesota, Nebraska, and Iowa. The region also drew migrants from eastern Canada, Manitoba, and other parts of Saskatchewan. Estevan became incorporated as a village in 1899 and by 1901 practically all of the land within eight to ten miles of the railway had been taken. In 1904, the Dominion Lands Agent reported all desirable homesteads taken up within twenty-five miles of any railway in the district. Land prices increased as settlers poured into the area, but that did not deter farmers from purchasing land in order to augment their farming operations. By 1903 half of the homesteaders in southeastern Assiniboia had purchased an adjoining quarter-section of railway land.[47]

The local history, *A Tale That Is Told*, provides information on fifty-four Canadian-born (thirty-four from Ontario, eleven returning from the United States, and nine coming from provinces other than Ontario) and fifty-one American-born settling in the rural municipality of Estevan.[48] Over 47 percent of the latter group were farmers prior to their move, while almost 10 percent were labourers, and another 10 percent came as children. The occupations of 17 percent are unknown, while the remainder filled a wide diversity of positions, including grain buyer, store owner, mill worker, drayman, railroad engineer, grocer, housewife, and livery business owner. Most of these migrants last resided in North Dakota, Minnesota, and Iowa. That many of this group moved to Saskatchewan to enter into agriculture is evident in the fact that 75 percent of American-born listed farming as their primary occupation in Estevan. Three operated stores in town, two ran waterwell drilling businesses, and one each occupied a variety of positions including drayman, carpenter, grain buyer, coal miner, fireman, and machinist. One of this group owned a coal mine, one operated a dray business, and one owned a livery business. Forty-two percent homesteaded, 27.5 percent purchased their land, 5.5 percent rented, and 25 percent did not enter farming. Seventy-six percent of this group remained in the Estevan area for the rest of their lives, but we must realize that the local histories are biased towards those who persist over time. Almost 44 percent of the American-born resided in the rural municipality for over forty years, 33 percent lived there between twenty-one and forty years, 13 percent stayed from ten to twenty years, and 2 percent stayed between six and ten years. Of the 24 percent who did not remain in Estevan, 11 percent moved elsewhere in Saskatchewan, 9 percent moved to British Columbia, and 4 percent returned to the United States.

Canadian-born displayed greater diversity in their occupational profiles both before and after the move to Estevan. Among those internal migrants born in Ontario, 32.4 percent were farmers prior to their coming to Estevan, 8.8 percent were labourers, 8.8 percent were blacksmiths, 5.9 percent were teachers, 5.9 percent came as children, and one each worked as a lumberman, steelworker, chief of police, storeowner, lawyer, housewife, pharmacist, salesman, and stone mason. Only 47 percent of this group listed farming as their major occupation after their move, while two went into retailing. One each worked primarily as a carpenter, implement dealer, clerk, grain buyer, teacher, engineer, labourer, pharmacist, undertaker, salesman, stone mason, and judge. One man owned a flour mill, one owned a real estate business, and one operated a hardware store. Eight of the Ontarians purchased their property upon arrival and six took up homesteads. Almost 83 percent of this group stayed in the rural municipality for the remainder of their lives. Over 31 percent of Ontarians lived in Estevan for over forty years, 40 percent resided in the rural municipality between twenty-one and forty years, 8.6 percent stayed between eleven and twenty years, 3 percent stayed for six to ten years, and another 3 percent lived in Estevan for less than five years.

Among the eleven Canadian-born return migrants, four were farmers in the United States, two were labourers, one was a sailor on a Great Lakes vessel, one was a lumberman in Minnesota, and one was a police inspector. Seven of these migrants took up farming, one worked as drayman, one was a veterinarian, one was a contractor, and one was a salesman. Six of the farmers homesteaded while the other purchased his original holding. Eight remained in Estevan for the remainder of their lives. Seven lived in the rural municipality for over forty years, two resided in Estevan for a period of twenty-one to forty years, and two lived there for eleven to twenty years.

Among the nine internal Canadian-born migrants from outside Ontario, seven came from Quebec. Two were children when they made the move and the occupation of one other is unknown. One each worked as a farmer, teacher, clerk, lumberman, carpenter, and lawyer. Six of this group took up farming in the rural municipality, one worked as a carpenter, one was a pharmacist, and the other was a lawyer. Three of the farmers purchased their land while the other three homesteaded. Seven re-mained in Estevan for the rest of their lives. Five lived there for over forty years, two resided in Estevan for twenty-one to forty years, one lived there for eleven to 20 years, and the remaining person stayed there less than ten years.

Although the local histories are very useful in capturing the patterns of return and internal Canadian migration and American emigration to western Canada, they say little about the settlement experiences of these groups. Fortunately, some of the accounts provide the reader with greater insight into the reasons for migration. For example, 27-year-old John M.

Denton of Emerson, Iowa, left that community in 1909 and settled in the Corrine area about twenty miles south of Regina. A year later, he and his family moved a short distance to Lang, where he homesteaded. In 1919, John and his family sold their farm and moved back to Emerson. Yet, as the local history recounts, "they found everything changed to what they had been used to and they decided to return to Canada." The following year they came to Estevan, where John was employed by Prairie Nurseries in the spring and summer and worked on a threshing crew in the fall. He later worked as a drayman and in winter hauled coal. During the war, John was employed by the CNR and afterwards worked a rented farm with his son. After thirty-seven years in Estevan, John died in 1957 at the age of 69.

Twenty-eight-year-old Frank Durick, born in Andover, South Dakota, came to Estevan in 1904. Prior to this move, he taught school in Pierpont, South Dakota, and homesteaded near Columbus, North Dakota, a few miles south of the Canadian border. He followed his brother Michael and some of his neighbours across the line and homesteaded in the Forest Glen school district on the southeast quarter of 20-1-7 W2. The local history includes notes from his son William, which give us insight into the nature of cross-border relations during this period.

Who living along the border had not smuggled at some time? The amount of traffic of goods across the border depended on the price differences in the U.S. and Canada. Woolen goods were usually cheaper in Canada for the Americans. While the return on farm products was usually greater in the States. As people on both sides were neighbours and attended one's dances and parties the exchange of foreign goods was common. Horses and wagons did not carry licence plates and so even grain and livestock sometimes crossed the border.[49]

Bill Hill was born in Bruce County, Ontario, in 1872 but moved with his family to Glenboro, in the Carberry district of Manitoba before 1880. Bill left home at the tender age of 12 and eventually took up a homestead in North Dakota. Besides farming, Hill took a turn as deputy marshall. In 1902, he married a girl from Rolla, North Dakota, sold his farm for $2,000, and moved to Saskatchewan where he homesteaded a quarter of section 34 in the fourth township of the second range in Alameda. The local history intimates that he was attracted by the opportunity to acquire free land. Bill's wife died in 1909, leaving him and their four boys, the youngest two dying shortly thereafter. In 1912 Bill and the two remaining boys moved into the town of Estevan, where he served one year on the police force. He then started a contracting and building moving business which he ran until he retired in 1946.

Despite the problems associated with the homestead records (see the Appendix), they are useful for examining the characteristics of many of the original settlers in the study area. The homesteaders who patented land in the rural municipality of Estevan arrived primarily after the construction of the Soo Line. Of those twenty-three entering their homestead before 1894, twenty-one were Canadians, all moving within Canada and most born in Ontario. Most of these early homesteads were located adjacent or close to the proposed Souris branch leading eastward into Manitoba. Only two settlers homesteaded between 1895 and 1899, although several others purchased land adjacent to the Soo and Souris rail lines.

The greatest influx of homesteaders (75.4 percent) patenting their property arrived during the 1900–4 period. Over 50 percent of all the homesteaders were not the original settlers on their quarter-sections; in fact, many were not even the second pioneer listed in the records. But all those previous settlers abandoned the homestead for various reasons. Over 86 percent of the other European-born homesteaders came during this period, followed by 83.3 percent of the British, 80.3 percent of the Scandinavians, 80 percent of the returning Canadian-born, 78.5 percent of the American-born, and 68.1 percent of the internal Canadian-born migrants. Many of the European-born migrants had previously resided in the United States. This rapid influx of settlers infiltrated all parts of the rural municipality. American-born were distributed widely although almost 48 percent located in the townships close to the border (Table 74). Almost 32 percent of the American-born had Swedish and Norwegian last names and so a significant degree of this migration can also be viewed as second-generation Scandinavian as well as first-generation American. Scandinavians were even more concentrated in these border townships, with 27.9 percent in Township 1, Range 7, 18 percent in Township 1, Range 8, and 14.8 percent in Township 1, Range 9. In contrast, Canadian-born were oriented more towards the north of the rural municipality with 40.1 percent homesteading in the third range of townships, 36.2 percent in the second tier, and 23.6 percent in the border townships.

The reasons for this geographic distribution of homesteaders involve many factors, some of which remain hidden from objective analysis. The fact that most homesteaders among all nativity groups filed for entry during the 1900–4 period indicates that date of settlement is not an important factor explaining this pattern. Except for the wooded slopes along the Souris, the region consisted of prairie grasses and so vegetative cover would seem not to be an important factor in location. Estevan lies in the dark brown soil region. North of the Souris River, medium-textured loam soils on glacial till modified by underlying shales dominate. Light-textured fine sandy soils on glacial lake alluvial deposits comprise most of the first townships of ranges 7 and 8 in the southeast corner of the rural municipality. Half of the first township of Range 9 consists of medium to heavy clay loams on glacial till moderated by underlying shales. These Trossach soils are less capable of supporting wheat cultivation but they are by no means unworkable. In many areas the topography is gently undulating to

Table 74 Location of Homesteaders by Township and Nativity, Estevan R.M.

Nativity	Twp1-R7			Twp2-R7			Twp3-R7			Twp1-R8			Twp2-R8		
	No.	Row %	Col. %	No.	Row %	Col. %	No.	Row %	Col. %	No.	Row %	Col. %	No.	Row %	Col. %
Scandinavian	17	27.9	28.3	4	6.6	6.9	3	4.9	5.4	11	18.0	20.0	2	3.3	4.9
British	1	5.6	1.7	6	33.3	10.3	1	5.6	1.8	1	5.6	1.8	0	0	0
Other European	1	3.4	1.7	1	3.4	1.7	1	3.4	1.8	1	3.4	1.8	3	10.3	7.3
American	31	19.0	51.7	18	11.0	31.0	8	4.9	14.3	25	15.3	45.5	5	3.1	12.2
Internal Canadian	8	4.4	13.3	24	13.2	41.4	42	23.1	75.0	16	8.8	29.1	31	17.0	75.6
Returning Canadian	2	13.3	3.3	5	33.3	8.6	1	6.7	1.8	1	6.7	1.8	0	0	0
Totals	60	12.8	100	58	12.4	100	56	12.0	100	55	11.8	100	41	8.8	100

Nativity	Twp3-R8			Twp1-R9			Twp2-R9			Twp3-R9			Totals		
	No.	Row %	Col. %	No.	Row %	Col. %	No.	Row %	Col. %	No.	Row %	Col. %	No.	Row %	Col. %
Scandinavian	3	4.9	7.0	9	14.8	15.5	3	4.9	7.7	9	14.8	15.5	61	100	13.0
British	2	11.1	4.7	2	11.1	3.4	4	22.2	10.3	1	5.6	1.7	18	100	3.8
Other European	8	27.6	18.6	6	20.7	10.3	1	3.4	2.6	7	24	12.1	29	100	6.2
American	11	6.7	25.6	22	13.5	37.9	20	12.3	51.3	23	14.1	39.7	163	100	34.8
Internal Canadian	16	8.8	37.2	19	10.4	32.8	11	6	28.2	15	8	25.9	182	100	38.9
Returning Canadian	3	20.0	7.0	0	0	0	0	0	0	3	20	5.2	15	100	3.2
Totals	43	9.2	100	58	12.4	100	39	8	100	58	12	100	468	100	–

Source: Homestead Records.

nearly level and most land is well drained, although there are a number of "burn out" pits, low knolls, and poorly drained flats and sloughs.[50] Yet, given the significant degree of uniformity, soil quality and topography would also seem to have played an insignificant role in location. Relations among these groups were generally harmonious and so they had little reason to avoid each other. Much of the land adjacent to the railways was homesteaded and purchased prior to the homesteader boom and so the influence of the railway would seem to be minimal in explaining the relative concentrations of the Scandinavians and Americans along the border and the Canadians north of the town of Estevan.

I suspect such geographic patterns are explained primarily by chain and cluster migration, although sporadic designation of kinship affiliation in the records makes such an assertion difficult to prove. Almost 24 percent of the American-born homesteaders shared the same last name with one or more of their fellow Americans, twenty-eight quarter-sections were occupied by American-born located adjacent to quarter-sections held by American-born with the same last name, and six American-born homesteaders with Scandinavian surnames located adjacent to Scandinavian-born settlers with the same last name, suggesting that a number of Scandinavians and Americans arrived with parents and children who filed in close proximity to one another. Almost 60 percent of those homestead records listing last place of origin for American-born and Scandinavian-born migrants include communities just across the border in North Dakota such as Bowbells, Bottineau County, and Kenmare. Of the eleven internal Canadian migrants for whom the homestead records list last place of residence, five came from somewhere else in the prairie region. Just over 19 percent of the internal Canadian-born homesteaders shared the same surname with one or more of their group, suggesting that a significant number of this group came to Estevan with other members of their families. Thirty-six quarter-sections were occupied by Canadians located adjacent to quarter-sections inhabited by people with the same last name, indicating that internal Canadian migrants also followed or accompanied relatives to Saskatchewan. This largely explains the clustering of this group in the northern part of the rural municipality. By contrast, only two among the returning Canadians shared the same surname.

The overwhelming majority of the homesteaders were male (Table 75). Seventy-five percent of the returning Canadians were married, reflecting the fact that this group was generally older, although ranking second in average age to those born in Britain. Internal Canadian migrants were generally younger than other homesteaders, indicating perhaps that for many of this group the move to Estevan represented the first, and what many hoped would be the last, significant stage in their migration histories. In contrast, many of the European-born were experienced in long distance migration, having come to America before emigrating to Estevan. The fact

Table 75 Estevan R.M. No. 5 Homesteader Characteristics by Nativity Group[1]

| Nativity | Sex | | | | % Married | No. of children for married homesteaders | | Age at entry (known) | | Age at patent (known) | | average no. of years before entry and patent issue |
| | Males | | Females | | | | | | | | | |
	No.	%	No.	%		ave.	s.d	ave.	s.d.	ave.	s.d.	
Canadian (internal)	178	97.8	4	2.2	54.8	4.4	2.5	31.6	10.5	36.2	10.7	4.8
Canadian (return)[3]	15	100	0	0	75.0	3.0	2.8	38.3	11.8	41.5	12.6	3.5
American	161	98.8	2	1.2	56.9	3.1	2.6	35.1	13.9	38.6	14.2	3.5
British[4]	18	100	0	0	57.1	2.3	1.0	41.8	13.4	45.6	12.8	3.7
Scandinavian[5]	58	95.1	3	4.9	49.2	2.4	1.4	35.4	13.7	39.3	23.3	4.3

| Nativity | $ value of all known improvements at statement[2] | | No. of cattle at statement | | No. of horses at statement | | No. of acres broken at statement | | No. of acres cropped at statement | |
	ave.	range	ave.	s.d.	ave.	s.d.	ave.	range	ave.	range
Canadian (internal)	868.55	10–1400	4.7	12.6	3.6	6.2	46.0	0–160	38.1	0–160
Canadian (return)[3]	349.33	80–700	3.1	4.2	3.1	1.9	62.2	25–110	51.5	18–80
American	350.08	20–2060	4	6.8	3.6	3.7	61.2	0–160	49.8	0–160
British[4]	495.83	0–1950	6.9	9.5	3.4	3.2	50.8	16–110	35.9	16–70
Scandinavian[5]	279.15	0–1150	3.6	5.5	2.5	2.9	57.6	0–145	48.8	1–145

Source: Homestead Records.

[1] not including other Europeans.

[2] houses, farm buildings, fences, wells, etc.

[3] never relinquished citizenship (N=4); American citizens (N=3); re-acquired Canadian citizenship (N=8).

[4] English-born–11, Irish-born–5; Welsh-born–1, Scottish-born–1, migrating from the U.S.–7.

[5] Norwegian/Swedish–45.9% emigrated to Saskatchewan from the United States.

that Canadian-born homesteaders had the largest families indicates that many of them were still in the child-rearing life-cycle stage, while many in the other groups had already experienced the departure of their older children prior to their move to western Canada. Yet we must recognize that over 50 percent of the Scandinavian-born and almost half of the internal Canadian migrants, American-born, and British-born were single. For the most part, unmarried homesteaders were younger than average.

Returning Canadians ranked first in terms of acreage broken and cropped, followed closely by American-born, and then by Scandinavian-born, British-born, and (internal) Canadian-born. Yet while the latter group registered lowest in terms of acreage cleared and cropped, they ranked well above the rest in terms of mean value of all known improvements at the time of their patent. In addition, they rate first (tied with American-born) in average number of horses and second to the British in average number of cattle. Thus, Canadians present a bit of a puzzle because one would expect the youngest families with the largest number of children and the lowest clearing rates to be among the poorest. Concrete reasons for this apparent anomaly cannot be discerned from the evidence at hand, but two possible explanations are offered. Canadians on average took longer to file for patent than other groups and so it is conceivable that some used this extra time to build farm buildings, wells, and fences. This might explain the higher average value for improvements and the lower average clearance and cropping rates.

The other possible explanation rests with the other homesteader groups. For a number of reasons, many of these individuals may have come to Canada with less capital in hand. Those who came directly from Europe may have spent a lot of their savings in getting to Estevan. Most European- and American-born came from north central states such as North Dakota, where adverse climatic conditions and rapidly increasing land prices in the late 1890s reduced farm income and made it more difficult for parents to provide for children. It is also possible that some of these groups from the United States had incurred expenses upon transferring land and/or capital to family members not accompanying them to Canada. But these explanations can only be conjectures.

Thus the homestead records present several difficulties in the study of migration and settlement. Yet they remain the richest source of information in the context of western Canada. I decided to link these records with the landholder information present in the Cummins Rural Directory Maps in order to trace persistence over time. The Cummins Map Company of Winnipeg, founded by Oliver F. Coumins (who later changed his name to Cummins), was a private business producing directory maps for commercial use. Originally located in Regina, this company began producing landowner maps based on local assessment rolls for the three prairie provinces in 1917. Although no one is certain about the rationale behind their selection of rural areas to be mapped, the primary market for the maps seems to have been residents of the regions shown, suggesting that Cummins mapped relatively heavily settled areas and avoided the sparsely populated southwestern part of Saskatchewan. The success of the 1917 series prompted them to expand their efforts into Ontario and Prince Edward Island and to create maps for 1918, 1920, 1926, and 1930, after which the depression felled the company. The original map series for 1917, 1920, 1922, 1926, and 1930 are available in the Saskatchewan Archives in Regina with a microfilm copy of the 1918 series.

I first consulted the Land Location Index to determine the file numbers for each homestead. I examined each homestead file and then traced each homesteader through the 1917, 1920, 1922, and 1926 Cummins maps (the 1930 map is not available). Table 76 clearly illustrates the notable transiency that characterized the homesteading period, even among those who stayed long enough to prove up their land. Scandinavian-born and internal Canadian migrants displayed a greater propensity to remain in situ; but there was considerable turnover among all groups, even when accounting for disappearance from the Cummins maps because of death. According to Conzen and Voisey, those settlers who had a "supplementary occupation" were considered to have greater economic stability, which, in turn, resulted in greater persistence.[51] For this study, supplementary occupation was taken to mean any additional seasonal work undertaken when absent from the homestead during the proving-up period for three to four months a year. A majority of the homesteaders worked off their homestead during their proving-up period (68.6 percent of the Canadians, 57.1 percent of the returning Canadians, 50.7 percent of the Americans, 50 percent of the other European group, 46.2 percent of the Scandinavians, and 33.3 percent of the British). Most worked in the vicinity, either in the coal mines of Bienfait, Roche Percee, or Coalfield, or as farm labourers for relatives or others. Yet homesteaders engaging in such activity were not more likely to persist than those who had always resided on their homestead land. Relative uniformity in terms of age profiles and land quality would seem to indicate that these factors did not play a significant role in determining persistence among the various nativity groups, but much remains hidden behind the statistics presented in Table 76.

A closer examination of Canadian-born moving within Canada shows that age was not a discriminator between persistent and transient (internal) Canadians as the average age and age standard deviation at date of patent was 34.9 and 35.3 for those persisting in Estevan until 1917, and 35.8 and 38.8 for those not present in the 1917 Cummins map (not including those settlers over the age of 65 who may have possibly died before this date). While the average Canadian persister (until 1917) only had $245.57 worth of improvements as compared to $465.29 for Canadian transients, the standard deviations for the former was $257.60 and

Table 76   Persistence among Homesteaders Receiving Patents before 1917 by National Origin, Estevan R.M. No. 5

Nativity	1917 %	1920 %	1922 %	1926 %
American	38.8	26.4	24.9	18.4
British	54.5	27.3	27.3	13.3
Canadian (internal)	41.5	32.8	27.9	20.8
Canadian (return)	20	13.3	13.3	0
other European	33.3	25	20.8	12.5
Scandinavian	57.9	42.1	39.5	26.3

Sources: Cummins Rural Directory Maps, 1917, 1920, 1922, 1926; Homestead Records.

$688.10 for the latter, indicating that those deciding to leave Estevan before 1917 varied greatly in terms of capital invested in improvements. Returning Canadians were less persistent in Estevan than internal Canadians, a fact that may be explained in part by their generally older ages (i.e., some may have died or moved elsewhere to retire before 1917), or their generally poorer situation as measured in terms of value of improvements and number of livestock. Yet evidence presented in the Border Crossing Records and the 1901 manuscript census for Assiniboia seem to indicate that returning Canadians were not substantially different than other Canadians or Americans in terms of income and property held, in spite of what was reported by the small number of returning Canadians homesteading in Estevan. While it is possible that acquisition of additional land encouraged persistence among Canadians and other groups, the cost of searching property records and assessment rolls ($2 per search) proved to be too great to pursue this inquiry.

Again the limitations of the homestead records and the difficulties associated with linking this and other sources clouds our understanding of the settlement experience of Canadians in Saskatchewan. But the evidence that is available seems to point to the presence of kinship not only as the most important factor in location but also in determining persistence. Over 47 percent of those internal Canadian migrants persisting until 1917 shared the same surname as another member within this group. Over 51 percent of this group were recorded in the 1926 Cummins map and of this number, 57 percent shared the same last name. The presence of kinship ties afforded by geographical proximity, itself the result of chain and cluster migration, discouraged turnover among Canadians and most likely among other nativity groups as well. The fact that only two of the returning Canadian group shared the same surname indicates that individuals not following relatives to Estevan dominated this group. Of course, the influence of friends in location or mobility decisions remains hidden from view.

CONCLUSION

While the data sources and strategies employed provide insight into the nature and pattern of Canadian and American migration to the Canadian prairies, they fail to reveal much about the settlement experiences of these groups. Such a detailed analysis awaits the release of the 1911 and 1921 manuscript censuses, which will make possible the tracing of persisters over time, and an intensive examination of assessment and property records, which will allow the researcher to understand better the circumstances and strategies of those who chose to move on. Only then will we be able to appreciate social and geographical mobility, agricultural production, property behaviour, family structure, and social class in this new frontier.

Pembina, North Dakota, 1897
(State Historical Society, North Dakota Heritage Center/Col.709-34)

PART FOUR

Conclusion

8 A Wall of Mirrors: Meanings and Interpretations of the Voyage

> We are not in the same boat but we are pretty much in the same waters.
> – Arthur Meighen, quoted in *Between Friends*, NFB documentary

> I may not know who I am, but I know where I am from.
> – Wallace Stegner, *Wolf Willow*

Writing any book is a personal journey. Just as the individual act of migration is an emotional as well as a physical odyssey, so has this voyage been. Tracing the experiences of Anglo-Canadian migrants at the turn of the twentieth century has prompted me to consider the significance not only of their movement but also of the place of "English" Canada within North America. And in this context, the study of the past has both clarified and confused the present.

In many ways, this has been an impossible task. Of all the immigrant groups in the United States, Anglo-Canadians were and continue to be the most invisible. There exists a widely held impression that Canadians and Americans are neighbours, similar in culture, economy, and composition, living in relative harmony with but little to distinguish them. So many elements of both societies are alike that the differences that exist are often hidden from view. Some argue that of all the regions in Canada, only Quebec can be distinguished as a nation unto itself, the implication being that the rest of Canada is the presence of an absence. In addition, the difficulty of finding sources that would allow one to break through this veil of invisibility has discouraged examination of this particular group.

The similarities between English Canada and the United States and the ease of passage across the border have meant that Canadians, both francophone and anglophone, and Americans have been unusually responsive to displacement and demand forces in effect in both countries at different times and that the act of migration has not exacted the degree of commitment required of other immigrants. Certain images of migration appear permanently etched in the national memory of the United States: fatigued immigrants waiting in line at Ellis Island, turn-of-the-century

340 With Scarcely a Ripple

tenements, millions of newcomers pulling themselves up by enormous effort in a land where such exertion is rewarded. But Anglo-Canadians are rarely included in this collection. Theirs was not a transatlantic adventure story but a less dramatic tale of movement. Over the years, millions have crossed the border in search of improved opportunities, although for many this movement was a strategy to maintain stability, whether for economic or family reasons. At several points along the border, trains, ferries, and automobiles cross with scarcely any more delay than in passing state or provincial lines. Many in the past chose to walk or drive their sleighs across the ice in winter. And so in physical terms, the "line" has always been inconsequential. But how significant has it been in economic and emotional terms?

THE BORDER

As much as I wanted to, I could not avoid the conundrum this question posed in my investigation of Anglo-Canadian migrants. The border metaphor materialized again and again in my mind, prompting me to reflect upon its significance in the context of this research. How should I approach this metaphor? What does it mean?

Geographers study boundaries both objectively and subjectively for what they reveal about landscape elements of neighbouring states and as part of larger investigations into relationships between those adjacent political units. The scientist classifies and defines, while the humanist considers the symbolic meanings of an artificial creation. To the empiricist, the Canadian-American border is understood by pertinent facts: at 5,524 miles, it is the longest continuous boundary line in the world; and with 130 crossing stations and more than 100 million people and over $200 billion in goods and services crossing each year, it is the busiest border on the planet.[1] To the humanist, this boundary can only be understood as an interpreted emotional experience, a symbolic marker defining a Canadian community, at least an Anglo-Canadian community.

The border itself is not a living entity, imbued with meaning; it is the people who live along it who give the border symbolic significance. The fact that 75 percent of all Canadians and only 12 percent of Americans live within one hundred miles of the border explains to some extent its greater influence on the lives of those who live north of the line. Yet more important than geographical propinquity is what the border represents to Canadians for the development of a "historically and geographically specific social system."[2]

Canada as a "historically contingent society," developing within the context of its own internal evolution, has always framed its "becoming" in its changing political, economic, and cultural relationships with the United States. The relationship with the United States functions as a barometer by which Anglo-Canadians measure their evolving identity. This is not surprising given the complex and varied nature of the ties linking various transborder regions. French Canadians have developed their own cultural boundaries within the country, shields serving to strengthen their own sense of national identity. At the same time, regional separation within Canada resulting from cultural plurality and geographical isolation, producing in effect internal borders, combined with different kinds of relationships with American border regions to create a variable settlement experience, produce different levels of attachment to the idea of Canada, and elicit different interpretations of the symbolic meaning of the border.

Borders, the one shared with the United States and those created internally, frame the Anglo-Canadian identity. Identity is a concept that is both discovered and invented. The Anglo-Canadian identity is not easily understood even by those who attempt to create it. The fact that the country exists in a dialectic of regional and ethnic tensions further complicates the search for identity. These internal borders of religious and ethnic division are reinforced by geographical separation and socio-economic distinction both within and between regions.

Yet it is misleading to view the Anglo-Canadians of the late nineteenth century as a completely fractious group, united only by common language. Despite their limited identities and regional outlooks,[3] Anglo-Canadians from every region created almost all of the country's political and legal infrastructure, systems borrowed from Britain but amended here. British ethnicity and loyalty to the mother country served as unifying forces but, as Akenson emphasizes, such identification was multi-dimensional and dynamic. British immigrants, he argues, did not identify with a monolithic British culture but instead associated with several distinct and perhaps even incompatible Anglo-Celtic cultures found in their homeland. In Canada, Australia, and New Zealand, Akenson maintains, "the melding of the several Anglo-Celtic cultures to establish a new and synthetic 'British' culture was coterminous with the creation of new national identities."[4] In other words, those of British origin were creating a culture in Canada not existing in Britain. Over time, disparate Anglo-Celtic cultures, sustained by Canada's geography, combined to produce a not easily defined but nevertheless substantial English-Canadian culture. This evolution required an infrastructure of institutions that was slow to develop and differed spatially and temporally in terms of impact. Eventually this culture served to create an association with the whole that transcended the region and increasingly replaced the affiliation with the past as represented by Britain.

Yet even as this evolution was taking place, Canada was increasingly influenced by the American presence. "The presence of American ideas and culture enlarged the English Canadian frame of reference ... their thought acquired a continental dimension which came to equal in importance the national and imperial sense in determining the lines along which the English Canadian outlook would be oriented."[5] Transplanted

British ideals and developing Canadian culture were juxtaposed against the growing presence of American culture and ideas. The contradictions, paradoxes, and complexities inherent in this compound extended the Anglo-Canadian's outlook beyond the region but at the same time presented a complicated and confusing cultural base upon which to erect a framework of identity. The region, Canada, Great Britain, and the United States served as the compass points of the voyager's experience as he set sail on his journey.

Regrettably, I was unable to discern the psychological dimensions of the voyage and had to appease myself with outward impressions as revealed in the chosen sources and tracing strategies. In addition, the study is not an examination of Anglo-Canadian mobility in all its forms and regional variations; it emphasizes in particular the persistence and migration experiences of Ontarians. While case histories are illuminating and reveal much about the circumstances and consequences of this migration, they do not allow us to draw broad conclusions about the adjustments made by the group as a whole. As such, our comprehension of this significant migration remains a blur but I would like to think this research has added structure, scale, and detail to our understanding.

THE CONTEXT OF MOBILITY

Most have viewed nineteenth-century mobility as primarily the result of immigration and natural increase. These two elements combined to produce unfavourable population/land ratios, which in turn served to push people out of the countryside and into the cities. David Gagan's influential book, *Hopeful Travellers*, focused on the question of continuing access to farm land and the associated dilemma of family inheritance. The crisis, as Gagan describes it, produced altered family strategies and inheritance patterns and stimulated out-migration.[6] Yet Ontario cities were slow to industrialize and thus unable to absorb this influx. As a consequence, many were impelled to seek opportunities elsewhere. For many, elsewhere meant the United States.

This is a uncomplicated and efficient interpretation, and contains a considerable degree of truth, but it is too simple. Upon closer inspection, we see a context that is much more complex than generally conceived. Revisionist studies of nineteenth-century Ontario reveal not uniformity but highly differentiated processes, which form the context of mobility. The decisions of persisters and movers must be seen against this varied and dynamic background. Marvin McInnis's overview of Ontario farms in 1861 shows a dominance of owner-occupied family farms between 70 and 170 acres, with few either very small or very large. He suggests that the Ontario farm economy was broadly egalitarian and devoid largely of either landless labourers or a landed elite.[7] Donald Akenson shows that many Irish

Catholics did not cluster in urban centres but instead settled in rural parts of the province, challenging the assumption that these particular immigrants served to swell the ranks of the urban proletariat.[8]

In the most critical challenge to traditional interpretations of Ontario's development to date, Darroch and Soltow demonstrate on the basis of their analysis of the 1871 manuscript censuses that propertied wealth was widely dispersed in Ontario even though there were considerable local variations. In 1871 about half of all adults owned land together with their own dwelling, and many more could expect to own property in time. While forces of changes acted to displace many, considerable numbers managed to achieve their quest for landed security.[9] This and previous studies by Akenson and Bruce Elliott[10] downplay the crisis in land availability argument and instead emphasize the means by which families attained and maintained landed status. Both persistence and migration, they show, were strategies revolving around the goal of providing family security.

My analysis of the Quinte families reinforces this argument. While earlier portraits of Ontario as a stable, rooted society were extreme, so too are more recent studies which focus almost exclusively on the notable geographical mobility of the population. That such a considerable degree of transiency existed is not surprising when, as Akenson argues, we consider that Ontarians "lived on a continent of frontiers."[11] Yet not everyone was a Wilson Benson, Michael Katz's famous prototype, who moved at least sixteen times and experienced over thirty occupational shifts. He and many others, Katz argues, were social flotsam, bouncing like atoms from job to job and place to place.[12] Movement for many had a purpose and was directed by social associations as well as perceived opportunities. What also emerges from this study is the fact that, despite such a high degree of population turnover, many individuals and families persisted in place. Rather than focusing exclusively on mobility, we need to balance the scales by recognizing the importance of persistence in development. Unless we trace the experiences of persisters and transients, then any comment regarding these related subjects is pointless. And only by recognizing the positive aspects of Ontario's development as well as the negative dimensions will we be able to achieve a more balanced picture of mobility strategies.

MIGRATION PATTERNS

The nature of this movement reflects a Ravenstein world in many ways, largely because his "laws" were a reflection of late nineteenth-century society. Several of his principles apply to this migration, including the importance of the economic motive, the friction of distance, the rural-urban directional focus, movement by stages, return migration, and the age and sex selectivity of the migration flow. Canadians leapfrogged to particular locations, usually not too distant, creating nodes from which they or their direct descendants migrated to newly opened areas. North America was an abundant migratory environment for native- and foreign-born alike. While it would be glib to say that the decision to emigrate was undertaken effortlessly, Canadians for the most part did not experience the same fateful sense of finality that many Europeans did. While an ocean separated European immigrants from their loved ones, only an accessible and porous border separated Canadians from family, friends, and home towns.

Many Europeans who came to Canada were in transit to American destinations, although some of this group did not continue across the border because of intervening opportunities. The fact that a significant number of European-born in the Index to Border Entries sample acquired Canadian citizenship before emigrating to the United States may be viewed as evidence of some connection with Canada. However, issues of citizenship and loyalty were probably not very significant to this group.

Most Anglo-Canadians moved in clearly defined streams determined by social and economic circumstances and family relationships. Inter-regional, intra-regional, and continental migration were framed by three concurrent processes: the decomposition of established rural societies, the expansion of urban-industrial opportunities, and the opening of new frontiers. While many who left their homes earlier in the nineteenth century hoped to preserve or expand their status as farmers, the majority of migrants following them sought opportunity in towns and cities either within their region or elsewhere. The catalyst for such movement was the displacement resulting from increasingly unfavourable human/land ratios or the increasing demand for labour in growing urban centres. As capital searched for investment opportunities, certain policies contributed to uneven economic development across North America, creating peripheries from which labour migrated and cores to which these workers moved. Yet we must be careful not to overemphasize the images of a crisis in access to land and dependence on staples exports so often associated with Ontario's development. Nor must we view individuals, families, and communities as completely dependent on forces of modernization. People and communities adjusted to change and actively participated in developing strategies to ensure some degree of continuity. Some were relatively successful, others were not; but what is important to realize is that they all attempted to mediate change.

The consequences of out-migration for origin communities varied. For many of the smaller centres, this selective outflow generated lower tax bases, aberrant sex ratios, unbalanced dependency ratios, and an increasingly aged population. The overall erosion of the rural community and general economic malaise could not have been unaffected by this demographic bleeding. Yet despite the stagnation and decline of many rural areas, many chose to remain in their regions of birth, taking advantage of the opportunities, however limited, that were present. In this context, the co-operation between and the support of families played a major role in ensuring persistence in place.

Many Canadians in eastern borderland states, unrestrained by distance, went home often. Migration to these areas from the Maritimes, Quebec, and Ontario was largely labour-seeking and more likely to include seasonal movement, whereas western migration was generally land-seeking. An unspecified but significant number of those moving to the upper midwest and the Great Plains regions migrated north across the border to take advantage of free homestead land in western Canada. This movement differs considerably from the classic return migration identified by Ravenstein. The majority of Canadian-born migrating from the United States to Saskatchewan were not returning to their home communities or even their regions of origin but instead were moving to another frontier which happened to be part of the country from which they originated. Affiliation with Canada may have played some role in the return migrants' decision-making, but besides the recollections of a limited sample in the local histories, we have no way of determining the relative importance of this factor. It is very clear that economic opportunity and the presence of kin and kith were influential factors in their decisions to move north of the forty-ninth parallel.

Canadian migration streams were self-sustaining. Because the distances for most were so often short, it was family and economic ties that mattered. People followed family and friends and economic opportunity and the border was not much of an impediment. For many Canadians, movement back and forth across the line was not unusual. The arrival of railways and the opening of new frontiers spurred longer-distance migration, and movement over time became more frequent and more urban-oriented. Yet migration for most remained short-distance even though the cumulative span of migration increased.

Besides attracting Canadian-born living in the United States, the settlement boom in western Canada at the turn of the century also attracted large numbers of people from the eastern part of the country, particularly from Ontario. This in effect changed the nature of internal migration in the country. Such movement was previously short-distance, rural-urban in orientation, and often proceeded in stages. But after the opening up of the west it became long-distance, rural in direction, and was frequently direct in character. Many did, however, move in stages, migrating to Manitoba and other parts of the prairies before taking up their land in Saskatchewan, the focus of our analysis.

The family continued to play an important role in migration throughout the nineteenth century, adapting to changes taking place in society. Within Ontario, inter-vivos and post-mortem transfers of property earlier in the century made possible by more readily available and less expensive land ensured greater persistence rates among children within regions of birth.

Because property was transferred primarily among the male line, daughters who married were more likely to move away from their birthplace. Yet transient males were as likely to move with or join female or maternal kin as they were to move with or join male kin. Kinship was a dominant mechanism in the increased movement out of the region taking place later in the century. Channels of migration were determined in large part by the advice, shelter, credit, jobs, and emotional support given by family members who had moved previously. Whatever the migration context, short-distance or long-distance, rural- or urban-directed, it is apparent that Anglo-Canadian families wanted to remain in close proximity to one another and so location decisions were often circumscribed by family considerations.

MIGRANT EXPERIENCES

Can we suppose a universal Anglo-Canadian immigrant experience? The answer based on this research is a qualified no. Anglo-Canadians differed in their degree of integration into the religious, economic, political, and social dimensions of American society. Such processes of integration and cultural survival were related to the size, composition, and structure of communities of origin and destination as well as personal characteristics of migrants such as age, sex, and family position. What appears to be consistent among most migrants is the importance assigned to the role of the family. The Anglo-Canadian family both facilitated and survived the migration.

The opinion of the host society towards immigrant groups is an important contextual variable of migration as it influenced ethnic association and integration as well as mobility patterns. American attitudes in the selected reception centres conformed to those held widely at this time, although it appears that Grand Forks was more inclined than Watertown and Syracuse to embrace all immigrant groups. Most Anglo-Canadians belonged to the white, Anglo-Saxon, Protestant majority in North America and thus cannot be identified with the conventional assimilative model that assumes the incorporation of "alien" groups into the host society. They were received very well in American society, so well in fact that they were looked upon as family rather than strangers. Anglophone Canada was perceived as being part of a larger North American community and thus Canadians fit the criteria to become good Americans. Certainly, the cultural-political context of this sense of common community and common identity was more one of continental expansion than of welcome accommodation of Anglo-Canadian immigrants. However, given this favourable outlook, it would appear that Anglo-Canadians faced an environment which was welcoming, or at least accommodating.

While the results of this study do not contradict the idea that Anglo-Canadians were one of the most assimilative groups in America, they do permit a reinterpretation of the accepted views of ethnicity and assimilation in terms of the Anglo-Canadian experience. This reinterpretation involves analysis of the immigrant experience at three different levels: the family, community, and ethclass.

The individual immigrant's degree of success in adapting to the change associated with migration varied in accordance with many factors, including nationality, recency of movement, and economic status. For many, however, the family in all its variant forms provided the means of support, economically, socially, and culturally, for newcomers in a new setting. Although they shared certain characteristics, Anglo-Canadian households in Watertown, Syracuse, and Grand Forks City differed in some fundamental ways. Generally Anglo-Canadians in Watertown took on some of the traits of the so-called "New" immigrants – a stronger reliance on kin and boarders of the same nationality in the family economy, more living in multiple dwelling units, more recent dates of arrival, younger household heads, a greater frequency of extended households, larger households – while the Anglo-Canadians in Syracuse were generally older, arrived at an earlier date, more likely to live in single dwelling units, and resided in smaller households. In both Grand Forks County and Grand Forks City there were few evident differences among all nativity groups in terms of household composition and household roles. The differences between Anglo-Canadians in Watertown and Syracuse in 1900 are explained largely by the longer period of residence in America by the Syracuse migrants. Yet Anglo-Canadians in both communities were among the immigrant groups most likely to share their homes with relatives, regardless of length of residence.

For newcomers, kinship connections were important in providing both accommodation and economic and social support, while for long term residents, such connections served to augment the household economy and maintain familial connections. Length of residence played little importance in determining differences among households of various groups in Grand Forks City. And, unlike their counterparts in the New York communities, Anglo-Canadians in Grand Forks City did not rank among immigrant groups most likely to share their homes with relatives. Yet their compatriots in the county did, reflecting the fact that family migration was more the norm for Anglo-Canadians settling in the countryside.

To John Bodnar, what gave the immigrants' experience coherence was their struggle to sustain the institution of the family household.[13] The family was fundamental in the adjustment of immigrants, many from rural backgrounds, to urban capitalism in the United States. Members found jobs through kinship ties and combined resources in order to survive. Here the experiences of Anglo-Canadians corresponded to that of other immigrant groups, although they did not depend so much on ethnic traditions to define their place within new urban settings. Yet dissimilar structural settings combined with variable characteristics of the immigrants themselves to ensure different levels of integration and produce different experiences.

We have demonstrated that there were significant differences in occupations among Anglo-Celtic Canadians living in Watertown, Syracuse, Manhattan, and Grand Forks in 1900. Anglo-Canadians in Watertown were largely working-class, many of whom, like blacksmiths and carpenters, followed the occupations they had learned as children on the farm. This group composed a major part of Watertown's blue-collar force, regardless of length of residence or stage of life. Their fellow countrymen in Syracuse, on the other hand, showed a greater diversity of occupations, with proportionately more engaged in clerical, professional, and business positions, although they were certainly more working-class in nature than Anglo-Canadians in Manhattan and Grand Forks. Anglo-Canadians and other immigrant groups in this city experienced a higher occupational status with length of residence, indicating that there were more opportunities for upward social mobility in Syracuse. It was also demonstrated that the rigid class division in Watertown hindered upward mobility for all immigrant groups, Canadians included, whereas greater opportunities existed for foreigners in Syracuse.

A comparison of the length of residence after 1880 shows that Anglo-Canadians in Manhattan were much more likely to achieve white-collar, business, and professional status than their Syracuse and Watertown counterparts. New York City, which was much larger and more diversified, offered a wide variety of opportunities and, consequently, more avenues of mobility. The city attracted Anglo-Canadians of various occupations but was especially inviting to those possessing certain professional skills such as doctors and nurses, business people who could take advantage of the huge local market, and clerical workers, both male and female, who found plenty of job opportunities in the city's expanding tertiary sector.

Although Grand Forks was the smallest of the four urban centres chosen for study, it was much different from Watertown, the city closest in size. The community was especially attractive to Anglo-Canadians who came to this region not to farm but to take advantage of opportunities accompanying the opening of a new frontier. They played a major role in the city's business, clerical, and professional sectors. Grand Forks presented an environment more open to the immigrant and Anglo-Canadians were well placed to take advantage of such a climate. Yet within a short period of time, many of these same Canadians would disappear from Grand Forks, some impelled to leave by the slow growth of the city and others drawn to new opportunities elsewhere.

Villages, towns, and cities are distinctive entities, socially produced and socially reproducing. While spatial structure alone does not determine patterns of social organization, there are definite relationships between the two, the ecology of the place of settlement affecting relations among home, workplace, and community. Residential clustering was shown to be more strongly related to national origin in Syracuse and Grand Forks City than in Watertown, where residential clustering was more pronounced in terms of class. There was a more diversified class structure in Syracuse as employment opportunities in business and industry were more widely spread. Yet both Watertown and Grand Forks City were so small that ethnic solidarity and identity were dependent not so much on residential congregation as on on formal and informal associations. The small size of the communities ensured interconnections among ethnic groups at places of work and recreation. The economic and social divisions among Anglo-Canadian in Syracuse ensured that no residential clustering would occur for this group. Neighbouring would have to transcend geographical and socio-economic separation. Anglo-Canadians in Grand Forks County showed greater tendency to congregate than those in the city, again revealing the importance of kinship forces and group migration in this particular case. While there is reason to believe that many Anglo-Canadian migrants felt culturally closer to Britons than Americans and in some cases associated themselves with ethnic clubs and societies, they were very familiar with American customs and did not generally feel disoriented in their new homes. Yet their earliest contacts in the United States were often former Canadians, a fact which may have enforced group cohesion and attachment to their Canadian identity.

Many emigrants set out on their journey with the intention of returning home. This goal regulated to some degree the immigrants' choice of employment, adaptation to the host culture, and investment in community building.[14] Some went to the United States with intentions of returning home, others had no such plans but were induced to move north because of circumstantial conditions. Did their American experience affect their outlook in any way? Probably so, although this is virtually impossible to discern.

The profile of the return migrant that emerges from the case studies reveals a generally older group, reflecting the fact that many had already passed through a number of life cycle and migration stages. The group differed greatly in cash and value of property both upon migration and during the proving-up period, and was no more likely than other groups to persist in place. Again, it is risky to make any conclusions based on the limited size of the Estevan sample, but it is important to note that at least in this part of the prairies, all groups, including returning and internal Canadians, displayed high rates of transiency. For many, including those who had already made a number of moves, Estevan and other parts of the prairies would represent just another temporary stage in their migration history.

There was no typical Anglo-Canadian migrant. Differentiated and even divided by religion, ethnicity, region, and level of attachment to Canada, Anglo-Canadian migrants varied in terms of circumstances and goals. They did occupy a distinctive position in their new homes. While French Canadians could identify with a distinctive ethnic identity derived from their religion, language, behavioural traits, and a sense of identity, there was no comparable monolithic Anglo-Canadian identity. In contrast to other immigrants, their homeland was nearby and their language, religion, and other cultural attributes provided common bonds with the native-born population. The experiences of James Pappa, R.B. Griffith, and others make clear the possibilities of social and economic success for Anglo-Canadian immigrants possessed of talent and industry. The relatively unencumbered access to local churches and local societies further contributed to the invisibility of the Canadian immigrant.

Yet the divergent character of the Anglo-Canadian migrant experience in New York and North Dakota leads us to question the assumption that this group underwent a complete and rapid assimilation. The Anglo-Canadian immigrant experience was more complex and contextual than is generally believed. Anglo-Canadians' role in the social and economic life of the community, their high degree of endogamy, their notable reluctance to acquiesce their Canadian citizenship, their strong reliance of family ties, and their continuing interest in Canadian life, all suggest that the Anglo-Canadian experience in Watertown was more similar to that of the great mass of immigrants than has heretofore been implied. While Anglo-Canadians in Grand Forks and Syracuse differed to some extent from their fellow countrymen and countrywomen in Watertown and from each other, they too were not carbon copies of native-born Americans. Ethnic identity, if it existed at all for Anglo-Canadians, was oriented towards the group's relationship with the structural setting in which they lived.

Yet while milieu played a major role in the adjustment of this group, the recent study of Darroch and Soltow on the wealth holding of Canadian emigrants in the United States in 1860 and 1870 shows that Canadians who journeyed south fared much worse than is generally assumed.[15] While Ontario, Maritime, and Quebec migrants were drawn to the prospect of achieving wealth south of the border, the evidence presented in the 1860 and 1870 manuscript censuses indicates that the position of the Canadian immigrant population in the United States actually deteriorated in this decade. Specifically, they found that just less than half of their 1860 and 1870 samples reported estates of $100 or more, evidence of extreme inequality of wealth in the United States; Canadian-born with estates of $100 or more held about 90 percent of the wealth among this group; about 60 percent of the Canadian-born in 1860 reported no estate at all; in that same year 20 percent of this group held 90 percent of all reported wealth and the top ten percent held about 80 percent of this total; prices increased rapidly during the decade but mean wealth and relative distribution of estate wealth remained constant; many of the Canadians emigrating after 1860 had attained no estate by 1870; by 1870 the Canadian-born were, on average, less prosperous than immigrants from Great Britain and Ireland; the relatively deprived economic circumstances of Canadians were not just a consequence of continuing emigration of the young and poor, as the age differential in wealth shrank considerably between 1860 and 1870 while increasing for the English, Scottish, Welsh, and Irish; and that this deterioration in wealth cannot be attributed primarily to the influx of Québécois who were more illiterate and less able to acquire homes than Anglo-Canadians. Their conclusions based on a cross-sectional analysis at the aggregate level combined with the results of this longitudinal tracing study at the micro-scale would seem to indicate that we have to rethink our assumptions about the emigrant Canadian experience.

While Anglo-Canadians were accepted by the host society, they too were new immigrants. They may have missed the culture shock of Ellis Island but they experienced adjustment problems. The nature and severity of these problems differed because of the varied nature of the migrants themselves and the different structural settings which they encountered. The degree to which their experience was influenced by these sometimes conflicting forces is all but impossible to determine. The answer may be that Anglo-Canadian immigrants occupied a middle ground. They generally fared better than several of the immigrant groups from eastern and southern Europe but there is reason to believe that in many areas they were no more successful and in fact less prosperous than immigrants from northern Europe. They were newcomers, conscious of their origins and in certain contexts they interacted with each other at different levels, whether by choice or by circumstance. They were perhaps invisible or not clearly discernable to those around them, natives and immigrants alike, but not to themselves.

Emigrating Canadians found themselves in a largely familiar ocean and through mutual cooperation based on family connections were able to navigate their voyages without creating too much of a ripple. There were many landmarks to offer guidance along the way, but the voyage was not smooth for all, and ripples indeed were made. It is noteworthy that Ontario attracted American tourists in the 1980s with television commercials that depicted the province as a place of interesting contrasts – friendly, familiar, foreign, and near – where one would be at home, but not quite at home. It may be that these same elements, broadly applied, informed the Anglo-Canadian experience in the United States at the turn of the century.

CODA: REFLECTIONS OF THIS VOYAGER

For Anglo-Canadians, Canada exists most clearly as a concept – an ideal sustained by a common will that transcends centrifugal forces. In this respect, the past reveals much about centripetal processes – both real and imagined – that created a sense of unity among the voyagers. In this historical geographic voyage, metaphors have served as lenses for viewing subjects, yet like all metaphors, "the border as mirror" and "the Anglo-Canadian as voyager" can only take us so far in our journey. Metaphors are by nature selective devices and so preclude other ways of viewing the world. Yet scholars have employed metaphors and concepts in their struggle to comprehend a subject that is by its very nature opaque.

It is worthwhile, I think, to inquire as to the place in which the voyager finds himself as this century draws to a close. Some things have not changed much. Canada still exists as a country with many layers of identity and possessing the same internal regional, cultural and economic divisions. Local places continue to provide the most important frame of reference and structure wider networks of economic, political and social interaction.

Yet while the voyager is still on his journey, the map has changed significantly, a transformation that has been decoded in different ways. For some, Canada at the end of the twentieth century represents the archetypical postmodern society. The noted Canadian novelist Robert Kroetsch portrays Canada as a fragmented postmodern country because it lacks unifying meta-narratives such as revolutionary genesis or a single, unifying National Dream.[16] Canadians, he believes, do not exist in a tight matrix of ideals; they come together because of the threat of death and disintegration. In such a postmodern society, "the forces of new technologies, globalization and 'time-space compression' have together created a sense of information flows, fragmentation and pace replacing what is ... perceived [even in Canada's case] to be a previous stability of homogeneity, community and place."[17] In this world of expanding horizons (for some) and dissolving boundaries, where space becomes less important in a society where accessibility via technology is freed from propinquity, places are no longer clear supports of identity.

The proponents of the Borderlands thesis claim that their theory is "part of a new paradigm for interpreting North American integration" and as such provides a basis for research to establish integrative elements operating in borderlands regions. Yet while the presentation of the Borderlands thesis is recent, the message behind the concept is not. In 1981, Joel Garreau in his book *The Nine Nations of North America* argued that except for Quebec, Canada "shares five perfectly respectable and different identities with the northern United States." The key to such integration, he contended, is the mobility of North American citizens, a mobility which erodes ties to old nations and strengthens links to new ones and effectively diminishes the significance of the boundary.

The irony of past mobility and present "placelessness" strikes me. Identity is rooted in place. For a Canadian, "here" is not only where but who I am. Identity develops as people engage in placemaking, in other words, "the way all of us as human beings transform the places in which we find ourselves into places in which we live."[18] The practice of placemaking and the development of identity in Canada has necessarily involved the creation of bounded territories which serve to strengthen and retard association with place at different levels.[19] While Canada in its infancy stage was struggling to find its identity, the political border it shared with the United States took on greater meaning. Identity was socially constructed through the establishment of internal and external boundaries. Identification with the past (i.e., Britain), and increasing association with the present (i.e., the United States), provided frames of reference for Anglo-Canadians as they struggled to find their place in North America and thus ensure their existence as distinct and sovereign people into the future.

Yet as migration has decreased over time, continental forces of integration have become stronger and ties to place have weakened. As cultures become less demarcated and differentiated in space in the form of places, "the continuity of identity is broken too."[20] Garreau concludes that the entire continent, including northern Mexico, is a single socio-economic unit where political and cultural boundaries have, in effect, lost all meaning. In such a framework, borders and national identity have little significance. Today, in the era of free trade and globalization, American distribution centres are treating regions of Canada as extensions of American networks. For many Canadians, "here" is becoming less relevant; interests are shifting elsewhere. The Canadian-American border is a wall of mirrors reflecting different meanings, meanings that in turn reflect different ideologies of nationalism. For Anglo-Canadians in particular, by examining the nature of our relations with America, we in turn see ourselves. What we see in the mirror is largely influenced by what we want to see, because ultimately nationalism, regionalism, and continentalism are territorial ideologies.

The vision I see in the mirror disturbs me greatly. The frames of reference are shifting elsewhere. In this new world order, regional differences are increasingly diminished in the face of homogeneous economic forces and a global culture which ironically promote simplification at the same time they make our lives more complex. Although regional circumstances continue to shape the impacts of broader forces, a gradual convergence is taking place and regional identities are vanishing, at least within the Anglo-American realm. The convergence Garreau's "Nine Nations" and the Borderlands concept represents reflects not only a dynamic, integrated global economy that knows no boundaries but a global culture which is increasingly dominated by an American mass culture.

Global culture, produced for the most part by media and corporate giants in New York and Los Angeles, has increased the sense that real life takes place somewhere else, not in Halifax, Nova Scotia, Gananoque, Ontario, Regina, Saskatchewan, Watertown, New York, or Grand Forks, North Dakota. I think of the people I know in Saskatchewan who watch the world go by on their satellite dishes and then I reflect upon the significance of Cable Regina replacing Williston television stations with those of Detroit. Instead of listening to North Dakota politicians reflecting on regional issues, we regularly get to view graphic pictures of the latest victims of drug-related murders.

I also think about an article I read a few years ago in which Alvin Toffler was quoted as saying that we have now entered an era of cultural technology in the sense that computers affect culture at its deepest levels. We now live in an age where, for many, place is more and more experienced through cable television, the VCR, the satellite dish, and the personal computer. We literally can select the time and place we want to see by the push of a button. Sack worries in particular about the power of television to misrepresent the meaning of place: "Television uproots and juxtaposes one context after another far more than other media, and this obscures the real historical and geographical depth of place and weakens its relation in space and time to other places and events ... Television's juxtaposition of places thins out their meanings and contexts and distorts them."[21]

Some may point to the re-emergence of place expressed in postmodern culture as evidence of a strong reaction against the homogenizing forces of modernity. Yet the creation of renovated warehouses, pedestrian malls, art-deco architecture, and commodified history that reflect something of the history and geography of the places in which they are situated and stand in direct contrast to the utilitarian, universal landscapes produced in the postwar period, are actually part of a culture and philosophy that is, arguably, the "latest ... expression of the transition from rationalist/ Modernist ... capitalism to an emergent, globalizing advanced capitalism."[22] The market for products sold in postmodern settings is geared primarily towards professionals, private-sector executives, management consultants, and so on, who make up the most important consuming section of society. It caters to a baby-boom generation whose tastes are imposed and shaped largely by media, cinema, and publishing, which for the most part is controlled by corporations. As Sack argues, consumption moulds people's consciousness of place and creates settings that cater to this sense; "from a geographical perspective, postmodernism assumes that the consumer's world is total."[23]

A material culture imposed from a disorienting global/American space is replacing local spaces or fashioning them into landscapes of consumption. Increasingly, places of consumption are as important as the items being purchased, and visits to these places take on an almost ritualistic flavour. It almost seems as if individuals and groups are deriving some sense of identity as they shop, eat, and drink in these consumer shrines. The settings are postmodern in the sense that they are an abstraction of the locality as it developed over time and place but modified to meet the manufactured aspirations of the consumer. The postmodern design, both in terms of historical preservation and construction of new structures, stresses developments of human proportions, pedestrian orientation, pluralism of colours and styles, historical and regional motifs, and acknowledgement of the local environment; yet the political-economic context of such development can be questioned.

Where does Canada fit in this new world order? Elements of our historical-geographical development and a different political culture have served to counteract the very powerful north-south pull that connects American and Canadian border regions. Yet the instruments bridging the island archipelago – a shared commitment to community and the public good, an extensive nationalized transportation linkage, a complex of government sustained cultural agencies, and redistributive policies designed to reduce regional and social disparity and humanize the marketplace – are in danger of collapsing under the weight of global economic restructuring. On the other hand, one could argue that, as was the case of the Mercier Bridge, the bridges are closing because of indifference rather than collapsing because of too little structural support.[24]

The "inbetweenness" of place and identity and the intermediary position of borders – internal and external – support my assertion that the concept of borderlands returns the symbol of the border to the fact of place. Researchers are now beginning to seek the middle ground between the extremes of nationalism and continentalism. The dialectic I mention has served a purpose, and that is to bring us to this middle ground in evaluating the problem of Canadian identity. Where is here? It is on the border that divides and joins Canadians and Americans, and Canadians from each other.

Yet in this new global environment, place is no longer the defining element of our identity because the meanings of borders and, as a consequence, borderlands are changing in such a way that their traditional functions are becoming blurred. Where is here? The geographic compass points which enabled the voyager to orient himself in time and space are disappearing. The promise of arrival that was such an important part of the journey no longer seems possible for many. Without the legend and conventions of the map, without the symbol of the border, the voyage is cancelled and the voyager is left adrift searching for a frame of reference.

Tracing Strategies and Sources

The manuscript census and city directory have been employed often in historical studies of immigration and community and their use has been well documented. The manuscript census in particular has constituted the major data source for decennial analyses of social structure and mobility. When the static cross-sections for different years are compared, an approximation can be made of net shifts in employment, residential mobility, and household organization. While the traditional cross-sectional approach is employed in this study, it is too delimited and episodic; chronology is treated somewhat arbitrarily for the sake of the data available and the methods employed. As Lawton points out, the patterns derived from this census-based classification obscure differences in the avenues produced by changes in the scale of economic organization.[1] And so I attempted to find records and devise strategies that would enable me to conduct a systematic and longitudinal investigation of individual movers.

The sources employed in tracing patterns of migration will presently be described but I should first mention something about the different strategies I designed to track the experiences of Anglo-Canadians as they moved about the continent (Figure 4). Sources were selected or rejected for record linkage on the basis of their availability, completeness, and compatability. Certain records that have proven useful in other studies of mobility were rejected if they did not fit these criteria, particularly that of availability. Rather than go into great detail about the problems I encountered and the decisions I had to make regarding use of sources, I instead direct the reader to Appendix A of Peter Knights's *Yankee Destinies*, which provides a thorough discussion of sources and issues in relation to record linkage.[2] Knights reviews many of the records I employed in my study and so little comment is offered here except for some of the particular problems I encountered using these sources in both Canada and the United States. More dis-

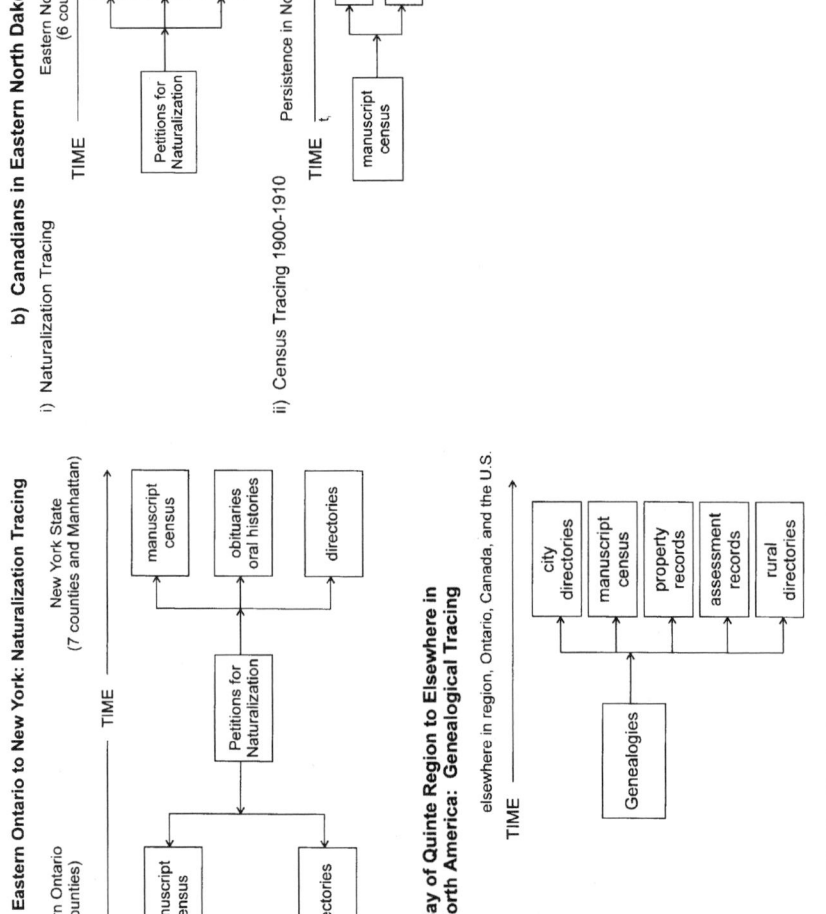

Figure 4 Tracing Strategies

cussion is tendered regarding those sources not employed by Knights – that is, naturalization records, border crossing records, local histories, and homestead records. Because genealogies comprised such an important basis for tracing the experience of the Bay of Quinte families, they were discussed in much detail in the introduction to Part Two.

PARTICULAR SOURCES

United States Naturalization Records

A little-used data source, the United States Naturalization Records, provides a potentially rich source of information about individual late nineteenth century immigrants from Canada. My research made use of two different types of naturalization records: the declaration of intention and the petition for naturalization.

The basis for the naturalization procedure was established in the Naturalization Act of 1795, which empowered any court of record to grant American citizenship to aliens after five years of residence in the country and one year in the state where naturalization would take place. In addition, a preliminary "declaration of intention" to become a citizen was to be made at least three years befor application for citizenship.[3] The two basic types of naturalization are these declarations of intention and the petitions for naturalization.

Both records generally are still in the custody of individual county courthouses, although the National Archives in Washington has abstracts of naturalization proceedings from the New England states from 1787 to 1906 and the District of Columbia from 1802 to 1926. The originals, however, are much more detailed and therefore are of much greater use in the study of migration.

Unfortunately, naturalization records prior to 1906 varied in format and completeness from place to place. Before that date, federal, state, district, and superior courts had the power to perform naturalizations, and a uniform set of guidelines as to what information was to be collected did not exist. In 1906 the federal government assumed responsibility for the citizenship process and the naturalization law of that year required that all courts provide a standard set of details on an alien's personal history before naturalization. While naturalization records dated after 1905 and stored in the federal archives are not available to researchers, those in custody of the individual county courthouses are open to inspection, with the stipulation that they are not to be photocopied.

When the decision was made to become a US citizen, the immigrant was required first to fill out a declaration of intention. This record includes the following information: full name; residence and occupation; date and place of birth; port of emigration and port of arrival; personal description (height, weight, colour of hair, complexion, colour of eyes); last foreign residence; intention to renounce their former allegiance; assurances that the applicant is not a practising or believing anarchist or polygamist; state and county where the declaration was filed; date of declaration; and signatures of declarant and clerk.

If the declaration was not filled out correctly, the petition for naturaliation was denied; declarations were frequently declared invalid. For instance, "during the period 1908 to 1918, 8.5% of all denials of naturalization petitions in the United States were on the grounds of 'declaration invalid'."[4] All responsibility for mistakes, even if they were the fault of the clerk, lay with the alien.

When the declaration was declared valid, the would-be citizen then had to file a petition for naturalization. This is a rich source of information, including the following: full name, residence, and occupation; date and place of birth; port of emigration and port of arrival; name of vessel or other mode of travel; date of departure and date of arrival; date and court of declaration of intention; marital status; wife's name, nativity and present residence, if applicable; number, names, birthplaces, and residences of minor children; assurances that the applicant is not a practising or believing anarchist or polygamist; intention to renounce former national allegiance and make permanent residence in the United States; ability to speak the English language; dates upon which the petitioner began residence in the United States and in what state; attachment to the principles of the Constitution; an assertion that this is the first petition for citizenship, or, if a former petition was denied, the reason for denial and the fact that this reason has been removed; and the affadivits of two witnesses who must declare on their oaths that they know the petitioner to have been a resident of the United States at least since a certain date not less than a year ago.

Until 1922, women automatically became citizens by virtue of the naturalization of their husbands. After that date, women were given equal status in naturalization with men and no longer lost their original citizenship nor gained that of their husbands by virtue of marriage. Children who emigrated with their parents were allowed to file their petitions two years later; however, it was customary for the courts to insist upon the age of 21 before granting citizenship. When the petition for naturalization was approved, the petitioner was then given a certificate of naturalization.

The naturalization records identify residential locations of migrants both before and after the move. This information is linked with other personal data sources in order to construct socio-economic and residential profiles of the individuals chosen for study.

Censuses

The Canadian and American published censuses contain only the crudest types of aggregate information. The birthplaces of individuals are enumerated but with no greater specificity than country or state of birth. From such data, the researcher can only establish gross patterns of migration. Yet this source is useful in describing general characteristics of the source and origin locations and the migrant groups.

In addition to the aggregate decennial census, available from 1790 onwards in the United States and 1851 onwards in Canada, use is also made of various state and manuscript censuses. When I started this research, the Canadian manuscript census was only available for the years 1842 (only partial), 1852, 1861, 1871, and 1881, as at that time there existed a one-hundred-year restriction on the use of this record. Since then, the time limit has been reduced to ninety-two years, so I have been able to include information from both the 1891 and 1901 censuses. Only a few of these censuses have been indexed. In the United States, individual counties hold some or all of the returns for a wide array of state censuses but because they are so few and far between, they were of little use in this study. The US manuscript census is available up to and including 1910 but unfortunately most of the 1890 census has been destroyed by fire. There is an eighty-year restriction on the use of this source and so I had to wait until 1990 in order to trace migrants in the 1910 census. I believe that this restriction has since been reduced to seventy years. The Soundex Index to the census proved to be very helpful in the use of this source although, as Knights has pointed out, it suffers from an annoying degree of incompleteness.

The Canadian decennial manuscript censuses vary from year in terms of types of data collected. While some years include schedules on agricultural and industrial characteristics, others do not. The 1851 and later censuses list for each member of the household name, age, occupation, religious affiliation, and birthplace (country or province). The 1871 and 1881 censuses list for each person father's origin or ethnic background. The 1891 census, in addition, asks if persons are French Canadian and for parents' birthplaces. The 1901 census includes household earnings but it appears that many did not choose to volunteer this information. The American censuses contain much of the same information found in the Canadian censuses and suffer as well from problems of under-enumeration. Again, for further discussion of the challenges this source presents, the reader is advised to read Appendix 1 of *Yankee Destinies*.

Directories

Directories are alphabetical lists of names and addresses. The information presented in city directories varies over time and with publisher, but most are limited to names of family heads with residential addresses and sometimes working members of families. By the latter part of the nineteenth century, directories became more complete in supplying, in the case of proprietors, the address of their business and providing information on the number of inhabitants, street names, public buildings, public persons, and so on. A major problem with directories is their tendency to neglect the less affluent.

Assessment Records

Assessment rolls are a rich source of information on land utilization. For rural townships, information is provided on the geographical location of each holding, the name of the lot holders, acreages cleared and uncleared, house type, the presence of mills or some other semi-industrial structures, figures on crop and livestock production, and rateable values for the properties concerned. The data for municipalities differ and vary over time but provide information on land use, land value, condition of tenure, and social and economic status. Unfortunately, assessment records are very scattered in terms of availability and distribution both in Canada and the United States and categories changed over time. Also, they refer only to property owners and ratepayers, thus leaving out a significant proportion of the population.

Although archives contain some assessment records, usually on microfilm, many are only available at the local level, which presents problems in terms of accessibility and quality. For instance, the assessment records for Oneida County, held in the basement of the county courthouse in Utica, are not arranged in any order, chronological or geographical. Thousands of assessment books, many in bad shape, are scattered all over a large room. After three days of frustration, I decided to abandon my search of these records. I was denied access to the assessment records in Syracuse. These records, which go back to about 1870, are pencil entries in leather-bound books that have been seriously damaged by basement storage. City officials are concerned that they will be further damaged if handled by researchers. The records for the city of Watertown were kept in an old barn outside the city and they were destroyed when the roof fell in following a heavy snowfall. Many of the county courthouses I visited in the United States followed the practice of destroying their older records, so I was very limited in terms of use of this source.

Probate Records

Wills and intestate administrations were probated in Ontario in county surrogate courts. These records are on LDS microfilms at the Public Archives of Ontario. They are of limited use in tracing persisters or out-migrants because few possessed enough to necessitate probate. In many parts of Ontario, most wills were not probated but were registered as deeds to record the transfer of real property. Those including lot and concession numbers were located in the Abstract Index to Deeds, while those not so specifying were recorded in county general registers, indexed by names. For further details on wills and probate records, see the articles by Osborne and Elliott.[5]

Land Records

Land records[6] were used to examine land transfers among the Bay of Quinte region families. In Ontario, most land records begin in the late 1700s. They include land patents, fiats and warrants, land grants and patents, and deeds. The Upper Canada land registry office was established in 1795 and individual deeds of property were recorded in each district office.[7] Several researchers have used these records to examine initial settlement and changing land ownership.[8] However, settlement in many cases, actually preceded the patent date. The process of land patenting in Upper Canada was a very complex procedure. Two kinds of procedures were followed in obtaining a patent.

Land Grant 1   There existed a regular procedure where the petitioners were the patentees. Eight steps were involved in this process. First the individual petitioned for a certain parcel of land. This was brought before the land commission and an order-in-council was dispatched. Then the location ticket was issued to the intending settler. The settler then proceeded to perform the settlement duties and when they were completed, he received a certificate noting the completion of these duties. At that time the attorney general's fiat was dispatched. This, in effect, was an arbitrary decree issued by the government which indicated their recognition of the individual's intention to settle. Finally, the surveyor general's description of the lot (chains, links, angles) was completed and the patent was issued.

The records involved in this process are found in three different archives. The petitions are in the National Archives of Canada because they are Executive Council Records. They are microfilmed and are available in the RG 1 L series. All subsequent documentation in the patent procedure stayed with the provincial governments and thus is available in Ontario. All of the records, from the order-in-council to the surveyor general's description, are available in the RG 1 series of the Ontario Archives. The copies of the original patents issued are available in the Provincial Secretary's office in the RG 8 series.

Land Grant 2   This procedure was followed when a person, after petitioning and receiving a location ticket, either died or legally assigned the land rights to someone else under certain circumstances before receiving the patent. When an individual died, a situation existed where the name on the petition and the name on the patent differed. In this case, a relative or even a complete stranger was issued the legal ownership of the lot. If the original petitioner died or assigned his rights to someone else, then the new claimant had to prove this claim before the Heir and Devisee Commission. The individual started this procedure by issuing a notice to the commission claiming the lot in question. This notice was posted on the courthouse doors for three weeks so all could read it in case there were counter claims. A hearing was established in which the counter claimants could file proof (wills, etc.) backing up their claims. The committee would then study the various admissions and decide to allow or disallow the claim. If the verdict was to disallow the claim, then someone else might make claim to the lot. If the claim was allowed, the government then prepared a patent in the new name.

There were other ways to register ownership of land besides patenting. Under the old registry system, the individual was not required to have a crown patent, but n 1846 this system was overhauled and the patentee was required to register his own patent. However, the registration of patents did not become compulsory until 1965 with the Public Lands Act.

Such a complex procedure meant that many individuals waited many years before starting the patenting procedure and so date of patent often does not indicate initial settlement. While date of patent has been used to signify initial occupation and to identify speculators,[9] the subsequent information regarding partial and complete transfers of land has been ignored until recently. In this context, the Abstract Index to Deeds has proven most useful. In the late 1850s, abstract books which convey data regarding land transactions were organized. Legislation of 1865 required each county registry to compile an abstract of the patent data. These records are available in each county registry and on microfilm in the Public Archives of Ontario. The abstracts summarize the history of title to a parcel of real estate property. They provide date of purchase, location of land, the parties involved in the transaction (grantor and grantee), and in some cases, the sales price and/or accompanying conditions involved in the transfer.

There are significant limitations to using abstract records for research besides the usual problem of legibility. In many cases, information regarding the sales price is missing. I suspect that certain transactions were not reported or were only recorded years after the transaction was finalized. Quite often the date of registry, which signifies the legal date of transfer and marks the completion of the transaction process, occurred at quite some time after the date of instrument which indicates for all practical purposes the transfer of property. In certain cases the individual owners sold their land to others before they actually registered their purchase of the property at the registry office. The local registry was, in many instances, too inaccessible to the two parties involved in the transaction. It is also conceivable that many persons were ignorant of the fact that registry of land transactions was necessary.

A major difficulty in using the abstract records is in determining the meanings of the instruments. Among the more common instruments present in the records are bargain and sale, quit claim, release of dower, will, discharge, sheriff's deed, deed of gift, grant and quit claim, release and quit claim, partition deed, grant, lease and mortgage. All but the last two are almost always interpreted by legal sources as transfers by sale or transfers by methods other than sales (for example, gift). Definitions of the most important instruments are offered below.

Bargain and Sale   This is a deed of contract between the bargainer and the bargainee where there is a bargain for money or equivalent consideration in goods, mineral, and timber rights. It signifies transfer of a property or a thing from one to another, upon valuable consideration, by way of sale.

Quit Claim   "This is a face-saving system of avoiding foreclosure. When a mortgagor has reached the point of no return by being absolutely unable to bring his mortgage arrears up to date, he can sit down with the mortgagee and work something like this out. It is a release of all the mortgagor's interests in his property."[10]

Grant   This is an instrument of conveyance transferring property.

Sheriff's Deed   This is a deed of contract between the sheriff of a district who has claimed the property of another for a certain reason and a prospective buyer. The original owner may have lost his property because of a failure to complete the settlement duties or to meet the financial responsibilities of the contract.

Mortgage   A mortgage "is an assignment of real estate to a person ... as security for the payment of a debt, on the condition that if the money is repaid according to the contract, the grant becomes void." The borrower is the mortgagor and the lender is the mortgagee. The borrower does not completely possess the property until the mortgage is paid off, although he can sell the land to another under conditions that the person he sells to assumes the mortgage obligations. When a person borrows money as a first mortgagor, he is left with an equity of redemption which signifies complete right to the property when the mortgage is paid off. If a mortgagor wants to borrow more money against the property, he mortgages his equity of redemption. This secondary mortgage is known as an equitable mortgage. What makes a mortgage first, second, third, and so on is the order in which it is legally entered in the deeds book.

Under land titles registration, mortgages do not involve transfers of property with the lender. Private loans were the most common type of mortgage money in early Ontario.[12] The time sequence of payments was agreed upon by the two parties involved and it usually included either the principal and interest or the interest paid on the addition to the payment.

Discharge   This signifies the payment of the mortgage and the completion of the transfer. The key date here is the date of registry. While date of instrument for other instruments means, for all purposes, the transfer of property, only the registry date of discharge has the force of conveyance.

I had planned to survey individual property records in my analysis of persistence and land-holding behaviour in Saskatchewan but found the $2 per search fee at the Land Titles offices too prohibitive.

US Canadian Border Crossing Records

The Canadian government did not keep lists of emigrants. Before 1847 there was no Canadian citizenship separate from British, and Canadians moved freely throughout the British Empire. Before 1895, when the United States government began keeping border crossing records, Canadians moved to the United States with few restrictions. The Family History Library in Salt Lake City and the National Archives in Washington have several collections of arrival indexes and manifests for persons crossing the United States–Canadian border. The most important and encompassing source is *St. Albans District Manifest Records of Aliens Arriving from Foreign Contiguous Territory* (Washington, DC: National Archives Record Service, 1986). The Family History Library has 937 rolls of microfilm that include Soundex cards and original manifests giving detailed information pertaining to border crossings.

All crossings from Maine to Washington are included between 1895 and 1915. Beginning in 1915, the records are limited to border crossing in the New York–Vermont region. However, this includes major eastern Canadian seaports where US officials processed ship passengers bound for the United States.

This collection includes the source used in this study, namely the *Soundex Index to Canadian Border Entries Through the St. Albans, Vermont District, 1895–1924.* It contains the original form filled out by border officials for every person entering the United States from Canada, regardless of origin. The four hundred rolls of index cards, part of the Records of the Immigration and Naturalization Service, Record Group 85, are arranged alphabetically using the Soundex phonetic system. They give complete geographic coverage to 1915. Some of these cards are the actual record of crossing; in those cases there is no original manifest. Another ninety-eight rolls of index cards are included in the *Soundex Index to Entries into the St. Albans, Vermont District Through Canadian Pacific and Atlantic Ports, 1924–1952.* They pertain to border crossings in the New York–Vermont area only. The forms include a bounteous variety of information on the migrant's social, ethnolinguistic, demographic, and occupational background, including: port of entry; date of entry; name; relationship, name and age of those accompanying the migrant; place of birth; age; sex; occupation; literacy; language spoken; race and nationality; last permanent residence; name, relationship, and age of reference person; indication of previous stay in the United States and if so for what period of time; the name of the person paying for passage, if applicable; the location to which the person is intending to travel and the relationships, name and ages of people whom the migrant will be joining, if applicable; the amount of money carried on the migrant's person; and the purpose in entering the United States (temporary or permanent stay).

This source proved to be useful in tracing migration patterns and discerning the characteristics of Canadian and non-Canadian migrants travelling to the United States from Canada. Yet as stated in chapter 2, it was not chosen as a basis for tracing migrants because it misses the period of greatest Canadian out-migration and because it is arranged alphabetically not geographically, thus making it difficult to trace in detail the experiences of migrants from specific Canadian origins to particular American destinations.

Canadian US Border Entry Records[13]

Prior to the railway, settlers entered western Canada by wagon and horse. With the construction of railways, customs offices opened at points such as Emerson, Manitoba, and North Portal, Saskatchewan, but officials were mainly concerned with collecting customs and only performed rudimentary immigration examinations as a favour to the Department of Immigration. The North West Mounted Police were responsible for catching border-jumpers and collecting customs duties at points where no customs office existed.

As the number of immigrants increased, the federal government turned over the responsibility of immigration and customs to the Department of the Interior in the fall of 1908. The department assumed responsibility for collecting information on in-migrants and remained in that capacity until 1919 when its duties were handed over to the Department of Immigration and Colonization.[14] The Border Crossing Records of the Department of the Interior have recently been released by the National Archives and are now available in various provincial archives and libraries across Canada.

The border crossing record includes: the day and month of admittance, name, age, sex, country of birth, country of citizenship, occupation, mode of travel, train number, the state from which the migrant came, destination, amount of cash carried, and a column for remarks which included the value of personal effects transported by those who travelled by freight car. Another sheet was prepared for the end of each month containing a list of those who were rejected for various reasons (for example, "tramp" or "black" on a couple of occasions). Often the immigration inspector wrote down the state where the migrant received his or her American citizenship rather than their country of citizenship, and sometimes state or province was included rather than country of birth.

It is unfortunate that more did not make such mistakes because the data included in the correctly filled records are not specific enough to allow one to trace the movements of individuals on the American side. Last state or province of residence, the latter referring to Canadians who travelled to western Canada through the United States, is included but there is no way of knowing if these origins coincide with the migrant's state or province of birth. Also, the records provide no clues for tracing the migration paths of European-born before leaving their last state of residence. The lack of specific information on birthplace and subsequent locations make it almost impossible to link the border crossing record with other personal sources to trace migrants backwards in space and time. And as mentioned in chapter 7, the destinations given to immigration officers were simply the places where migrants planned to disembark and so are of little use in tracing the migrants forward movements.

Homestead Records[15]

Homestead practices in Canada were patterned after those in the western United States. Homesteading began in Canada in 1872 and ended in 1930, when the Prairie provinces assumed control of the crown lands within their borders. Homestead regulations were modified over time but generally settlers were required to follow a number of steps. The homesteader, any male 18 or over or a widow with dependants, had to pay a $10 registration fee, $5 for homesteads of 80 acres or less. The settler was to appear at the Dominion Lands Agency for the district, declare his intention to become a British subject if not one already, pay the fee, and secure entry for the land he had selected.

Homesteaders were required to live six months of the year on their claims, construct a habitable house, and bring at least 15 acres under cultivation within three years. Raising twenty head of cattle and providing buildings for their shelter could substitute for cultivation. Settlers could reside with their parents or upon a previous homestead instead of on their homesteads, provided they stayed in the same or an adjoining township.

At the end of three years, homesteaders appeared with witnesses before the homestead inspector or before the local agent of the Dominion Lands Office and applied for the patent, submitting evidence that the duties had been performed. Up until 1890, homestead entrants were entitled to take up an adjacent quarter-section as a pre-emption by paying a fee of $10 and, after obtaining the patent, purchasing it at the price prevailing at the time of entry. Pre-emptions were abandoned because they interfered with the sale of private property and because many homesteaders were so anxious to acquire more land that they lost everything, including their original homesteads, by extending their mortgages too far. Pre-emptions were reinstituted in 1908 with new requirements: three years of additional residence and cultivation of 50 acres, both of which might be applied to the original homestead or the pre-emption quarter, provided the acreage was in addition to that performed in earning the homestead. After fulfilling these conditions a settler could patent the pre-emption for $3 an acre.

The homestead files in the Public Archives of Saskatchewan contain records of the federal Department of the Interior and the Provincial Lands Branch, the bulk of the material created by the former. The Lands Branch of the former Department of the Interior was in charge of settlement on Dominion Lands from 1871 to 1930 when the Transfer of Resources Agreement turned over crown land to the provincial Ministry of Natural Resources. Until land was patented in the name of the settler or corporate body, the right to the land remained in the hands of the Dominion government. Documents relating to the homesteading experience were forwarded to Ottawa by the local land agency, where a number was assigned to the file and subsequent correspondence regarding the land was entered into the same file. When the patent was issued, land was registered at the local land title office in the name of the new owner and the homestead file was closed unless seed liens or other debts remained against the land. The files also contain records in connection with various types of land scrip issued by the federal government (for example, militia grants, half-breed grants).[16]

Most files contain the application for entry, the application for letters patent, and notification that the patent had been granted. A relatively small number also include other documents, such as declaration of abandonment, certificates of naturalization, and claims for inspection. Unfortunately, many of the files only have the basic documents that had to be completed to meet the regulations. Archivists believe that the files were culled before they were returned to the Saskatchewan Archives in the 1950s. The index to the files and the originals are housed in the archives branch in Saskatoon while some microfilm copies are in Regina. The Church of the Latter Day Saints took on the huge task of microfilming the files but abandoned it a third of the way through, continuing to film only the three basic documents. Researchers interested in accounts of problems encountered not only by the homesteader after receiving the patent but others who preceded him or her must thus travel to Saskatoon to examine the original files.

Local Histories

Although local histories from all over Canada and the United States were investigated in various stages of this research, including the Writers' Project of North Dakota local histories employed by John Hudson in his research on migration to North Dakota,[17] they were used most intensively in the investigation of migration to Saskatchewan. In Saskatchewan, a combination of several factors – rural depopulation and community disintegration, the deaths of the original pioneers, and anniversary celebrations of Canada and the province – served to launch many local history studies at the end of the 1970s and throughout the 1980s. Local history committees asked people living in rural municipalities as well as descendants of families who had left the area to write down the oral histories of their families. Many of the community-sponsored histories were assisted by John Archer, former president of the University of Regina and a distinguished Saskatchewan historian. The typical Saskatchewan history contains three to five hundred family biographies, including important name and place information. Although historians studying western Canada have largely ignored this source, Paul Voisey believes that the community histories are valuable for quantitative research because they include "all sorts of random facts" about ordinary individuals.[18] This "mass detail," when linked to traditional historical sources, can provide the raw material for many kinds of scholarly analysis.

The more than five hundred Saskatchewan community histories located in the Prairie History Room of the Regina Public Library have several advantages over the local histories used by Hudson. They are not elitist; no family had to pay to include their history in the monograph. Secondly, because the settlement period was only two to three generations from the time in which the histories were written, memories of the era are still fairly accurate. Finally, while the quality of the histories varies, many contain detailed information about the migration of settlers, homesteaders and purchasers of land alike. However, the histories are biased towards those who persisted in place as these were the families most likely to have responded to requests for information.

Other Records

Many other sources were used to supplement the basic information derived from the records just described. Newspapers, county histories, obituaries, annual reports of various government departments, family papers, oral histories, and correspondence with descendants all served to add flesh to the story.

For any (masochistic) readers who might wish to embark on a similar study, I offer these thoughts. In 1985, I spent forty-five days travelling over 8,000 kilometres through fifteen states visiting communities in which my Quinte family migrants located. The typical day involved arising at 6:00 a.m., packing my tent, driving 300 to 500 kilometres to a town or city which housed county courthouses, libraries, or archives and spending the rest of the day until closing time frantically searching through directories, assessment records (if available), and local histories for information about my migrants. More often than not, I was unsuccessful. It was only after this that I learned about the marvellous collection of genealogical sources at the Family History Library in Salt Lake City. Fortunately, I had the opportunity some years later to spend a few months in this facility completing my family profiles (as best I could). The lesson in all this is: look before you leap. Yet I must stress that I did come across sources on my summer of voyaging that are not housed anywhere else but the locations in which I found them. And I would like to think that I somehow acquired some insight into the migration experience just by travelling to the same destinations as my voyagers.

Notes

PART ONE: INTRODUCTION

1 James Pappa's life story is compiled from an obituary appearing in the 12 March 1925 edition of the Watertown *Daily Times*. The obituary contains excerpts from an interview conducted with Mr Pappa before his death.
2 Michael Percy, "Migration Flows during the Decade of the Wheat Boom in Canada, 1900–1910; A Neo-Classical Analysis" (Ph.D. dissertation, Queen's University, Kingston, 1977), 4.
3 Watertown *Daily Times*, 12 March 1925, 6.
4 See Rowland Berthoff, *British Immigrants in Industrial America* (Cambridge, Mass.: Harvard University Press, 1953), and Charlotte Erickson, *Invisible Immigrants* (Coral Gables: University of Miami Press, 1972). Both view British immigrants as being "invisible"; that is, they adapted readily to American life. But I would argue that English-speaking Canadians from predominantly Anglo-Celtic backgrounds, the Anglo-Canadians to which I refer, were even less visible in the American scene. While the English, Scots, Irish, and Welsh often formed cultural groups and associations, anglophone Canadians rarely identified themselves as a distinct group. Map 1 in chapter 2 is reprinted with the permission of Professor Berthoff.
5 For further discussion of this point, see Michael Cross, *The Frontier Thesis and the Canadas: The Debate on the Impact of the Canadian Environment* (Toronto: Copp Clark Publishing Co., 1970).
6 For examples, see Ralph E. Vedder and Lawrence E. Galloway, "Settlement Patterns of Canadian Emigrants in the United States, 1850–1960," *Canadian Journal of Economics* 3 (1970), 477–86; Percy, "Migration Flows." Of importance for the study of migration between Canada and the United States are

the volumes by Fred Landon, *Western Ontario and the American Frontier* (Toronto: Ryerson Press, and New Haven: Yale University Press, for the Carnegie Endowment for International Peace, Division of Economics and History, 1941); and, by the same publishers, John B. Brebner, *North Atlantic Triangle: The Interplay of Canada, the United States and Great Britain* (1946); and George Parkin de Twenebrokes Glazebrook, *A History of Transportation in Canada* (1938). Recommended articles include Paul Coats, "Two Good Neighbours: A Study of Exchanges in Populations," Proceedings, Canadian-American Affairs Conference (Kingston: Queen's University, 1937), 116–17; and Karel D. Bicha, "The North Dakota Farmer and the Canadian West, 1896–1914," *North Dakota History* 29 (1962), 297–302.

7 Such work includes: I. Podea, "Quebec to Little Canada: The Coming of French Canadians to New England in the Nineteenth Century," *New England Quarterly* 2, 3 (1950); Ralph Vicero, "French Canadian Settlement in Vermont Prior to the Civil War," *Professional Geographer* 23, 4 (1971), 290–4; John P. Allen, "Migration Fields of French Canadian Immigrants to Southern Maine," *Geographical Review* 62 (1972), 366–83; Tamara Hareven and Randolph Langenbach, *Amoskeag: Life and Work in an American Factory City* (New York: Pantheon Books, 1978); Dean Louder and Eric Waddell, eds., *Du continent perdu a l'archipel rétrouvé: le Québec et l'amerique française* (Québec: Presses de l'université Laval, 1983); and B. Craig, "Early French Migration to Northern Maine, 1785–1850," *Maine Historical Society Quarterly* 25 (1986), 230–47. Besides my work, I know of no other research that attempts to trace the migration experiences of Anglo-Canadians at the micro-level with the exception of the research completed by Alan Brookes and the current research conducted by Bruno Ramirez and his team. Brookes was the first to study Maritime out-migration within a larger borderlands framework and published his results in four articles: "Out-Migration from the Maritime Provinces, 1860–1900: Some Preliminary Considerations," *Acadiensis* 5, 2 (1976), 26–55; "Islanders in the Boston States, 1850–1900," *The Island Magazine* 2 (1977), 11–15; "The Golden Age and the Exodus: The Case of Canning, Kings County," *Acadiensis* 11, 1 (1981), 57–82; "Family, Youth and Leaving Home in Late Nineteenth Century Rural Nova Scotia: Canning and the Exodus, 1868–1893," in Joy Parr, ed., *Childhood and the Family in Canadian History* (Toronto: McClelland and Stewart, 1982), 93–108.

Ramirez's work, using the Index to Canadian Border Entries to the United States to trace the experiences of 40,000 Canadian out-migrants, promises to shed much light on this subject. Unfortunately for my investigation, this source was not available until the summer of 1986, when much of my research was already completed. However, several of the questions asked, sources used, and strategies employed serve to distinguish our two studies in many ways. For example, while Ramirez's work promises to present a more in-depth and representative analysis of Anglo-Canadian emigration at the pan-

Canadian level, my research compares and contrasts Anglo-Canadian immigrant experiences with those of other immigrant groups in different kinds of communities and also addresses the important dimension of return migration. In addition, Ramirez refers largely to Canadian emigration after 1910 while my research is focused largely on movement taking place during the greatest period of out-migration. Use is made of the Index to Canadian Border Entries in tracing the migration patterns of Canadian-born and foreign-born entering the United States from Canada in chapter 2. See Bruno Ramirez, "Canada's Place in the North Atlantic Migrations, 1860–1930," unpublished paper presented at the Eleventh International Economic History Congress, Milan, Italy, September 1994.

8 These are the critical dimensions that emerge from the considerable body of literature that has been directed towards the immigrant experience, particularly in the United States and among more distinguishable ethnic groups. They are discussed in the introduction to Part Three.

CHAPTER 1

1 Group for the Advancement of Psychiatry, *Us and Them: The Psychology of Ethno-nationalism* (New York: Brunner/Mazel Publications, 1987), 11.

2 E. Barkan, "French Canadians," in S. Thernstrom, A. Orlov, and O. Handlin, eds., *Harvard Encyclopedia of American Ethnic Groups* (Cambridge, Mass.: Harvard University Press, 1980), 392.

3 Northrop Frye, *The Bush Garden: Essays on the Canadian Imagination* (Toronto: Ananasi, 1971), ii, 220.

4 R. Cole Harris, "Regionalism and the Canadian Archipelago," in Larry D. McCann, ed., *Heartland and Hinterland*, 1st ed. (Scarborough: Prentice-Hall, 1982), 459–84.

5 Canadian Broadcasting Corporation, *Journey Without Arrival* (1975) (film).

6 Northrop Frye, *Divisions on a Ground* (Toronto: Anansi, 1982), 59 (edited by James Polk).

7 The understanding of self in the context of community is most fully developed in the political philosophy of Charles Taylor, a philosophy which stands in direct contrast to the Lockean individualism which one associates with American perception of self-identity. See Charles Taylor, *Sources of the Self* (Cambridge, Mass.: Harvard University Press, 1989); *The Malaise of Modernity* (Concord: Anansi, 1991); and *Reconciling the Solitudes* (Montreal and Kingston: McGill-Queen's University Press, 1993).

8 R. Cole Harris, "The Pattern of Early Canada," *Canadian Geographer* 31 (1987), 207.

9 Donald H. Akenson, *Being Had: Historians, Evidence and the Irish in North America* (Port Credit: P.D. Meany, 1985), 43.

10 Bernard Bailyn, *The Peopling of North America* (New York: Alfred A. Knopf, 1986), 25, 36–7.

11 R. Cole Harris and John Warkentin, *Canada before Confederation: A Study in Historical Geography* (New York: Oxford University Press, 1974),319, 321.

12 Donald H. Akenson, "The Historiography of English-speaking Canada and the Concept of Diaspora: A Sceptical Appreciation," *Canadian Historical Review* 76, 3 (1995), 394, 396. Akenson makes the important point that migrants from Britain were not a single, amorphous cultural group but were divided by the very same differences that I associate with Anglo-Canadians.

13 Goldwin Smith, "The Political Destiny of Canada," *Canadian Monthly and National Review* 11, 6 (1877), 610.

14 Charles Mair, "The Political Future of Canada," *Canadian Monthly and National Review* 8, 2 (1875), 163–4.

15 Harris and Warkentin, *Canada before Confederation*, 323.

16 William Westfall, "On the Concept of Region in Canadian History and Literature," in David Taras, Beverly Rasporich, and Eli Mandel, eds., *A Passion for Identity: An Introduction to Canadian Studies* (Scarborough: Nelson Canada, 1993), 338–9.

17 David Bell and Lorne Tepperman, *The Roots of Disunity* (Toronto: McClelland and Stewart, 1979), 249.

18 Thomas Acheson, "The Maritimes and 'Empire Canada'," in David J. Bercuson, ed., *Canada and the Burden of Unity* (Toronto: Macmillan, 1977), 94–5.

19 For further discussion, see R. Douglas Francis, "Changing Images of the West," in Taras, Rasporich, and Mandel, *A Passion for Identity*, 453; Paul Phillips, "National Policy, Continental Economics and National Disintegration," in Bercuson, ed., *Canada and the Burden of Unity*, 19–43; Douglas Owram, *The Promise of Eden*, vol. 2 (Toronto: University of Toronto Press, 1992), 178.

20 This quotation appears in Donald B. Smith, "A Look Backwards: Canada in 1892, 1927 and 1967," Association of Canadian Studies *Newsletter* 14, 3 (1992), 10.

21 J.M.S. Careless, *Frontier and Metropolis: Regions, Cities and Identities in Canada before 1914* (Toronto: University of Toronto Press, 1989), 91.

22 Northrop Frye, "Northrop Frye's Canada," *Globe and Mail*, 15 April 1991, A17.

23 Louis Hartz et al., *The Founding of New Societies* (New York: Harcourt Brace and World, 1964); R. Cole Harris, "The Simplification of Europe Overseas," *Annals, Association of American Geographers* 67, 4 (1977), 469–83; Donald Meinig, *The Shaping of Atlantic America: A Geographical Perspective on 500 Years of History, Volume 1: Atlantic America* (New Haven: Yale University Press, 1986), 221.

24 Jehu Mathews, "The Political Future of Canada," *Canadian Monthly and National Review* 8, 1 (1875), 55; William Norris, "Canadian Nationality and Its Opponents," *Canadian Monthly and National Review* 8, 3 (1875), 237.

25 Patricia Marchak, "Given a Certain Latitude: A (Hinterland) Sociologist's View of Anglo-Canadian Literature," in Paul Cappon, ed., *In Our House: Social*

Perspectives on Canadian Literature (Toronto: McClelland and Stewart, 1978), 178–205.

26 Ibid., 180.

27 Roy Daniels, "Confederation to the First World War," in Carl F. Klinck, ed., *Literary History of Canada*, vol. 1 (Toronto: University of Toronto Press, 1976), 208.

28 Allan Smith, "The Imported Image: American Publications and American Ideas in the Evolution of the English Canadian Mind" (Ph.D. dissertation, University of Toronto, 1972), 294.

29 Charles Mair, "The New Canada: Its Resources and Productions," *Canadian Monthly and National Review* 8, 2 (1875), 163.

30 Paul Cappon, "Introduction," in Cappon, ed., *In Our House*, 60.

31 Roswell Fisher, "Canada's Alternatives," *Canadian Monthly and Journal Review* 8, 5 (1875), 429.

32 Karen C. Altfest, "Canadian Literary Nationalism" (Ph.D. dissertation, City University of New York, 1979), 235–8.

33 Russell Brown, "The Written Line," in Robert Lecker, coordinating editor, *Borderlands: Essays in Canadian-American Relations* (Toronto: ECW Press, 1991), 13.

34 Anthony Cohen, *The Symbolic Construction of Community*, Key Idea Series, No. 1 (Chichester: Ellis Horwood, 1985), 58.

35 Patrick McGreevy, "The End of America: The Beginning of Canada," *Canadian Geographer* 32, 4 (1988), 307, 313.

36 This argument is most closely associated with Seymour Martin Lipset, *Continental Divide: The Values and Institutions of the United States and Canada* (New York and London: Routledge, 1990).

37 Ibid.

38 Northrop Frye, "Sharing the Continent," in Tara, Rasporich, and Mandel, *A Passion for Identity*, 255.

39 Louis Hartz, *The Liberal Tradition in America* (New York: Harcourt, Brace and World, 1955); Hartz et al., *The Founding of New Societies*; S.F. Wise, "Upper Canada and the Conservative Tradition," in E.G. Firth, ed., *Profiles of a Province* (Toronto: Ontario Historical Society, 1967).

40 Wise, "Upper Canada and the Conservative Tradition," 31.

41 Daniel Drache, "The Crisis of Canadian Political Economy Dependency Theory versus the New Orthodoxy," *Canadian Journal of Political and Social Theory* 7 (1983), 44.

42 David J. Cheal, "Ontario Loyalism: A Socio-Political Ideology in Decline," *Canadian Ethnic Studies* 13, 2 (1981), 40.

43 Gad Horowitz, "Conservatism, Liberalism and Socialism in Canada: An Interpretation," *Canadian Journal of Economic and Political Science* 32 (1966), 143–71.

44 S.D. Clark, *The Social Development of Canada* (Toronto: University of Toronto Press, 1940); Wise, "Upper Canada and the Conservative Tradition."

45 See, for example, George Rawlyk, "The Federalist-Loyalist Alliance in New Brunswick, 1784–1815," *Humanities Association Review* 27, 2 (1976), 142–60; Katherine Bindon, "Kingston: A Social History, 1785–1830" (Ph.D. dissertation, Queen's University, 1979); Jane Errington and George Rawlyk, "The Loyalist-Federalist Alliance of Upper Canada," *American Review of Canadian Studies* 14, 2 (1984), 157–76; Jane Errington, *The Lion, the Eagle, and Upper Canada: A Developing Colonial Ideology* (Kingston and Montreal: McGill-Queen's University, 1989).

46 Errington and Rawlyk, "The Loyalist-Federalist Alliance," 159.

47 J.L. Granatstein and N. Hillmer, *For Better or Worse: Canada and the United States to 1990* (Toronto: Copp Clark Pitman Ltd., 1991), xiv.

48 Bruce Wilson, *As She Began: An Illustrated Introduction to Loyalist Ontario* (Toronto: Dundurn Press, 1981), 10.

49 Mathews, "The Political Future of Canada," 58.

50 Mair, "The New Canada," 161.

51 The J.S. Larned Report, 1871, as contained in the U.S. Senate Document 80, Second Part, 1911 (6092), 1285. This quote, with permission of the author, comes from David R. Smith, "Crossing the Border: Canadian Migration to the Great Lakes," paper presented at the Association for Canadian Studies in the United States Biennial Conference, New Orleans, 1993.

52 Granatstein and Hillmer, *For Better or Worse*, 17.

53 Goldwin Smith, *Canada and the Canadian Question* (Toronto: Hunter, Rose, 1891).

54 Smith, "The Political Destiny of Canada," 613.

55 These comments were taken from a New York *Sun* interview with Erastus Wiman and reprinted in the 8 October 1888 edition of the Toronto *Empire*. This interview in turn is quoted in Watson Griffin, "A Canadian-American Liaison," *Magazine of American History* (February 1889), 123.

56 Heather Jo Hammer and John W. Gartrell, "American Penetration and Canadian Development: A Case Study of Mature Dependency," *American Sociological Review* 51, 2 (1986), 203.

57 Sara Jeanette Duncan, *The Imperialist* (Toronto: McClelland, Goodchild and Stewart, 1904), 266.

58 Lauren McKinsey and Victor Konrad, *Borderlands Reflections: The United States and Canada*, Borderlands Monograph Series No. 1 (Orono: Canadian-American Center, University of Maine, 1989), iv; Victor Konrad, "Borderlands: A Concept for Reinterpreting North America," *Association of American Geographers Annual Meeting Program and Abstracts* (Washington: Association of American Geographers, 1990), 127.

59 McKinsey and Konrad, *Borderlands Reflections*, 2.

60 Victor Konrad, "Borderlines and Borderlands in the Geography of Canada–United States Relations," in Stephen Randall, Herman Konrad, and Sheldon Silverman, eds., *North America without Borders? Interpreting Canada, the United States, and Mexico* (Calgary: University of Calgary Press, 1992), 199.

61 Graeme Wynn, "New England's Outpost in the Nineteenth Century," in Stephen Hornsby, Victor Konrad, and James Herlan, eds., *The Northeastern Borderlands: Four Centuries of Interaction* (Orono and Fredericton: Canadian-American Center, University of Maine and Acadiensis Press, 1989), 64–90.

62 Wynn, "New England's Outpost," 68–77.

63 Ibid., 77–86.

64 Fred Landon refers to Smith's gazetteer in his book *Western Ontario and the American Frontier* (Toronto: Ryerson Press and New Haven: Yale University Press, 1941), 21.

65 For a comprehensive study of Ontario to Michigan migration patterns during the first half of the nineteenth century, see Gregory Rose, "The Origins of Canadian Settlers in Southern Michigan, 1820–1850," *Ontario History* 89, 1 (1987), 31–52.

66 Thomas McIlwraith, "Transport in the Border Lands, 1763–1920," in Lecker, *Borderlands*, 54–79.

67 W. Raymond Wood and Thomas D. Thiessen, "Introduction," in W. Raymond Wood and Thomas D. Thiessen, eds., *Early Fur Trade on the Northern Plains: Canadian Traders among the Mandan and Hidatsa Indians, 1738–1818* (Norman: University of Oklahoma Press, 1985), 1–6.

68 Barry Kaye, "The Trade in Livestock Between the Red River Settlement and the American Frontier, 1812–1870," *Prairie Forum* 6 (1981), 163.

69 Arthur S. Morton, *A History of the Canadian West to 1870–71*, 2nd ed. (Toronto: University of Toronto Press, 1973), 853.

70 David Whiteley, "Letters Home: Correspondence to and from the Red River Settlement," *Manitoba History* 26 (1993), 21–5.

71 John Warkentin, "The Desert Goes North," in Brian Blouet and Merle P. Lawson, eds., *Images of the Plain: The Role of Human Nature in Settlement* (Norman: University of Oklahoma Press, 1975), 161.

72 Paul Sharp, "The Northern Great Plains: A Study in Canadian-American Regionalism," *Mississippi Valley Historical Review* 39 (1952), 68–70.

73 McIlwraith, "Transport in the Border Lands," 76.

74 Robert and Wynona Wilkins, *North Dakota: A Bicentennial History* (New York: W.W. Norton and Co., 1977), 38.

75 Harold Troper, *Only Farmers Need Apply* (Toronto: Griffin House, 1972), 86–7.

76 Sharp, "The Northern Great Plains."

77 David D. Harvey, *Americans in Canada: Migration and Settlement since 1840* (Lewiston, New York and Queenston, Ontario: The Edwin Mellen Press, 1991), 156–9.

78 Marcus Lee Hansen and John Bartlett Brebner, *The Mingling of the Canadian and American Peoples, Volume 1: Historical* (New Haven: Yale University Press, 1940).

79 R. Bruce Shepard, "American Influence in the Settlement and Development of the Canadian Plains" (Ph.D. dissertation, Canadian Plains Research Centre, University of Regina, 1994).

378 Notes to pages 34–42

80 See David Breen, *The Canadian West and the Ranching Frontier, 1874–1924* (Toronto: University of Toronto Press, 1983); Warren Elofson, "Adapting to the Frontier Environment: The Ranching Industry in Western Canada, 1881–1914," in Donald H. Akenson, ed., *Canadian Papers in Rural History*, vol. 8 (Gananoque: Langdale Press, 1992), 307–27; Simon Evans, "American Cattlemen on the Canadian Range, 1874–1914," *Prairie Forum* 4 (1979), 121–35; Simon Evans, "The Origin of Ranching in Western Canada: American Diffusion or Victorian Transplant?" in L.A. Rosenvall and Simon Evans, eds., *Essays on the Historical Geography of the Canadian West* (Calgary: Department of Geography, University of Calgary, 1987), 70–94.

81 Frances Kaye, "Borderlands: Canadian/American Prairie/Plains Literature in English," paper submitted to the Borderlands Project, 1. This quote appears in Konrad, "Borderlines and Borderlands," 202.

82 Seymour Martin Lipset, *Agrarian Socialism: The Cooperative Commonwealth Federation in Saskatchewan: A Study in Political Sociology*, rev. ed. (New York: Doubleday, 1968). This book was originally published in 1950 by University of California Press, Berkeley. See also Mildred Schwartz, "Political Protest in the Western Borderlands: Can Farmers Be Socialists?" in Lecker, *Borderlands*, 46.

83 For a discussion of the concept of gateway cities, see Andrew Burghardt, "A Hypothesis about Gateway Cities," *Annals, Association of American Geographers* 61 (1971), 269–85.

84 Sharp, "The Northern Great Plains," 63, 75–6.

85 Shepard, "American Influence on the Settlement and Development of the Canadian Plains," 342.

86 F.W. Howay, W.N. Sage, and H.F. Angus, *British Columbia and the United States*, 2nd ed. (New York: Russell and Russell, 1970), 18–19, 23–100.

87 Donald Meinig, *The Great Columbia Plain: A Historical Geography, 1805–1910* (Seattle: University of Washington Press, 1968).

88 Howay, Sage, and Angus, *British Columbia and the United States*, 109–38.

89 Ibid., 184–8.

90 Charles Fedorak, "The United States Consul in Victoria and the Political Destiny of the Colony of British Columbia," *B.C. Studies* 79 (1988), 11–12, 23.

91 John Bradbury, "British Columbia: Metropolis and Hinterland in Microcosm," in McCann, *Heartland and Hinterland*, 343.

92 Joseph Leavitt, *A Vision Beyond Reach* (Ottawa: Deneau Publishers, 1982).

93 Thomas White, "The Immigrant in Canada," *Canadian Monthly and National Review* 2, 1 (1872), 8; Fisher, "Canada's Alternatives," 43.

94 Hammer and Gartrell, "American Penetration and Canadian Development," 203.

95 Granatstein and Hillmer, *For Better or Worse*, 20.

96 James Douglas Jr, "The Intellectual Progress of Canada during the Last Fifty Years, and the Present State of Its Literature," *Canadian Monthly and National*

Review 7, 6 (1875), 473; J.W. Langley, "Canadian Literature," *Maritime Monthly* 2, 3 (1873), 257–61.
97 Smith, *The Imported Image*, 2, 7, 46.

CHAPTER 2

1 Portions of this chapter originally appeared in three of my articles: "Belleville and Environs: Continuity, Change and the Integration of Town and Country During the Nineteenth Century," *Urban History Review* 19, 1 (1991), 181–208 (reprinted by permission of Becker Associates); "Scale and Context: Approaches to the Study of Canadian Migration Patterns in the Nineteenth Century," *Social Science History* 12, 3 (1988), 269–303 (reprinted by permission of Duke University Press); "Motivation and Scale: A Method of Identifying Land Speculators in Upper Canada," *Canadian Geographer* 23, 4 (1979), 337–51.
2 Sylvia Pedroza-Bailey, "Immigration Research: A Conceptual Map," *Social Science History* 14, 1 (1990), 62–3.
3 For elaboration of Giddens's theory of structuration and examples of this approach in historical geographic research, see Anthony Giddens, *New Rules of Sociological Method* (London: Hutchinson, 1976); Anthony Giddens, *The Constitution of Society: Outline of the Theory of Structuration* (Cambridge: Polity Press, 1984); Derek Gregory, *Regional Transformation and Industrial Revolution: A Geography of the Yorkshire Woollen Industry* (London: Macmillan, 1984); Alan Pred, "Place as Historically Contingent Process: Structuration and the Time-Geography of Becoming Places," *Annals, Association of American Geographers* 74 (1984), 279–297; Alan Pred, *Power, Place and Structure* (Cambridge: Polity Press, 1986). Gregory emphasizes structuration in his analysis of regional transformation and class struggle in the late eighteenth and early nineteenth-century West Riding textile industry. Pred's studies of mercantile urban development in the eastern United States and rural settlement in Sweden are intended to integrate the experiences and actions of merchants and farmers with their structural contexts.

All social sciences face the problem of theorizing on human agency. Questions of agency and structure are ontological. In this study, locality is viewed as a context which does not determine but rather delimits action. Individuals are never fully capable of understanding the conditions of their action and yet at the same time neither are they completely conditioned by structure. Time and space are the constituitive elements of human existence and thus the important dimensions of context. Yet these dimensions of context are extremely difficult to comprehend, particularly when the study is of the inaccessible past.

Individuals are not only conditioned by wider structural forces but by human relations as well. People interpret the conditions of their existence through the shared experience of the various local groups to which they belong (family, ethnic, social, class). Space plays a major role in this media-tion between structure and agency. Social space is created through interac-tion with the environment; society creates and relates to space through prac-tices of social production and reproduction. As Thrift maintains, people learn what group categories they belong to and what is expected of them in those categories at particular times and in particular places or locales. In many ways, culture is locally defined. I believe that such locally defined culture was very important in the mobility experiences of the Anglo-Canadians compris-ing this study. Yet in order to acquire insight into the workings of the individ-ual mind and the group, we have to move beyond the observable hard data of experience to the less concrete realm of inference and the subjective. But how do we do this? For elaboration of this argument, see A. Warde, "Reasons for a Prodding: a Comment on Locality," *Antipode* 21 (1989), 274–81, 279–80; Nigel Thrift, "On the Determination of Social Action in Space and Time," *Environment and Planning D: Society and Space* 1 (1983), 23–58.

4 Michael Percy, "Migration Flows during the Decade of the Wheat Boom in Canada, 1900–1910" (Ph.D. dissertation, Queen's University, Kingston, 1977), 2–4.

5 David Montgomery, *The Fall of the House of Labour* (Cambridge: Cambridge University Press, 1987).

6 For further discussion of the neo-Marxian view of Canadian development, a perspective more varied and widely interpreted than addressed here, see Wal-lace Clement, *The Canadian Corporate Elite* (Toronto: McClelland and Stewart, 1975); Tom Naylor, *Industrial Development, The History of Canadian Business, 1867–1914: Volume 2* (Toronto: James Lorimer and Company, 1975).

7 Pedroza-Bailey, "Immigration Research," 62.

8 Alan Kulikoff, "The Transition to Capitalism in Rural America," *William and Mary Quarterly*, 3rd series, 46, 1 (1989), 120–44.

9 See, for example, Charles Grant, *Democracy in the Connecticut Frontier: Town of Kent* (New York, 1961); James Lemon, *The Best Poor Man's Country: A Geograph-ical Study of Early Southeastern Pennsylvania* (Baltimore: The Johns Hopkins Press, 1972).

10 See, for example, Michael Merrill, "Cash is Good to Eat: Self-Sufficiency and Exchange in the Rural Economy of the United States," *Radical History Review* 3 (1977), 42–71; James Henretta, "Families and Farms: Mentalite in Pre-Industrial America," *William and Mary Quarterly*, 3rd series, 35, 1 (1978), 3–32; Christopher Clark, "The Household Economy, Market Exchange and the Rise of Capitalism in the Connecticut Valley, 1800–1860," *Journal of Social History* 13 (1979), 169–89; Winnie B. Rothenberg, "The Emergence of a Cap-italist Market in Rural Massachussetts, 1730–1838," *Journal of Economic History* 45, 4 (1985), 781–808.

11 Kulikoff, "The Transition to Capitalism," 122–3, 127.

12 This theory was first articulated in J.M.S. Careless, "Frontierism, Metropoli-tanism, and Canadian History," *Canadian Historical Review* 35, 1 (1954), 1–21.

13 See, for example, Fred Dahms, "The Process of Urbanization in the Countryside: A Study of Huron and Bruce Counties, 1891–1981," *Urban History Review* 12 (1984), 1–18; Chad Gaffield, "Social Structure and the Urbanization Process: Perspectives on Nineteenth Century Research," in Gilbert Stelter and Alan Artibise, eds., *The Canadian City: Essays in Urban and Social History* (Ottawa: Carleton University Press, 1984), chapter 12; Gilbert Stelter, "A Regional Framework for Urban History," *Urban History Review* 13 (1985), 193–206; Larry S. Bourne, "Urbanization, Migration and Urban Research in Comparative Context: An Urban Systems Perspective," *Canadian Journal of Development Studies* 8, 1 (1987), 69–80.

14 N.S.B. Gras, *Introduction to Economic History* (New York: Harper and Row, 1922).

15 Walter Christaller, *Central Places in Southern Germany*, trans. C.W. Basken (Englewood Cliffs, NJ: Prentice-Hall, 1970).

16 James Vance, *The Merchant's World: The Geography of Wholesaling* (Englewood Cliffs, NJ: Prentice-Hall, 1970).

17 See, for example, Hal C. Barron, *Those Who Stayed Behind: Rural Society in Nineteenth Century New England* (Cambridge: Cambridge University Press, 1984). In his recent comprehensive treatment of transatlantic migration, Walter Nugent finds "modernization as a general theory ... too vague to be testable." Walter Nugent, *Crossings: The Great Transatlantic Migrations, 1870–1914* (Bloomington: Indiana University Press, 1992), 164.

18 This is one of the major points made by Gerald Hodge and Mohammed Qadeer in their book *Towns and Villages in Canada: The Importance of Being Unimportant* (Toronto: Butterworths, 1983).

19 Steven Hahn and Jonathan Prude, eds., *The Countryside in the Age of Capitalist Transformation* (Chapel Hill: University of North Carolina Press, 1985); David Gagan, *Hopeful Travellers: Families, Land and Social Change in Mid-Victorian Peel County, Canada West* (Toronto: University of Toronto Press, 1981).

20 David Gagan, "Geographical and Social Mobility in Nineteenth-Century Ontario: A Microstudy," *Canadian Review of Sociology and Anthropology* 13, 2 (1976), 153.

21 Frederick Mendels, "Social Mobility and Phases of Industrialization," *Journal of Interdisciplinary History* 2, 3 (1976), 216.

22 E.G. Ravenstein, "Census of the British Isles, 1871"; "Birthplaces and migration," *Geographical Magazine* 3 (1876), 173–7, 201–6, 229–33; "The Laws of Migration," *Journal of the Royal Statistical Society* 48 (1885), 167–227; "The Laws of Migration," ibid., 52 (1889), 214–301.

23 This point is emphasized by Robert Woods in his book *Theoretical Population Geography* (London: Longman, 1982).

24 For example, see Everett S. Lee, "A Theory of Migration," *Demography* 3 (1966), 47–57.

25 Richard Harris and Eric Moore, "An Historical Approach to the Study of Migration," *Professional Geographer* 32, 1 (1980), 22–8.

26 Herbert Mays, "'A Place to Stand': Families, Land and Permanence in Toronto Gore Township, 1820–1890," Canadian Historical Association, *Historical Papers* (1980), 186.

27 John Warkentin, "Southern Ontario: A View from the West," *Canadian Geographer* 10, 3 (1966), 163.

28 For example, G.P. deT. Glazebrook, *Life in Ontario: A Social History* (Toronto: University of Toronto Press, 1968).

29 In the past two decades students of nineteenth-century Ontario have focused attention on various themes which contradict this uni-dimensional view. See, for example, Michael Katz, *The People of Hamilton, Canada West* (Cambridge, Mass.: Harvard University Press, 1975); Gregory Kealey, *Toronto Workers Respond to Industrial Capitalism, 1867–1892* (Toronto: University of Toronto Press, 1980); Gagan, *Hopeful Travellers.*

30 See, for example, Gilbert Patterson, "Land Settlement in Upper Canada," in Alexander Fraser, ed., *Sixteenth Report of the Bureau of Archives for the Province of Ontario* (Toronto: Clarkson W. James, 1921); Lillian Gates, *Land Policies of Upper Canada* (Toronto: University of Toronto Press, 1968); A. Wilson, *The Clergy Reserves of Upper Canada* (Toronto: University of Toronto Press, 1968).

31 Gates, *Land Policies,* 15. Under the regulations of 1783, field officers received 1,000 acres; captains, 700 acres; and subalterns, staff officers, and warrant officers, 500 acres.

32 Thomas Talbot and William Dickson were two notable individuals who acquired large blocks of land in return for their sponsorship of settlement. Thomas was granted a vast amount of land along the shore of Lake Erie from St Thomas to Simcoe while Dickson was given control of Dumfries Township.

33 For discussion of the speculative behaviour of surveyors, see Randy William Widdis, "Speculation and the Surveyor: An Analysis of the Role Played by Surveyors in the Settlement of Upper Canada," *Histoire Sociale* 15, 30 (1982), 443–58.

34 L.A. Johnson, "Land Policy, Population Growth and Social Structure in the Home District, 1793–1851," *Ontario History* 63, 1 (1971), 41.

35 Robert Gourlay, *A Statistical Account of Upper Canada,* 2 vols (London, 1822), ccccxlviii–ix.

36 D'Arcy Boulton, *Sketch of His Majesty's Province of Upper Canada* (1805), 8–9.

37 Harold Adams Innis, *Essays in Canadian Economic History* (Toronto: University of Toronto Press, 1956); Douglas McCalla and Peter George, "Measurement, Myth and Reality: Reflections on the Economic History of Nineteenth-Century Ontario," *Journal of Canadian Studies* 21, 3 (1986), 72.

38 Chad Gaffield, "Children, Schooling, and Family Reproduction in Nineteenth-Century Ontario," *Canadian Historical Review* 62, 2 (1991), 168.

39 David Gagan, "Class and Society in Victorian English Canada: An Historiographical Reassessment," *British Journal of Canadian Studies* 4, 1 (1989), 76–7.

40 J. Ladell and M. Ladell, *A Farm in the Family: The Many Faces of Ontario Agriculture over the Centuries* (Toronto: Dundurn Press, 1985), 88.

383 Notes to pages 54-7

Douglas Baldwin, "Political and Social Behaviour in Ontario, 1879–1901: A Quantitative Approach," (Ph.D. dissertation: York University, 1973), 74–6.

42 William Marr, "Tenant vs. Owner Occupied Farms in York County, Ontario," in Donald H. Akenson, ed., *Canadian Papers in Rural History*, vol. 4 (Gananoque: Langdale Press, 1984), 53. Wilson suggests that freeholding was not such an obsession among Ontario residents as many believe. Tenancy for many, she argues, was regarded as a viable strategy until enough money could be saved to purchase a farm. And for some, such as certain of the Irish Protestant tenants living on Amherst Island, tenancy was actually preferred. See Catherine Anne Wilson, *A New Lease on Life: Landlords, Tenants, and Immigrants in Ireland and Canada* (Montreal and Kingston: McGill-Queen's University Press, 1994).

43 For discussion of mortgaging in nineteenth-century Ontario, see David Gagan, "The Security of Land, Mortgaging in Toronto Gore Township," in F.H. Armstrong, et al., eds., *Aspects of Nineteenth Century Ontario* (Toronto: University of Toronto Press, 1974).

44 James Gilmour, *Spatial Evolution of Manufacturing, Southern Ontario, 1851–1891* (Toronto: University of Toronto Press, 1972).

45 Tom Naylor, *The History of Canadian Business, 1867–1914, Vol. 1* (Toronto: James Lorimer and Company, 1975), 4; Ian Drummond, "C.H.R. Dialogue: Ontario's Industrial Revolution, 1876–1941," *Canadian Historical Review* 69, 3 (1988), 288.

46 Baldwin, "Political and Social Behaviour," 67–70.

47 Gilmour, *Spatial Evolution of Manufacturing*, 141.

48 Baldwin, "Political and Social Behaviour," 93–4.

49 *Census of Canada, 1921*, I: 234–41.

50 Brian S. Osborne, "Kingston in the Nineteenth Century: A Study in Urban Decline," in J. David Wood, ed., *Perspectives on Landscape and Settlement in Nineteenth Century Ontario* (Toronto: McClelland and Stewart, 1975), 179.

51 R. Cole Harris and John Warkentin, *Canada Before Confederation: A Study in Historical Geography* (New York: Oxford University Press, 1974), 154–6.

52 For a detailed discussion of urban development in Ontario, see Jacob Spelt, *Urban Development in South-Central Ontario* (Toronto: University of Toronto Press, 1972).

53 This perception of land is discussed in Fred Landon, *Western Ontario and the American Frontier* (Toronto: Ryerson Press and New Haven: Yale University Press, 1941) and Glazebrook, *Life in Ontario*.

54 J.K. Johnson, "The Businessman as Hero: The Case of William Warren Street," *Ontario History* 65, 3 (1973), 128.

55 For example, see Boulton, *Sketch of His Majesty's Province*, and William Catermole, *Emigration: The Advantages of Emigration to Canada* (London: Simpkin and Marshall, 1831); and David Gagan, "'The Prose of Life': Literary Reflections of the Family, Individual Experience and Social Structure in Nineteenth Century Canada," *Journal of Social History* 9, 3 (1976), 369.

56 Mobility, social and geographical, was less possible for women than men in nineteenth-century Ontario. Males almost exclusively owned property and women were subordinated within the patriarchal household and in society as well. Positions of various institutional powers were occupied predominantly by men. The status of females was determined largely through their husband's or father's position and their roles were largely confined to the family. There were few opportunities outside the home although these would increase as society became more urbanized.

Yet in pioneer society, women worked along with men in the clearing of fields and the management of the household. After the farm was established, they involved themselves in the important tasks of maintaining the household: spinning, weaving, butter- and cheese-making, hauling water, tending the animals, keeping fires going, washing, cleaning, and cooking for the family. Cohen believes that the transformation from self-sufficient to commercial production actually undermined the economic importance of farm women. Yet the reality for most women during the nineteenth century was that opportunities for social mobility were severely restrained. The major avenue of advancement for many lay in marriage. See Marjorie Cohen, *Women's Work: Markets and Economic Development in Nineteenth-Century Ontario* (Toronto: University of Toronto Press, 1988).

57 Russell Hann, *Farmers Confront Industrialization: Some Historical Perspectives on Ontario Agrarian Movements* (Toronto: New Hogtown Press, 1975), 4, 13.

58 Ibid., 13–21.

59 Bryan D. Palmer, "The Changing Face of Labour Protest," in R.L. Gentilcore, ed., *Historical Atlas of Canada, Vol. 2: The Land Transformed 1800–1891* (Toronto: University of Toronto Press, 1993), 145; David Sutherland, "A Changing Society," in ibid., 135.

60 Sutherland, "A Changing Society," 133–4.

61 Peter Laslett, "The Character of Familial History, Its Limitations and the Conditions for Proper Pursuit," *Journal of Family History* 12, 1–2 (1987), 273–4.

62 R.L. Gentilcore, D. Measner, and D. Doherty, "The Coming of the Loyalists," in Gentilcore, *Historical Atlas of Canada*, 24.

63 Harris and Warkentin, *Canada Before Confederation*, 116.

64 Jean-Claude Robert, "An Immigrant Population," in Gentilcore, *Historical Atlas of Canada*, 21.

65 Harris and Warkentin, *Canada Before Confederation*, 118.

66 Donald H. Akenson, *The Irish in Ontario: A Study in Rural History* (Montreal and Kingston: McGill-Queen's University Press, 1984), 18–19, 32–3.

67 B.S. Osborne, J.C. Robert, and D. Sutherland, "Population in the Canadas and the Maritimes to 1851," *Historical Atlas of Canada*, 30.

68 Harris and Warkentin, *Canada Before Confederation*, 118.

69 Marvin McInnis, "Childbearing and Land Availability: Some Evidence from Individual Household Data," in *Population Studies in the Past* (Centre for Advanced Study in the Behavioural Sciences, 1977), 202.

70 Peter Russell, "Upper Canada: A Poor Man's Country? Some Statistical Evidence," in D.H. Akenson, ed., *Canadian Papers in Rural History*, Vol. 3 (Gananoque: Langdale Press, 1982), 137–8.
71 Bouchard argues that equivalent systems have been identified elsewhere in North America, including Quebec. He also makes the point that Gagan's model of this system relied solely on wills and other inheritance arrangements, ignoring other types of family transmission and missing other types of transfers and holdings taking place before this stage. See David Gagan, "The Indivisibility of Land: A Microanalysis of the System of Inheritance in Nineteenth-Century Ontario," *Journal of Economic History* 36, 1 (1976), 126–41; Gerard Bouchard, "Family Reproduction in New Rural Areas: Outline of a North American Model," *Canadian Historical Review* 75, 4 (1994), 475–510.
72 Marvin McInnis, "Fertility Patterns in Late Nineteenth-Century Ontario and Quebec," paper presented at the 13th annual meeting of the Social Science History Association, Chicago, 1988.
73 This trend has been noted by both McInnis in Ontario and Easterlin in the United States. See R. Easterlin, "Factors in the Decline of Farm Fertility in the United States: Some Preliminary Research Results," *Journal of American History* 63, 3 (1976), 600–14.
74 Jean-Claude Robert, "The People," in Gentilcore, *Historical Atlas of Canada*, 77; Alan A. Brookes and Catharine A. Wilson, "'Working Away' from the Farm: the Young Women of North Huron, 1910–30," *Ontario History* 77, 4 (1985), 282.
75 Percy, "Migration Flows," 2–4; U.S. Bureau of the Census, *12th Census of the United States, 1900*, Population Part II, Volume II (Washington: Government Printing House, 1902).
76 W.T. Easterbrook and H.G.J. Aitken, *Canadian Economic History* (Toronto: Macmillan and Co., 1956), 396.
77 Paul Coats, "Two Good Neighbours: A Study of Exchanges in Populations," *Proceedings*, Canadian-American Affairs Conference (Kingston: Queen's University, 1937).
78 Ralph E. Vedder and Lawrence E. Galloway, "Settlement Patterns of Canadian Emigrants in the United States," *Canadian Journal of Economics* 3 (1970), 477–86.
79 Rowland Berthoff, *British Immigrants in Industrial America* (Cambridge, Mass.: Harvard University Press, 1953).
80 U.S. Bureau of the Census, *10th Census of the United States, 1880*, Vols. 1 and 2 (Washington: Government Printing Office, 1882).
81 Ibid.
82 *12th Census of the United States.*
83 Alan Brookes, "Out-Migration from the Maritime Provinces, 1860–1900: Some Preliminary Considerations," *Acadiensis* 5, 2 (1976), 46.
84 Previous residence is defined as living in the United States for a period of six months or more.

85 These interpretations were included in the reports submitted to the Lieu-tenant-Governor of Ontario by Richard McPherson, the commissioner of the Department of Immigration.
86 Alan Brookes, "British Canadians," in S. Thernstrom, A. Orlov, and O. Handlin, eds., *Harvard Encyclopedia of American Ethnic Groups* (Cambridge: Harvard University Press, 1980), 193.
87 Patricia Thornton, "The Problem of Out-Migration from Atlantic Canada, 1871–1921: A New Look," *Acadiensis* 15, 1 (1985), 17.

PART TWO: INTRODUCTION

1 Much of the following discussion on the use of genealogical sources comes from my article "Generations, Mobility and Persistence: A View From Genealogies," *Histoire Sociale* 25, 49 (1992), 125–50 (reprinted by permission of *Histoire Sociale*).
2 For examples of how the manuscript censuses have been used in analysis, see David Gagan and Herbert Mays, "Historical Demography and Canadian Social History: Families and Land in Peel County, Ontario," *Canadian Historical Review* 54 (1973), 27–47; Marvin McInnis, "Childbearing and Land Availability," in *Population Studies in the Past* (Centre for Advanced Study in the Behavioural Sciences, 1977), 201–22.
3 Chad Gaffield, "Theory and Method in Canadian Historical Demography," *Archivaria* 14 (1982), 124.
4 Darrell Norris's study of Adolphustown is a notable exception. See D.A. Norris, "Household and Transiency in a Loyalist Township: The People of Adolphustown, 1784–1822," *Histoire Sociale* 13 (1980), 399–415.
5 Gerard Bouchard, "Family Structures and Geographical Mobility in Laterriere, 1815–1935," *Journal of Family History* 2 (1977), 368.
6 Torsten Hagerstrand, "The Domain of Human Geography," in Richard Chorley, ed., *Directions in Human Geography* (London: Methuen, 1973); Tamara Hareven, "The Family as Process: The Historical Study of the Family Cycle," *Journal of Social History* 7 (1978).
7 Bruce Elliott, *Irish Migrants in the Canadas: A New Approach* (Montreal and Kingston: McGill-Queen's University Press, 1988).
8 I have communicated with the authors of two of the five genealogies and spent an entire summer travelling to the majority of American destinations of the descendants of the five primogenitors. Much of the census information was collected from microfilmed manuscripts housed in the Ontario Archives in Toronto and the Burton Library in Detroit. I also made use of the excellent collection of census, property, local history, and border crossing records housed in the Family History Library operated by the Mormon Church in Salt Lake City. For more information about sources and tracing strategies, see Appendix on p. 357.

CHAPTER 3

1 Most of the material in this chapter appeared in Randy William Widdis, "Belleville and Environs: Continuity, Change and the Integration of Town and Country during the Nineteenth Century," *Urban History Review* 19, 1 (1991), 181–208.

2 This brief summary of the region's physical geography was taken from Robert L. Jones, *History of Agriculture in Ontario, 1613–1880*, 2d ed. (Toronto: University of Toronto Press, 1977), 1–22, and Lloyd G. Reeds, "The Environment," in R. Louis Gentilcore, ed., *Ontario*, Studies in Canadian Geography Series, Louis Trotier, ed. (Toronto: University of Toronto Press, 1972), 1–4.

3 The government was quick to realize that improved wild land had almost no immediate value and this, combined with poor markets, the high price of imported goods, the need for large quantities of food, and primitive methods of farming, made it obvious that large acreages were necessary to support pioneer families. The basic grants of 50 acres for each colonist and 100 acres for heads of families were increased to 200-acre lots for each adult Loyalist and 100 acres for their children. Military grants ranged from 200 acres for privates to 5,000 acres for field officers. To encourage the immigration of people of means and education, further grants were awarded to merchants and professional people. Grants were also given to justices of the peace, members of council, and surveyors in lieu of salaries. And any Loyalist who could prove his military service could also apply for additional lands. For further information on the system of land granting in Upper Canada, see Lilian Gates, *Land Policies of Upper Canada* (Toronto: University of Toronto Press, 1968); and Gilbert Patterson, "Land Settlement in Upper Canada," in Alexander Fraser, ed., *Sixteenth Report of the Bureau of Archives for the Province of Ontario* (Toronto: Clarkson W. James, 1921).

4 Gerald Boyce, *Historic Hastings* (Belleville: Ontario Intelligencer, 1967), 33.

5 *The Illustrated Historical Atlas of the Counties of Hastings and Prince Edward, Ontario* (Toronto: H. Belden and Co., 1878), vi (reprinted by Mika Silk Screening Ltd., Belleville, 1972).

6 Jane Goddard Bennett, *Hans Waltimeyer* (Cobourg: Haynes Printing, 1980), 322.

7 Ibid., 282.

8 Nick and Helma Mika, *The Grand Junction Railway* (Belleville: Mika Publishing Company, 1986), 8.

9 Ibid.

10 Boyce, *Historic Hastings*, 54.

11 Archives of Ontario (AO) RG-A-IV, vol. 23, Schedules under the Assessment Act of 1820.

12 Robert Gourlay, *A Statistical Account of Upper Canada*, 2 vols. (London, 1822).

13 Douglas McCalla, "The Internal Economy of Upper Canada: New Evidence

on Agricultural Marketing Before 1850," *Agricultural History* 59, 3 (1985), 400; *Hastings County Directory, including Belleville, 1860–61* (Belleville: Hastings County Council, 1972), 27.

14 Quoted in Gerald Boyce, *Hutton of Hastings* (Belleville: Hastings County Council, 1972), 27.

15 Boyce, *Historic Hastings*, 20; *Hastings County Directory*, 280.

16 Boyce, *Hutton of Hastings*, 20.

17 Susanna Moodie, *Roughing It in the Bush* (London: Richard Bentley, 1852), 317.

18 Jones, *History of Agriculture*, 250, 257.

19 Boyce, *Historic Hastings*, 107.

20 *Hastings County Directory*, 30–1.

21 Mika and Mika, *The Grand Junction Railway*, 35–6.

22 Elizabeth Bloomfield et al., *Industry in Ontario Urban Centres, 1870: Accessing the Manuscript Census* (Research Paper 1, Department of Geography, University of Guelph, 1986).

23 This information comes from the manuscript censuses on Industrial Establishments for the County of Hastings.

24 Bloomfield et al., *Industry in Ontario*, 48–9.

25 R.T. Naylor, *The History of Canadian Business, 1867–1914*, Vol. 1 (Toronto: James Lorimer and Company, 1975), 4.

26 AO, RG 18, Series B-3, *Commission to Inquire and Report Upon the Financial Affairs of the Town of Belleville with Things Connected Therein, 1875–1877*.

27 Boyce, *Hutton of Hastings*, 156.

28 Belleville *Intelligencer*, 9 July 1880.

29 Ibid., 27 July 1880.

30 Jacob Spelt, *Urban Development in South-Central Ontario* (Toronto: University of Toronto Press, 1972), 77.

31 The decline is evidenced in the prices obtained at the Belleville market and the quantities grown in Hastings. On Saturday, 3 January 1880, fall wheat, spring wheat, barley no. 1, barley no. 2, rye, oats and buckwheat fetched bushel prices of $1.25–$1.30, $1.20–$1.30, 60 cents, 50 cents, 75 cents, 35–7 cents and 50 cents respectively on the Belleville market. On Thursday, 14 February 1901, the same items were sold for 65 cents, 65 cents, 40 cents, 38 cents, 48 cents, 28 cents, and 45 cents respectively. Between 1882 and 1900 there was a 69.2%, 38.4%, and 41.5% decrease in the number of bushels of fall wheat, barley, and rye produced in Hastings County. This information was collected from: Belleville *Intelligencer*, 18 May 1891, 14 February 1901; and AO, Ontario Bureau of Industry, Agricultural Returns, First Annual Report, 1900, Part I, *Agricultural Statistics*, 1901, 43.

32 Belleville *Intelligencer*, 18 May 1891.

33 *Belleville City Directory, 1900* (Ingersoll: Union Publishing Company, 1900).

34 James Gilmour, *Spatial Evolution of Manufacturing, Southern Ontario, 1851–1891* (Toronto: University of Toronto Press, 1972), 60.

35 Leo Johnson, *History of the County of Ontario, 1615–1875* (Whitby: Corporation of the County of Ontario,), 342.

36 Biographical sketches of these individuals are included in *Pioneer Life on the Bay of Quinte, including genealogies of old families and biographical sketches of respectable citizens* (Toronto: Rolph and Clark Ltd., 1904), reprinted in Canadiana Series No. 20 (Belleville: Mika Silk Screening, 1972). I would like to thank Darrell Norris for drawing my attention to this volume.

37 Marjorie Cohen, "C.H.R. Dialogue: Ontario's Industrial Revolution, 1876–1941," *Canadian Historical Review* 69, 3 (1988), 309.

CHAPTER 4

1 C.M. Warner, "Some Early Amusements of the County," *Lennox and Addington Historical Society*, Papers and Records, Vol. 1 (1909), 61.

2 W.S. Wallace, "The Loyalist Migration Overland," *Proceedings of the New York State Historical Association*, 11 (1914), 164.

3 In 1797 Hallowell Township was created by the cutting off of the northern part of Marysburgh and the southern part of Sophiasburgh. Ameliasburgh was divided into two townships, Ameliasburgh and Hillier, in 1823. In 1890 Hallowell was divided into Athol and Hallowell. This information was obtained from D.K. Redner, *Its Good to Get Home: More Stories of Prince Edward County and Beyond* (Belleville: Mika Publishing Company, 1983), 13.

4 Audrey Kirk and Robert Kirk, "Approaches to UEL Research," in Don Wilson, ed., *Readings in Ontario Genealogical Sources. A Selection of Presentations Given at the Conference on Ontario Genealogical Sources, October 27–29, 1970* (1970), 108; Janice Potter-MacKinnon, *While the Women Only Wept: Loyalist Refugee Women in Eastern Ontario* (Montreal and Kingston: McGill-Queen's University Press, 1993), 19; *The Illustrated Historical Atlas of the Counties of Hastings and Prince Edward* (Toronto: H. Belden and Co., 1878), vii.

5 Potter-MacKinnon, *While the Women Only Wept*, 19–20.

6 The most important point to make about this volume is that it offers a data set which is at once both rich and seriously incomplete. It does not provide a complete list of all the regional migrants settling in the Quinte region but is a sample of 325 families. Moreover, some of the family articles are genealogical only while others are family histories only, though the majority are both. For the purpose of this study, only those sketches that use both types of information are analysed.

Unfortunately, the data for individual families are not always complete, and the amount of information varies from case to case. Often, for instance, there is no information about the marital status and number of children at the time of migration. Similarly, with respect to origins and destinations, many entries state country only; others record more specific information (i.e., state or province, county, and, sometimes, even lot and concession). This results in variable sample sizes. Only place of settlement and number of children are

390 Notes to pages 118–21

given for successive generations, except for a few notable persons who distinguished themselves in politics, business, or land ownership. In addition, only a selected number of second- and third-generation genealogies include information on names and locations.

Thus, it is possible only to trace the distance and direction of movement of first-generation migrants, along with a selected sample of the second- and third-generations. Even then, it must be acknowledged that many of the people may have lived in other places before settling in the locations mentioned in the book. The dates that they settled in these locations are not available either, and we do not know for sure that they stayed there.

The examination of patterns of initial migration is much more straightforward and detailed than the analysis of inter-generational migration patterns because of the nature of this source. Thousands of moves are mentioned in the Quinte volume but I decided to trace those moves known to have been made by the first-, second-, and third-generation sons of the original pioneers who settled permanently in Sidney, Adolphustown, and Sophiasburgh townships. These were the most heavily populated townships in the original migrant population. To simplify the presentation of the results, only those moves made by the Adolphustown descendants were mapped. Daughters were not included because their moves were almost entirely directed by males, that is, husbands or fathers. These maps are included in my article "Pioneer Life on the Bay of Quinte: An Evaluation of Genealogical Source Data in the Study of Migration," *Canadian Geographer* 27, 3 (1982), 273–82.

7 Norman Crowder, "More about the Loyalists in Ontario," *Families* 23, 3 (1984), 131.

8 Anne Christie, "The Settlement of the County of Lennox and Addington by United Empire Loyalists," *Women's Canadian Historical Society of Ottawa, Transactions*, Vol. 7 (1917), 22.

9 *The Illustrated Historical Atlas of the Counties of Frontenac, Lennox and Addington* (Toronto: J.H. Meacham and Co., 1878) (reprinted by Mika Silk Screening Ltd., Belleville, 1972), 13.

10 Rosa Eaton, "The Early History of Prince Edward County" (MA thesis, Queen's University, 1934), 11, 13.

11 Christopher Moore, "The Disposition to Settle: the Royal Highland Emigrants and Loyalist Settlement in Upper Canada, 1784," *Ontario History* 76, 4 (1984), 314.

12 Eaton, *The Early History*, 14–15, 32–3; *Historical Atlas of Hastings and Prince Edward Counties*, iv.

13 Walter S. Herrington, "Pioneer Life on the Bay of Quinte," *Lennox and Addington Historical Society, Papers and Records*, Vol. 6 (1915), 9.

14 Potter-MacKinnon, *While the Women Only Wept*, 129.

15 AO, RG 1-C-1-8, Indexes for Docket Books, Vol. 8, Simcoe A-4, 1796–1799, Midland District.

16 Darrell Norris, "Household and Transiency in a Loyalist Township: The People of Adolphustown, 1784–1822," *Histoire Sociale* 13 (1980), 403, 405.

17 In order to reduce costs, a detailed reconstruction of the Denyes and Morden patrilineal lines, originally included in an appendix, has been omitted. These two family groups were selected for intensive investigation because their records are the most complete, and because both progenitors were privates, thereby making any differences between them relevant to the story of mobility and persistence. Those interested in looking at these reconstructions, which review the locational and property-holding histories of all male descendants, and maps tracing the generational migration patterns of these same individuals, can contact me at the Department of Geography, University of Regina.

18 Genealogical information about the Denyes families was collected from Drury Denyes, *The Denyes Family, 1750–1982* (Bloomfield, 1982). Additional information from this and other family genealogies was collected by the author from sources both in Canada and the United States.

19 Information on the Morden families was collected from an unpublished and anonymous genealogy housed in the Lennox and Addington Historical Society Museum in Napanee, Ontario, and from an unpublished genealogy compiled by Mrs Marjorie Van Damme. I wish to thank Mrs Van Damme for granting me permission to use her genealogy.

20 Information on the Laughlins was collected from an unpublished genealogy compiled in 1955 by M.E. and E.R. Laughlin.

21 Potter-MacKinnon, *While the Women Only Wept*, 22.

22 Information on the Hudgins family was collected from Charles L. Proctor, *200 Years of Hudgins, 1776–1976* (Picton: Picton Gazette Co. Ltd., 1976) and the Burleigh Collection housed in the Queen's University Archives.

23 AO, MS 622, Sir Frederick Haldimand Papers, 1758–1784, General Abstract of Men, Women, and Children Settled on the New Townships on the St. Lawrence, beginning at No. 1 Lake St. Francis and Running Upwards, Montreal, July 1784.

Information on the Ruttan family was collected from *Pioneer Life on the Bay of Quinte*; the McIlreath Papers housed in the Kingston Public Library; an unpublished genealogy compiled by H. Stevenson housed in the Lennox and Addington Historical Society Museum; and a detailed letter dated 8 August 1988 sent to me by Mrs Mary Pazuick of Trail, British Columbia.

24 Brenda Hudson, *Pride of Place: Story of the Settlement of Prince Edward County* (Belleville: Mika Publishing Co., 1982), 27.

25 *Census of Canada, 1931*, Vol. II, Table 12, 61–77; *Census of Canada, 1880–81*, Vol. III, Table 22, 78–84; *Census of Canada, 1890–91*, Vol. II, Table 16, 272–300.

26 Robert Taylor Jr, "The Olin Tribe: Migration, Mutual Aid and Solidarity of a Nineteenth Century Rural American Kin Group" (Ph.D. dissertation, Kent State University, 1979).

27 Patrilineal transfer figures are only offered for the Denyeses, Mordens, and Laughlins because of the low incidence of such transfer among the Hudgins and Ruttans.

28 Catherine Anne Wilson, *A New Lease on Life: Landlords, Tenants, and Immigrants in Ireland and Canada* (Montreal and Kingston: McGill-Queen's University Press, 1994).

29 Michael Katz, *The People of Hamilton, Canada West: Family and Class in a Mid-Nineteenth Century City* (Cambridge, Mass.: Harvard University Press, 1975).

30 John Bodnar, *The Transplanted: A History of Immigrants in Urban America* (Bloomington: University of Indiana Press, 1987), 212.

31 Hans Medick, "The Protoindustrial Family Economy: The Structural Function of the Household During the Transition from Peasant Society to Industrial Capitalism," Social History 3 (1976).

PART THREE: INTRODUCTION

1 Rowland Berthoff, *British Immigrants in Industrial America* (Cambridge, Mass.: Harvard University Press, 1953), 28; Michael Percy, "Migration Flows during the Decade of the Wheat Boom in Canada, 1900–1910: A Neo-Classical Analysis" (Ph.D. dissertation, Queen's University, Kingston, 1977), 76.

2 Marcus Lee Hansen and John Bartlett Brebner, *The Mingling of the Canadian and American Peoples, Vol. 1: Historical* (New Haven: Yale University Press, 1940),188, 189–95, 192–3, 196, 204, 205–7, 208, 210, 217, 227.

3 US Bureau of the Census, *11th Census of the United States, 1891*, Vol. I and II (Washington: US Census Office, 1891); ibid., *12th Census of the United States, 1901*, Vols. I, II, V, VIII.

4 J. Gavit, *Americans by Choice* (New York: Harper, 1922), 241, 244.

5 E. Barkan, "French Canadians," in S. Thernstrom, A. Orlov, and O. Handlin, eds., *Harvard Encyclopedia of American Ethnic Groups* (Cambridge, Mass.: Harvard University Press, 1980), 392, 394–5.

6 W. Gregory, ed., *American Newspapers* (New York: H.W. Wilson Co., 1937).

7 Alan Brookes, "British Canadians," in Thernstrom, Orlov, and Handlin, eds., *Harvard Encyclopedia of American Ethnic Groups*.

8 For greater discussion of the relationship between ethnicity and class, see G. Carchedi, *On the Economic Identification of Social Classes* (London: Routledge and Kegan Paul, 1977) and J. Scott, Corporations, Classes and Capitalism (London: Hutchinson and Company, 1979).

9 Milton Gordon, *Assimilation in American Life: The Role of Race, Religion and National Origins* (New York: Oxford University Press, 1964).

CHAPTER 5

1 Portions of this chapter originally appeared in three of my articles: "With Scarcely A Ripple: English Canadians in Northern New York at the Beginning

of the Twentieth Century," *Journal of Historical Geography* 13, 2 (1987), 169–92; "'We Breathe the Same Air': Eastern Ontario Migration to Watertown, New York in the Late Nineteenth Century," *New York History* 68, 3 (1987), 261–80 (reprinted by permission of the New York State Historical Association); "Tracing Eastern Ontarian Emigrants to New York State, 1880–1910," *Ontario History* 81, 3 (1989), 201–33 (reprinted by permission of the Ontario Historical Society).

2 The chosen eastern Ontario and northern New York study areas were both important source and destination regions in the total Ontario-to-New York migration flow. The naturalization records are available only after 1906 and refer to migrations taking place after 1880. Petitions for naturalization filed by source region emigrants during the period 1880 to 1910 comprised 58.4 percent of the total number of petitions filed from eastern Ontario emigrants (that area from Hastings in the west to the Quebec border) and 6.3 percent of the entire number of petitions filed by immigrants in the state. The seven New York counties chosen varied in terms of importance as reception areas but they were selected on the basis of their relative proximity to the source region and their varied environments.

3 Robert L. Jones, *History of Agriculture in Ontario, 1613–1880* (Toronto: University of Toronto Press, 1977), 206–7.

4 This vignette was constructed from the 1871 and 1881 manuscript censuses and the Petitions for Naturalization records.

5 This information was contained in a letter written by Janet Snedley of Erinsmore, Ontario, and dated 29 November 1981. John Salisbury was the grandfather of Mrs Snedley's husband.

6 *Census of Canada, 1880–81*, Vol. 1, Table II, 162–9, Table III, 264–85.

7 Many books have been written on the subject of Orangeism in Ontario. Three of the best are Donald H. Akenson, *The Orangemen: The Life and Times of Ogle Gowan* (Toronto: James Lorimer and Company Publishers, 1986); Cecil Houston and William Smyth, *The Sash Canada Wore: A Historical Geography of the Orange Order in Canada* (Toronto: University of Toronto Press, 1980); and Hereward Senior, *Orangeism: the Canadian Phase* (Toronto: McGraw-Hill Ryerson, 1975).

8 *Census of Canada, 1880–81*, Vol. 2, Table XIV, 280–99.

9 Marvin McInnis, "Childbearing and Land Availability," in *Population Studies in the Past* (Centre for Advanced Study in the Behavioural Sciences, 1977), 202.

10 Arthur R.M. Lower, "The Character of Kingston," in Gerald Tulchinsky, ed., *To Preserve and Defend: Essays on Kingston in the Nineteenth Century* (Montreal and Kingston: McGill-Queen's University Press, 1976), 25.

11 Paul Gates, "Agricultural Change in New York State, 1850–1890," *New York State History* 50, 2 (1969), 117, 128–39.

12 David Ellis et al., *A History of New York State* (Ithaca: Cornell University Press, 1969), 504–10.

13 The average wage figure, however, does not take into account short-term and seasonal unemployment in the calculation of average earnings. It also does not account for wide variations in pay among different occupations both within firms and among different establishments.

14 Ellis et al., *A History of New York State*, 513, 526.

15 W.F. Galpin, *Central New York: An Inland Empire*, Vol. 1 (New York: Lewis Historical Publishing Company, Inc., 1941), 106.

16 Ellis et al., *A History of New York State*, 527.

17 V. Crisafulli, "Commerce and Industry," in *The History of Oneida County* (Utica: Oneida County, 1977), 103.

18 Galpin, *Central New York*, 106.

19 Unfortunately, the prior experiences of these individuals remain indiscernible because of the lack of data and thus subsequent analysis of the characteristics of the naturalization group will focus on those individuals born in the origin region. The recently released Index to Canadian Border Entries will make it possible for Ramirez and his team to undertake an analysis of European migrants who spent some time in Canada before moving on to the United States. See note 7, Introduction to Part One.

20 The nature of the naturalization records seriously underestimates the participation of females in the migration process. As stated in the Appendix, women until 1922 automatically became US citizens by naturalization of their husbands. Thus, Canadian women in many cases acquired citizenship when they married Americans or when their Canadian husbands became American citizens. Only those women who chose to file for naturalization before marrying were included in these records.

21 "Old Steamers of the St. Lawrence," Watertown *Daily Times*, 7 May 1943.

22 This information was compiled from an obituary appearing in the 6 October 1940 edition of the Watertown *Daily Times* and from the Petitions for Naturalization.

23 This story was conveyed to me in a letter written by Mrs Thelma Smith of Adams, New York, daughter of Clarence Shangraw, and dated 30 November 1981.

24 These sketches were derived from the Petitions for Naturalization.

25 However, we must be suspicious of the directories which in some cases have been known to under-represent residents in a city.

26 This account was communicated to me in a letter written by Mrs Iris Avery, granddaughter of Mrs Samuel Avery, and dated 28 July 1982.

27 These two vignettes were compiled from the Petitions for Naturalization, the Declarations of Intention, and the Watertown city directories.

28 1900 US Manuscript Census for Watertown, New York.

29 Edward Hungerford, "A North County Town in the Nineties," *New York History* 26 (1945), 136–40.

30 Ibid., 142.

31 Howard Thomas, *Black River in the North Country* (Prospect: Prospect Books, 1963), 116–17.
32 *Boyd's Directory of Watertown* (Watertown: Boyd and Company, 1900).
33 E.C. Gould, *Centennial History of Watertown* (Watertown: T.C. Oakes Advertising, 1969), 23.
34 Watertown *Daily Times*, 31 March 1900, 2.
35 This fact was related to me by local historian Alex Duffy.
36 Ellis et al., *A History of New York State*, 268.
37 W.F. Galpin, *Central New York*, 77.
38 *12th Census of the United States*, Vol. II, Population, Part II, Table 35 (Washington: US Census Office, 1901), 800–3.
39 Ibid., Census Bulletin 159, 25 April 1902, 15.
40 Bruce Bigelow, "Ethnic Stratification in a Pedestrian City: A Social Geography of Syracuse, New York in 1860" (Ph.D. dissertation, Syracuse University, 1978), 74.
41 Watertown *Daily Times*, 15 August 1902, 3.
42 Ibid., 25 April 1902, 2.
43 An interview with an elderly patient (whose name I unfortunately lost) conducted at Watertown Mercy Hospital in June 1980 indicates, at least in her opinion, that ethnic and social differences were a major dimension of the city's character during this period. The comments she offers provides us with a fascinating insight into the community.

I was born right here in Watertown in 1895. My father was a lawyer. I lived here until I married and then I moved to New York City. When my husband died I came back to Watertown ... I can remember very clearly the fourth of July parade in 1900. My father took us to see it. My sister and I sat often sat on the balcony right outside my father's office window where we could look right down on the activity in Public Square. I once saw Teddy Roosevelt ride his horse in the square. It was the centre of the city; everything happened there, not like today. Working people walked up to the square from Mill Street on their way home from work. There were a lot of saloons on the way and many didn't make it home until quite some time after work ... Italians lived in the Sand Flats area; that's the area around Bellew Avenue near the fairgrounds. Irish people were originally there but moved up town as they became wealthier. There were Hungarians there also. The Italians were labourers and many sold vegetables. After they had been there a few years, many got jobs in the factories and moved to other parts of the town ... Canadians, mostly French, lived on the north side. They had different festivals to raise money to build their church [Our Lady of the Sacred Heart]. I think a lot of them worked in the paper mills. They really took care of themselves ... There was a big difference between the north and south sides. The north side was much poorer. There was a mix of different people on that side while

Americans lived mostly on the south side. You know, there were almost fifty millionaires in Watertown in 1910 and they all lived on the south side ... Watertown was full of cliques based on how much money you had and where you came from. There was a strong anti-Catholic feeling and wealthy people had their own societies, clubs and groups. The north side was always referred to as "over the river". The Water Street area was especially off limits to "good" people. It was the red light district and was not spoken of in "proper" circles.

44 Watertown *Daily Times*, 28 February 1900, 2.
45 Ibid., 1 March 1890, 2.
46 Syracuse *Herald-Journal*, 19 March 1899, 4.
47 J.L. Reese, "A Comparative Study of Jewish and Italian Intergenerational Occupational Mobility in Syracuse" (Department of Sociology, University of Syracuse, 1975), 8.
48 Syracuse *Herald-Journal*, 19 March 1899, 4.
49 *Century*, vol. 28 (September 1884).
50 Syracuse *Post-Standard*, 27 April 1900, 2.
51 Figures for Syracuse are derived from a stratified sample computed by weight factors. The sample procedure was designed after consultation with Dr Thomas Stroud of the Department of Mathematics, Queen's University, and David Howes, a fellow graduate student in the Department of Geography at Queen's.
      The technique for 1900 was based on the stratified random sampling procedure. Stratified sampling was chosen because it best enables the researcher to gain a precise estimate of characteristics of the whole household head population and thus best to approximate reality. Because the Watertown sample is the total population, the statistics cited are descriptive of reality and thus cannot be questioned as to representativeness. The stratified sampling technique computed by weight factors for Syracuse best approximates the entire population and thus allows me to avoid statistical tests of representativeness. For further explanation of this procedure see my Ph.D. dissertation, "With Scarcely A Ripple: The Eastern Ontarian Immigrant Experience in Northern New York at the Turn of the Century" (Kingston: Queen's University, 1984), Appendix 4, 484–9.
52 The information for these case studies originates from obituaries of naturalization members appearing in the Watertown *Daily Times*. These obituaries, collected by the Genealogical Department of the Flower Memorial Library in Watertown, provide detailed histories of eastern Ontarians. Unfortunately, no such readily available collection exists in Syracuse where a fewer number of naturalizations are concealed within a much larger population.
53 Watertown *Daily Times*, obituary, 15 August 1969 edition.
54 This example was constructed from the city directories, the Petitions for Naturalization, and the Declarations of Intention.
55 The index of dissimilarity is calculated according to electoral districts and measures the proportion of one group that would have to change its location

in order to be distributed identically with another group. For example, Table 37 shows that only 9.9 percent of other Americans would have to move to be consistent with the residential location of New Yorkers; but 57.5 percent of the Italians would have to change residence to be identical to New Yorkers. A lack of segregation yields a minimum index of o, complete segregation 100; the cutoff point is usually accepted as 25. The formula for the index of dissimilarity is:

$$Id = 1/2 \sum_{i=1}^{k} Ixi{-}yiI$$

For further discussion of this technique, see: R.J. Johnston, ed., The Dictionary of Human Geography (Oxford: Oxford University Press, 1981), 162–163.

56 Kathleen Conzen makes note of the mutual tendency of both these groups to avoid each other in her study of Milwaukee. See Kathleen Conzen, *Immigrant Milwaukee, 1836–1860: Accommodation and Community in a Frontier City* (Cambridge, Mass.: Harvard University Press, 1976).

57 The occupational classification devised by Peter Goheen in his *Victorian Toronto: 1850 to 1900* (Chicago: University of Chicago Press, 1970), was used in this study. For the coding used in this research, see my Ph.D. dissertation, "With Scarcely a Ripple," 463–5.

Unskilled: these include those who were employed as casual labourers outside the factory and at the bottom of the hierarchy in the factory. They possessed no discernible skills which could be applied at their place of occupation. *Semi-skilled and skilled*: like the unskilled, they belonged to the proletariat, that is, they were producers of surplus value but did not own the means of production (unless specified by the census). This group includes both manual and non-manual labourers. *Petty capitalists*: this includes those individuals who controlled their own means of production and labour power but did not employ labour or, if they did, only on a very small scale. *Large capitalists*: they differ from the petty bourgeois in terms of the scale of their operation and control. They not only controlled their own labour power and means of production but employed labour and generated surplus income. *Middle (new business) class*: this group includes those not involved in the production of surplus value but rather in the sale of finished commodities (e.g., managers, accountants). In this sense, they were performing the function of capital. The capital of this group rested in knowledge and control. This category also includes professionals who may be viewed as the petty bourgeoisie. They are distinguished, however, more by the provision of technical expertise than by their control of the means of production. *Private means*: this includes a miscellaneous group, ranging from women whose occupations were not specified, meaning that they may be included in all classes, to gentlemen who may also may be either working class or bourgeoisie.

58 For discussion of the role of working-class institutions, see T. Cumbler,

"Transatlantic Working Class Institutions," *Journal of Historical Geography* 6, 3 (1980), 279.

59 Watertown *Daily Times*, 3 May 1910, 4.

60 W. Gregory, ed., *American Newspapers* (New York: H.W. Wilson Company, 1937).

61 Although the Orange Order was common to all Protestant groups of British descent, and was supported most by those of Protestant Irish background, in Watertown it was essentially an institution organized by former Canadians, although many of them were first- and second-generation Irish. The Watertown lodge was established in 1897 with G.A. Sexsmith, a Canadian immigrant, as treasurer; Murray Ackerman, an American, as chairman of the reception committee; G.C. Crawford, an American whose parents came from Canada, as chairman of the decorating committee; H.J. Becker, a Canadian immigrant, as general chairman; and W.R. Sexsmith, also a Canadian, as secretary. This information was derived from the 22 April 1936 edition of the *Daily Times*.

62 Wages for specific occupations in Watertown at the turn of the century are discussed in the 11 July 1951 edition of the *Daily Times*.

63 Ibid., 15 August 1969.

64 This case history was compiled from the city directories, Petitions for Naturalization, and the Declarations of Intention.

65 Ibid.

66 Transients include those who disappeared from the directories without any indication of their deaths. It is possible that the directories failed to mention the deaths of all Canadians residing in the city and so the numbers may be inflated.

67 Nathan Glazer and Daniel Patrick Moynihan, *Beyond the Melting Pot* (Cambridge, Mass.: MIT Press, 1970).

68 The stratified sampling strategy does not include the very small number of Canadians who fit into this category.

CHAPTER 6

1 This quote appears in John Lee Coulter, "Industrial History of the Valley of the Red River of the North," *Collection of the State Historical Society of North Dakota*, Vol. 3 (Bismarck: State Historical Society of North Dakota, 1910), 540–1.

2 Anonymous, "Pembina: Meeting Place of Nations" (Bismarck: State Archives of North Dakota, 1964).

3 William Sherman, *Prairie Mosaic: An Ethnic Atlas of Rural North Dakota* (Fargo: North Dakota Institute for Regional Studies, 1983), 99.

4 Coulter, "Industrial History of the Valley," 550–1; Jesse Tanner, "Foreign Immigration into North Dakota," in *Collections of the State Historical Society of North Dakota*, Vol. 1 (1906), 184.

5 Ted Quanrud, "English/Celtic," in Francie Berg, ed., *Ethnic Heritage in North Dakota* (Washington: Attiyeh Foundation, 1983), 184. The present-day states of North and South Dakota were not created until 1889. Prior to that date they were both included in the Dakota Territory.

6 John Gillette, "Study of Population Trends in North Dakota," *North Dakota Historical Quarterly* 9 (1942), 185.

7 Sherman, *Prairie Mosaic*, 100.

8 R. Wilkins and W. Wilkins, *North Dakota: A Bicentennial History* (New York: W.W. Norton, 1977), 38.

9 Kenneth Norrie, "The Rate of Settlement of the Canadian West, 1870–1911," *Journal of Economic History* 33 (1975), 410.

10 Elwyn B. Robinson, *The History of North Dakota* (Lincoln: University of Nebraska Press, 1966).

11 Tanner, "Foreign Immigration," 185.

12 T. Dwight Connor, "The Population of North Dakota from 1890 to 1960: A Geographic Study" (M.Sc. thesis, University of North Dakota, 1963), 8.

13 William Sherman and Playford Thorson, eds., *Plains Folks: North Dakota's Ethnic History* (Fargo: North Dakota Institute for Regional Studies, 1988), 6–7.

14 Quanrud, "English/Celtic," 153.

15 Connor, "The Population of North Dakota," 17.

16 Hiram Drache, *The Challenge of the Prairie: Life and Times of Red River Pioneers* (Fargo: North Dakota Institute for Regional Studies, 1970), 316.

17 John Hudson, "Migration to an American Frontier," *Annals, Association of American Geographers* 66 (1976), 256.

18 Sherman, *Prairie Mosaic*, 101.

19 Walsh County Historical Society, *Walsh Heritage*, Vols. 1–4 (Grafton, 1976), 28, 1061.

20 The sample of petitions for naturalization in the six Red River valley counties is too small to reconstruct any meaningful spatial patterns of migration.

21 Centennial Committee, *They Came to Stay: Grand Forks, North Dakota Centennial, 1874–1974* (Grand Forks: Grand Forks Centennial Corporation, 1974), 4–5; Norene Roberts and Joe Roberts, *Historical Research Report: Summer 1981 Historical and Architectural Survey of Downtown Grand Forks, North Dakota* (Minneapolis: Historical Research Inc., 1981), 1–2; D. Jerome Tweton, *Grand Forks: A Pictoral History* (Norfolk: The Donning Company Publishers, 1986), 10.

22 Centennial Committee, *They Came to Stay*, 5; Tweton, *Grand Forks*, 10–11.

23 Robert Anderson, "A Social History of Grand Forks, North Dakota" (MA thesis, University of North Dakota, 1951), 134.

24 Centennial Committee, *They Came to Stay*, 8, 10, 62.

25 *11th Census of the United States, 1890–91*, 648–9.

26 Centennial Committee, *They Came to Stay*, 43.

27 Anderson, "A Social History of Grand Forks," 143.

28 Roberts and Roberts, *Historical Research Report*, 32–6.

29 Grand Forks Historical Preservation Commission, "Historic Reeves Drive and South 6th Street Walking and Driving Tour" (Grand Forks, n.d).

30 Grand Forks Heritage Book Committee, *Grand Forks County Heritage Book: A History of Grand Forks County* (Grand Forks, 1976), 11.

31 Grand Forks Historical Preservation Commission, "Historic Grand Forks: Selected Sites on the National Register of Historic Places" (pamphlet) (Grand Forks, n.d.). The Nonpartisan League, which first appeared in 1915, sought a more equitable relationship with outside buyers and merchants. North Dakota farmers were tired of seeing their produce sold at a profit by grain exchange officials.

32 Grand Forks *Herald*, 3 July 1885, 3.

33 Grafton *Herald News and Times*, 19 April 1890, 2.

34 Grand Forks *Herald*, 9 June 1883, 2.

35 *The Record*, Vol. 5, 2 (Fargo, 1899), 12.

36 Indices of dissimilarity were calculated for wards instead of electoral districts because in Grand Forks City the wards were smaller units.

37 1900 manuscript census for Grand Forks, North Dakota. The numbers of North Dakota-born (N=5) and Austro-Hungarians (N=11) were so small that little of significance can be said about the residential patterns of these groups.

38 Anderson, "A Social History of Grand Forks," 134; Roberts and Roberts, *Historical Research Report*, 41.

39 Drache, *The Challenge of the Prairies*, 235.

40 Sherman and Thorson, *Plains Folk*, 420–1.

41 Hudson, "Migration to an American Frontier," 257.

42 Centennial Committee, *They Came to Stay*, 12; Drache, *The Challenge of the Prairies*, 235; and Sveinbjorn Johnson, "The Icelandic Settlement of Pembina County," *Collections of the State Historical Society of North Dakota*, Vol. 1 (Bismarck, 1906), 117.

43 Wilkins and Wilkins, *North Dakota*, 39.

44 *Compendium of History and Biography of North Dakota* (Chicago: George A. Ogle Publishers, 1900).

45 Tweton, *Grand Forks*, 24, 58.

46 Robert P. Wilkins, "People of the British Isles," in Sherman and Thorson, *Plains Folks*, 54–5.

47 *12th Census of the United States*, Vol. 1, 775; *13th Census of the United States*, Vol. 1, 808; ibid., Vol. III, 348–58.

CHAPTER 7

1 Portions of this chapter originally appeared in my articles "Saskatchewan Bound: Migration to a New Canadian Frontier," *Great Plains Quarterly* 12, 4 (1992), 254–68 (reprinted by permission of Great Plains Quarterly); and "American-Resident Migration to Western Canada at the Turn of the

Twentieth Century," *Prairie Forum* 22, 2 (1997) (reprinted by permission of *Prairie Forum*).

2 John Dales, "Some Historical and Theoretical Comment on Canada's National Policies," *Queen's Quarterly* 7 (1964), 297–316.

3 David Hall, "Clifford Sifton: Immigration and Settlement Policy, 1896–1905," in Richard Francis and Howard Palmer, eds. *The Prairie West: Historical Readings* (Edmonton: Pica Pica Press, 1985), 289.

4 Patricia McCormick, "A Historical Geography of the Districts of Saskatchewan and Assiniboia in 1904" (MA thesis, University of Saskatchewan, 1977), 78.

5 Hall, "Clifford Sifton," 290–7.

6 Kenneth Norrie, "The Rate of Settlement of the Canadian West, 1870–1911," *Journal of Economic History* 33 (1975), 410, 426.

7 H.G. Strange, "The Western Canada Semi-arid Area – Its History and Probable Future," an address presented to the Winnipeg Bankers Lecture Club, Fort Garry Hotel, 6 February 1935 (Winnipeg: Wallingford Press, 1935), 1–30.

8 Harold Troper, *Only Farmers Need Apply* (Toronto: Griffin House, 1972), 41.

9 Don Loveridge and Barry Potyondi, *From Wood Mountain to Whitemud: An Historical Survey of the Grasslands National Park Area* (Ottawa: Parks Canada, Department of Indian and Northern Affairs, 1977), 244.

10 Karl Bicha, "The North Dakota Farmer and the Canadian West, 1896–1914," *North Dakota History* 29 (1962), 297–302.

11 David D. Harvey, *Americans in Canada: Migration and Settlement since 1840* (Lewiston, New York, and Queenston, Ontario: The Edwin Mellen Press, 1991), 42.

12 Ditlaw Frederickson, *The Land Laws of Canada and the Land Experience of the United States* (Canora, Saskatchewan, 1907), 5.

13 Andre Lalonde, "Colonization Companies in the 1880s," *Saskatchewan History* 24 (1971), 101, 108–9.

14 McCormick, "A Historical Geography," 105–6.

15 Chester Martin, *Dominion Lands Policy* (Toronto: Macmillan, 1938); Norman Macdonald, *Canada: Immigration and Colonization, 1841–1903* (Toronto: Macmillan, 1966).

16 John Culliton, "Assisted Emigration and Land Settlement," *National Problems of Canada* (Montreal: McGill University Economic Studies Number 9, 1928), 23.

17 These statistics were taken from an editorial entitled "A Good Record" appearing in the Moose Jaw *Times*, 27 January 1893.

18 John Archer, *Saskatchewan: A History* (Saskatoon: Western Producer Prairie Books, 1980), 140.

19 Alan Anderson, "Ethnic Identity in Saskatchewan Bloc Settlements: A Sociological Appraisal," in Howard Palmer, ed., *The Settlement of the West* (Calgary: University of Calgary Press, 1977), 188, 190.

20 Ronald Rees, *New and Naked Land: Making the Prairies Home* (Saskatoon: Western Producer Prairie Books, 1988), 45.

21 Minister of the Interior, *Immigration Facts and Figures* (Ottawa, 1910).

22 1906 Census Bulletin, *Immigrants of the Agricultural Class in the Northwest* (Ottawa, 1906).

23 *Canadian Sessional Papers, Number 25* (Ottawa, 1912).

24 Harvey, *Americans in Canada*, 215.

25 Dominion of Canada, *Report of the Department of Immigration and Colonization for the Fiscal Year Ended March 30, 1930* (Ottawa, 1931), 8.

26 Bicha, "North Dakota Farmer," 299.

27 These rural municipality local histories are: Key West RM 70, *Prairie Grass to Golden Grain*; Maryfield RM 91, *Across Border and Valley*; Cymri RM 36, *Plowshares to Pumpjacks*; Foam Lake 276, *They Came From Many Lands*; Caledonia RM 99, *From Prairie Plow to Now*; Mervin RM 499, *Turtleford Treasures*; Pittville RM 169, *Hazlet and Its Heritage*.

28 These rural municipality local histories are: Argyle RM 1, *Autumn Leaves, Gilded Sheaves*; Mount Pleasant RM 2, *A Stake in the West*; Enniskillen RM 3, *From Dream to Reality and Furrow to the Future*; Cambria RM 6, *Our Prairie History*; Happy Valley RM 10, *Happy Valley Happenings*; Cymri RM 36, *Plowshares to Pumpjacks*; Laurier RM 38, *Radville-Laurier: The Yesteryears*; Old Post RM 43; Brock RM 64, *Arcola-Kisbey: Golden Heritage*; Weyburn RM 67, *As Far As the Eye Can See*; Key West 70, *Prairie Grass to Golden Grain*; Pinto Creek RM 75; Wise Creek 77, *Cadillac Prairie Heritage*; Maryfield RM 91, *Across Border and Valley*; Caledonia RM 99, *From Prairie Plow to Now*; Wolseley RM 155, *Bridging the Past*; Pittville RM 169, *Hazlet and Its Heritage*; Canaan RM 225, *Pioneer Trails to Demaine*; Victory RM 226, *Looking Back to Victory*; Snipe Lake RM 259, *Grass to Grain*; Chesterfield RM 261, *Captured Memories*; Foam Lake RM 276, *They Came From Many Lands*; Milton RM 292, *Captured Memories*; St Phillips RM 301, *History Coming Alive*; Invermay RM 305, *Parkland Trails*; Arborfield RM 456, *Echoes From the Past*; Mervin RM 499, *Turtleford Treasures*.

29 *A Tale That Is Told: Estevan 1890–1980* (Estevan: Estevan Book Committee, 1981).

30 For an engaging discussion of the Prairies, see Don Gaynor, *The Wheatgrass Mechanism: Science and Imagination in the Western Canadian Landscape* (Saskatoon: Fifth House Publishers, 1990).

31 Rees, *New and Naked Land*, 52.

32 Arthur Morton, *History of Prairie Settlement* (Toronto: Macmillan Company of Canada, 1938), 170–1.

33 Marcus Lee Hansen and John Bartlett Brebner, *The Mingling of the Canadian and American Peoples, Vol. 1: Historical* (New Haven: Yale University Press, 1940).

34 Moose Jaw *Times*, 3 March 1893.

35 Regina *Leader*, 28 July 1910.

36 The 1900 and 1910 Soundex Indexes were used in tracing migrants in the United States.

37 Foam Lake RM 276, *They Came From Many Lands*, 357.

38 Caledonia RM 99, *From Prairie Plow to Now*. McCartney left for Michigan in the mid-1890s and was in Canada by 1900 and so does not appear in any census records.

39 Happy Valley RM 10, *Happy Valley Happenings*.

40 Pittville RM, 169, *Hazlet and Its Heritage*.

41 Snipe Lake RM 259, *Grass to Grain*.

42 Milton RM 292, *Captured Memories*.

43 This background comes from J. Mitchell, H. Moss, and J. Clayton, *Soil Survey of Southern Saskatchewan*, Soil Survey Report 12 (Saskatoon: University of Saskatoon, 1962); *Department of Mineral Resources, Inventory and Outlook of Saskatchewan's Mineral Resources* (Regina: Government of Saskatchewan, 1976), 8–11, 15, 16–17.

44 Estevan Book Committee, *A Tale That Is Told: Estevan 1890–1980* (Estevan, 1981), 13.

45 Myrl Leyton-Brown, "The History of Estevan During the Territorial Period" (MA thesis, University of Regina, 1982), 36, 49.

46 Michael Freedman, "A Geographical Analysis of the Estevan Coalfield, 1880–1966" (MA thesis, University of Saskatchewan, 1968), 36.

47 Leyton-Brown, "The History of Estevan," 58.

48 Estevan Book Committee, *A Tale That Is Told*, 706.

49 Ibid., 740.

50 Mitchell, Moss, and Clayton, *Soil Survey*, 87–90.

51 Michael Conzen, *Frontier Farming in an Urban Shadow* (Madison: University of Wisconsin Press, 1971); Paul Voisey, *Vulcan: The Making of a Prairie Community* (Toronto: University of Toronto Press, 1988).

CHAPTER 8

1 John Robert Colombo, *1001 Questions about Canada* (Toronto: Doubleday Canada, 1986); Marci Macdonald, "Fields of Force," *Maclean's*, 3 July 1989, 26–30.

2 Alan Pred, "Place as Historically Contingent Process: Structuration and the Time-Geography of Becoming Places," *Annals, Association of American Geographers* 74 (1984), 281.

3 The concept of limited identities was first articulated by Maurice Careless although the initial germ of this idea was suggested by Ramsay Cook. See J.M.S. Careless, "Limited Identities in Canada," *Canadian Historical Review* 50, 1 (1969), 1–10.

4 Donald H. Akenson, "The Historiography of English-speaking Canada and the Concept of Diaspora: A Sceptical Appreciation," *Canadian Historical Review* 76, 3 (1995).

5 Allan Smith, "The Continental Dimension in the Evolution of the English-Canadian Mind," in Allan Smith, ed., *Canada: An American Nation?* (Montreal and Kingston: McGill-Queen's University Press, 1994), 56.

6 David Gagan, *Hopeful Travellers: Families, Land and Social Change in Mid-*

Victorian Peel County, Canada West (Toronto: University of Toronto Press, 1981).

7 Marvin McInnis, "The Size Structure of Farming, Canada West, 1861," *Research in Economic History,* Supplement 5 (1989), 313–29.

8 Donald H. Akenson, *The Irish in Ontario: A Study in Rural History* (Montreal and Kingston: McGill-Queen's University Press, 1984).

9 Gordon Darroch and Lee Soltow, *Property and Inequality in Victorian Ontario: Structural Patterns and Cultural Communities in the 1871 Census* (Toronto: University of Toronto Press, 1994), 63.

10 Bruce Elliott, *Irish Migrants in the Canadas: A New Approach* (Montreal and Kingston: McGill-Queen's University Press, 1988).

11 Akenson, *The Irish in Ontario,* 334.

12 Michael Katz, *The People of Hamilton, Canada West* (Cambridge, Mass.: Harvard University Press, 1975).

13 John Bodnar, *The Transplanted: A History of Immigrants in Urban America* (Bloomington: Indiana University Press, 1987).

14 Mark Wyman, *Round-Trip to America: The Immigrants Return to Europe, 1880–1930* (Ithaca: Cornell University Press, 1993).

15 Darroch and Soltow, *Poverty and Inequality,* 161–83.

16 Robert Kroetsch, *The Lovely Treachery of Words* (Toronto: Oxford University Press, 1989).

17 E. Carter, J. Donald, and J. Squires, "Introduction," in E. Carter, J. Donald, and J. Squires, eds., *Space and Place: Theories of Identity and Location* (London: Lawrence and Wishart, 1993), viii.

18 Linda Schneekloth and Robert Shibley, *Placemaking: The Art and Practice of Building Communities* (New York: John Wiley and Sons, 1995), xii.

19 Sack aptly describes territory as "the backcloth of geographical context." See Robert Sack, *Human Territoriality: Its Theory and History* (Cambridge: Cambridge University Press, 1986), 216.

20 D. Morley and K. Robins, "No Place Like Heimat: Images of Home(land) in European Culture," in Carter, Donald, and Squires, *Space and Place,* 5.

21 Robert Sack, *Place, Modernity and the Consumer's World* (Baltimore: The Johns Hopkins Press, 1992), 98–9.

22 Paul Knox, "The Restless Urban Landscape: Economic and Sociocultural Change and the Transformation of Metropolitan Washington, D.C.," *Annals of the Association of American Geographers* 81 (1991), 203.

23 Sack, *Place, Modernity and the Consumer's World,* 9.

24 In the summer of 1991, a 77-day armed stand-off between an armed band of Mohawk warriors, the Quebec Provincial Police, and the Canadian armed forces took place at Oka, Quebec, a village of approximately 1,500 natives and whites. The Mohawks were particularly upset with the development of a golf course and the building of houses on land not settled by treaty. A gunfight ensued and a Quebec police officer was killed. Mohawks at Kahnawake erected a sympathy blockade at the Mercier Bridge, a major link between the

island of Montreal and the south shore of the St Lawrence. The incident is a damning comment on the land claims settlement process in Canada; but at another level, both the standoff and the blockade of the Mercier Bridge may be seen as symbolic of the distance separating whites and natives and perhaps the indifference shown by regionally bound Canadians towards others who live in this country.

APPENDIX

1 Richard Lawton, "Mobility in Nineteenth Century British Cities," *Geographical Journal* 145, 2 (1979), 210.
2 Peter Knights, *Yankee Destinies: The Lives of Ordinary Nineteenth-Century Bostonians* (Chapel Hill: University of North Carolina Press, 1993).
3 Gary Kocolowski, "Alternatives to Record Linkage in the Study of Urban Migration: The Uses of Naturalization Records," *Historical Methods* 14, 3 (1981), 139.
4 J.P. Gavit, *Americans by Choice* (New York: Americanization Studies Series, 1922), 98.
5 Brian S. Osborne, "Wills and Inventories: Records of Life and Death in a Developing Society," *Families* 19 (1980); Bruce Elliott, "Sources of Bias in Nineteenth-Century Ontario Wills," *Histoire Sociale* 18, 35 (1985), 125–32.
6 Much of this discussion of land records comes from Randy William Widdis, "Tracing Property Ownership in Nineteenth Century Ontario: A Guide to Archival Sources," in Donald H. Akenson, ed., *Canadian Papers in Rural History*, Vol. 2 (Gananoque: Langdale Press, 1980), 83–102.
7 Richard Steacy, *Canadian Real Estate: How to Make It Pay* (Toronto: P. Martin Associates, 1968), 8–9.
8 For example, see Leo A. Johnson, "Land Policy, Population Growth and Social Structure in the Home District, 1793–1851," *Ontario History* 13, 1 (1971); John Clarke, "Geographical Analysis of Colonial Settlement in the Western District of Upper Canada, 1788–1850" (Ph.D dissertation, University of Western Ontario, 1970); Alan Brunger, "A Spatial Analysis of Individual Settlement in Southern London District, Upper Canada, 1800–1836" (Ph.D dissertation, University of Western Ontario, 1973).
9 See, for example, John Clarke, "The Role of Political Position and Family and Economic Linkage in Land Speculation in the Western District of Upper Canada, 1788–1815," *Canadian Geographer* 19, 1 (1975).
10 Steacy, *Canadian Real Estate*, 28.
11 Ibid., 15.
12 David Gagan, "The Security of Land: Mortgaging in Toronto Gore Township, 1835–1895," in F.H. Armstrong, H.A. Stevenson and J.D. Wilson, eds. *Aspects of Nineteenth Century Ontario* (Toronto: University of Toronto Press, 1974).
13 Most of the discussion of this source comes from Randy William Widdis, "An Evaluation of Canadian Border Crossing records in the Study of American-

Resident Migration to the Canadian West," *Proceedings, The Association of North Dakota Geographers*, vol. 39 (Grand Forks: University of North Dakota Department of Geography, 1989), 18–35.

14 This information was provided by Kenneth Aitken of the Regina Public Library.

15 Much of the discussion of the homestead records comes from Widdis, "Saskatchewan Bound."

16 Lyle Rodwell, "Saskatchewan Homestead Records," *Saskatchewan History* 18 (1965), 10–11.

17 John Hudson, "Migration to an American Frontier," *Annals, Association of American Geographers* 66 (1976).

18 Paul Voisey, "Rural Local Histories and the Prairie West," *Prairie Forum* 10 (1985), 335.

Index